THE TWENTY-SIX WORDS THAT CREATED THE INTERNET

THE TWENTY-SIX WORDS
THAT CREATED
THE INTERNET

JEFF KOSSEFF

CORNELL UNIVERSITY PRESS
ITHACA AND LONDON

First published 2019 by Cornell University Press

Printed in the United States of America

Library of Congress Cataloging-in-Publication Data

Names: Kosseff, Jeff, 1978– author.
Title: The twenty-six words that created the Internet / Jeff Kosseff.
Other titles: 26 words that created the Internet
Description: Ithaca [New York] : Cornell University Press, 2019. |
   Includes bibliographical references and index.
Identifiers: LCCN 2018042989 (print) | LCCN 2018044648 (ebook) |
   ISBN 9781501735783 (pdf) | ISBN 9781501735790 (epub/mobi) |
   ISBN 9781501714412 | ISBN 9781501714412 (cloth: alk. paper)
Subjects: LCSH: Internet—Law and legislation—United States. |
   Web sites—Law and legislation—United States. | Liability (Law)—
   United States. | Freedom of speech—United States. | United States.
   Communications Decency Act of 1996.
Classification: LCC KF390.5.C6 (ebook) | LCC KF390.5.C6 K67 2019
   (print) | DDC 343.7309/99—dc23
LC record available at https://lccn.loc.gov/2018042989

This book is dedicated to Judges Leonie M. Brinkema and Milan D. Smith Jr. Working for them was the greatest privilege of my career, and they taught me how to love the law, even if I didn't always agree with it.

CONTENTS

Acknowledgments   ix

Introduction   1

Part I. The Creation of Section 230   9

1. Eleazar Smith's Bookstore   11

2. The Prodigy Exception   36

3. Chris and Ron Do Lunch   57

Part II. The Rise of Section 230   77

4. Ask for Ken   79

5. Himmler's Granddaughter and the Bajoran Dabo Girl   103

6. The Flower Child and a Trillion-Dollar Industry   120

7. American Exceptionalism   145

Part III. The Gradual Erosion of Section 230   165

  8. A Lawless No-Man's Land?   167

  9. Hacking 230   190

Part IV. The Future of Section 230   207

10. Sarah versus the Dirty Army   209

11. Kill. Kill. Kill. Kill.   228

12. Moderation Inc.   239

13. Exceptional Exceptions   252

Conclusion   273

Notes   281

Index   307

Acknowledgments

Thanks to the many lawyers, litigants, scholars, and others who spoke with me for this book.

It was particularly difficult to track down documents and information from many cases in the 1990s and early 2000s, and I greatly appreciate all who helped me as I researched and wrote the book, providing me with old case files and leads and serving as sounding boards for my many thoughts and questions about Section 230. Special thanks to Timothy Alger, Jerry Berman, Chris Brancart, Bill Burrington, Bob Butler, Pat Carome, Danielle Citron, Sophia Cope, Lydia de la Torre, Dennis Devey, Brant Ford, Leo Kayser, Jeannine Kenney, Mary Leary, Alex Levy, Paul Levy, Stephen Rohde, Peter Romer-Friedman, Barbara Wall, and Kurt Wimmer.

I am particularly grateful to Brian Frye, Mike Godwin, Eric Goldman, Bob Hamilton, and Daphne Keller for their thorough reviews of the manuscript and immensely helpful comments.

Thanks to Emily Andrew and her colleagues at Cornell University Press for seeing the potential in a book about twenty-six words in an arcane federal law and for providing absolutely essential assistance in shaping the book over more than a year. Thanks to Karen Laun and Romaine Perin for meticulous editing, and to Liz Seif for outstanding cite-checking.

As always, I am eternally thankful to my family, especially Crystal Zeh, Julia, Chris, and Betty Kosseff, and Eileen Peck for their tireless support.

I am indebted to my colleagues and midshipmen at the United States Naval Academy (Hooyah!) for taking the time to talk through the legal, moral, and ethical complexities of Section 230. All views expressed in this book are only mine and do not represent those of the Naval Academy, Department of Navy, or Department of Defense. This book is not intended to be legal advice and is not a substitute for guidance from a lawyer.

Many of the legal disputes in this book arise from offensive, inappropriate, and vulgar content. It is important to publish the unedited words to allow the reader to assess the full scope of the harms suffered by victims. For filings from many of the cases discussed in this book and updates about Section 230, visit jeffkosseff.com.

THE TWENTY-SIX WORDS THAT CREATED THE INTERNET

INTRODUCTION

"During my service in the United States Congress,
I took the initiative in creating the Internet."

So said Al Gore in a March 9, 1999, broadcast on CNN, as the vice president prepared to launch his presidential bid. That sentence was one of many factors that would contribute to his electoral college loss to George W. Bush the following year. The phrase "Al Gore invented the Internet" became a frequent late-night talk show joke (even though Gore had said "creating" and not "inventing"). His political opponents pointed to the CNN interview as evidence of his being a liar or, at the very least, a master-class exaggerator. After all, how could a member of Congress single-handedly create the Internet? Since the 2000 election, history has been kinder to Gore. Some commentators have since noted that Gore did, in fact, take the lead on a 1991 bill that funded new technology and allowed the private sector to develop networked computing technology that the Defense Department had been developing for decades.[1] Gore was not crazy to suggest that Congress was responsible for creating the Internet—at least, the Internet as we know it today. The dynamic, communal, and vicious public square exists because of one federal law.

But this law wasn't born from the bill that Gore sponsored. Twenty-six words in an entirely different federal statute have created the modern Internet:

> No provider or user of an interactive computer service shall be treated as the publisher or speaker of any information provided by another information content provider.[2]

Those words are part of Section 230 of the Communications Decency Act of 1996, written by an odd pairing of congressmen: California Republican Chris Cox and Oregon Democrat Ron Wyden. The twenty-six words would come to mean that, with few exceptions, websites and Internet service providers are not liable for the comments, pictures, and videos that their users and subscribers post, no matter how vile or damaging. The services retain this broad immunity even if they edit or delete some user content. As the name of the law suggests, Cox and Wyden, working with technology companies and civil liberties groups, wrote the bill hoping to encourage early online services such as America Online and Prodigy to moderate pornography, filthy jokes, violent stories, and other words and images that could harm children.

Section 230 was a direct and swift response to a Long Island, New York, state court judge's 1995 ruling against Prodigy, then the largest online service in the United States. Relying on a tangled web of First Amendment decisions dating to the 1950s, the judge ruled that because Prodigy moderated some content and established online community policies, and it failed to delete posts that allegedly defamed the plaintiff, Prodigy could be sued for those posts regardless of whether it knew of them. Had Prodigy taken an entirely hands-off approach to its users' posts, the First Amendment might have protected it from the lawsuit. This court opinion stirred concerns that online services would not set family-friendly guidelines, fearing being sued into oblivion. By immunizing all online services from lawsuits over materials that their users upload, Cox and Wyden hoped to encourage the companies to feel free to adopt basic conduct codes and delete material that the companies believe is inappropriate.

But there was another reason that Cox and Wyden provided such sweeping immunity. They both recognized that the Internet had the potential to create a new industry. Section 230, they hoped, would allow technology companies to freely innovate and create open platforms for user content. Shielding Internet companies from regulation and lawsuits would encourage investment and growth, they thought.

The bill's proposal and passage flew under the radar. Section 230 received virtually no opposition or media coverage, as it was folded into the more controversial Communications Decency Act, which was added to the Telecommunications Act of 1996, a sweeping overhaul of U.S. telecommunications laws. Beltway media and lobbyists focused on the regulation of long-distance carriers, local phone companies, and cable providers, believing that these companies would shape the future of communications. What most failed to anticipate was that online platforms—such as websites, social media companies, and apps—would play a far greater role in shaping the future of the Internet than would the cables and wires that physically connected computers. Section 230 addressed a tiny niche that few outside the technology policy world paid much attention to in 1995.

Even Cox and Wyden had little inkling of the Internet that Section 230 would create. Only forty million people *worldwide* had any Internet access, a tiny sliver of the more than three billion today. Many companies did not even have websites, and even fewer had viable plans to make money from the Internet. Apple would not introduce the first iPhone for more than a decade. Mark Zuckerberg was eleven years old. "I always thought the bill was going to be useful," Wyden, now a U.S. senator, said, speaking in his Washington, D.C., office in 2017, "but I never thought that its reach would be this dramatic."[3]

This book is a biography of Section 230. Yes, a biography of a law. More precisely, a biography of a law within a law. Or, to be exact, twenty-six words of a law within a law within a law. Few federal statutes are worthy of an entire book. But Section 230 is. In the two decades since Section 230's passage, those twenty-six words have fundamentally changed American life.

The technology and protocols that undergird the Internet were under development for decades before Congress passed Section 230. Yet Section 230 created the legal and social framework for the Internet we know today: the Internet that relies on content created not only by large companies, but by users. The multibillion-dollar social media industry. The hateful comments beneath news stories. The power of a consumer to tell the world about a company's scams and rip-offs. The unfounded claims by anonymous cowards that can ruin an individual's reputation. The ability of the victims of those allegations to respond freely. Without Section 230, companies could be sued for their users' blog posts, social media ramblings, or homemade online videos. The mere prospect of such lawsuits would force websites and online service providers to reduce or entirely prohibit user-generated content. The Internet would be little more than an electronic version of a traditional newspaper or TV station, with all the words, pictures, and videos provided by a company and little interaction among users.

Consider the ten most popular websites in the United States as of 2018.[4] Six—YouTube, Facebook, Reddit, Wikipedia, Twitter, and eBay—primarily rely on videos, social media posts, and other content provided by users. These companies simply could not exist without Section 230. Two of the other top ten websites—Google and Yahoo—operate massive search engines that rely on content from third parties. Even Amazon, a retailer, has become the trusted consumer brand it is today because it allows users to post unvarnished reviews of products. Only one of the top ten sites—Netflix—mostly provides its own content.

Section 230 has allowed third-party content–based services to flourish in the United States. Many of the largest and most successful social media sites are based in the United States. Other jurisdictions—even Western democracies such as Europe and Canada—provide weaker protections for distributors of third-party content. Typically, if a website receives a complaint about an allegedly defamatory or illegal user post, it must remove the content immediately or be forced to defend its legality in court. Sometimes, the sites are expected to screen content in advance and prevent harmful third-party content from ever appearing on their sites. So it is not an accident that U.S. websites are relatively liberal with third-party content; Section 230 allows them to take those liberties. Imagine an Internet where armies of volunteers could not crowd edit Wikipedia entries, where Americans could not share their views about politics on Facebook, where unhappy consumers could not leave one-star reviews on Amazon. That would be the Internet without Section 230.

The history of Section 230's passage suggests that Congress sought to allow platforms to best determine how to moderate objectionable third-party content, and to allow a new industry to grow with minimal interference from courts and regulators. Yet it has evolved into one of the greatest protections of free online speech in the world. As Marvin Ammori accurately described in a *Harvard Law Review* essay, a platform such as Twitter considers itself a "medium for free speech."[5] Section 230 is a jarring megaphone that amplifies all speech, for better or worse (the worse is often what gets attention in the courts and media, and the better is the quotidian communication that we take for granted).

The United States is more likely than many other countries to favor free expression over other values, such as privacy and law enforcement. The First Amendment's protections for free speech are not absolute,[6] but they are more comprehensive than the free speech rules in other countries. For instance, the United States Supreme Court's First Amendment decisions have made it difficult for public figures to sue for libel and for governments to prohibit newspapers from publishing stories. Those constitutional protections do not exist, or are much weaker, in many other countries. Section 230 applies those First Amendment values to the Internet. Section 230 recognizes the unique role that online platforms play in allowing billions of people to communicate freely, and it unshackles those platforms from regulations and crippling lawsuits.

As with other free speech protections, Section 230 has significant social costs. Victims of online defamation, harassment, and other wrongs may be unable to track down the anonymous Internet user who posted the harmful material. In many cases, Section 230 prevents the victims from suing the website or other online platform, even if the platform encouraged the user to post horrific content and refused to remove it. As trolls and criminals figure out new ways to exploit the Internet, Section 230 is increasingly under attack. In the eyes of many critics, Section 230 enables terrorist recruitment, online sex trafficking, discriminatory housing sales, and vicious harassment. Some online platforms fail to adequately police such bad acts. Others turn a blind eye. And some even encourage users to post scurrilous rumors. Victims' advocates are increasingly asking members of Congress to amend Section 230 and carve out situations in which online intermediaries are not immune. Some courts have interpreted Section 230 in novel ways that allow them to avoid immunizing online services. These attempts to chip away at Section 230 reflect the well-established trade-off between free speech and other important values, including privacy and security. Some websites exist for no other reason than to enable their users to harm others. Such bad actors have been the focus of recent debates over Section 230.

This book seeks to inform that debate by taking a broad view of Section 230, from its origins, through two decades of courts' struggles to apply the law in tough cases, to the benefits and challenges that Section 230 has created today. By telling the story of Section 230, the book tells the stories of the people, companies, and ideas that have been affected—for good and bad—by the twenty-six words. This book shows how a deliberate policy choice by Congress in the infancy of a technology can alter the economic and social landscape for decades to come.

The book is based on dozens of interviews with members of Congress and staffers who drafted Section 230, plaintiffs and defendants in some of the most difficult Section 230 cases, lawyers who argued those cases, and judges who decided how to apply Section 230. The volume also relies on thousands of pages of documents from state and federal courts. I began writing the book in Section 230's twentieth year, in part because I wanted to document the law's history. I found that memories of Section 230's early days were already fading. Some of the key players did not recall important details of how the law was passed and litigated. Some had passed away. Courts already had destroyed the records of some of the most important Section 230 cases. Many of the mid-1990s websites that documented the Section 230 debate were offline, their articles lost in the ether. Understanding the history of Section 230 is vital as we consider how the Internet will look in the future. To explain the role that Section 230 plays in the modern Internet, this book explores the past, present, and future of the law.

Part I traces the origins of Section 230. It examines the decades of First Amendment court rulings that left online services vulnerable to lawsuits stemming from third-party content and provides an oral history of Section 230's proposal and zigzag path to passage as part of a much larger telecommunications law. Part II examines the rise of Section 230, as courts in the late 1990s and early 2000s broadly interpreted the statute to provide sweeping immunity to online services, even in terribly difficult cases. Part II also explains how Section 230 stands out from the rules for intermediary liability in other Western economies, and the role that the robust immunity has played in promoting innovation in and the growth of online services in the United States. Part III documents the gradual decline of Section 230. Beginning in 2008, courts carved out exceptions to Section 230 for particularly egregious cases. Although Section 230 remains the law of the land, it is weaker than it was in its early days. Finally, Part IV explores the future of Section 230. As Section 230 enters its third decade, criminals and other bad actors are using the Internet in new ways to troll innocent victims, organize terrorist plots, and traffic children for sex. The future of Section 230 depends, in large part, on whether Congress and courts believe that online services should shoulder the responsibility for such acts. I also examine the content moderation policies and practices that online services have voluntarily adopted based on consumer demand, as Congress intended when it passed Section 230 in 1996.

I did not come to this project as an unbiased observer. I am a former journalist and lawyer for newspapers and websites, and I have an unabashed enthusiasm for free speech. As a media lawyer, I often invoked Section 230 on behalf of websites in response to demands to remove user content. One of my mentors referred to such responses as "pound sand" letters. But this book is a biography. Not a love story. Not a tribute. And, hopefully, not an obituary. I do not dismiss the concerns of Section 230's critics as unreasonable. In fact, as I read hundreds of court opinions to research this book, I felt deep sympathy for many plaintiffs. Small businesses that lost customers because of nasty and false online consumer reviews. Women harassed by pseudonymous stalkers. Victims of terrorists recruited on social media. There is not an easy moral answer to the Section 230 debate.

Section 230 has fostered the innovation and freedom that has allowed an industry to grow and thrive for more than two decades. Section 230's broad immunity has been a net benefit to American society. But I can understand why someone could reach the exact opposite determination because of the real problems that have arisen as a result of irresponsible online platforms. I reach my conclusion by confronting some of the most troubling Section 230 cases head on: a lawyer whose career was in shambles after a website posted a false claim that she was a descendant of a Nazi leader; an actress whose photo and contact information was posted without her consent or knowledge on a dating website, leading to harassment and threats; and a White House staffer falsely accused of spousal abuse.

Whether those very real harms outweigh the free speech benefits of Section 230 depends on how much you cherish free speech as compared to other legitimate values, such as privacy.

There is a second story about Section 230 that also needs telling, a story that goes beyond the standard debate about whether Section 230 is good or bad. This book tells the story of the impact that twenty-six words in Title 47 of the United States Code can have on an entire industry. In the early days of the Internet, the United States went its own way when Congress passed Section 230. It adopted a law that provided more protection for online third-party speech than does any other country in the world. Twenty years later, Section 230's protections are so entwined in our everyday lives that it would be impossible to start from scratch without those twenty-six words. This book explains how Section 230 created the Internet that we know today.

The history of Section 230 helps to guide its future—and the future of the Internet. As I explain in Part IV, I believe that Section 230—like all laws—can be modestly amended to deal with real social problems such as online sex trafficking. But any such changes must be done with great deliberation, caution, and sense of responsibility. Severely limiting or eliminating Section 230 would fundamentally change the Internet. Websites, apps, and other platforms would face a duty to prescreen content, lest they face company-ending liability. Instagramming, Facebooking, tweeting, and Snapchatting in their current forms would be nearly impossible. The modern Internet in the United States is built on more than two decades of reliance on Section 230. To remove those twenty-six words from the United States Code would unravel the Internet that we know today. This book examines why Congress passed Section 230, the impact it has had on the United States, and some of the biggest challenges to its future.

The story of Section 230 is the story of American free speech in the Internet age. In 1996 Congress decided how to govern online speech. More than two decades later, we can finally step back and examine the effects of that choice.

Part I

THE CREATION OF SECTION 230

The discussion about Section 230 often begins in 1996, when President Bill Clinton signed the law as part of a broad overhaul of U.S. communications law. But that tells only part of the story. The United States' journey to Section 230 started decades earlier.

As Jack Balkin observed in 2008, Section 230's protections for online platforms are not a constitutional mandate, but a policy choice of Congress. Nonetheless, he wrote, Section 230 "has been one of the most important guarantors of free expression on the Internet, at least in the United States." Section 230 "has had enormous consequences for securing the vibrant culture of freedom of expression we have on the Internet today. The reason is that section 230 has protected the conduits and online service providers from being sued for the speech of strangers that they carry. Because online service providers are insulated from liability, they have built a wide range of different applications and services that allow people to speak to each other and make things together."[1]

Congress passed Section 230 because the First Amendment did not adequately protect large online platforms that processed vast amounts of third-party content. In fact, the First Amendment rules that the courts developed throughout the twentieth century created a disincentive for service providers to set content policies and moderate user posts. To fully understand why Congress passed Section 230—and its impacts—it first is necessary to understand the limits of First Amendment protections for distributors of speech.

For more than a half century, the United States Supreme Court has recognized that, under the First Amendment, bookstores, newsstands, and other intermediaries have a limited amount of immunity for legal claims arising out of the words and images created by others. Courts had good reason to create this protection: if businesses could face multimillion-dollar fines—or even jail time—merely because the pictures and articles that they distribute are illegal, those companies might err on the side of not selling books, magazines, and videos. Recognizing that such prudence could create a chilling effect on speech, the courts restricted liability to only the companies that actually know or should know that the material is illegal.

This rule has a major blind spot: the First Amendment immunity does not apply to all distributors. Distributors generally are not protected if they knew or should have known of the illegal content and failed to take action. And, at least under one court's interpretation of the First Amendment, some companies may not even qualify as distributors if they were able to edit the third-party content. These limits on the First Amendment protection for neutral distributors rattled the earliest Internet service providers such as Prodigy and America Online. If the online services took even the slightest steps to moderate their third-party content—such as deleting posts that contained pornographic images—then they take the risk of being held legally responsible for the millions of posts that proliferated their bulletin boards.

Section 230's authors and advocates hoped that the twenty-six words would repair this glitch. What they didn't know is that the law would shape the Internet as we know it.

1

ELEAZAR SMITH'S BOOKSTORE

In the fall of 1956, a North Dakota broadcaster aired a fringe Senate candidate's unhinged speech. Exactly three weeks later, a Los Angeles bookstore clerk sold a tawdry erotic book to an undercover cop. Legal disputes stemming from these two unrelated events would reach the United States Supreme Court and set precedent that would lay the groundwork for passing Section 230 forty years later. The two cases differed from typical free speech battles because their outcomes did not depend on the rights of the speaker or author. Instead, the cases turned on the rights of the intermediaries: the broadcaster and the bookseller. In both cases, the Supreme Court provided limited legal protections to the distributors. The court ruled that companies receive some protection from liability for distributing books, videos, and other material if the companies are unaware that the content is illegal. However, the protection is not absolute and depends on the state of mind of the distributor, the court would rule in the second case. The disputes eventually would establish the fundamental constitutional protections for distributors of information, including not only bookstores and broadcasters but also websites and ISPs. The weaknesses of these protections eventually led to the passage of Section 230.

Knowing when the Constitution protects radio stations, bookstores, and other content distributors is essential to understanding why Congress provided websites and other online intermediaries with Section 230's extraordinary benefits.

The 1956 U.S. Senate campaign in North Dakota was not supposed to be dirty. The incumbent Republican, Milton Young, and the mainstream Democratic challenger, Quentin Burdick, ran campaigns focused on issues that mattered to North Dakotans, such as farm policy. That comity ended when WDAY, a television and radio broadcaster in North Dakota, aired a fiery speech by independent candidate Arthur C. Townley on the evening of October 29, 1956, about a week before the election. Townley was notorious throughout the state for his rhetoric. A former socialist organizer, Townley had founded the Nonpartisan League, which pushed for the government to take over agricultural businesses. After many political and business failures, he used his bully pulpit to speak against communism.[1] This advocacy included unfounded charges that his opponents were communists.

In the WDAY speech, Townley attacked his Democratic and Republican opponents for being puppets of the state farmers union, a powerful force in North Dakota politics. Consider a snippet of the speech:

> For ten years, Senator Young has used the power and prestige of the high office that he holds to serve this Farmers Union. He has not raised his voice or hand to stay the communist viper gnawing at your private ownership and liberty. . . . Young and Burdick both support the Democrat Farmer program. Both men take orders from Communist controlled Democrat Farmers Union and now this amazing fact—Communist infiltration and power has gone so far in North Dakota that the Democratic Party supports 100% the Democratic Farmers Union candidate and the Republican Party supports 90% the Democratic Farmers Union candidate. The Communists can't lose unless the Americans wake up and wake up fast.[2]

WDAY's station managers recognized that Townley's speech would be controversial, and they warned Townley's campaign that the speech might be defamatory if false. But WDAY believed that a federal communications law prohibited the station from requiring Townley to change or redact the speech. During the 1956 campaign, WDAY had broadcast speeches by Young and Burdick. Townley demanded that WDAY provide him with an opportunity to broadcast his message. He was legally entitled to such an opportunity. Section 315 of the federal Communications Act of 1934 mandated that any broadcaster who allowed a candidate to broadcast a message "shall afford equal opportunities to all other such candidates" for the office. The law stated that the broadcaster "shall have no power of censorship" over material that the broadcaster must air under the equal time requirement.[3]

A week after the broadcast of the Townley speech, Young won reelection with more than 60 percent of the vote. Townley received a mere .38 percent, or 937 votes.[4] Despite Townley's failure to make a blip in the election, his fiery speech attracted attention. Perhaps the angriest were not his opponents but the North Dakota division of the Farmers Educational and Cooperative Union of America. The union filed a defamation lawsuit in the state trial court in Cass County, North Dakota.[5] Instead of suing only Townley, the union also sued WDAY for broadcasting the speech, seeking $150,000 from both the candidate and the broadcaster. The union argued that, by broadcasting the speech and allowing Townley to use its facilities, WDAY was equally liable for harm to the union's reputation.[6]

WDAY asked Judge John C. Pollock to dismiss the claims against it, and Pollock granted the broadcaster's request on May 23, 1957. Because federal communications law required WDAY to broadcast Townley's speech—and prohibited the station from censoring it in any way—WDAY's participation was limited to "the mechanical preparation, taping, and recording of the script and film," Pollock wrote.[7] The union appealed to the Supreme Court of North Dakota, which on April 3, 1958, affirmed the trial court's dismissal in a 4–1 decision. Writing for the majority, Judge P. O. Sathre concluded that because the federal statute required WDAY to air the full, uncensored speech, the statute effectively immunized the station from any lawsuits against the station that arose from the broadcast. WDAY, he wrote, "was under compulsion to publish the speech by direct mandate of a federal statute. It had no choice other than to broadcast the speech."[8] Judge James Morris dissented; he did not believe that Congress intended to prohibit broadcasters from *any* censorship of political content. For instance, he reasoned, broadcasters could censor obscene or blasphemous content. If WDAY could censor the speech, Morris wrote, it should not receive absolute immunity from a defamation lawsuit.[9]

The union filed a petition to the U.S. Supreme Court, requesting that it review the North Dakota court's ruling. The Supreme Court agrees to hear only a small fraction of requested appeals, so the odds were not in the union's favor that the court would even agree to review the case. U.S. solicitor general J. Lee Rankin, who represented the federal government in the Supreme Court, urged the court to hear the case. Rankin wanted the court to adopt the government's position that the federal communications law "precludes any deletion by a station licensee of material in a broadcast by a legally qualified candidate for public office because of its possible or even probable defamatory nature." The Supreme Court agreed to review the North Dakota court's ruling. On March 23, 1959, the high court held oral arguments.[10]

The union focused on the need to verify the accuracy of claims made in advertisements intended to influence voters. Edward S. Greenbaum, a prominent New York lawyer representing the union, told the justices that if the court read the statute as requiring the stations to air any political content provided to them *and* immunizing the stations from lawsuits from those broadcasts, politicians would fill the airwaves with lies and libel. "We think this statute, if affirmed, would open up the doors for a field day for the future Hitlers and Stalins that will arise in this country," Greenbaum said. "They will get free from any liability, except on their own part and they have none, stations such as this one."[11] WDAY urged the justices to focus on the unfair consequences that would arise from denying immunity to broadcasters. WDAY lawyer Harold W. Bangert argued that even though the federal communications law does not explicitly immunize stations for broadcasting equal time political speeches, the Supreme Court should read the statute as implicitly providing immunity. "We are in a position of being required to subject ourselves to an action for libel and the—and unable to protect ourselves," Bangert told the justices.[12]

Throughout the argument, the justices and lawyers debated whether broadcasters had the same editorial discretion as other media, such as newspapers. Douglas A. Anello, representing the National Association of Broadcasters, argued that broadcasters were unlike print media, with full discretion to reject content provided by third parties. "Newspapers may print what they please," Anello told the justices. "They may excise. They may edit. They have no regulatory body to whom they must account every three years, nor any Section 315 telling them what they may or may not do."[13] The justices and lawyers seemed to agree on one point: the station could be immune from the union's lawsuit only if the federal statute prohibited WDAY from refusing to air libelous political speeches. If WDAY could edit the speeches, then there was no way it could be immune.

Three months after the oral argument, a divided Supreme Court issued its opinion. Writing for the five-justice majority was Justice Hugo Black, who was among the most adamant defenders of the First Amendment to ever sit on the United States Supreme Court. A former U.S. senator from Alabama appointed to the court by Franklin Roosevelt in 1937,[14] Black believed that the First Amendment's text—"Congress shall make no law . . . abridging the freedom of speech"—meant just that. Unlike most other jurists, who recognized exceptions to the First Amendment for emergencies or compelling government interests, Black believed that the First Amendment prohibited any government regulation of speech. No exceptions.[15] Not surprisingly, Black ruled for WDAY. He could have done so in a narrow, technical manner, interpreting the plain text of Section 315 to determine whether it immunized the station. But he did not do that. Instead, he used the case to make a bold statement about free speech. In his opinion, Black concluded that the federal statute prohibited any censorship of political speeches that were required under this federal equal time rule and that the statute therefore immunized stations from any lawsuits stemming from those speeches. Justice Black explored the practical effect that censorship would have on free speech. Although he did not explicitly state that this would violate the First Amendment, he stressed that Section 315's purpose was to apply "this country's tradition of free expression to the field of radio broadcasting."[16] A station's individual evaluation of a candidate's speech for libel would be "far from easy," Black reasoned.[17] "Whether a statement is defamatory is rarely clear," he wrote, noting that the screening would occur "during the stress of a political campaign, often, necessarily, without adequate consideration or basis for decision."[18]

Encouraging such censorship, Black wrote, would cause an overall reduction in speech by political candidates, particularly about hot-button issues. If stations could censor such broadcasts, "a station so inclined could intentionally inhibit a candidate's legitimate presentation under the guise of lawful censorship of libelous matter."[19] Because campaign seasons are short, he wrote, it would be difficult for the candidate to successfully challenge that censorship in court before the election. Black then concluded that in light of this absolute prohibition on censorship, "traditional concepts of fairness" require stations to be immune from liability for the broadcasts of the uncensored political speeches.[20] He acknowledged that a station could avoid lawsuits by refusing to air any political content, but he concluded that such a result is contrary to the entire purpose of the equal time rule. "While denying all candidates use of stations would protect broadcasters from liability," Black wrote, "it would also effectively withdraw political discussion from the air."[21]

Justice Felix Frankfurter, joined by three other justices, dissented from Black's ruling. He agreed that the federal statute would have prohibited WDAY from deleting Townley's speech. But he disagreed with Black's decision to immunize the station.[22] Requiring the station to air an uncensored speech, even if that speech could expose the station to liability, could create "a burden, even unfairness," Frankfurter acknowledged. "But there may be unfairness too, after all, in depriving a defamed individual of recovery against the agency by which the defamatory communication was magnified in its deleterious effect on his ability to earn a livelihood." The court's job was limited to interpreting the laws passed by Congress, he wrote. And Congress simply did not provide liability protection in Section 315. "We are dealing with political power, not ethical imperatives," he asserted.[23] Black's opinion was particularly troubling to Frankfurter because it allowed broadcasters to avoid state libel laws. This usurped the states' rights to chart their own course and decide whether to impose liability on harmful and untrue broadcasts, Frankfurter believed, claiming that "states should not be held to have been ousted from power traditionally held in the absence of either a clear declaration by Congress that it intends to forbid the continued functioning of the state law or an obvious and unavoidable conflict between the federal and state directives."[24]

The *Farmers Educational* opinion marks the Supreme Court's first clear recognition of the need to protect not only speakers and publishers but also the passive distributors of information. Although the opinion does not even mention the First Amendment, its entire basis is grounded in the need to allow free and robust debate. *Farmers Educational* provides two important guideposts for determining whether a neutral distributor could be liable for content it did not create. First, the opinion reflects the Supreme Court's desire to avoid requiring private parties to censor content provided by third parties. The court could have decided the case on narrow grounds: the plain text of the statute appears to prohibit broadcasters from censoring the equal time political speeches, and it therefore seems fair and logical to immunize a broadcaster from any claims arising from content it is legally required to air. Rather than confining the opinion to this reasoning, Black grounded his decision in the need to promote robust political debate. Despite the lack of explicit discussion about the First Amendment, Black's entire reasoning stems from a desire to promote free speech and avoid any liability rules that would cause neutral intermediaries to overcensor. Second, *Farmers Educational* creates a strong presumption for distributors: if they cannot censor third-party content, then it is only fair for a court to find they are immune from lawsuits.

Soon after it issued its *Farmers Educational* opinion, the Supreme Court would once again protect the rights of neutral parties to distribute speech. And this time, the dispute would be more scandalous than a politician's on-air rant. Justice Black's opinion paved the way for more than a half century of U.S. court opinions that consider the free speech implications of laws that burden intermediaries.

Three weeks after WDAY broadcast Townley's speech, William Rothweiler sold a book.

Rothweiler worked in Eleazar Smith's bookstore on South Main Street in Los Angeles, an area that now teems with lofts and hipsters but then was the heart of the city's skid row. On November 19, 1956, police arrested Rothweiler when he sold the book *Sweeter Than Life* to Joseph E. Wing, an undercover officer on the Los Angeles Police Department vice squad.[25] Wing believed that *Sweeter Than Life*, and other books and magazines he purchased from Rothweiler, violated Section 21.01.1 of the Los Angeles Municipal Code. The ordinance stated: "It shall be unlawful for any person to have in his possession any obscene or indecent writing, book, pamphlet, picture, photograph, drawing . . . in any place of business where ice-cream, soft drinks, candy, food, school supplies, magazines, books, pamphlets, papers, pictures or postcards are sold or kept for sale."[26]

Rothweiler's arrest was noteworthy not merely because he allegedly violated an ordinance that banned the possession of obscene materials. Such ordinances were increasingly commonplace. The United States Supreme Court had ruled that "obscene" content is not entitled to First Amendment protection and could therefore be prohibited by federal, state, and local governments. The historical significance of Rothweiler's arrest came from the City of Los Angeles's seeking to hold the bookstore—and not the book's author or publisher—liable for merely distributing the obscene material.

Prosecutors eventually charged the bookstore's owner, septuagenarian Eleazar Smith, with violating the Los Angeles ordinance, and he faced a short jail sentence if convicted. Smith had lived a low-profile life until his criminal trial and was not the typical activist or journalist at the center of a major free speech battle. Other than the filings in his court case, little trace of him remains in the public record. He was born in Lomza, Poland, on December 23, 1884, according to a U.S. citizenship application he filed in 1936. Before coming to the United States, he lived in Winnipeg, Canada, where he met his wife, Polly, and they moved to the United States in 1923. As of 1936, the couple had no children, according to the application.[27] On the draft card he filed with the Selective Service in 1942, he listed his job as "own employer," though it is unclear if he was running the bookstore at that time. If an average Joe like Smith could face jail time for merely selling a book—even if he had never read the book and had no reason to suspect it was obscene—then every bookseller, newsstand owner, and librarian would have a duty to review the content of every book and magazine before selling it or allowing it to be borrowed. Although Smith apparently never sought to become a First Amendment icon, his unusual criminal charges thrust him into the spotlight.

Perhaps because of the high stakes of his case, Smith was represented, not by a run-of-the-mill criminal defense attorney, but by Stanley Fleishman, a renowned First Amendment attorney who just five months earlier had argued an obscenity case before the U.S. Supreme Court.[28] Fleishman had represented the operator of a mail-order business convicted under California obscenity laws.[29] The Supreme Court ruled against Fleishman's client, but in doing so, it set a high bar for prosecutors to prove that material is obscene. Writing for a six-justice majority, liberal lion William J. Brennan Jr. articulated the test for determining whether material is obscene: "whether, to the average person, applying contemporary community standards, the dominant theme of the material taken as a whole appeals to prurient interest."[30] For a book or movie to lose its First Amendment protection because it is obscene, the work must be outside of the community standards. Fleishman was a First Amendment warrior.

A few months after arguing the landmark case in the U.S. Supreme Court, Fleishman was defending Eleazar Smith in the far more modest courtroom of Judge James H. Pope in the Los Angeles Municipal Court. Smith's two-day trial began on September 23, 1957.[31] The judge, lawyers, and witnesses focused on two issues: whether *Sweeter Than Life* was obscene and whether Smith, as a merchant, could be held responsible for the book.

Even those with encyclopedic knowledge of American literature likely have not heard of *Sweeter Than Life*. The book, written by Mark Tryon and published in 1954 by the Vixen Press, appears to have had only one printing but still sometimes sits on the shelves of used bookstores. The publisher apparently recognized the potential controversy of the book and began with a disclaimer that the book was "a work of fiction and is purely a product of its author's imagination." *Sweeter Than Life* tells the story of Nym Bardolph, a Florida realtor unhappy in her marriage to a powerful and wealthy man. Most of the book focuses not on Bardolph's sexual exploits but on a fraudulent real estate development scheme that she plans. Still, the book contained enough sex to raise the eyebrows of Officer Wing. The remaining court documents do not specify the exact passages that Wing deemed obscene. Among the more controversial passages of the book, one describes a sexual encounter that Bardolph has with the "trim little blonde" secretary named Lynn in her real estate office. Among the most graphic scenes is the description of Lynn's "blue-veined breasts that were so full that they seemed swollen, their great dark eyes gleaming dully against the white flesh." Further describing the encounter, Tryon writes: "And as Nym sank slowly before her, Lynn started sobbing softly and her body arched in frantic ecstasy. And then there were no sounds in the office but the sounds of love."[32]

Sweeter Than Life is a poorly written book with a weak plot and unbelievable dialogue. In the most charitable light, it reads like a parody of erotic literature. Bad writing is not a crime. By twenty-first-century standards, such words do not even come close to being obscene. In the 1950s, however, community standards left little room for such graphic depictions of sex, particularly when the sex is between members of the same gender. At the very least, Judge Pope's standards left no room for that smut. The book shocked Judge Pope to the point that it became the sole focus of a First Amendment case that would reach the U.S. Supreme Court. At Smith's trial, the lawyers and judge avoided a long discussion of the salacious details of *Sweeter Than Life* but clarified that of all the books and magazines that Officer Wing had purchased, *Sweeter Than Life* was the most likely to be considered indecent.

"*Sweeter Than Life*, I thought, was depravity," Judge Pope declared at trial. "Just straight out depravity, with no redeeming feature. It carried no plot. It didn't even explain why the woman in the book had separated from her husband; they just separated, leaving her with the secretary, young woman secretary, and her designs thereafter, which she carried out."[33] Fleishman acknowledged that "there is much that can be said about the book that it is not good" but that *Sweeter Than Life* "should be killed by the Saturday review or the *New York Times* Book Section, not by law."[34] Fleishman tried to convince Judge Pope that although *Sweeter Than Life* was not highbrow literature, it was not obscene. To make his case, he called to the stand an expert witness, Robert R. Kirsch, who then was the daily book columnist at the *Los Angeles Times*. Kirsch, who claimed to read about thirty books a week, was prepared to testify that the materials that Rothweiler sold to Wing followed contemporary community literary standards.[35] Fleishman failed to convince Pope, who refused the request to allow Kirsch to testify as an expert witness. Pope also refused to allow the expert testimony of a psychologist who was prepared to testify about the community standards for sexual behavior and expression.

Simply put, *Sweeter Than Life* sickened Judge Pope, and it was abundantly clear that no book critic, psychologist, or other expert could convince him that the book was not obscene. He noted that he had "reviewed" the book three times. And he emphasized that he had taken no joy in the task. "The effect on me was one of depression," Pope said. "I would not choose to read such material, and I think the ordinary prudent person who had some of these books come to his attention would read possibly a page in some cases."[36] Apparently recognizing that Judge Pope would not suddenly declare the book to be in line with community standards, Fleishman moved on to his next argument: even if the book was obscene, Smith could not be held liable as a passive distributor who had not even read the book. Throughout his questioning of Smith and Rothweiler, Fleishman tried to show that Smith did not—and could not—know the contents of *Sweeter Than Life* and the thousands of other books and magazines in the store. Officer Wing acknowledged to Fleishman that, at the time of the arrest, Rothweiler had stated that he was merely a clerk who had no involvement with ordering books for the store. Rothweiler testified that he had no idea that any books or magazines in Smith's shop were obscene because he did not read them. "I have got to watch people," Rothweiler said. "I have certain duties to perform, and I haven't got time to read."[37]

Smith, seventy-two at the time of his trial, testified that he also read none of the books or magazines that the prosecutors alleged to be obscene. Smith said that he would need about three months to read a single book. It simply would be impossible, he said, for him to know the content of the thousands of books and magazines in his store. Most books and magazines arrived at his store by freight train from a supplier.[38] Prosecutor William Doran was incredulous. He noted that while Smith forbade minors under twenty-one from browsing adult magazines such as *Exotique*—one of the magazines that Officer Wing purchased with *Sweeter Than Life*— minors could browse comics.

"If you have never read *Exotique*," Doran asked Smith, "what is there about it that you don't want the juveniles to handle?"

"Knowing the character of this kind of magazine, so we know it," Smith responded. "We don't let them do it. That is all. So we don't take any chance."[39]

Judge Pope concluded that Smith was guilty of violating the obscenity ordinance, although the court files and transcripts that remain from the trial do not fully explain his reasoning. After determining that *Sweeter Than Life* was obscene, Judge Pope sentenced Smith to thirty days in city jail.[40] Smith appealed the ruling, and on June 23, 1958, a divided three-judge panel of the Appellate Department of the Superior Court of Los Angeles County affirmed Smith's conviction. The two judges in the majority concluded that municipalities may hold booksellers criminally liable for possessing obscene books, even if the booksellers are unaware that the books are obscene. The judges reasoned that a bookseller "may not, with impunity, adopt as his rule of conduct: 'Where ignorance is bliss, 'Tis folly to be wise.'"[41] The two judges also appeared incredulous that Smith was unaware that his skid row bookstore sold obscene books and magazines. "Those who are engaged in selling articles of a particular class to the public," the judges wrote, "have the first and best opportunity to know or be on notice of their characteristics, even though possession and not sale is involved."[42] The dissenting judge noted the existence of a state obscenity law much like the Los Angeles ordinance, with one key difference: the state law applied only to those who "willfully and lewdly" sold the obscene materials. "This is a wise and just provision because those proprietors customarily buy books from advertisements sent out by the publishers," the judge wrote. "Such dealers order books without an opportunity to read them in advance."[43]

Fleishman and another First Amendment attorney at his law firm, Sam Rosenwein, asked the U.S. Supreme Court to review the ruling. If the Supreme Court did not agree to rehear the case, then the California court opinion—and Smith's jail sentence—would stand and could not be subject to any further challenge. In their petition to the Supreme Court, Fleishman and Rosenwein wrote that the Los Angeles ordinance "throws upon the proprietor the absolute duty to know the contents of every book and writing in his establishment."[44] Requiring such omniscience, they wrote, was unrealistic. "It is not the price of the book, nor the quality of its paper with which the proprietor is required to be familiar," Fleishman and Rosenwein wrote, "but knowledge of the sexual purity of the contents of each and every book is the burden of the proprietor."[45] Fleishman and Rosenwein also argued that *Sweeter Than Life* was not obscene and that the trial judge should have allowed the expert testimony. The arguments apparently persuaded at least some of the Supreme Court justices, and they agreed to rehear the case.

Defending the content of the book might not have been a successful strategy for Fleishman and Rosenwein. Paul Bender, who clerked for Justice Frankfurter at the time, later recalled that Frankfurter described *Sweeter Than Life* as "horrible filthy junk," and was appalled when he learned that Bender's wife had viewed the book. "He was apoplectic about the fact that an innocent young woman like my wife should see this," Bender said.[46]

On October 20, 1959, Fleishman and Rosenwein appeared before the nine justices of the United States Supreme Court. Fleishman and Rosenwein each took half the argument. After Fleishman explained to the justices that *Sweeter Than Life* was not obscene under the Supreme Court's First Amendment standards, Rosenwein argued that the Los Angeles ordinance violated the First Amendment by holding a bookseller criminally liable even though the bookseller was unaware of the book's contents. In other words, Rosenwein argued that the ordinance was unconstitutional because it applied even if Smith lacked any intent, knowledge of illegality, or other culpable state of mind (in legal terms, known as *scienter*).

Justice Brennan, the stalwart liberal, was the first to question Rosenwein. What state of mind, Justice Brennan asked, would the prosecutors need to prove to bring criminal charges against the bookseller?[47]

"I would say, as a minimum, they would of course have to prove that he had knowledge of the contents of the book," Rosenwein responded.[48] Justice Brennan said that, based on the record of Smith's criminal trial, there was no evidence that Smith knew about the contents of *Sweeter Than Life*. Rosenwein agreed. "He took the stand and testified he's a man of 72 years of age, that he had not read this book," Rosenwein recounted. "He hadn't read for some time, as a matter of fact, and he was in the business of buying books."[49]

At this point, Justice Potter Stewart joined the discussion. Stewart was a centrist on a divided Supreme Court, so his swing vote was valuable. Stewart is perhaps most famous for a single sentence he wrote in another obscenity case, *Jacobellis v. Ohio*. In that case, the government alleged that a movie was hard-core pornography unprotected by the First Amendment. In a short concurring opinion, Stewart wrote that the movie was not hard-core pornography. "I shall not today attempt further to define the kinds of material I understand to be embraced within that shorthand description; and perhaps I could never succeed in intelligibly doing so," Stewart wrote. "But I know it when I see it, and the motion picture involved in this case is not that."[50] That phrase, "I know it when I see it," has become common shorthand for a bold conclusion that is not accompanied by a detailed explanation.

For Smith's case, however, Stewart was more equivocal. "Under your view, a man who couldn't read could sell anything with impunity, is that right?" Stewart asked Rosenwein.

"Well, no, that isn't quite accurate, Your Honor," Rosenwein replied. "I mean, there are different ways of proving guilty knowledge. I would say also, and we would be ready to concede, that if there was a reckless disregard of the facts which a person should have known in some way, I would say that that too might be included in the area of scienter."[51] However, Smith had no reckless disregard, Rosenwein argued. "We're dealing with a situation where the person admittedly is innocent. He has no intent. He just doesn't have knowledge of the contents of the book. He's in the business of buying books, selling them, and he has thousands of books in his shelf."

Roger Arnebergh, the Los Angeles City Attorney, told the justices that the ordinance did not violate the First Amendment and had not had the chilling effect on speech that Fleishman and Rosenwein alleged. "This ordinance has been on our books in Los Angeles since 1939 and it has not been amended in any respect that affects this," Arnebergh said, "and we still have a great many bookstores in Los Angeles." Arnebergh argued that Smith's professed ignorance of the contents of the books was simply immaterial. "Is bigness a defense?" Arnebergh asked. "If we had to prove that the defendant knew that the book that he sold was obscene, then he would be setting the standard. Not the community. Not the average person." Rather than expand on that line of thinking, Arnebergh pivoted to a novel argument. Essentially, he argued that because copyright law protected the book, the book was property and not speech. So, he reasoned, the First Amendment did not protect the book's distribution.

This was a mistake.

Justice Black was taken aback by the proposition that if copyright law protects a work, the First Amendment does not apply. "Do you think the fact that the book is copyrighted takes away the right of people to read it under the First Amendment?" Black asked.

Arnebergh quickly clarified. "My point is this," he said. "I think that, first of all, in this case, we were dealing with the free speech of the defendant. That he is the one that's charged and his free speech was not in any way violated because he wouldn't even read what he was selling. To him, he was selling a piece of property." Because the book was merely property, Arnebergh said, Los Angeles could not have violated the author's right to free speech. "The book was copyrighted and then the author has sold the copyright to the publisher and the publisher held the copyright," he pointed out. "And furthermore, under the law as frequently expressed by this and other courts, when you copyright something you acquire a property right in it, and you are then dealing with property."

"But it's still a book," Black shot back.

The copyright debate with Black and other justices consumed most of Arnebergh's valuable oral argument time. Arnebergh's arguments were not persuasive. Less than two months after the oral argument, on December 14, 1959, the Supreme Court issued an opinion reversing the California court and concluding that the Los Angeles ordinance violated the First Amendment. In the majority opinion, Brennan did not even mention Arnebergh's copyright argument. Instead, he focused on the Los Angeles ordinance's chilling effect on speech.[52] Brennan acknowledged that the First Amendment allows the restriction of obscenity. But that "narrow" exception does not permit the government to regulate non-obscene books, Brennan reasoned. He predicted that the Los Angeles ordinance "would tend seriously to have that effect, by penalizing booksellers, even though they had not the slightest notice of the character of the books they sold."[53] Such penalties, Brennan concluded, will discourage stores from selling any books or magazines they have not personally reviewed. Otherwise, the vendors could face massive fines or jail time. "If the contents of bookshops and periodical stands were restricted to the material of which their proprietors had made an inspection, they might be depleted indeed," Brennan wrote. "The bookseller's limitation in the amount of reading material with which he could familiarize himself, and his timidity in the face of his absolute criminal liability, thus would tend to restrict the public's access to forms of the printed work which the State could not constitutionally suppress directly."[54]

Brennan's opinion—which ultimately led to the vacating of Smith's conviction—stemmed from a concern about far more than the rights of Smith and other booksellers. Brennan worried that the ordinance would restrict the ability of authors and publishers to reach their audiences. If laws such as the Los Angeles ordinance cause bookstores to self-censor non-obscene speech, Brennan reasoned, they raise the same First Amendment concerns as laws that directly prohibit legal speech. That is not to say that Brennan believed that the First Amendment protects booksellers from *any* restrictions on the materials they sell. Prohibition of distributing obscene materials may be constitutional, he wrote, as long as the regulation contained a state-of-mind requirement. He did not say whether that state of mind needed to be actual knowledge or simply having a good reason to suspect that the materials were obscene. Brennan wrote that it was unnecessary for him to delve too deeply into that question because the

Los Angeles law required absolutely no inquiry into the distributor's state of mind before imposing liability. Such expansive liability, he reasoned, was unconstitutional.

"We need not and most definitely do not pass today on what sort of mental element is requisite to a constitutionally permissible prosecution of a bookseller for carrying an obscene book in stock," Brennan wrote, "whether honest mistake as to whether its contents in fact constituted obscenity need be an excuse; whether there might be circumstances under which the State constitutionally might require that a bookseller investigate further, or might put on him the burden of explaining why he did not, and what such circumstances might be." However, Brennan left open the possibility of holding a distributor liable even if the bookseller claimed to have not seen the specific illegal content that triggered the prosecution: "Eyewitness testimony of a bookseller's perusal of a book hardly need be a necessary element in proving his awareness of its contents. The circumstances may warrant the inference that he was aware of what a book contained, despite his denial."[55]

Three of the justices who joined Brennan's opinion issued separate concurring statements. Frankfurter, whose clerk later recalled his disgust with *Sweeter Than Life,* wrote to clarify that the ruling did not entirely prevent prosecutions of booksellers who sold obscene materials.[56] "Obviously the Court is not holding that a bookseller must familiarize himself with the contents of every book in his shop," Frankfurter wrote. "No less obviously, the Court does not hold that a bookseller who insulates himself against knowledge about an offending book is thereby free to maintain an emporium for smut."[57] Frankfurter signed on to Brennan's opinion, but it appeared that he did so reluctantly.

Black, the First Amendment absolutist, agreed that the Los Angeles ordinance was unconstitutional, but not just because it punished unknowing booksellers. Black wrote in his concurrence that any restrictions on speech are unconstitutional, period. "While it is 'obscenity and indecency' before us today, the experience of mankind—both ancient and modern—shows that this type of elastic phrase can, and most likely will, be synonymous with the political and maybe with the religious unorthodoxy of tomorrow," Black wrote. "Censorship is the deadly enemy of freedom and progress. The plain language of the Constitution forbids it. I protest against the Judiciary giving it a foothold here."[58] Similarly, Justice William Douglas, who like Black was a fervent First Amendment advocate, wrote that it is unconstitutional to punish an author or distributor of a book such as *Sweeter Than Life,* regardless of his or her mental state.[59]

Justice John Marshall Harlan, a conservative member of the court, was the only justice to not fully sign on to Brennan's majority opinion. He agreed that the court should overturn Smith's conviction, but not because of the constitutionality of the Los Angeles ordinance. Instead, he believed that the trial judge was incorrect in rejecting the introduction of certain evidence. But Harlan disagreed with Brennan's conclusion that the court should convict Smith only if he knew that the book was obscene.[60]

The public record does not reveal whether Smith continued to sell erotic books and magazines after the Supreme Court vindicated him. Smith died in Los Angeles on January 16, 1965, five years after the Supreme Court ruled in his favor, according to federal records.[61]

Despite the widely divergent views among the justices, eight of the nine agreed with the reasoning in Brennan's majority opinion, which endures to this day: the First Amendment prohibits content distributors—such as bookstores—from being held legally responsible for the content they distribute unless a prosecutor or plaintiff makes some concrete demonstration about their scienter—for instance, that they either knew of the illegal content or had reason to know. This First Amendment rule applies to more than just obscenity. If, for instance, a bookstore sells a book that contains false and damaging allegations about an individual, the *Smith* rule would apply. The *Smith* rule also applies to more than just bookstores. All distributors of third-party content, including television stations, magazine distributors, Internet service providers, and websites, are entitled to some First Amendment protection. The opinion's impacts were far-reaching. Five years later, in the landmark defamation case, *New York Times v. Sullivan,* the Supreme Court would rely on *Smith v. California* in its conclusion that public officials must demonstrate actual malice—a high bar—to recover damages in a defamation case. "A rule compelling the critic of official conduct to guarantee the truth of all his factual assertions—and to do so on pain of libel judgments virtually unlimited in amount—leads to a comparable 'self-censorship,'" Brennan wrote in the *New York Times* opinion.[62] Eleazar Smith's challenge to a thirty-day jail sentence would forever upend First Amendment law.

Still, *Smith's* First Amendment rule led to a paradox: distributors might reduce their risk of liability by turning a blind eye to whether the books, newspapers, and online user comments were illegal. Once a distributor reviews the content, the First Amendment protection offered by *Smith* may no longer apply. The *Smith* rule does not offer absolute protection to distributors such as bookstores and broadcasters, for it exposes a company to liability if the company has any knowledge of the content it is distributing. And the Supreme Court left open the possibility of liability for a distributor that recklessly disregards illegality, even if the distributor had not actually known of the specific third-party content. For the next half century, courts would elaborate on that rule and articulate the limits of *Smith's* distributor immunity.

To understand fully the gaps in *Smith's* protection, it helps to examine the cases of two people who claim they were wronged: an iconic 1950s child actor and one of the most vocal feminists of the 1980s.

Unlike many child television stars, Kenneth Osmond made good after the network canceled his show. Osmond, who played Wally Cleaver's sycophantic friend Eddie Haskell on the sitcom *Leave It to Beaver* from 1957 to 1964, avoided a life of crime and drugs. Instead, he ended up on the opposite side of the law. Throughout the 1970s and into the 1980s, he was a Los Angeles Police Department officer. He lived a largely quiet life with his wife and two children, sometimes reappearing on *Leave It to Beaver* spin-off shows and public events.[63] Osmond was thus understandably surprised when the LAPD's internal affairs department summoned him, as he recalled in his 2014 autobiography. A detective showed him a photo of a shirtless man who slightly resembled Osmond. The man in the picture was John Holmes, one of the most popular male pornography stars of the 1970s, Osmond wrote. The internal affairs detective asked Osmond to pull down his pants. Osmond complied, and he recalled that the detective took a quick peek and said, "Okay. You're free to go. Return to duty."[64]

A chain of California adult bookstores, Le Sex Shoppe, was selling copies of a movie titled *Supercock*, and the cover of the cassette claimed that the movie starred "John Holmes, who played 'Little Eddie Haskell on the *Leave it to Beaver*' show."[65] Osmond was the only actor who had played Eddie Haskell. And Osmond was certain that he had never appeared in such a film. A friend of Osmond's, another LAPD officer, dropped in to a Le Sex Shoppe store and asked a clerk about the claim that the movie starred the actor who played Eddie Haskell, and the clerk replied that other films in the store were also made by porn actors who were "stars" before "going into the movies."[66]

Osmond sued Le Sex Shoppe's owner, EWAP Inc. (the abbreviation was short for Erotic Words and Pictures), claiming that the stores defamed him by selling tapes that announced that he acted in a porn film. EWAP asked the California state trial court to dismiss the lawsuit, arguing it was a passive distributor of the tapes.[67] EWAP's president, Howard Green, and vice president, Melvin Starkman, stated in written declarations that EWAP merely purchased films for sale in their outlets and did not publish or produce the films that they sold in its stores.[68] They claimed that they did not prescreen the movies that wholesalers provided for them to sell.[69] Green and Starkman stated that until the lawsuit, they had not even known who portrayed Eddie Haskell.[70] They said they did not recall seeing the packaging for the video that claimed to star Osmond.[71] During discovery, Osmond acknowledged that he had no evidence that EWAP or any of its employees or executives knew that they were selling a film that contained false statements about Osmond.[72] The trial judge granted summary judgment in favor of EWAP and dismissed the case.[73]

Osmond appealed, and a three-judge panel of the Court of Appeals of California, Second District, unanimously upheld the dismissal. Relying on *Smith,* Judge Armand Arabian wrote that "one who merely plays a secondary role in disseminating information published by another, as in the case of libraries, news vendors, or carriers, may avoid liability by showing there was no reason to believe it to be a libel."[74] Adult bookstores, such as Le Sex Shoppe, may also receive this protection, Arabian wrote.[75] Because Osmond failed to demonstrate that EWAP "knew of the libelous nature of the statement on the film carton or knew of facts which imposed a duty to investigate," Arabian concluded, the trial court was correct to dismiss the lawsuit.[76] Osmond's claims were not frivolous; his reputation likely suffered because of the false claims that he went from *Leave It to Beaver* to pornography. Yet the firm rule in *Smith* prevented him from holding EWAP accountable. Had Osmond produced any evidence that EWAP's executives or employees selected movies based on the claims on the packaging—or even reviewed the covers—then the court might not have dismissed his case. EWAP was rewarded for its ignorance. Had the retailer tried to review the content of the movies in its stores, but sold the *Supercock* film, then it probably would receive no First Amendment protection from Osmond's lawsuit. Because EWAP took no precautions to ensure the accuracy of the claims made on the covers of its films, it managed to dodge liability.

Although Arabian ruled in favor of EWAP, his opinion was not entirely a win for distributors. While Justice Brennan emphatically avoided the issue of what state of mind a distributor must have in order to be held liable for third-party content, Arabian left open the possibility that the First Amendment immunity does not apply to a defendant who has "reason to believe" that the third-party content is libelous. This goes beyond having actual knowledge of specific defamatory content.

The *Smith* rule provides a strong incentive for distributors to take a hands-off approach regarding the materials they sell to the public. However, willful blindness will go only so far. If a distributor should have known about illegal content—or recklessly disregarded it—a court might conclude that the First Amendment immunity does not apply. These limits were seen in two court cases that stemmed from a feminist activist's feud with one of the country's most notorious pornographers.

Thirty years after the City of Los Angeles tried to prohibit the sale of obscene books and magazines, Andrea Dworkin also wanted to ban pornography. However, her tactics were less conventional.

By the 1980s, it was tough to convince a court that a pornography ban was constitutional. In 1973 the Supreme Court had significantly narrowed the scope of pornography it considered "obscene,"[77] leading to a proliferation of pornography theaters and to the widespread sale of hard-core magazines such as *Hustler*. Some commentators dubbed the 1970s and early 1980s the "golden age of porn."[78]

Dworkin was among the most prominent feminist activists of the 1970s and 1980s. Rather than focusing on obscenity, Dworkin wrote books and articles in which she asserted that pornography is a civil rights issue. She viewed pornography as the source of violence against women.[79] Dworkin worked with the Indianapolis City Council to pass an ordinance that would allow victims to sue pornography distributors, but a federal appeals court struck down the law as unconstitutional in 1985.[80] Dworkin became an enemy of the porn industry. Her most notorious adversary was Larry

Flynt, the publisher of *Hustler* and a fervent First Amendment advocate. His campaign against Dworkin intensified in 1984, when he published features about her. In the February issue, for instance, a cartoon depicted two women engaged in sexual relations, with one woman saying, "You remind me so much of Andrea Dworkin, Edna. It's a dog-eat-dog world."[81] In March the magazine ran a feature entitled "SO MANY DYKES—SO LITTLE TIME," which included a picture of women engaged in a sex act, with the caption stating that they were members of the "Andrea Dworkin Fan Club."[82]

Dworkin sued for defamation, and famed Wyoming trial lawyer Gerry Spence represented her. The outcome of a court case often depends on where the trial occurs, so lawyers strategically seek the most friendly locale for the trial. If the lawyer or client is particularly well liked in that town, they will try to hold the trial in state court, where they are more likely to find a friendly local judge and jury than if the trial took place in federal court. Spence was a local legend, so Dworkin probably stood a better chance of success in state court in Jackson, Wyoming, than, say, in a court in Los Angeles or New York. There was a slight problem: Dworkin lived in New York, and *Hustler* was incorporated in California, so Wyoming's courts lacked jurisdiction over a case involving only Dworkin and the magazine. Possibly in an effort to address this problem, Dworkin sued along with two Wyoming residents who were members of the National Organization for Women.

Including the Wyoming plaintiffs in the lawsuit allowed Dworkin to sue in Wyoming. But she faced yet another procedural hurdle: if none of the plaintiffs were residents of the same states as the defendants, then federal law allowed the defendants to move the case from Wyoming state court to Wyoming federal court. Possibly in an attempt to keep the case in state court, Dworkin sued not only *Hustler* but also Park Place Market, a Jackson, Wyoming, store that sold *Hustler*.[83] The defendants nonetheless removed the case to federal court, arguing that the plaintiffs were incorrect to name Park Place Market as a defendant. The plaintiffs argued that the market could be held liable and requested that Wyoming-based federal judge Clarence Addison Brimmer Jr. send the case back to state court.[84] The only way that Brimmer could grant their request would be to conclude that they had a viable claim against Park Place Market.

As in Osmond's case against Le Sex Shoppe, the outcome turned on whether the store could be held liable for the content it sold. Did Park

Place Market know or have reason to know that it was selling magazines that defamed Dworkin? Park Place Market's co-owner and president, Michael Lynch, stated in documents for the case that when the store sold the magazines, he and his employees were unaware of the magazine's statements about Dworkin or even that they "might be libelous in nature."[85] When the magazines were sold in 1984, the Lynch family owned Park Place Market, recalled Charlie Callaway, who said he purchased the store from the Lynches in 1985 and owned it until 1999. In a 2017 interview, Callaway recalled that Park Place Market was one of the only stores in the area to sell "smut magazines," such as *Hustler*. Around 1996, Callaway stopped selling pornography, concerned that the clientele who sought such magazines harmed the store's community reputation and its sales.[86]

On June 18, 1985, Brimmer ruled for Park Place Market and concluded that the market was not a legitimate defendant in the lawsuit against *Hustler*. Relying on the Supreme Court's decision in *Smith*, Brimmer wrote that Park Place Market could not be held responsible for any defamatory statements in *Hustler* unless the market knew of the damaging statements at the time of the sale. Brimmer pointed to the Supreme Court's concern in *Smith* that requiring bookstores to self-censor would harm the public's free exchange of information: "To avoid such private censorship, courts have required a specific showing of scienter, knowledge of the defamatory material, before allowing mere distributors to be held liable," Brimmer wrote. "The plaintiffs have produced no evidence of such scienter on the part of Park Place."[87]

The plaintiffs asserted that because *Hustler* had a reputation for being "scandalous" and that Flynt had been sued for defamation, Park Place Market was "on notice" that *Hustler* might publish defamatory statements and therefore had a duty to inspect the magazines before selling them. Judge Brimmer swiftly dismissed those arguments: "If that was the proper standard, every distributor of publications, such as the *National Enquirer*, or such respected publications as *Time* and *The New York Times*, which have also had their fair share of libel suits, would have to check each issue, at his peril, for possible libelous statements about people or events of which the average publication distributor might have no basis for judgment. Such a standard is not in our society's best interests; it would foster excessive censorship, and would deprive the public of reading educational

and entertainment materials, all in direct contradiction of the right of freedom of the press guaranteed by the First Amendment."[88]

Dworkin and the other plaintiffs also pointed to evidence that Lynch
had asked female job applicants whether they would have "reservations"
about working at a store that sold *Hustler*. Such questions, they claimed,
demonstrated that Lynch knew what was in the pages of the magazine.
Brimmer rejected this argument. Even though Lynch may have known
that *Hustler* contained adult or controversial content, he reasoned, there
would be no reason for him to know that the magazine printed damaging
lies about Dworkin and others: "Many publications are offensive to one
group or another, but that does not mean that these groups should have
the power to stop others from purchasing otherwise protected publications. The near absolute freedom of speech and of the press guaranteed by
the First Amendment has its costs. All citizens must live with the realiza-
tion that every other citizen also has protected rights."[89]

Brimmer eventually transferred the case against *Hustler* to federal
court in Los Angeles. The Los Angeles judge dismissed the claims, and
the United States Court of Appeals for the Ninth Circuit affirmed the dismissal, concluding that the First Amendment protected Hustler features
as "opinion" pieces.[90]

This would not be the last time that *Hustler* and Park Place Market
would face a libel lawsuit in Wyoming court.

Spence's vigorous representation of Dworkin made him a target of
Flynt's sharp pen. The July 1985 issue of *Hustler* bestowed Spence with the
honor of "Asshole of the Month." The photo illustration placed Spence's
face on a naked rear end, with this caption: "Many of the vermin-infested
turd dispensers we name Asshole of the Month are members of that group
of parasitic scum-suckers often referred to as lawyers. These shameless
shitholes (whose main allegiance is to money) are eager to sell out their
personal values, truth, justice, and our hard-won freedoms for a chance
to fatten their wallets. The latest of these hemorrhoidal types to make this
page is Gerry Spence, our Asshole of the Month for July."[91] Spence's investigator stated that he notified a Park Place employee on May 28, 1985,
that the July issue of *Hustler* contained a defamatory statement and asked
the store to stop selling it. Two days later, the investigator says, he made
the same request to the manager, and later that day the magazine was
removed from the store shelves.[92]

Spence filed a libel lawsuit in the same Wyoming state court, again listing *Hustler*, Flynt, and Park Place Market among the defendants. However, this time he was the plaintiff. In his complaint, Spence asserted that because Lynch had already been deposed in Dworkin's lawsuit, he "gained sufficient knowledge about the nature of the contents of *Hustler* Magazine so as to put him on notice that future issues of *Hustler* Magazine would contain materials scandalous in nature."[93] The defendants once again removed the case to federal court, arguing that Park Place Market was not a legitimate defendant. As in Dworkin's lawsuit, Spence asked Judge Brimmer to send the case back to state court because Park Place Market could be held liable for the magazines that it sold.[94] This time, Brimmer granted the request to send the case back to state court. Reaching the exact opposite conclusion he had with Dworkin's lawsuit, he concluded that Park Place Market might be held responsible for the allegedly defamatory content of *Hustler*. The key difference in Spence's case, he wrote, is the likelihood that when Park Place Market sold the July 1985 edition of *Hustler*, the store already knew of the controversial nature of the magazine because Dworkin already had sued the store.[95] (However, Judge Brimmer did note that the affidavits from the parties "are in conflict in regard to whether the manager and Mr. Lynch knew of the Spence article prior to talking to the investigator.")[96]

"Jackson, Wyoming is a relatively small community in which news of Gerry Spence, one of its most famous citizens, travels fast," Brimmer wrote. "The dispute between Mr. Spence and *Hustler* was well-known to Mr. Lynch. This was simply not a case of an innocent magazine seller unwittingly disseminating allegedly libelous material. Rather, we have a distributor who possessed detailed knowledge of the ongoing bitter battle between *Hustler* and Spence, and who, after receiving a complaint about the magazine, failed to investigate and continued to sell it."[97]

The very different results in the two *Hustler* cases were not outliers or misreadings of the *Smith* rule. The same judge decided both cases, and they involved the same magazine and even the same convenience-store defendant. Brimmer's refusal to dismiss Spence's case shows the limits of the First Amendment protections for distributors under *Smith*. Park Place Market could dodge Dworkin's lawsuit by claiming ignorance of the vile and potentially defamatory words in *Hustler*. But the market could not use that defense the second time it faced a *Hustler*-related lawsuit because by that time it knew at least of the possibility of the magazine's publishing damaging allegations, and it had received a complaint about the magazine.

As difficult as it was to apply *Smith v. California* to videotape covers and magazines, the rule would become unworkable as people began connecting their computers to the Internet.

2

THE PRODIGY EXCEPTION

Smith v. California struck a balance in First Amendment doctrine: a government regulation on distributors of speech must contain some requirement that addresses the distributor's state of mind. The regulation, criminal prosecution, or lawsuit cannot hold distributors strictly liable for third-party speech. That balance became more difficult for courts to apply in the early 1990s, as consumers began connecting their computers to online services that stored more information than the largest bookstores in the world. It may have been reasonable to expect Park Place Market eventually to be on notice that *Hustler* might defame people. But an Internet service provider or website with millions of customers simply cannot review every word that its users transmit unless it radically changes its operations and business model.

Although the Internet had long been under development by the U.S. Department of Defense and academic institutions, by the early 1990s, customers connected their home computers to mainly three commercial online service providers: CompuServe, Prodigy, and America Online.

CompuServe was owned by H&R Block Inc., and Prodigy was owned by IBM and Sears, Roebuck and Co. America Online was an independent upstart that came around after its more established rivals; it eventually became the market leader. The services ultimately would have millions of subscribers in the United States. Customers connected their computers to their home phone lines and dialed in to the Internet at speeds that were glacial compared with those of today's broadband. The companies charged per-minute and per-month rates that could bring monthly bills to hundreds of dollars an hour, particularly if teenagers were online.

These early online services differed from what is offered on the Internet we know today because they began as closed communities, curated by the companies that provided them. Rather than connecting to any websites around the world, these services offered curated information, such as electronic versions of newspapers, newsletters, and financial advice. The services also allowed users to post comments on bulletin boards, open to other members, and to communicate in chat rooms. Unlike what is available on the modern Internet, the services initially were not interoperable. For example, a CompuServe user could see only posts, articles, and pictures provided by other CompuServe users or the newsletters and other online information portals available on CompuServe but could not see posts on America Online bulletin boards.

By modern standards, this closed system of information might seem rather limited. But in the 1980s and early 1990s, the services were revolutionary. Within seconds, researchers could access articles that otherwise would have required a trip to the library and searches through dusty microfiche boxes to find. Newspapers provided "electronic editions" on these services, allowing a customer to read the news the night it was written, rather than wait for the thud of the paper on the doorstep the next morning. Never before had so much information been available so readily. Further, perhaps the most extraordinary innovation was the interactive nature of these new services. Until CompuServe and Prodigy came along, media consumption was largely a one-way experience. Consumers read newspapers, listened to the radio, and watched television. These online services marked a shift to two-way media consumption. Rather than wait for the monthly edition of the *Photographic Journal* to learn about the latest lenses, a camera enthusiast in Salt Lake City, Utah, could dial up

Prodigy and chat with a professional photographer in Sandusky, Ohio, on a photography bulletin board.

A 1985 article in the *New York Times* described the new services with awe: "By hooking up the modem and dialing local numbers, computer callers log on to the many special-interest bulletin boards to exchange information. At CompuServe, there are close to 100 bulletin boards to choose from, where you can pick up tips on everything from Apple computers to home gardening and, of course, leave your own comments. It's even possible to 'chat' by computer with another computer user live on the other end of the line (that's called Citizens' Band Simulator, after the popular CB radio exchange on the road)."[1] This unprecedented deluge of information created a dilemma for service providers such as CompuServe and Prodigy: What steps should they take to control the quality of the information that their users received? Should the services review materials before providing them to subscribers? Should they create and enforce community standards to prevent subscribers from being exposed to profane or indecent articles or pictures? The companies took different approaches, with some, such as CompuServe, adopting a hands-off approach. Prodigy, on the other hand, created and enforced user conduct standards. Under *Smith v. California*, CompuServe's Wild West approach provided it with far greater protection from lawsuits than Prodigy's attempt to create community standards.

Bob Blanchard recognized the power of these emerging online information services and wanted to create a news business that harnessed the possibilities of this power. Blanchard had been a local television journalist in Rhode Island and New York for more than a decade and had won three Emmy awards for consumer investigative reporting.[2] Blanchard and his friend David Pollak in 1986 founded Cubby Inc., which developed products and services for the growing computer industry.[3] In 1990, as entities such as CompuServe and Prodigy provided subscription-based news services on particular topics, Cubby launched *Skuttlebut*, an "electronic grapevine" about the broadcast industry.[4] Because *Skuttlebut* was not yet affiliated with a company such as CompuServe or Prodigy, it distributed its newsletters to customers mainly by fax machine. "The technology was so primitive then," Blanchard later recalled.[5]

Another company, however, had already delivered, through the computer, a broadcast industry newsletter similar to *Skuttlebut*. *Rumorville* was published by a company run by journalist Don Fitzpatrick.[6] It was available to CompuServe customers on CompuServe's Journalism Forum, an industry-focused bulletin board managed by Cameron Communications Inc. (CCI).[7] Blanchard, a CompuServe subscriber, was surprised to see his new company as the focus of the April 12, 1990, edition of *Rumorville*, in an article titled "Scuttlebutt on 'Skuttlebut': New Dish-rag Often Wipes an Empty Plate." The article accused *Skuttlebut* of accessing *Rumorville* "through some back door" and stealing news items from *Rumorville*.[8] However, Blanchard said that he was a CompuServe subscriber and thus had legitimate access to *Rumorville*.

The next day, *Rumorville* amped up its attack on Skuttlebut by unmasking Blanchard as the "name" and "face" of *Skuttlebut*. The newsletter took a particular interest in Blanchard's departure from WABC, the New York ABC television affiliate, a few years earlier. "From what we've been able to piece together, he was bounced at WABC about three years ago. Since then he has worked on a number of projects, mostly out of the TV biz. Several people told us that he had been programming several 900 and 976 numbers across the country. They weren't sure where the locations for the numbers were, or what types of material could be found on those pay-per-use numbers."[9] Blanchard says he was stunned to read the claim that the New York television station had fired him. "I wasn't bounced," Blanchard recalled. "I left on good terms with the station. I wasn't going back into broadcasting."[10] Blanchard was angry. He contacted Leo Kayser, a New York attorney, to file a defamation lawsuit on behalf of himself and Cubby in Manhattan federal court. Kayser typically was on the other side of defamation lawsuits, defending book publishers, authors, and media personalities. Besides suing Fitzpatrick, the publisher of *Rumorville*, Blanchard also sued CompuServe for distributing the newsletter. The October 5, 1990, lawsuit claimed that the false statements constituted business disparagement of Cubby and libel of Blanchard.[11] The suit also claimed that the newsletter engaged in unfair competition because *Skuttlebut* intended "to retain its subscribers without reducing its higher fee structure to meet the new competition."[12]

Blanchard's suit is the first on record that seeks to hold an online service liable for a third party's words. As Kayser and his colleague, Declan Redfern, would concede in a brief in Blanchard's case, they could not find a single court opinion that "delineates and characterizes the respective role of the participants where news and information is transmitted and received through computer database networks."[13] They were in uncharted territory, and the only guidance they had were the court opinions that arose from acts that had nothing to do with computers, such as WDAY's broadcast of Townley's speech, Eleazar Smith's sale of *Sweeter Than Life*, and Park Place Market's distribution of *Hustler* magazine.

Seven months after Blanchard sued, CompuServe moved for summary judgment, asking Judge Peter Leisure to dismiss the claims against it. President Ronald Reagan appointed Judge Leisure, a former federal prosecutor, to the Manhattan federal court bench in 1984. Robert W. Hamilton and Steven J. McDonald, respected media lawyers at the Ohio-based Jones Day law firm, defended CompuServe against Blanchard's suit. In their briefs asking Judge Leisure to dismiss the lawsuit, Hamilton and McDonald did not even attempt to argue that *Rumorville*'s claims about Blanchard were not defamatory. Instead, the gist of their argument was that CompuServe was merely a passive distributor of *Rumorville*. They argued that CompuServe did not even have the ability to control the words that *Rumorville* published.[14] The Supreme Court's First Amendment precedent from *Smith v. California*, he wrote, required evidence of the distributor's state of mind regarding the specific comments.[15]

Eben L. Kent, CompuServe's manager for news and reference products, told the court in a written statement that CompuServe did not employ Fitzpatrick to produce the *Rumorville* newsletter, nor did it directly contract with him. CompuServe, he wrote, did not exercise "any editorial control" over *Rumorville*'s content before it was uploaded to CompuServe. Kent also noted that he "would have been informed of any significant complaints," and he had not been told of any complaints about *Rumorville*.[16] The contract between CompuServe and CCI, the contractor that provided the Journalism Forum to CompuServe, stated that its management of the Journalism Forum would be "in accordance with editorial and technical standards and conventions of style as established by CompuServe."[17] But CCI said that it was unable to review *Rumorville*'s contents in advance, according to a written affidavit from CCI president Jim Cameron.[18] Fitzpatrick's contract with CCI stated that Fitzpatrick's company had "total responsibility" for the contents of *Rumorville*.[19]

In CompuServe's summary judgment motion, Hamilton and McDonald pointed Judge Leisure to *Smith v. California*'s protection for distributors.

CompuServe, they wrote, "acts no differently than do the New York City Public Library, Rizzoli's Bookstore and any news vendor with respect to hard-copy books, magazines, and newspapers."[20] Like its offline counterparts, they wrote, CompuServe had "no control" over the information it distributed. CompuServe had no editorial control over *Rumorville,* they wrote, and CompuServe "had no reason to, and did not, know of the alleged defamations before they were distributed."[21]

Penalizing CompuServe for *Rumorville's* words, Hamilton and McDonald wrote in their brief in *Cubby,* would "seriously restrict the free flow of information that the First Amendment was designed to encourage and protect."[22] To Hamilton and McDonald, holding CompuServe responsible for the *Rumorville* newsletter would not differ from sending Eleazar Smith to jail for selling *Sweeter Than Life.*

Blanchard's attorney, Kayser, bristled at that comparison. He argued in his opposition brief that CompuServe could not have the First Amendment protection of *Smith v. California* because CompuServe was more like a publisher than a bookstore: "The information electronically published and distributed by CompuServe was distributed to subscribers by CompuServe's own service and database. CompuServe thus controlled the method of distribution and the means for the defamatory material to reach the customer."[23] Kayser challenged Hamilton and McDonald's claim that CompuServe did not control *Rumorville's* stories. He pointed to the contract between CompuServe and CCI, which required CCI to "meet CompuServe's technical and editorial standards and conventions of style."[24] Paradoxically, Kayser then argued that CompuServe exercised no controls to prevent defamatory comments and that its "failure to adequately monitor the content or otherwise supervise the content of the material that was being published through its data base was grossly irresponsible."[25] Kayser's focus on editorial control apparently prompted Judge Leisure to address whether CompuServe's editorial control—or lack thereof—allows it to receive the First Amendment protections afforded to distributors such as bookstores. In cases against bookstores, broadcasters, and newsstands, the courts typically assumed that the defendants were distributors, and the judges merely needed to determine whether the defendants knew of the harmful content. Kayser argued that CompuServe was not even entitled to the First Amendment protection that newsstands received, because CompuServe published *Rumorville;* it was not a passive distributor of information like a newsstand. This dispute shifted the focus of the First Amendment inquiry from one of mere state of mind to one of editorial control. At first glance, this may appear to be a minor difference. But these are separate issues. It would be possible for CompuServe to have the legal authority to edit content but have no knowledge that *Rumorville* contained any defamatory articles. Yet even if CompuServe lacked any ability to edit *Rumorville,* it might know about the general scurrilous nature of the claims it published.

Judge Leisure ruled for CompuServe on October 29, 1991.[26] He became the first judge in the United States to decide whether an online service such as CompuServe could be held liable for third-party content. At first glance, his dismissal might appear to be a major win for the rapidly growing online service industry. For online services such as CompuServe, however, this eventually would prove to be a Pyrrhic victory: before the services could even receive the First Amendment protection afforded to bookstores and other offline intermediaries, a judge needed to determine they were distributors of the content. Leisure began his opinion by recognizing that the Supreme Court in *Smith v. California* "struck down an ordinance that imposed liability on a bookseller for possession of an obscene book, regardless of whether the bookseller had knowledge of the book's contents."[27] Leisure devoted much of the opinion to a discussion of whether CompuServe acted as a "distributor." If CompuServe was a distributor, it could be held responsible only if it knew or should have known of the defamatory content:

> High technology has markedly increased the speed with which information is gathered and processed; it is now possible for an individual with a personal computer, modem, and telephone line to have instantaneous access to thousands of news publications from across the United States and around the world. While CompuServe may decline to carry a given publication altogether, in reality, once it does decide to carry a publication, it will have little or no editorial control over that publication's contents. This is especially so when CompuServe carries the publication as part of a forum that is managed by a company unrelated to CompuServe.
>
> With respect to the Rumorville publication, the undisputed facts are that [Don Fitzpatrick Associates] uploads the text of Rumorville into CompuServe's data banks and makes it available to approved [CompuServe] subscribers instantaneously. CompuServe has no more editorial control over

such a publication than does a public library, book store, or newsstand, and it would be no more feasible for CompuServe to examine every publication it carries for potentially defamatory statements than it would be for any other distributor to do so.[28]

Leisure's conclusion was partly rooted in pragmatism. He recognized that holding CompuServe liable for every word on its services would effectively undercut its entire business model. After this lengthy determination that CompuServe qualified as a distributor, Leisure applied the *Smith v. California* test and determined that CompuServe was immune from the lawsuit. Leisure wrote that Cubby and Blanchard had failed to establish any significant dispute "as to whether CompuServe knew or had reason to know of Rumorville's contents," and, therefore, "CompuServe, as a news distributor, may not be held liable if it neither knew nor had reason to know of the allegedly defamatory Rumorville statements."[29] Although Leisure dismissed the libel claim against CompuServe because CompuServe did not know of the allegedly defamatory articles, the opinion's focus on editorial control would forever change the discussion about service provider liability for third-party content. Leisure effectively created a two-step test for an online service to be protected from claims over third-party content. First, the judge must conclude that the online service does not exercise significant editorial control before content is published and thus is merely a distributor (although the opinion is not clear as to precisely the degree or type of editorial control that might ever deprive a defendant of "distributor" status). Second, the service must establish that it had no knowledge or reason to know of the objectionable content. Leisure's discussion of "editorial control" could provide an online service with reason to stop taking *any* steps to moderate content. Of course, that is not to say that CompuServe had absolutely no control over *Rumorville*, as Leisure acknowledged. CompuServe could have terminated the contract that allowed the newsletter's publication, just as Eleazar Smith could have asked his wholesaler to stop shipping a particular type of book.

Had CompuServe taken more steps to control the quality of the newsletters it distributed, Blanchard's lawsuit may have survived CompuServe's summary judgment motion and been tried before a jury (or CompuServe would have settled). But CompuServe's lack of responsibility and accountability for *Rumorville* contributed to Leisure's decision to immunize the company from the lawsuit.

Blanchard could have appealed to the United States Court of Appeals for the Second Circuit. Indeed, he recalled that after reading Judge Leisure's decision, he largely agreed with the result: "I thought it was decided correctly. I did not want to appeal."[30] His reluctance to appeal partly stemmed from his journalism roots. He recognized that online services such as CompuServe offered tremendous potential for distributing news and information. "I did not want to be part of something that would adversely affect the development of the Internet," Blanchard said. "I felt it would have a chilling effect on the free flow of information. I didn't want to have my name part of that."[31]

Blanchard was not alone in his overall assessment that Judge Leisure was correct. Kayser, too, agreed with the opinion. Kayser said he felt that Judge Leisure correctly determined that CompuServe was not liable for the contents of the online newsletter.[32] Kayser believed that Judge Leisure's opinion provided limited protection for online intermediaries; CompuServe was immune only because it did not know of the newsletters' claims. "Essentially, what Judge Leisure did was require notice to be given to the company," Kayser asserted. "After they had given notice, the implication was that they'd be liable if they failed to act after notice."[33]

Because Judge Leisure was a judge on a trial court and not an appellate court, no other judges in the United States needed to follow his analysis if they presided over a similar claim against an online service provider. But because the *Cubby* case (as it soon came to be known) was the first opinion dealing with such a claim, it quickly attracted national attention as the de facto standard. Two days after Judge Leisure's decision, the *Wall Street Journal* ran a story on the front of its Marketplace section, calling the opinion "a major boost for free speech in the computer age." But the article presciently noted that the decision "won't necessarily benefit" CompuServe's primary rival at the time, Prodigy. That is because Prodigy warned its subscribers it will not carry messages that are "obscene, profane or otherwise offensive."[34] If Prodigy exercised substantial editorial control over its users' posts, or if it knew of the objectionable content, then it might not satisfy the new test that Judge Leisure developed in *Cubby*.

Prodigy's moderation of user content distinguished the company from its competitors such as CompuServe. A *Los Angeles Times* column stated, "Prodigy, which bills itself as a family oriented service, is one of the few bulletin boards in the country to screen all electronic messages for potential improprieties. Some observers liken Prodigy to a newspaper publisher which is ultimately responsible for what appears in print."[35] Prodigy's potential liability was not just mere speculation. The week before Judge Leisure issued his *Cubby* decision, the Anti-Defamation League criticized Prodigy for anti-Semitic user posts.[36] Could Prodigy be held liable for those posts just because it reserved the right to remove objectionable content? Legal experts simply did not know the answer, even in the days after the *Cubby* opinion. "The law has never been very good at assimilating new technologies," Harvard law professor Laurence Tribe said shortly after the *Cubby* opinion.[37]

Commentators generally welcomed the *Cubby* opinion. An article in *George Mason Independent Law Review* shortly after the decision argued that Judge Leisure's opinion held that "undue restrictions should not be placed on new types of communications simply because they assume an unfamiliar form."[38] No court ever determined whether Prodigy was liable for the anti-Semitic posts. But a defamation case against Prodigy a few years later would show the limits of the First Amendment protection that *Cubby* provided.

Daniel Porush was the president of Stratton Oakmont, a securities brokerage based on Long Island, New York. Porush entered a guilty plea on charges of financial crimes in 1999 and served thirty-nine months in federal prison. Jonah Hill's character in the 2013 movie *The Wolf of Wall Street* reportedly was based on Porush, although Porush has contested many of the details in the movie as inaccurate.[39]

Besides making an indelible mark on the securities industry, Porush forever changed the Internet. Five years before he pleaded guilty, Porush was a plaintiff in a civil lawsuit that would eventually lead Congress to pass Section 230. On October 21, 1994, Stratton Oakmont underwrote the initial public offering of Solomon-Page Group Ltd., an employee recruitment company.[40] Also on that day, Stratton Oakmont and Solomon-Page issued a prospectus revealing that Solomon-Page's largest client, Union Bank of Switzerland, was dropping Solomon-Page.[41] This announcement led a Prodigy user to post a message on Prodigy's Money Talk online bulletin board. Unlike CompuServe's Journalism Forum, which published newsletters from outside contractors, Money Talk allowed Prodigy users to post comments and reply on a public forum. Two days after the Initial Public Offering and announcement about UBS, a user of the Prodigy account registered to "David Lusby" posted this message on October 23, 1994, at 7:25 A.M.:

THANK GOD! THE END OF STRATTON OAKMONT WILL FINALLY COME THIS WEEK. THIS BROKERAGE FIRM HEADED BY PRESIDENT AND SOON TO BE PROVEN CRIMINAL—DANIEL PORUSH— WILL CLOSE THIS WEEK. STRATTON TOOK PUBLIC AN IPO THURSDAY CALLED SOLOMON PAGE!!!!!! (SYMBOL SOLP)

THE STOCK WENT PUBLIC AT $5.50 A SHARE THURSDAY AND CLOSED FRIDAY AT $6.50 A SHARE

FRIDAY 4:15 (15 MINUTES AFTER THE MARKET CLOSED). SOLOMON PAGE WALL ST. NEWS:

SOLOMON PAGE LOSES ITS LARGEST CUSTOMER (UNION BANK OF SWITZERLAND) RESPONSIBLE FOR 40% OF SOLOMON PAGES 1992, 1993, 1994 REVENUES.

THE COMPANY GOES PUBLIC ON THURSDAY AND LOSES ITS LARGEST CUSTOMER ON FRIDAY.

THIS IS FRAUD, FRAUD, FRAUD, AND CRIMINAL!!!!!!!!

MY HEART GOES OUT TO ANYBODY WHO PURCHASED THIS STOCK. OVER 10 MILLION SHARES WERE TRADED THURSDAY AND FRIDAY. MONDAY MORNING: 1 OR 2 THINGS WILL HAPPEN!!!!!!!!

1. THE TRADING OF THIS COMPANY WILL BE HALTED IMMEDIATELY, WHILE THE NASD (NATIONAL ASSOCIATION OF SECURITIES DEALERS) AND THE SEC (SECURITIES AND EXCHANGE COMMISSION) INVESTIGATE THE ILLEGALITIES OF THE ABOVE MENTIONED—IPO—

2. IF THE STOCK DOES OPEN IT WILL INSTANTLY DROP FROM $6.50 A SHARE TO BETWEEN $1.00-$3.00 A SHARE, AT WHICH POINT TRADING WILL BE HALTED.

I AM NOT A SHAREHOLDER OF THIS STOCK. I AM AN ATTORNEY WHO SPECIALIZES IN BUSINESS FRAUD. MY RECOMMENDATION

IS TO BE CALM. WAIT AND SEE WHAT HAPPENS MONDAY. NEWS
WILL BE FLYING IN ALL YOUR MAJOR PUBLICATIONS.

I AM ALREADY POTENTIALLY REPRESENTING 20–30 SHARE-
HOLDERS OF THIS STOCK. MOSTLY PERSONAL FRIENDS AND AC-
QUAINTENANCES. BY MONDAY I SHOULD HAVE A LIST OF ABOUT
100–200 SHAREHOLDERS OF THIS STOCK.

REMAIN CALM YOU DO HAVE RECOURSE!!!!!!!!

I WILL GIVE YOU FURTHER DIRECTION MONDAY AFTER THE
NEWS HITS. REST EASY THEYRE ARE SOLUTIONS.[42]

Seven hours later the David Lusby account user posted this message:

STRATTON IS NOT STUPID. THEY DEFINITELY HAVE A GAME
PLAN. YOU ARE VERY GULLIBLE IF YOU THINK STRATTON KNEW
NOTHING ABOUT THE NEWS. IN ANY CASE IT IS FRAUD FOR SOLB
TO GO PUBLIC KNOWING THERE #1. CUSTOMER WAS TERMINAT-
ING BUSINESS.

I AM NOT AN ATTORNEY TRYING TO STIR UP TROUBLE THAT
DOESN'T EXIST. THIS DEAL IS MAJOR CRIMINAL FRAUD. YOU
CAN NOT FAULT THE STRATTON CUSTOMERS. STRATTON OAK-
MONT IS A CULT OF BROKERS WHO EITHER LIE FOR A LIVING OR
THEY GET FIRED.

MONDAY WILL SHOW YOU THIS SITUATION AND THE FRAUD
COMMITTED ARE FACTUAL.[43]

The poster was not finished with the screeds about Stratton Oakmont
and Porush. Two days after those posts, on October 25, 1994, at 5:00 A.M.,
the user of the David Lusby account posted another message to Money Talk:

MR. PORUSH,

HAD A MEETING MONDAY A.M. WITH HIS STAFF OF BRO-
KERS. HE WAS TELLING THEM TO TELL THEIR CUSTOMERS NOT
TO WORRY BECAUSE HE KNEW 2 MONTHS AGO THAT SOLP HAD
LOST THEYRE #1 ACCOUNT THE BANK OF SWITZERLAND. THIS
IS 100% CRIMINAL FRAUD (TO KNOW BEFORE THE DEAL THEY
LOST THEIR #1 ACCOUNT AND NOT TO DISCLOSE THIS UNTIL
THE DAY AFTER THE COMPANY IS TAKEN PUBLIC)

ALL THE STRATTON BROKERS WERE ADMITTING THE ABOVE
FACT TO THEIR CLIENTS MONDAY. I HAVE 4 CLIENTS WHO TAPE

RECORDED THEIR CONVERSATIONS WITH THEIR BROKERS MONDAY CONFIRMING THE ABOVE MENTIONED FACT . . .

WITHOUT THE BANK OF SWITZERLAND ACCOUNT SOLP BOTTOM LINE IS VERY MUCH IN THE RED.

THE SUPPORT OF THIS STOCK, AND THE ISSUANCE OF THE IPO CONCEALING ALL THE ABOVE MENTIONED FACTS IS CRIMINAL FRAUD COMMITTED BY BOTH SOLP AND DANIEL PORUSH STRATTON OAKMONT. THE OUTCOME OF THIS CRIMINAL FRAUD IS IMMINENT.[44]

Porush contacted Jake Zamansky, a New York lawyer who had represented Stratton Oakmont on securities issues. Zamansky had never filed an online defamation lawsuit, but he believed that Porush had a strong case, Zamansky recalled in an interview: "Those posts were defamatory. There was no criminal proceeding. There were no fraud charges."[45] On November 7, 1994—a few weeks after the posts—Zamansky filed a lawsuit on his clients' behalf against "David Lusby" and Prodigy for a number of claims focused primarily on libel and negligence. The suit, filed in state court in Nassau County, New York, on behalf of Porush and Stratton Oakmont, sought more than one hundred million dollars in damages and a court order to remove the posts.[46]

Justice Stuart Ain, who was sixty-six at the time, presided over the case. (In New York state courts, trial judges are called justices.) He had served on the Long Island court since 1985. Ain came with his own controversy. In 1990, while presiding over a trial in a civil case, he had asked a defense attorney, "You're not an Arab, are you?" When the attorney answered that he was an Arab, Justice Ain responded, "You're our sworn enemies." The attorney tried to clarify that he was a Christian Arab from Lebanon, and Justice Ain said, "You're still our enemies, and here's what I have to say to you," while extending his middle finger. "What the fuck do you people want, anyway?" Justice Ain asked the attorney. Later, Ain defended his conduct as a joke. Still, the New York Commission on Judicial Conduct concluded that Justice Ain had violated various judicial conduct rules and that his "hostile and insulting words and gestures were intemperate, inappropriate and conveyed the impression that he was biased against [the defense attorney] because of his ethnic background." Rather than remove Justice Ain from the bench, the commission unanimously censured him on September 21, 1992.[47]

Two years after his censure, Justice Ain would preside over a case that would shape the Internet for decades to come. Among his first decisions in the case, Justice Ain allowed the parties to conduct limited discovery about the posts. The plaintiffs learned that the David Lusby associated with that Prodigy account was not an attorney, as claimed in the posts. Rather, David Lusby was a former Prodigy manager who had left the company in 1991. "He said someone had hacked or used his internal email to post that," Zamansky recalled.[48] Two months after suing, Stratton Oakmont and Porush amended the complaint to drop David Lusby as a defendant, instead suing anonymous defendants "John Doe" and "Mary Roe." In the new complaint, the plaintiffs noted that Lusby's Prodigy account was an internal Prodigy "test ID" and that at least thirty Prodigy employees were assigned access to the account.[49] The new complaint alleged that on November 3, 1994, Lusby told Prodigy customer service that another individual had written the posts under his account and that on November 11, 1994, Prodigy had terminated the account, which prevented Prodigy and the plaintiff from tracking down the identity of the actual poster.[50] As of 2017, Zamansky said he did not know the identity of the poster.[51]

Although Prodigy removed the posts in November 1994, Stratton Oakmont and Porush continued to pursue the hundred-million-dollar suit against Prodigy and the anonymous defendants.[52] Stratton Oakmont and Porush then asked Ain to rule that Prodigy was the "publisher"—and not the mere distributor—of Money Talk.[53] This determination could make or break that hundred-million-dollar lawsuit. Under the test set forth in Judge Leisure's ruling in *Cubby,* a finding that Prodigy was a publisher might mean that Prodigy would be responsible for the David Lusby posts even if the company did not know of the alleged defamation. If Prodigy was merely a distributor, then the plaintiffs would need to prove that the company knew or had reason to know of the alleged defamation.

During Lusby's deposition, Zamansky said, Lusby described the editorial control that Prodigy and its employees and contractors had over bulletin boards such as Money Talk. "It looked like Prodigy was editing things the way a newspaper would," Zamansky said. The crux of Zamansky's argument was that Prodigy distinguished itself from CompuServe and other competitors by setting standards for third-party content and removing objectionable posts. Prodigy had adopted "content guidelines" that, among other things, required posters to use their real names rather than pseudonyms and prohibited harmful material such as defamation.[54] The company also warned that it would "delete or remove" posts that violated the guidelines and that it may cancel the accounts of "problem posters."[55] In a deposition for the lawsuit, Jennifer Ambrozek, who managed Prodigy's bulletin board service, said that historically, Prodigy "scanned notes that went on the bulletin boards," and AOL and CompuServe did not.[56]

Zamansky found support in Prodigy's public statements. Throughout the early 1990s, Prodigy aggressively promoted its family-friendly environment. In a 1990 article, Prodigy spokesman Brian Ek said, "What we do with our bulletin boards is identical to the policy taken by most newspapers on letters to the editor. No obscenity, no slander, no libel, no commercialism."[57] That statement was particularly damaging for Prodigy in the Stratton-Oakmont lawsuit, as Zamansky repeatedly cited it in his briefs. Zamansky also emphasized that Prodigy aggressively marketed its content moderation. This was not just a minor technical difference; it was a selling point. "Prodigy has held itself out to the public as the 'family-oriented' on-line service which exercises 'editorial control' over the content of messages posted on its bulletin boards as a marketing strategy intended to differentiate Prodigy from its competition," he wrote in a brief.[58]

Zamansky focused on the actual editorial control that Prodigy exercised over Money Talk. Since 1993, Prodigy had contracted with Charles Epstein to serve as the "Board Leader" of Money Talk. In a deposition, Epstein said that Prodigy required a "dignified level of discussion" and that he was responsible for "policing" Money Talk and deleting posts that failed to conform to the Prodigy guidelines. Epstein testified that Board Leaders could remove a posting and replace it with a prepared message explaining why the post was deleted, "ranging from solicitation, bad advice, insulting, wrong topic, off topic, bad taste, et cetera." For instance, Epstein stated that he would remove posts that accused others of being criminals or of engaging in "fraudulent activity," as such posts would be "insulting."[59] Epstein said that the three posts about Stratton Oakmont and Porush were "insulting" and "should have been removed."[60]

Zamansky seized on such characterizations and asked Ain to recognize "the 'Prodigy Exception' to the *Cubby* rule."[61] Under this view, if an online service provider exercised control over third-party content, then the provider was a publisher, not a distributor that was entitled to the protections of *Cubby* and *Smith*. If Justice Ain were to adopt this view, then Prodigy still could be held liable for the three posts even if the company had not known about them. Prodigy would be held liable just like a newspaper that published a defamatory letter to the editor. Prodigy implored Justice Ain to avoid creating such an exception. Prodigy claimed that when the anonymous user posted the messages about Stratton Oakmont in October 1994, Prodigy no longer manually reviewed bulletin board posts before publication.[62] Ek's comparison of Prodigy to letters pages in newspapers, Prodigy wrote, was made in 1990—more than four years before the posts about Stratton Oakmont. Ek's statement "reflects Prodigy's nascent policy toward the bulletin boards," and as of October 1994, the company had long since stopped any manual review of user posts.[63] The rapidly growing use of Prodigy made such vetting impossible, the company argued. As of 1994, users posted about sixty thousand daily messages on Prodigy.[64]

Prodigy claimed that as of October 1994, its only prescreening occurred through automated software, which searched for certain words and "does not involve any judgment or evaluation of the subject matter or substance of the message containing that language."[65] Under its new procedures, Prodigy removed posts only after the company was notified of a breach of its content policy. "Prodigy's approach is thus the direct opposite of the editorial discretion exercised by a publisher, which is predicated upon subjective consideration and evaluation of all content," the company wrote. "To the extent that any subjective consideration and evaluation by Prodigy of individual 'Money Talk' messages occurs, it takes place only after those messages are brought to the attention of Prodigy, or the Board Leader."[66]

Board Leaders such as Epstein are contractors, not employees, Prodigy wrote. They are not "editors" and instead are expected "to participate in board discussions, and undertake promotional efforts, to encourage usage and increase the number of bulletin board users."[67] Ambrozek, Prodigy's bulletin board manager, described Epstein as "very much a free agent." By distinguishing Board Leaders as contractors rather than employees, Prodigy was trying to convince Justice Ain that the company did not edit bulletin board posts as newspapers edit letters to the editor.

Justice Ain did not agree with Prodigy's portrayal of itself as a neutral intermediary. On May 24, 1995, Justice Ain ruled for Porush and

Stratton Oakmont, and in doing so, he would forever change the future of Internet law.[68]

Justice Ain questioned Prodigy's claims that it no longer manually reviewed bulletin board posts, noting that there was no written evidence of the policy change.[69] Unlike CompuServe, Justice Ain wrote, Prodigy publicly marketed its user content moderation. Indeed, to Ain this was a key selling point that distinguished Prodigy from competitors: "By actively utilizing technology and manpower to delete notes from its computer bulletin boards on the basis of offensiveness and 'bad taste,' for example, Prodigy is clearly making decisions as to content . . . and such decisions constitute editorial control. That such control is not complete and is enforced both as early as the notes arrive and as late as a complaint is made, does not minimize or eviscerate the simple fact that Prodigy has uniquely arrogated to itself the role of determining what is proper for its members to post and read on its bulletin boards."[70]

Justice Ain emphasized that he agreed with Judge Leisure's opinion in *Cubby* and that such online services typically received the protections afforded to neutral distributors such as libraries and bookstores. Prodigy's "conscious choice" to moderate, he reasoned, prevented it from receiving this immunity: "It is Prodigy's own policies, technology and staffing decisions which have altered the scenario and mandated the finding that it is a publisher."

Justice Ain's opinion, however, failed to articulate precisely how to draw the line between distributor and publisher. Prodigy clearly exercised more granular control over its third-party content via moderators and policies than CompuServe did. However, as Judge Leisure noted, CompuServe had at least some ability to control newsletters such as *Rumorville* by refusing to carry it altogether. Justice Ain's opinion reduced "editorial control" to a binary choice when the reality was far more complicated.

Justice Ain's ruling did not sit well with Bob Hamilton, who had represented CompuServe before Judge Leisure. To Hamilton, Justice Ain simply misread the case law and had no support for imposing different liability based on the editorial control that a service exercised. "No amount of 'editorial control' could make one who 'distributes' content liable for 'publishing' the content unless he has knowledge (or reason to know) of the content he is disseminating at the time he is disseminating it," Hamilton wrote in a 2018 email. Hamilton would write an influential treatise chapter that made this point with historical case citations and present this argument at national media law conferences.

Ain apparently recognized that some critics might argue that his ruling would compel online bulletin boards to take a hands-off approach to user posts, although he sought to minimize those concerns. "For the record, the fear that this Court's finding of publisher status for Prodigy will compel all computer networks to abdicate control of their bulletin boards, incorrectly presumes that the market will refuse to compensate a network for its increased control and the resulting increased exposure," he wrote in the opinion. "Presumably Prodigy's decision to regulate the content of its bulletin boards was in part influenced by its desire to attract a market it perceived to exist consisting of users seeking a 'family-oriented' computer service."

Justice Ain correctly predicted the far-reaching implications of his ruling. The opinion quickly attracted national attention. Zamansky received media interview requests from around the world. "Every network was covering this," he recalled.[71] Two days after Ain issued his opinion, *Time* wrote that the ruling "sent chills through the online world."[72] An editorial in the trade publication *Advertising Age* criticized the decision, observing that Justice Ain punished Prodigy for an attempt to reduce racist and obscene user content: "The solution is not to force online services to flee from any attempt at supervising their bulletin boards—or to stop offering them altogether. This would make cyberspace even wilder than it is today, or deprive businesses and consumers of one of the true benefits of emerging communications technologies."[73]

In October 1995, Prodigy agreed to apologize publicly for the posts, stating that "Prodigy is sorry if the offensive statements concerning Stratton and Mr. Porush, which were posted on Prodigy's Money Talk bulletin board by an unauthorized and unidentified individual, in any way caused injury to their reputation."[74] Although the statement was short of a full-throated and sincere apology, it was enough to persuade the firm to agree to drop its lawsuit. Zamansky characterized the statement as an apology, which he says was all that his clients had wanted. "We also raised the level of awareness of the industry on the potential damage that can result from false and defamatory messages, and the need for on-line providers to examine their responsibility with regard to how they will protect subscribers and third parties," Zamansky told the *New York Times* at the time.[75]

Although Prodigy could avoid paying a single cent to Stratton Oakmont and Porush, Justice Ain's opinion finding Prodigy to be a publisher
was still on the books. Typically, a company would not be that concerned
about the ruling of a single state trial judge, as courts are bound by only
the rulings of appellate courts. But only two judges—Judge Leisure and
Justice Ain—had ever addressed the liability of an online service provider
for third-party content. When other courts faced similar claims against
Prodigy, they would immediately look to Justice Ain's *Stratton Oakmont*
opinion for guidance. And that opinion would lead them to the conclusion
that Prodigy was a publisher—not a distributor—and the company could
be held responsible for harm caused by all user bulletin board posts even
if Prodigy did not know of the posts.

In the same month that Prodigy apologized to Stratton Oakmont and
Porush, Prodigy asked Justice Ain for a reargument of his determination
that Prodigy was a publisher. Prodigy stated that two of its employees, in
their depositions for Stratton Oakmont's lawsuit, may have overstated the
amount of editorial control that Prodigy exercised. Stratton Oakmont did
not oppose the request for reargument. Zamansky said in 2017 that Stratton Oakmont was not seeking to make money from the lawsuit. Rather,
the lawsuit merely sought to clarify the public record. "It's a brokerage
firm," Zamansky said. "They make money with stocks and bonds. We
had changed the law. We got an apology. We thought we won."[76]

Still, on December 11, 1995, Justice Ain denied the request for reargument. In a rare move for a judge, Ain acknowledged the media attention
that his decision had received, and he acknowledged that his opinion offered "some guidance" to the burgeoning online services industry. "What
was once a tool used only by a handful of researchers and scientists has
become a means of entertainment, education and business which is used
by millions of people on a daily basis," he wrote.[77] Yet he refused to dis-
card his earlier legal analysis of the publisher/distributor issue just because
Prodigy and Stratton Oakmont had settled. "The Court finds that this is
a developing area of the law (in which it appears that the law has thus
far *not* kept pace with the technology) so there is a real *need* for some
precedent," Ain continued. "To simply vacate that precedent on request
because these two parties (or this Plaintiff) has lost interest or decided
that the litigation would be too costly or time consuming would remove
the only existing New York precedent in this area, leaving the law even
further behind the technology."[78]

The opinion makes clear that Justice Ain knew that his ruling would set precedent for this new industry. He had analyzed Prodigy's business model and determined that it would be unfair to provide Prodigy—and companies like it—with the same immunity that booksellers like Eleazar Smith had received for decades.

By 1995, online service providers were moving from the closed bulletin board system to the much broader Internet, with the development of World Wide Web browsers. This presented exponentially greater opportunities for consumers to share their thoughts with millions of other people and to read the creations of others around the world. The *Stratton Oakmont* decision received wide attention for potentially holding the growing Internet industry responsible for the actions of millions of consumers. "The Prodigy (example) is not a good one from the perspective of people who provide online services because it still leaves them in an ambivalent position," Bill Coats, a Silicon Valley attorney, said in a 1995 article.[79]

The year after Justice Ain's decision, an *Arkansas Law Review* article correctly highlighted the logical inconsistencies in the opinion. "Beyond its implications on constitutional rights, *Prodigy* also could hamper consumers and the computer industry," noted the author. "If computer companies must face legal liability if they make some efforts to monitor computer communications, they most likely will stop all monitoring or simply stop providing communication services. Either way, the public will be harmed, and a valuable, emerging technology will be stifled."[80] David Ardia explained the "perverse upshot" of the *Stratton Oakmont* decision: "Any online service provider who made an effort to restrict or edit user-submitted content, even for purposes of ensuring a family-friendly environment, faced a much higher risk of liability if it failed to eliminate all tortious material than if it simply did not try to control or edit the content of third parties at all. As Judge Ain anticipated, the decision in *Stratton Oakmont* created quite an uproar."[81]

Just as venture capitalists were pouring millions of dollars into technologies that would commercialize the Internet and connect people across the globe, a single Long Island judge could throw a wrench into the entire industry. All eyes were on his opinion, and as Internet service providers and websites began to emerge and transmit the words, images, and eventually videos of their users, they needed to figure out how to avoid becoming the next Prodigy.

The answer to this was straightforward and painful: online services needed to avoid claiming *any* control over their users' content. No codes of conduct. No automatic or manual monitoring. And definitely no deletion of objectionable bulletin board posts.

The *Stratton Oakmont* rule not only provided incentives for illogical corporate policies, but the ruling could make it easier for Internet users to spread defamatory and damaging bulletin board postings. If a company like Prodigy or CompuServe even had a policy of deleting posts that accused others of serious crimes such as murder, the company could risk losing its status as a "distributor" and be held liable for every hateful utterance of millions of customers. If Justice Ain intended to make a splash with the opinion, he succeeded. This ruling shook the foundations of the burgeoning Internet sector.

And Congress was watching.

CHRIS AND RON DO LUNCH

In 1995, Chris Cox was entering his seventh year representing Orange County, California, in the United States House of Representatives. He was a rising star in the Republican Party, and by the time his party took control of the House in January 1995, he had achieved the position of fifth-ranking Republican in the House. Cox wanted to make his mark with legislation. Unfortunately for Cox—and every other member of Congress—the Republican takeover of Congress led by the new Speaker, Newt Gingrich, came with a surge of partisanship and infighting between Democrats and Republicans that would lead to two government shutdowns. With Republicans controlling both the House and Senate for the first time since 1954 and a Democrat in the White House, any meaningful attempt at legislating would grind to a halt in partisan gridlock.

Shortly after the Republican takeover, Cox had lunch in the Capitol's private, members-only dining room with Ron Wyden, a liberal Democratic congressman from Portland, Oregon. That day, Cox recalled, most tables were entirely Democratic or entirely Republican: "It was like boys and girls at an eighth-grade dance."[1] Cox and Wyden bemoaned the partisan segregation and worried that Congress had never been so divided across party lines (an observation that, during a 2017 interview, Cox acknowledged was quaint). They represented the West Coast in Congress, but their districts were nothing alike. Orange County's sunny beaches and mainstream conservative politics bore little resemblance to Portland's drizzly grunge and strident liberalism. Like their districts, Cox and Wyden had little in common.

Cox, a Minnesota native, had earned graduate law and business degrees from Harvard, toiled at a corporate law firm, cofounded a company that translated the Soviet *Pravda* newspaper into English, and worked as a lawyer in the Reagan White House. Cox was straight out of central casting for a Republican congressman from Orange County. Wyden was the son of Jewish immigrants who had escaped Nazi Germany. His father was a journalist and author who wrote about Hiroshima, Hitler, and the Bay of Pigs. Wyden was raised in Palo Alto and, as a lanky teenager, played high school basketball. He went to the University of California at Santa Barbara to play basketball and later transferred to Stanford. After graduating from the University of Oregon School of Law, Wyden founded a senior citizen advocacy group. He shocked the entrenched Portland political establishment in 1980 when he successfully challenged a Democratic incumbent in the primary and then handily won the general election. Despite their different personal backgrounds and political beliefs, the two struck a close friendship. In an interview in later years at his Senate office in Washington, D.C., Wyden smiled as he recalled "kibbutzing" with Cox and getting ice cream together. "I just always thought he was smart, and I enjoyed being around him," Wyden said. "Chris Cox and I had become friends because we both liked to talk about ideas, and thought that not enough about government was ideas driven."[2]

The duo worried that the partisan rancor—exacerbated by tensions between President Clinton and Gingrich—would make it even harder for members of Congress to find common ground to pass any meaningful legislation. They recognized that it would be impossible to find consensus on hot-button social issues, which lawmakers had debated for years with little common ground. Rather than rehash those well-debated topics, Cox and Wyden agreed to identify issues so new that political parties and interest groups had not yet developed an entrenched position. "The idea that you're limited to those handful of very predictable questions and answers is folly," Cox said. "So we decided to make a pact to think about cutting-edge issues where people haven't thought through it fully. They'd have to approach it without a knee-jerk response."[3] Neither of them could immediately think of such a novel issue during their lunch. So they each agreed to give it some thought.

Soon after the lunch, Cox was on his weekly flight to Washington from California, and he read a newspaper article about *Stratton Oakmont*. Unlike many other members of Congress, who at the time had never used an online service, Cox was a subscriber to both Prodigy and CompuServe. His *Pravda* translation company employed fifty translators, and he communicated with them through both services. As a user, Cox knew that although Prodigy and CompuServe drew on different marketing tactics, they essentially provided the same services. To Cox, it made little sense that Prodigy could be exposed to multimillion-dollar legal penalties because, unlike CompuServe, it tried to moderate third-party content.

When Cox was back in Washington, he discussed the problem with Wyden, who agreed that this was a prime issue for Congress to address. Although Wyden did not share all of Cox's free market conservative ideals, he was interested in fostering growth in the technology sector. He had long advocated for Oregon's timber industry, which was in decline. Wyden saw the technology industry as the future for Oregon. Throughout the 1990s, some of the state's largest private employers were technology companies such as Intel and Tektronix. Although Oregon is not immediately associated with the technology sector to the same degree as are Silicon Valley and Seattle, the Portland area has a dense concentration of tech workers who care deeply about policies that promote their industry's sustainability and growth. By 1995, the Internet seemed to Wyden the engine that could drive the creation of even more innovation and technology jobs. At the time, few of his colleagues paid much attention to the Internet and had little understanding of the technology of business model. Wyden took an interest and had begun working with the technology sector on ways to promote the growth of the industry, such as a moratorium on online sales taxes. In the process, Wyden earned a reputation as a go-to member of Congress on technology issues—something that he says his teenage children found humorous.

Wyden thought that the *Stratton Oakmont* rule could hamper the potential for the growth of the technology industry. "I said, 'I don't know everything about the Internet, but that's crazy,'" Wyden recalled. "Why would anybody invest in a technology company if they thought they would be held personally liable?"[4] Wyden and Cox discussed how to provide online services such as Prodigy and CompuServe with the proper incentives to moderate content. They realized that overregulation could imperil the development of new online services. CompuServe and Prodigy, they recognized, not only created their own content but also relied on material provided by millions of users. Under the *Stratton Oakmont* rule, these providers had a strong disincentive to take *any* steps to moderate third-party content because any moderation would trigger the responsibility for all third-party content. They knew that it would simply be impractical to expect them to ensure the community standards of every single posting that each user uploaded. They did not yet know what form their bill would take, but they knew that they wanted to prevent *Stratton Oakmont* from becoming the law of the land. Their rough idea was to empower Internet companies—and their subscribers—to figure out the rules that govern their communities and decide on the best ways to prevent minors from accessing pornography and other harmful material online. "What we were trying to do was make sure the people who were in the best position to clean up the Internet would do so," Cox said. "We knew that right now there was a disincentive for them to do it."[5]

Both Cox and Wyden said that they stumbled on this problem when they learned of *Stratton Oakmont* and that Internet companies did not bring this issue to their attention. It was the rare type of problem that was so under the radar that Cox and Wyden could start from scratch on crafting a solution. "Nobody in Congress had heard of *Stratton Oakmont*," Cox said. "To the extent that eventually the handful of Internet-related businesses became aware of it, it was after we patiently explained to them what we were doing and why it was important. There was zero industry impetus for this."[6] The duo saw a window of opportunity to pass technology-related legislation, for Congress was deep in the weeds of drafting a bill to overhaul the Communications Act of 1934, which set the overall framework for regulating telecommunications. The sixty-year-old law set the framework for regulation of telephone service, and most agreed that it needed an update to address new communications technologies.

At the time, the primary focus of the telecommunications law debate was allowing the Baby Bell telephone companies to offer long-distance service in exchange for letting competitors use their lines to offer competing local service. The Internet was a shiny new object, but online platforms were largely an afterthought. The lobbyist armies were battling over the future of landline telephone service. "The Telecom Act was a huge deal," recalled former Congressman Rick White, a Republican who represented the Washington State district that included Microsoft's headquarters. "Everyone was focused on the telephone side and cable TV side. The Internet was new. It didn't have much of a constituency pro or con."[7] The revamp of federal communications law seemed like a perfect opportunity for Wyden and Cox to tuck in an amendment that promoted the growth of Internet communities while encouraging service providers to moderate third-party content.

Justice Ain issued the *Stratton Oakmont* opinion on May 24, 1995, when both the House and the Senate were already years into negotiations over a telecom reform bill. Passage was rumored to be months away. And Cox and Wyden had only a rough idea of how they wanted to address the *Stratton Oakmont* opinion in legislation. They needed to draft a bill. Quickly. The two had met with a small group of like-minded advocates, including Jerry Berman, the head of the Center for Democracy and Technology; Bob Butler, a lawyer for Prodigy; and Bill Burrington, an America Online lawyer. Throughout June 1995, the group often convened to map out legislation that would absolve online providers of liability for user content while also encouraging the companies to develop market-based standards for user content. "There was a real sense of responsibility," Burrington recalled. "We said, 'We've got to really get this right. We need to be very cautious about regulating this thing in its infancy.'"[8]

There was a problem: Cox and Wyden were late to the game. One other member of Congress had already taken up the banner of promoting online decency, but he took a different tack. Senator James Exon introduced the Communications Decency Act of 1995 on February 1, 1995—nearly three months before Justice Ain had ruled in *Stratton Oakmont*. Exon was shocked by the vast amount of pornography on the Internet. He printed pornographic images that were freely available online and compiled them in a binder, which became known on Capitol Hill as his "Blue Book."

He would show the Blue Book to his colleagues in the Senate cloakroom to convince them of the urgency of passing a law to crack down on on-line indecency.[9] Among the key proposals within the larger telecommunications overhaul was the creation of a program known as E-Rate, which would levy a fee on telephone companies to fund Internet access in schools and libraries. Exon was a conservative Democrat from Nebraska and had long aligned with family values groups. He supported E-Rate but was concerned about the prospect of children using school and library computers to access online smut. "He was a grandfather," said Chris McLean, who was Exon's legislative counsel. "He genuinely had a concern about what kids would be exposed to. It was the Wild West. The Internet was not well organized then. You could stumble into almost anything."[10]

Rather than adopting the laissez-faire approach that Wyden and Cox were developing, Exon took a punitive route. The first draft of Exon's bill amended telephone harassment laws from the 1960s to include Internet-based harassment and threats.[11] However, that draft was criticized for lacking adequate defenses. On June 14, 1995—about three weeks after the *Stratton Oakmont* decision—Exon succeeded in adding a new version of the bill to the telecommunications overhaul moving through the Senate. That version of Exon's legislation addressed some criticism of the first bill. It prohibited the use of a telecommunications device to knowingly make available "indecent" material to minors under eighteen. Violating this prohibition would lead to a fine of up to one hundred thousand dollars or up to two years in prison.[12] The threat of criminal penalties mobilized opposition across the political spectrum. Six days after the Senate added Exon's proposal to the Senate's telecommunication's law, House Speaker Gingrich said the legislation was "clearly a violation of free speech" and "a violation of the right of adults to communicate with each other."[13]

Exon's bill concerned civil liberties groups, but many free speech advocates believed that their best plan of action was to allow the Exon bill to pass and challenge it in court. Surely, they believed, courts would strike it down as a violation of the First Amendment. Berman, of the Center for Democracy and Technology, disagreed. A lawyer and longtime advocate for civil liberties, Berman had been the director of the Electronic Frontier Foundation, a group that often challenges civil liberties violations in court. Before that, he served as chief legislative counsel at the American Civil Liberties Union, which often litigates against laws that it believes are unconstitutional. In 1994 Berman founded the Center for Democracy and Technology, a more D.C.-centric group that focused, not on suing, but on lobbying the government to make sure that the laws were not unconstitutional in the first place. So Berman teamed up with Prodigy and America Online, which viewed Exon's bill—and the threat of criminal penalties not only to users but companies—as an existential threat. The companies also had huge practical difficulties in complying with the bill. How would a service provider even be able to determine, with certainty, that a picture or post was indecent? "Art from the Louvre in Paris could be considered indecent," Burrington, the lawyer from America Online, said.[14] Cox and Wyden likewise saw Exon's approach as unworkable. "Exon was pushing this concept of the federal government being the nanny for all of this stuff," Cox said. "It was a preposterous concept if you understood the volume of Internet traffic even back then. You could sympathize with people who wanted to deal with pornography, but it was a foolish approach."[15] But Cox, Wyden, and the technology companies could not merely oppose Exon's legislation. The Internet industry in 1995 was much smaller than it is today, and it had far less political clout. They were up against family values coalitions in a year when conservatives had taken over the House. On top of that, *Time* magazine had recently run a cover story expose on the growing amount of "cyberpornography" available on the Internet.

As the ad hoc group hammered out the details of the Cox-Wyden proposal, they viewed it not just as a solution to the *Stratton Oakmont* problem but also as an alternative to Exon's bill. Rather than just criticizing Exon's bill, they wanted to address the problem of online indecency with a different solution. Early computer programs such as NetNanny and Surf-Watch allowed parents to prevent their children from viewing online pornography and other objectionable websites. The Cox-Wyden group saw such "user empowerment" as the primary alternative to Exon's proposal. Rather than imposing penalties on Internet posters and their service providers, the group argued that it would be more effective and fair to allow individuals and companies to set their own standards.

As Exon's Blue Book and threats of criminal prosecution attracted worldwide attention and criticism, Wyden and Cox quietly pressed on with developing their parallel approach to Internet regulation, keeping in mind their goals of encouraging innovation and responsible content moderation. Wyden, Cox, and their staffers spent weeks in meetings with Berman, Burrington, and Butler, figuring out the details. The group agreed on two primary goals. First, they wanted to encourage companies to develop interactive online services without being held liable for third-party content. Second, they hoped that the services would be free to set their own standards for user content, as Prodigy did. The market, they believed, would encourage the companies to develop conduct codes that are most appropriate for their audiences. "We really were interested in protecting the platforms from being held liable for the content posted on their sites and being sued out of existence," Wyden said. "And we were interested in allowing the platforms to take down some content that they believe shouldn't be on their site without being held liable for all the content on the site, so that you could really encourage responsible behavior."[16] On June 30, 1995—two weeks after the Senate added Exon's Communications Decency Act to its large telecommunications reform bill and five weeks after Justice Ain ruled in *Stratton Oakmont*—Cox and Wyden proposed H.R. 1978, the Internet Freedom and Family Empowerment Act. The bill would create a new section of the Communications Act of 1934 known as Section 230.[17]

Tracking Wyden and Cox's two main goals, Section (c) of the bill has two primary components, both under the subheading "Protection for 'Good Samaritan' Blocking and Screening of Offensive Material." First are the twenty-six words at the heart of the bill, now known as subsection (c)(1) of Section 230: "No provider or user of an interactive computer service shall be treated as the publisher or speaker of any information provided by another information content provider."[18] At first glance, those words might not seem particularly society changing. They don't mention anything about shielding companies from multimillion-dollar lawsuits or promoting the growth of third-party content. What is an "interactive computer service?" What is "another information content provider?" What does it mean to treat someone as a "publisher or speaker?" The bill provided some guidance. It defines "interactive computer service" as "any information service, system, or access software provider that provides or enables computer access by multiple users to a computer server, including specifically a service or system that provides access to the Internet and such systems operated or services offered by libraries or educational institutions."[19] This term covered not only closed services such as Prodigy and CompuServe; courts would later conclude that it also encompassed Internet service providers and websites, apps, and other online forums. The bill defines "information content provider" as "any person or entity that is responsible, in whole or in part, for the creation or development of information provided through the Internet or any other interactive computer service."[20]

This immunity created a new legal landscape for online services. The bill provides companies with sweeping protection from claims arising from the words, images, videos, or other content provided by third parties. However, the precise scope of that protection would not be certain until courts decided what it means to treat an interactive computer service as the publisher or speaker of content provided by another information content provider. If courts were to adopt a broad reading of subsection (c)(1), the bill would create immunity that is far more expansive than the First Amendment protection for distributors under *Smith v. California*. Under this defendant-friendly interpretation, Section 230 would protect a company even if the company knew or should have known of illegal or defamatory third-party content. Yet of the two main parts of Section 230, this received considerably less attention in Congress and in the media coverage.

The second main component of the bill, subsection (c)(2), prohibits providers or users of interactive computer services from being held liable for "any action voluntarily taken in good faith to restrict access to or availability of material that the provider or user considers to be obscene, lewd, lascivious, filthy, excessively violent, harassing, or otherwise objectionable, whether or not such material is constitutionally protected" or giving information content providers the "technical means" to limit access to such material.[21] This "good faith" provision aims to encourage service providers to set their own user content standards. Although this portion of Section 230 has received less attention over the past two decades than the twenty-six words that immunized intermediaries, it helped to promote Section 230 as an alternative to the Exon proposal that helped to reduce indecency online.

Both the twenty-six words and the "good faith" action provisions at first were in the same section, (c), of the Cox-Wyden bill, but throughout the legislative process they were divided into two subsections, with the 26 words in (c)(1) and the "good faith" provision in (c)(2). Taken together, (c)(1) and (c)(2) mean that companies will not be considered to be the speakers or publishers of third-party content, and they will not lose that protection only because they delete objectionable posts or otherwise exercise good-faith efforts to moderate user content.

Cox and Wyden included a few narrow exceptions to this protection. The bill does not apply to online service providers for their users' violations of intellectual property laws.[22] If, for example, a YouTube user posts an entire episode of a television show, the TV network could sue YouTube for copyright infringement. (In 1998 Congress would pass a separate bill, the Digital Millennium Copyright Act, which provides companies with a safe harbor from copyright lawsuits if they remove user content after receiving notice from the copyright holder.) The Cox-Wyden bill also does not protect companies from enforcement of federal criminal laws.[23] The bill does shield providers from *state* criminal laws. Section 230's immunity does not apply to the federal Electronic Communications Privacy Act—which prohibits unauthorized wiretapping and access to stored communications—or similar state laws.[24] The law also states that it must not be interpreted "to prevent any State from enforcing any State law" that "is consistent with" Section 230, and lawsuits cannot be brought under "any State or local law that is inconsistent with this section."[25]

Figuring out what to exempt from the immunity was particularly challenging, recalled Butler, the Prodigy lawyer. Too many exceptions would render Section 230 toothless. But absolute immunity with no exceptions could attract opposition from law enforcement or industry groups. "We had to cut out criminal law," Butler said. "We had to cut out intellectual property. We knew the copyright people would kill us on that. It was a developing area. We were flying by the seats of our pants trying to make sure we got all the language in that we needed." The small group also made sure to include enough guidance for courts to understand that Section 230 did, indeed, provide broad immunity.

The bill begins with a description of the factual findings that led Cox and Wyden to write the bill. The bill declares that the Internet represents "an extraordinary advance in the availability of educational and informational resources to our citizens" and that it offers "a forum for a true diversity of political discourse, unique opportunities for cultural development, and myriad avenues for intellectual activity." The Cox-Wyden bill observes that Internet services provide users with a "great degree of control over the information that they receive" and that they have "flour-ished, to the benefit of all Americans, with a minimum of government regulation."[26] These findings came from a Center for Democracy and Technology report on user empowerment. Not to leave any confusion about their intent to promote their goals, Cox and Wyden also included a section in the bill that describes the "policy" that they intended to pro-mote with the bill. They listed many goals, including "to promote the continued development of the Internet and other interactive computer services and other interactive media" and "to encourage the development of technologies which maximize user control over what information is received by individuals, families, and schools who use the Internet and other interactive computer services."[27]

The "findings" and "policy" sections would serve as a road map for courts trying to sort out what Congress meant by the twenty-six words in Section 230. Cox and Wyden wanted to leave no doubt about their intent: they wanted the bill to strongly protect intermediaries, and by doing so they would protect online speech, allow innovation, and encourage com-panies to develop their own content moderation processes.

Even with the factual findings, policy statement, and definitions, the entire text of the bill is fewer than nine hundred words.

Despite its monumental statements about a new, hands-off approach to the Internet, the bill was virtually unopposed on Capitol Hill. Lobbyists focused primarily on the telecommunications bill's impacts on phone and cable television service. "We were dealing with the Telecommunications Act," Berman said. "This was not the center of the fight. The Internet was a footnote."[28] Wyden and Cox's proposal also received barely any media attention. The few newspaper articles that even mentioned the bill in the month after its introduction focused mainly on the Exon bill. A July 18, 1995, column published in the *Star-Tribune* newspaper of Casper, Wyo-ming, mentioned the Cox-Wyden bill as an alternative to Exon's proposal but described it as prohibiting Federal Communications Commission regulation of the Internet and putting "the responsibility squarely where it belongs, on the user."[29] While that observation is true, it missed the far bigger picture. What that column—and nearly every other word of media coverage of the time—failed to even briefly mention was the sweeping immunity that service providers and websites would receive from law-suits. The twenty-six words—and the rest of Section 230—were under the radar. And this proved to be essential to the bill's success. While Exon's proposal pitted civil liberties advocates against family rights groups, Section 230 quietly received the support of both sides, plus the technology lobbyists.

There is little evidence—or recollection by Section 230's architects—that interest groups mounted any significant opposition to the bill or even raised much criticism of it. This indifference likely stemmed from the relatively small size of the Internet industry; America Online and Prodigy were large, but they were only a fraction of the size that Google and Facebook would become in the following two decades. As the Internet economy grew, Section 230 would prevent individuals from recovering damages from some of the largest companies in the United States.

The Senate added Exon's proposal to its telecommunications bill in June, and then had finalized its bill. But the House had not yet completed drafting its own version of the telecom bill. Once the House passed its telecommunications bill, key members from the House and Senate would meet in a conference committee to hash out a final bill that combined portions of the House and Senate versions, and that final bill would receive an up-or-down vote from both the House and Senate. For the conference committee to even be able to consider including Section 230 in the final bill, Cox and Wyden first needed to persuade their House colleagues to amend their proposal to the House telecommunications bill. Their opportunity arrived on August 4, 1995, when the House debated and voted on amendments to its telecommunications bill. The House floor debate that day could not have been more promising for Section 230's supporters. Including Cox and Wyden, nine members of Congress spoke about the Cox-Wyden bill, and none encouraged colleagues to vote against it. Only one—Missouri Democrat Pat Danner—expressed even the slightest reservations about the bill. Danner said that although she strongly supported the Cox-Wyden bill, she remained concerned about children having "untraceable" access to obscene online material. She had a solution. Danner noted that phone companies must inform customers of the telephone numbers to which they make long-distance calls. "I believe that if computer online services were to include itemized billing, it would be a practical solution which would inform parents as to what materials their children are accessing on the Internet," she told Wyden on the House floor.[30] Wyden delicately responded to Danner's suggestion, promising to "certainly take this up with some of the private-sector firms that are working in this area."[31]

That exchange revealed precisely the challenge that Wyden, Cox, and the ragtag technology coalition faced when they talked with other members of Congress about Internet regulation. Danner's comments revealed an utter lack of understanding about the entire nature of the Internet. Emails simply are not like long-distance telephone calls, and they never were. Providers do not bill customers per email sent or website visited, and if they did, there would be an outcry from consumer and privacy advocates. At that time, however, members of Congress had little experience with communications outside of plain old telephone service. "This is 1995," White, the former Washington state congressman, said later. "By that time, email was prevalent, but a couple years before it wasn't. Members of Congress were older, and they hadn't focused on the Internet much." Congress's overall lack of exposure to the Internet, White said, may have helped him and other supporters of Section 230. "People didn't understand the impact of it," he said.[32]

The remainder of the House floor debate consisted primarily of praise for the Cox-Wyden bill and opposition to Exon's proposal. Joe Barton, a Texas Republican and influential member of the House Energy and Commerce Committee, said that Section 230 "is a much better approach than the approach that has been taken in the Senate by the Exon amendment."[33] Zoe Lofgren, a Democrat who represented Silicon Valley, agreed, comparing Exon's bill to "saying that the mailman is going to be liable when he delivers a plain brown envelope for what is inside it."[34] Barton and Lofgren had little in common politically. Yet the Texas conservative and the California liberal found common ground on a bill that took a light touch to regulating a new industry while also allowing companies the flexibility to block objectionable content from children. This bipartisan agreement perhaps explains how Section 230 moved through Congress so quietly.

The House members stressed that Section 230 empowered users and companies—rather than the government—to protect children. Speaking to his colleagues on the House floor, White said that as a parent of four small children, he wanted to protect them from improper online influences, but "the last person I want making that decision is the Federal Government."[35] They also discussed the other goal of Section 230: allowing online services to thrive and innovate without excessive regulation and lit-igation. Virginia Republican Bob Goodlatte alluded to the *Stratton Oak-mont* decision, arguing that it was impossible for those organizations that provided Internet access to "take the responsibility to edit out information that is going to be coming in to them from all manner of sources onto their bulletin board."[36] Cox used his floor debate time to clarify, for the record, that he intended the bill to reverse the *Stratton Oakmont* decision, which he called "backward." While acknowledging that his proposal was an alternative to Exon's bill, Cox also explained the need to encourage innovation and growth in a promising new sector. Section 230, Cox said on the House floor, "will establish as the policy of the United States that we do not wish to have content regulation by the Federal Government of what is on the Internet, that we do not wish to have a Federal Computer Commission with an army of bureaucrats regulating the Internet because frankly the Internet has grown up to be what it is without that kind of help from the Government."[37]

With no vocal opposition on the House floor, the House voted 420–4 to add Section 230 to the House version of the telecommunications re-form bill. As with Section 230's initial proposal in June, the House's over-whelming approval of the bill received barely any media attention. An article published in the *Washington Post* the day after the House vote—one of the few that even mentioned the Cox-Wyden amendment—stated that the legislation "expressly prohibits Internet censorship by the govern-ment" and "is based on the principle that technologies are already avail-able to help parents control what children can find on the Internet."[38] Consistent with much of the news coverage of Section 230 as it moved through Congress, the article failed to even mention the unprecedented protection that the bill would provide to online services.

The House continued to refine the telecom bill and passed the legisla-tion on October 12, 1995. The Cox-Wyden Section 230 proposal was in the House bill. Exon's proposal was not. "That was, for us, an enormous victory," Berman said.[39]

The technology coalition may have been optimistic, but the battle was not over. The House and Senate needed to reconcile their bills into a final draft in conference committee. The conference committee—a small group of members from the House and Senate chosen by leadership to negotiate a final bill—was free to reject Section 230. A budget showdown between Gingrich and Clinton led to a shutdown of the federal government in November 1995, so the conference committee did not convene until December, a month when Congress is in a hurry to pass appropriations bills before the winter recess. Neither Cox nor Wyden was on the conference committee, so they were not in the room to advocate for Section 230's inclusion in the final bill. But White, a Section 230 supporter and technology industry ally, was on the committee. Because of the significant attention that online pornography had received, White said, it would have been impossible to block Exon's proposal from being in the final bill. Throughout 1995, Congress had amended Exon's bill to address critics' concerns and increase the likelihood that a court would uphold the indecency provisions after an inevitable legal challenge by civil liberties groups.

In its final version, Exon's bill contained two subsections that instilled fear among technology companies and civil liberties groups. The first prohibited the use of a telecommunications device to transmit any content that was "obscene or indecent, knowing that the recipient of the communication is under 18 years of age, regardless of whether the maker of such communication placed the call or initiated the communication."[40] The second section prohibited an individual from knowingly sending or displaying content that depicted or described "in terms patently offensive as measured by contemporary community standards, sexual or excretory activities or organs."[41] Violators of both sections faced fines and up to two years in prison, as did individuals who knowingly permitted their telecommunications facilities to violate those prohibitions. The bill contained exceptions for those who took "good faith, reasonable, effective, and appropriate actions" to block minors from the materials.[42]

In the conference committee, White had two goals: tone down Exon's criminal prohibition on indecency and ensure that Section 230 was in the final bill. For his first goal, White almost succeeded in amending Exon's bill to apply it to only content harmful to minors, but conservatives ultimately blocked him. Exon's indecency amendment stayed in the final bill. However, White succeeded in ensuring that Section 230 was included in the final telecommunications bill. He recalls that Section 230 was not particularly controversial among other members of the conference committee, so it was not difficult to persuade colleagues to keep it in the final bill as long as the Exon amendment stayed in. "It was two sides of the same coin," White said. "We wanted the Internet to be open. We also had this age-old issue of indecency. For a lot of people at the time, indecency was their main concern about it."[43]

McLean, who was Exon's legal counsel and point person on the telecommunications law, believes that the conference committee included both Section 230 and the Exon amendment as a compromise. The Exon amendment addressed the family values groups' concerns about the proliferation of online pornography. Section 230 provided the technology sector with a safe harbor to help ensure that it would not be held responsible for use content. He doubts that either Section 230 or Exon's indecency bill could have passed without the other. "They were symbiotic," McLean said. "Section 230 was a concession to the industry that made our provision more palatable."[44] On his congressional office's website in late 1995, White touted what he called the "White Internet Compromise": combining the Cox-Wyden bill with some of the penalties of the Exon bill. "The network of networks called the Internet is growing at an extraordinary rate and should be allowed to grow without federal regulation," White's website stated at the time. "The White proposal ensures that the federal government does not stifle the growth and innovation for education and commerce on the Internet."[45]

The involvement of technology companies such as America Online and Prodigy made this negotiation different from those involving other free speech and civil liberties issues in Congress. Exon and his supporters did not want the public to see them as attacking huge corporations. And huge corporations did not want to be seen as peddling smut to minors. "It's one thing to fight with the Electronic Frontier Foundation," McLean said. "It's another thing to fight with IBM and Sears. And IBM and Sears didn't want to be associated with pornography either. It was one of those moments of politics being the art of the possible. Both sides genuinely sat down and listened."[46]

The conference committee included both Section 230 and Exon's indecency amendment in its final bill. Because both proposals dealt with the Internet and related to the indecency debate, the conference committee combined them into Title V, which it named the Communications Decency Act of 1996, borrowing the title from Exon's initial bill. Conference committees are not open to the public, so it is impossible to know precisely why the committee members decided to include Section 230. But a report accompanying the final bill explains at least part of the members' thinking. The committee wrote that by including Section 230, it intended to overrule *Stratton Oakmont,* which created "serious obstacles to the important federal policy of empowering parents to determine the content of communications their children receive through interactive computer services."[47]

The telecommunications bill moved back to the full House and Senate. Because both chambers needed to pass identical bills, it was not open to further amendments. On February 1, 1996, the Telecommunications Act of 1996 passed the House in a 414–16 vote and the Senate in a 91–5 vote. President Clinton signed the forty-six-thousand-word bill on February 8. Section 230 now appears in Title 47 of the United States Code—the official compendium of federal statutes—under the title "Protection for private blocking and screening of offensive material." In his statement at the bill signing, Clinton discussed telephone industry competition and broadcast station ownership and did not allude to either part of the Communications Decency Act. Cox and Wyden had succeeded in passing a law to overrule *Stratton Oakmont.* But the law also included Exon's criminal prohibitions on indecent content—legislation that had the civil liberties community up in arms.

A week before President Clinton signed the Telecommunications Act, Wyden won a tight special election to replace Senator Bob Packwood, who had resigned in a sexual harassment scandal, and as of 2017, Wyden had risen to be the top Democrat on the powerful Senate Finance Committee. Although he is firmly stationed in the liberal wing of the Senate, he has continued to find areas of bipartisan agreement. For instance, Wyden's 1996 Senate race against Republican Gordon Smith was heated and divisive. Months later, Smith won Oregon's other Senate seat when Mark Hatfield retired. Although they were fierce opponents in 1996, Wyden and Smith quickly became known as the congressional "odd couple," working on Oregon-focused issues for the twelve years that Smith served in the Senate. Cox served in the House until 2005, when President George W. Bush nominated him to chair the Securities and Exchange Commission. After leading the commission for nearly four years, he moved back to Orange County to practice law.

Cox and Wyden still often chat on the phone. They also see each other at technology industry events, where they both receive awards for their work on technology policy. In later years Cox and Wyden became heroes of the technology community. In 1996, however, their achievement was largely unnoticed by the public. Media coverage barely acknowledged the passage of Section 230. Articles and TV segments focused on mainly the Exon indecency prohibitions, which civil liberties groups were already planning to challenge in court the day it passed.

HOW THE DECENCY FIGHT WAS WON. SAVVY POLITICAL VET-ERANS TROUNCED NAIVE FREE SPEECH ADVOCATES WHEN CONGRESSIONAL DEBATE SHIFTED TO FAMILY SAFETY FROM ON-LINE TECHNOLOGY.

This was the headline in the March 3, 1996, business section of the *San Jose Mercury News*, which then was the bible of the Silicon Valley tech world. The three-thousand-word article began by declaring that the "Internet's free speech supporters lost their historic battle over cyberspace decency standards because they were outgunned, outflanked, out-connected and out-thought in the most crucial battle of the on-line community's brief history" and described Section 230 merely as focusing on "software that would put parents in control, sidestepping the main censorship question." The article mentioned in passing that Section 230 also was in the final bill but cast the new telecommunications law as a brutal loss for the technology sector.[48]

This sort of media coverage explains how Section 230 could quietly slip into the United States Code. The lobbyists and moneyed industry interests focused on the battle between local and long-distance telephone companies. When the media coverage was not following the money, it homed in on flashy issues, like the prospect of a librarian going to prison for emailing an article about breast cancer to a teenager.

It was as though Section 230 was invisible.

Exon's indecency amendment, on the other hand, quickly became one of the most visible parts of the Telecommunications Act of 1996. On the day that Clinton signed the bill, the ACLU and nineteen other civil liberties advocates sued to prevent the government from enforcing Exon's indecency amendment. Four months after Clinton signed the bill, a special three-judge panel in Philadelphia ruled that those criminal prohibitions violated the First Amendment. The Justice Department immediately appealed the ruling to the Supreme Court.

On June 26, 1997, the Supreme Court unanimously struck down Exon's indecency sections.

The government defended the Exon law mainly relying on a 1978 Supreme Court decision, *FCC v. Pacifica Foundation*,[49] that allowed the FCC, the Federal Communications Commission, to penalize a radio station for broadcasting George Carlin's monologue containing the "seven dirty words." In *Reno v. ACLU*, Justice John Paul Stevens disagreed. Writing for all nine justices, he declared the Internet to be a different medium from those of television and radio stations. Broadcast spectrum is limited and controlled by a handful of content creators, whereas the Internet allows anyone to publish his or her thoughts and creations: "This dynamic, multifaceted category of communication includes not only traditional print and news services, but also audio, video, and still images, as well as interactive, real-time dialogue. Through the use of chat rooms, any person with a phone line can become a town crier with a voice that resonates farther than it could from any soapbox. Through the use of Web pages, mail exploders, and newsgroups, the same individual can become a pamphleteer."

Like Cox and Wyden, Justice Stevens recognized the potential of the Internet to thrive by attracting large communities of content creators. By imposing criminal penalties on people who knowingly transmit indecent material to minors, Stevens reasoned, the law would also prevent adults from receiving that material—something that they're constitutionally permitted to do. "Given the size of the potential audience for most messages, in the absence of a viable age verification process, the sender must be charged with knowing that one or more minors will likely view it," Stevens wrote. "Knowledge that, for instance, one or more members of a 100-person chat group will be a minor—and therefore that it would be a crime to send the group an indecent message—would surely burden communication among adults."

The government also had argued to the Supreme Court that regulating online indecency is necessary for the development of nascent Internet-based industries. If the Internet gained a reputation as a porn-filled cesspool, the government argued, customers would go offline. Justice Stevens scoffed at that suggestion, calling it "singularly unpersuasive." Again with a line of argument that could have come out of the mouths of Cox or Wyden,

Stevens wrote that *less* regulation of the Internet is essential to its growth. "The record demonstrates that the growth of the Internet has been and continues to be phenomenal," he added. "As a matter of constitutional tradition, in the absence of evidence to the contrary, we presume that governmental regulation of the content of speech is more likely to interfere with the free exchange of ideas than to encourage it. The interest in encouraging freedom of expression in a democratic society outweighs any theoretical but unproven benefit of censorship."

The Supreme Court's ruling struck down Exon's indecency law, but it did not affect Section 230. After the Supreme Court's opinion, all that remained of the Communications Decency Act was Section 230. The ad hoc technology coalition had not only succeeded in ultimately defeating Exon's bill; they had also established Section 230's immunity from claims that stemmed from third-party content. "The irony is that the Communications Decency Act became the Communications Freedom Act," Berman said. "Going through the pornography fight was a destiny that let the Internet be free."[50] The technology companies knew that they had scored a victory. But in the months after President Clinton signed the Telecommunications Act, it was not clear exactly how courts would interpret the twenty-six words. Few judges had ever confronted lawsuits involving the Internet. And Congress had never before passed a law like Section 230. Would the courts broadly interpret Section 230? Or would the courts immunize only some companies, as Justice Ain did in *Stratton Oakmont*?

There were two very different ways to interpret the twenty-six words. If a court were to agree with Justice Ain's binary distinction between "publishers" and "distributors," Section 230 would merely mean that all online services must be treated as distributors, and they become liable for third-party content if they receive notice but fail to remove the content. But a court also might conclude that Section 230's prohibition on treating online services as "publishers" or "speakers" of third-party content means that these platforms have absolutely no liability for this content unless an exception applied. Neither the text of the statute nor the committee report directly and clearly indicated which approach would prevail.

Clarity would soon emerge, thanks to a man named Ken from Seattle. And this would forever alter the Internet's legal landscape.

Part II

THE RISE OF SECTION 230

When President Clinton signed the Telecommunications Act into law on February 8, 1996, John Perry Barlow was in a hotel in Davos, Switzerland, where he had attended the World Economic Forum.[1] The former Grateful Dead songwriter, who founded the Electronic Frontier Foundation, was furious about the Exon Amendment. He typed out an email to hundreds of friends. The email became known as "A Declaration of the Independence of Cyberspace." Addressed to "Governments of the Industrial World," Barlow pronounced cyberspace to be a realm that is not subject to traditional government laws and regulations. "We are creating a world where anyone, anywhere may express his or her beliefs, no matter how singular, without fear of being coerced into silence or conformity," Barlow wrote. "Your legal concepts of property, expression, identity, movement, and context do not apply to us. They are all based on matter, and there is no matter here." The 844-word declaration went viral (by 1996 standards), and *Wired* magazine reprinted it in its June 1996 issue.

Barlow's declaration represented a new mind-set known as Internet exceptionalism. Under this philosophy, the Internet simply is different from the media that came before it, such as newspapers and television. The Internet carries exponentially more content from exponentially more providers. The Internet also presents greater social benefits than old-school media. Because the Internet is different, the government should not burden it with traditional regulations and laws.

Internet exceptionalism is at the heart of Section 230. During the brief congressional floor debate in August 1995 about the Cox-Wyden proposal, Cox spoke about the need to nurture the amazing potential of this burgeoning technology. "We are talking about the Internet now, not about telephones, not about televisions or radios, not about cable TV, not about broadcasting, but in technological terms and historical terms, an absolutely brand-new technology," Cox said. "The Internet is a fascinating place and many of us have recently become acquainted with all that it holds for us in terms of education and political discourse."[2]

The Internet is different.

The Supreme Court appeared to agree with the general principle of Internet exceptionalism when it struck down the Exon Amendment. Justice Stevens's opinion was not nearly as extreme as Barlow's declaration, but the opinion carried a strong tinge of Internet exceptionalism. Stevens wrote that the Internet allows "tens of millions of people to communicate with one another and to access vast amounts of information from around the world" and is "a unique and wholly new medium of worldwide communication."[3]

The Internet is different.

Internet exceptionalism would only grow in the following year, as courts began to interpret what remained of the Communications Decency Act: Section 230. The first judges to interpret Section 230 could have concluded that it applies in only narrow circumstances. They did not. They read it as broadly as possible, making Section 230 the vehicle for Internet exceptionalism in the United States.

4

Ask for Ken

As Congress was quietly drafting Section 230 in 1995, Kenneth Zeran began receiving phone calls. A lot of phone calls. Angry calls. Hang-up calls. Media calls. These calls eventually would lead to a court opinion that caused judges around the country to interpret Section 230 broadly and immunize websites against claims from sympathetic plaintiffs.

Zeran was a middle-aged filmmaker and real estate agent who was living in his parents' house in Seattle. When he arrived home on April 25, 1995, Zeran discovered hang-up calls on his answering machine. He then received a call from Neff Hudson, a reporter at the *Army Times*.[1] Hudson told Zeran that an America Online user, with the pseudonym KEN ZZ03, was advertising T-shirts with offensive slogans about the bombing of the Alfred P. Murrah Federal Building in Oklahoma City that had occurred six days earlier. Hudson told him that the posting, in the Michigan Military Movement forum on AOL, instructed people to call Zeran's home phone number.[2]

Zeran was befuddled. He didn't even have an America Online account, so he couldn't view the post that Hudson was asking him about. And he knew nothing about Oklahoma City T-shirts. Zeran called America Online and spoke with a legal department staffer. He insisted that he was not behind the posts. The staffer told Zeran that the company would remove the post, but she refused to publish a retraction of the post's claims. Over the rest of the evening, he received several angry calls, including death threats, from strangers who apparently had viewed the post.[3]

The ad soon disappeared. But a new post materialized on America Online the next day, and the angry phone calls continued. Zeran also received calls from reporters at the *Oklahoman* newspaper in Oklahoma City and the *Oakland Press* in Pontiac, Michigan. Zeran explained to the reporters that he was not involved in any way with the posts, and the Michigan reporter faxed a copy of the "ad" to Zeran.[4] When he received the one-page fax, he saw his first name and phone number on a one-page bulletin board message, posted at 2:23 P.M. Eastern time on April 26, 1995. The subject was "GREAT OKLAHOMA T-SHIRTS," and the poster was "KEN ZZ033," just one character off from the name used in the previous post. The post read:

EXECERCISE [*SIC*] YOUR FREEDOM OF SPEECH

NEW OKLAHOMA T-SHIRTS ORDER YOURS TODAY !!!!

Item# slogan

#520—"Rack'em, Stack'em, and Pack'em—Oklahoma 1995" SOLD OUT

#522—"Shit happens. . . . . . to EXPLODE—Oklahoma 1995"

#524—"Dear IRS. . . . . . The check is in the van—Oklahoma 1995"

#568—"Visit Oklahoma . . . It's a BLAST !!!"

#569—"Putting the kids to bed. . . . . . . Oklahoma 1995" ONLY SMALLS LEFT

#583—"McVeigh for President 1996"

NEW ITEMS

#633—"2nd floor ladies apparel, 1st floor dead babies—Oklahoma 1995"

#637—"Forget the rescue, let the maggots take over—Oklahoma 1995"

#651—"Finally, a day care center that keeps the kids quiet—Oklahoma 1995"

*** *I WILL BE DONATING $1 FROM EVERY SHIRT TO THE VICTIMS* ***

→ $14.95 each plus $2.00 shipping/handling
→ Shirts are a white cotton 50/50 blend with black ink.
→ SIZES: Small, Medium, Large, X-Large, XX-Large
→ Please order by number and size
→ All orders are shipped out same day
Please call [phone number redacted]
Ask for Ken
Due to high demand please call back if busy[5]

Zeran's phone continued to ring incessantly, with angry America Online subscribers on the other end. By then, Zeran said, his phone was ringing so much that it had become useless. Because Zeran used the phone number for his business, changing the phone number was not a viable option.

On April 27 and 28, he repeatedly called American Online but received voice mail. He left messages and continued to call until the afternoon of April 28, when he reached an America Online employee named Pamela, who told him that dial-up accounts associated with the posts originated from a phone number with a Massachusetts area code. Pamela also suggested that Zeran contact law enforcement. He immediately called the Seattle office of the Federal Bureau of Investigation to file a report, and he called Pamela again to request the deletion of the message. She assured him that AOL would soon delete the post and disable the account.[6]

More Oklahoma posts emerged on America Online, containing Zeran's phone number. By the end of April, he was receiving angry calls on average every two minutes. A staffer from the tabloid television show *Hard Copy* called him.[7] His troubles worsened on May 1, when Mark Shannon, a radio host at KRXO in Oklahoma City, read the T-shirt slogans on the air, provided listeners with his home phone number, and encouraged them to call.[8] This was just two weeks after that city had experienced a domestic terrorist attack that killed 168 people, including 19 children, and injured hundreds more.[9]

The pace of the phone calls increased, as did the intensity. Some callers were grieving relatives and friends of Oklahoma City bombing victims. For days after the broadcast, Zeran received death threats.[10] Unable to reach an America Online lawyer on the phone, Zeran faxed and mailed a letter to AOL lawyer Ellen Kirsh, begging her to "withdraw and not list any entries referring to my name and/or phone number effective immediately." He received no response that day.[11]

As his phone continued to ring around the clock, Zeran had trouble sleeping. The next day, a Portland-based Secret Service agent interviewed Zeran and advised him to correct the record in the press. Zeran called America Online again and spoke with AOL lawyer Jane Church, who said she was unaware of the letter. She told Zeran that the company would remove the postings.[12] Over the next two days, the angry calls continued, and Zeran called the local police. The police increased its surveillance around Zeran's home. One of the officers told Zeran that he had spoken with Church, who had assured the officer that AOL had purged the posts and conducted a "system check."[13]

As the angry phone calls continued to roll in at a steady pace, Zeran took the Secret Service agent's advice and told his story to a reporter for the *Oklahoman,* the daily newspaper in Oklahoma City. On May 7, 1995—twelve days after the phone calls began—the *Oklahoman* ran a story on page A-16 titled "Online T-Shirt Scam Jolts Seattle Man." It began:

> Ken is an easygoing fellow who claims to have no enemies.
>
> But he's made a few thousand—maybe tens of thousands—enemies worldwide since the Oklahoma City bombing.
>
> What's frustrating is that the anger and threats being hurled at him aren't justified. They're due to a heartless computer hacker using technology to transform Ken from a docile Seattle real estate agent into a nervous figure forever looking over his shoulder.
>
> "I'm a victim here," he said. "A target."[14]

After the article ran, Zeran received some apologies from people who had called him earlier, but he also continued to field threatening calls. By the following week, Zeran was so sleep deprived and emotionally exhausted that he saw his doctor, who prescribed tranquilizers.[15]

Zeran received a response to his letter to America Online on May 22—twenty-one days after he faxed the letter to Kirsh, the AOL lawyer. In a letter dated May 17, AOL lawyer Church wrote that the "information you have provided is insufficient for us to locate the alleged postings which you claim are causing you problems," and informed Zeran that he "should be aware that America Online does not have the ability to physically screen every posting subscribers make to the America Online service before they are posted."[16]

Zeran retained Leo Kayser—the New York lawyer who represented Blanchard and Cubby in the case against CompuServe, discussed in chapter 2. Kayser recalled that his former law school roommate, a lawyer in Seattle, connected Zeran with Kayser.[17] In 1995, Kayser was one of only a handful of lawyers who had ever tried to hold an online service accountable for third-party content, so he would be a logical choice. Kayser wrote a six-page letter to Church on June 26, 1995, describing the torrent of phone calls and the "considerable injury" that Zeran had suffered. Pointing to Judge Leisure's ruling in the *Cubby* case, Kayser asserted that America Online "is legally liable for much of this injury for its failure to delete the bogus material upon receiving notice from Mr. Zeran."[18] When Kayser wrote the letter, America Online's primary legal defense arose from the First Amendment. Section 230 was still being drafted and negotiated on Capitol Hill.

On January 4, 1996, Zeran sued KRXO, the Oklahoma City radio station, in Oklahoma federal court. On April 23, 1996—nearly three months after President Clinton signed Section 230 into law—Zeran sued America Online in the same Oklahoma federal court. Zeran sued America Online not for defamation but for negligence. Negligence means that the defendant owed a duty of care to the plaintiff and failed to meet that duty, leading to injury to the plaintiff. For instance, a customer who fell on a department store's wet floor might sue the store for negligence, arguing that, at the very least, the retailer had a duty to post a wet-floor sign. "There was a standard of care that America Online was obligated to engage in," said Kayser, who litigated the case for Zeran.[19]

Zeran argued that when he first called America Online to complain about the posts, the company was placed on notice of the false and harmful posts and that it was obligated to immediately delete them and mitigate damage by informing subscribers that the posting was false. The company also had a duty to monitor for additional false posts about Zeran, he argued in the complaint.

The Oklahoma court transferred the case to a federal court in Virginia, the home of America Online's headquarters. The case was assigned to Judge T. S. Ellis III, a Reagan appointee who then was fifty-six years old. Many lawyers who practice in Virginia have Judge Ellis stories. The former naval aviator is notorious for writing long opinions that leave no fact or argument unaddressed.[20] He also holds hearings throughout the day and well into the night, and will keep the lawyers in the courtroom until they have exhaustively argued every last detail. Ellis has presided over the high-profile criminal cases of American Taliban member John Walker Lindh, former congressman William Jefferson, and former Trump campaign chairman Paul Manafort. Before he sentences criminal defendants to years in prison, he often reminds them that life is about "making choices and living with the consequences of the choices that you make."[21]

Judge Ellis hears cases in the United States District Court for the Eastern District of Virginia's Alexandria courthouse, a building just outside Washington, D.C., in a cluster of unremarkable beige office buildings such as the headquarters for the Patent and Trademark Office. However, the Alexandria court's docket is extraordinary. Because the Pentagon and Central Intelligence Agency are in the court's boundaries, the judges preside over many national security cases. The Alexandria court also is known as the "Rocket Docket." Unlike many other federal courts, in which cases can drag on for years, the judges in Alexandria take pride in requiring the parties to rapidly file motions and conduct discovery, and the judges swiftly issue their rulings.

On January 28, 1997, America Online asked Judge Ellis to dismiss Zeran's case. Representing America Online was Patrick Carome, a highly regarded First Amendment media lawyer at Wilmer, Cutler & Pickering (now known as WilmerHale), one of the largest firms in Washington, D.C. Carome's brief did not even mention *Smith v. California*. Instead, he relied solely on Section 230, which had been law for less than a year. Carome's strategy carried some risk. No court in the United States had issued a written opinion interpreting Section 230, so Carome was starting from scratch. This was vastly different from the standard defamation case, in which both sides relied on decades of First Amendment rulings from the Supreme Court. Carome could not cite a single case that interpreted Section 230 because none existed in January 1997. Carome had to carefully walk Judge Ellis through the statute and why he believed it afforded America Online such sweeping protections.

To interpret Section 230, Carome relied heavily on the statements that the bill's supporters made throughout Section 230. He pointed Judge Ellis to the "policy" section that Cox and Wyden included in the text of the bill and argued that "Congress recognized that a regulatory regime under which interactive computer service providers faced potential liability as publishers or speakers of content produced by others inevitably would lead such providers to censor the content of speech on their networks to avoid the risk of liability, or even cause such providers to stop offering their services altogether."[22]

But did the statute protect America Online from Zeran's lawsuit? The twenty-six key words from the law state that "no provider or user of an interactive computer service shall be treated as the publisher or speaker of any information provided by another information content provider." There was little doubt that America Online provided an interactive computer service. So Carome had to persuade Judge Ellis to agree with him on two points: first, that the Oklahoma City posts were "information provided by another information content provider" and, second, that Zeran's suit treated America Online as the "publisher or speaker" of those posts. The T-shirt posts, Carome wrote, were provided by another information content provider—the anonymous poster (or posters). AOL's role, he wrote, was "merely that of a distributor of someone else's information."[23]

The harder task for Carome was to convince Judge Ellis that Zeran's lawsuit sought to treat America Online as the publisher or speaker of that content. Kayser's decision to sue for negligence was deliberate. Kayser had carefully drafted the complaint to avoid suing for defamation—the typical claim that a plaintiff would bring against a newspaper or other media outlet that published a false and harmful article. Carome argued that the difference between negligence and defamation was immaterial under Section 230. "In every respect, imposing liability upon AOL for these messages would treat AOL as if it had actually been the originator and publisher (or speaker) of the messages—precisely the treatment of an 'interactive computer service' provider that the statute was designed to proscribe."[24]

Because Judge Ellis heard cases in the Rocket Docket, Kayser had little over two weeks to respond to Carome's request to dismiss the lawsuit. Kayser devoted most of his response brief to arguing that Section 230 simply did not immunize AOL. Section 230, Kayser argued, only prevented interactive computer services from being treated as *publishers* or *speakers* of third-party content. Zeran's lawsuit, on the other hand, never claimed that America Online was the publisher or speaker of the Oklahoma City posts, nor was it necessary to treat the company as the publisher or speaker to find that it had been negligent. Instead, Kayser asserted, the negligence lawsuit merely alleged that America Online was the *distributor* or "secondary publisher" of the posts.[25]

The distinction between distributor and publisher was at the heart of Kayser's argument. By classifying America Online as a distributor, Kayser was trying to convince Judge Ellis that America Online was not entitled to immunity under Section 230 because the lawsuit did not treat the company as a "publisher." As a distributor, he argued, America Online received only the basic First Amendment protections afforded under *Cubby*. Under this line of reasoning, America Online would be liable for the Oklahoma City posts if the company was on notice that those posts were on its bulletin boards yet failed to promptly remove them. In Kayser's view, Section 230 did not provide the sweeping immunity that Carome claimed. He wrote that the statute merely overruled *Stratton Oakmont*'s classification of Prodigy as a publisher because Prodigy had adopted content policies and reserved the right to moderate content.[26]

Under Kayser's interpretation, Section 230's only change to online liability law was to place online services such as Prodigy and AOL in the "distributor" category, holding them liable for user posts if they knew or should have known about the harmful content. Zeran's case differed from Porush's, Kayser wrote, because Zeran's repeated complaints to America Online put the company on notice of the defamatory posts. So Zeran can sue America Online as a negligent distributor, Kayser argued. "AOL is not being held liable for the messages themselves as it argues, but rather for failure to take appropriate action to block the posting after actual notice," Kayser wrote.[27] By overruling *Stratton Oakmont*, Kayser reasoned, Congress simply intended for all online services to receive the immunity of *Cubby v. CompuServe*. Kayser's client Blanchard lost in the *Cubby* case because the court determined that CompuServe did not know about *Rumorville*'s contents. Had CompuServe received a complaint about *Rumorville* but failed to act on it, the outcome may have been different.

In 2017 Kayser said that he still believed that Congress intended merely to reaffirm that the *Cubby* rule applies to all online services. Even though Kayser's client lost that case, he conceded that Judge Leisure had correctly decided the *Cubby* case. "You can't hold the library or the newsstand or the billboard or the website responsible unless you give them the notice that there's something defamatory or actionable in some way," Kayser said.

Judge Ellis held a hearing on America Online's motion on February 28, 1997. Judge Ellis, like many judges and lawyers in the Alexandria court, takes great pride in the court's local traditions and procedures. If the primary lawyer on a case is not from the Washington, D.C., area, he or she typically partners with "local counsel" who understands the Rocket Docket's unique procedures and often is known to the judges. Because Kayser worked in New York, he partnered with John S. Edwards, a lawyer and Virginia state senator who had been the U.S. attorney for the Western District of Virginia in the administration of President Jimmy Carter. (Virginia is divided into two federal judicial districts—the Western District and the Eastern District, which is the location of the Alexandria court.) Edwards's office was in Roanoke, about two hundred miles from Alexandria.

The hearing got off to a bumpy start for Zeran. Judge Ellis admonished Edwards for filing documents by fax machine, in violation of the local court rules. " 'Local counsel' typically means local," Ellis said. "Roanoke is not terribly local, but I am going to permit it. But if there is a hardship that results, it will fall on the plaintiff."[28] Carome presented his arguments first, telling Judge Ellis that the lawsuit sought to render America Online liable as the publisher of the anonymous user's postings. Section 230, he said, simply prevented such lawsuits, regardless of whether they claimed defamation or negligence. Judge Ellis appeared to have some trouble accepting Carome's view that this new law provided such broad protections to online services. Allowing America Online to be sued for user posts, Carome told Judge Ellis, would mean that the company would "have to essentially have a legion of investigators on hand to investigate that complaint, just as a newspaper would."

"But a newspaper does have responsibility," Ellis responded.

"That is absolutely right," Carome said. "And a newspaper is—when you sue a newspaper for the content in the newspaper, you have treated that newspaper as the publisher of that content. . . . And that's perfectly permissible as to a newspaper."

"If you substituted a newspaper for America Online in the hypothetical I gave you," Ellis said, "there probably would be liability."

"Absolutely, your Honor," Carome said. "It is very clear that Section 230 was intended to eliminate liability for entities such as America Online."

"Now, let's suppose," Ellis said, "that instead of something appearing on America Online about some or one of their subscribers, that America Online decided for one reason or another to defame somebody and started putting stuff on. Is there any liability?"

"Yes," Carome said, "there potentially would be liability, your Honor, because—"

"Why?" Ellis asked.

"Section 230 states that no provider or user of an interactive computer service—that is, America Online—shall be treated as the publisher or speaker of any information provided by another," Carome replied.

Ellis moved on to question Carome about more technical legal issues, mainly whether Section 230 could retroactively apply to a lawsuit involving bulletin board postings that occurred before Congress passed the statute. But it was clear from the transcript that he had misgivings about shielding America Online from any liability. Kayser's oral argument was smoother, and Judge Ellis interrupted him only a few times, mainly to ask clarification questions or to agree with him. "This case is not just a defamation case," Kayser told Judge Ellis. "The telephone number of the plaintiff was used. If that telephone number had been blocked out—it actually goes directly to a direct privacy issue—then these phone calls that have threatened his life couldn't have happened in the wake of what did occur here."

In the Rocket Docket, judges often announce their rulings at the end of a hearing, to avoid the delays associated with writing a long opinion. At the end of the *Zeran* hearing, Ellis did not announce his decision, but instead would write a full opinion "chiefly because it is novel." Three weeks after the hearing, Ellis issued a nearly eight-thousand-word opinion with twenty-seven footnotes. Purely on the basis of Ellis's questions during the oral argument, Zeran appeared to have a reasonable chance of defeating America Online's motion to dismiss, allowing the case to proceed and possibly go to trial. However, Ellis agreed with Carome and granted America Online's motion to dismiss the case. Ellis rejected Kayser's argument that

Section 230 did not apply to distributors such as America Online. Distributors, Ellis reasoned, are one "species" of publisher. Zeran could not skirt Section 230's immunity, Ellis wrote, by labeling America Online a "distributor." "It follows that Zeran's attempt to impose distributor liability on AOL is, in effect, an attempt to have AOL treated as the publisher of the defamatory material," Ellis wrote.[29] Ellis also agreed with Carome that holding America Online liable for the anonymous postings would contradict Congress's intent "to encourage the development of technologies, procedures, and techniques" that moderate offensive content. "If this objective is frustrated by the imposition of distributor liability on Internet providers, then preemption is warranted," Ellis wrote. "Closely examined, distributor liability has just this effect."[30]

Ellis's ruling marked the first time that any U.S. court had ever interpreted Section 230 in a written opinion. It was the only opinion that other courts could look to when deciding whether Section 230 shielded an online service from lawsuits. Because the opinion was issued by a district judge, and not an appellate court, it was not binding precedent, so any judge (including other federal judges in Alexandria) was free to disregard it in other cases. This lack of binding precedent soon would change, as Zeran quickly appealed his loss to the United States Court of Appeals for the Fourth Circuit. In his brief for Zeran to the Fourth Circuit, Kayser primarily reargued that Zeran's complaint treated America Online as a distributor and not a publisher: "The lower court's opinion results in the absurd position that Congress has enacted legislation that utterly vitiates any remedy an injured party has against a computer service provider, which is distributing defamatory or other objectionable matter which can foreseeably injure someone, after such provider is given express notice of the situation, has or should have had the ability to prevent or mitigate the injury, but, nevertheless has failed to respond adequately to such notice. Congress enacted no such legislation. What Congress did was make it easier for computer service providers to respond to notices without subjecting themselves to increased exposure by deeming themselves 'publishers.' "[31]

To many reasonable observers, Ellis's ruling resulted in not only an absurd reading of an obscure statute but also an outcome that was fundamentally unfair to plaintiffs such as Zeran, who could not track down and sue the actual poster. Unfortunately for Zeran, the Fourth Circuit could not reverse Ellis's ruling on the grounds that it was merely unfair or absurd. Kayser needed to convince the judges that Ellis misinterpreted Section 230. Carome argued that Ellis had correctly applied the new law. He told the Fourth Circuit in his response brief that Kayser's attempts to cast America Online as a "distributor" rather than a "publisher," and to sue for negligence rather than defamation, was a distinction without a difference. "If Section 230 were construed so as to permit Zeran's 'negligence' claim to survive, then virtually any claim that is barred by Section 230 could be restated in the same fashion," Carome wrote. "Congress obviously did not intend for the protections it created in Section 230 to be so easily eviscerated."[32]

The Fourth Circuit hears appeals from all federal district courts in Virginia, Maryland, West Virginia, North Carolina, and South Carolina. In the late 1990s, it had a reputation for being more conservative than many other circuits, with many Republican appointees. As with all other federal appeals courts, the panels of three randomly chosen judges hear the appeals.

Some federal appeals courts notify lawyers—and the public—of the identities of the three panel judges weeks or months before arguments, allowing the lawyers to tailor their briefs or oral arguments to the three judges' philosophies. For instance, some judges subscribe to the "textualist" philosophy that they should interpret statutes based only on the plain language in the statute and nothing else. Other judges more broadly consider the legislature's purpose, looking at statements that members of Congress issued during debate on the bill and reports that committees issued when considering the legislation. The composition of a panel can make or break a lawyer's case. However, the Fourth Circuit has a long-standing policy against announcing the judges' names in advance. Carome and Kayser learned the names of the three judges when they arrived at the Fourth Circuit's Richmond, Virginia, courthouse for arguments on the morning of October 2, 1997.

This was a decade before iPhones, so the lawyers could not conduct a quick search for the judges' biographies. It was even before the Black-Berry, so they couldn't ask coworkers to email them information. In fact, most people did not even have flip cell phones at that point. As soon as Carome learned the judges' names at the court clerk's office, he rushed to a courthouse pay phone to make a call to ask a colleague to quickly research the three judges' backgrounds.

J. Harvie Wilkinson III, the chief judge of the Fourth Circuit, was on the panel. At first, Carome recalled, he was concerned because Wilkinson had a reputation for being rather conservative. Wilkinson was a Justice Department official early in the Reagan administration, and Reagan later appointed him to the Fourth Circuit.[33] A conservative might not want to be the first judge in U.S. history to grant wide immunity to Internet companies for scurrilous user posts. But Carome's colleague gave Carome a ray of hope: in the late 1970s and early 1980s, after he clerked for Supreme Court justice Lewis Powell and taught law at the University of Virginia, Wilkinson was the editorial page editor of the *Virginian Pilot* newspaper. Perhaps Wilkinson's newspaper roots might tilt him toward a ruling that promoted free speech? One tidbit from Wilkinson's biography was not readily apparent from his official biography: he had known Kayser for decades, dating to when they were undergraduates at Yale University. They later attended law school at the University of Virginia and served on the law review together. "I always used to pull his leg and joke with him all the time," Kayser recalled.

The two other panel judges were harder to read. Donald S. Russell had been a Democratic governor and U.S. senator from South Carolina before President Lyndon Johnson appointed him to be a federal district judge in 1966. President Richard Nixon appointed him to the Fourth Circuit in 1971.[34] Russell was ninety-one when he heard arguments in the *Zeran* case. The final judge was Terrence Boyle, a former aide to Republican senator Jesse Helms. Boyle was a judge on a federal district court in North Carolina, appointed by Reagan. Although he was not an appellate judge, the Fourth Circuit, like most other appellate courts, allows district judges to sit "by designation" on a panel to help reduce the caseload on the full-time Fourth Circuit judges. (President George H. W. Bush had nominated Boyle to the Fourth Circuit, but Democrats blocked his confirmation, as they would again when President George W. Bush renominated him.)[35]

Because his client was appealing Ellis's decision, Kayser argued first. The Fourth Circuit has purged the recording of the *Zeran* oral argument, and none of the lawyers who worked on the case had retained a recording or transcript. Carome recalls that the judges peppered Kayser fairly aggressively, particularly about whether there was a distinction between "distributor" and "publisher." By the time Carome stood up to deliver his argument, he had decided to say less than he had first planned, and he later recalled that he ended his argument before his allotted time was up.

By late 1997, interactive websites and online services were proliferating, part of the early stages of the first dot-com boom. Although the judges' decision would be binding only on courts in the Fourth Circuit, it was increasingly apparent that the first appellate opinion on Section 230 would be enormously influential nationwide. If at least two of these three judges accepted Kayser's reading, then Section 230 would provide little protection to Internet companies. If the judges agreed with Carome, these new companies could develop new platforms that rely on third-party content, with little reason to worry about lawsuits.

The technology community did not have to wait long to learn the future of Section 230. On November 12, 1997, forty-one days after oral argument, the panel issued a unanimous opinion, affirming Ellis's dismissal of the case. Section 230, the judges concluded, prevented Zeran from successfully suing America Online. Wilkinson wrote the opinion, which was little more than half the length of Judge Ellis's. Despite the brevity, Judge Wilkinson clearly adopted an exceptionally broad view of the immunity that Section 230 provided to Internet companies. Section 230's purpose "is not difficult to discern," Wilkinson wrote. "Congress recognized the threat that tort-based lawsuits pose to freedom of speech in the new and burgeoning Internet medium. The imposition of tort liability on service providers for the communications of others represented, for Congress, simply another form of intrusive government regulation of speech."[36] Section 230 did not prevent a plaintiff from suing the person who wrote the harmful content, Wilkinson reasoned. But Congress made a clear "policy choice," he wrote, to absolve the online platforms of responsibility for whatever terrible things their users posted. To do otherwise, he predicted, would have an "obvious chilling effect" on online speech.[37] "It would be impossible for service providers to screen each of their millions of postings for possible problems," Wilkinson wrote. "Faced with potential liability for each message republished by their services, interactive computer service providers might choose to severely restrict the number and type of messages posted."[38]

Wilkinson's opinion was the clearest characterization of Section 230 as an independent enabler of free online speech. The "policy" and "findings" sections that Wyden and Cox included in Section 230 suggest that one of their intentions was to bolster free speech protections. Those sections state that the purposes of Section 230 included the promotion of the "continued development" of the Internet[39] and the preservation of "the vibrant and competitive free market" for such services.[40] The sections also discuss the goal of encouraging technologies that "maximize user control" over the information received via the Internet, and the promotion of blocking and filtering technologies.[41] They discuss the potential that the Internet and related services pose as a "forum for a true diversity of political discourse, unique opportunities for cultural development, and myriad avenues for intellectual activity."[42] Democratic congresswoman Zoe Lofgren, a supporter of the Cox-Wyden bill, said during the House floor debate in 1995 that the bill preserved "the First Amendment and open systems on the Net,"[43] and Republican congressman Robert Goodlatte, another supporter, said the bill "doesn't violate free speech or the right of adults to communicate with each other."[44] While it is clear from the legislative history that Congress envisioned Section 230 as a protector of online speech, Wilkinson explained *how* the new statute provides that protection.

Wilkinson rejected Kayser's argument that Section 230 applied to only publishers, and not to distributors. Like Ellis, Wilkinson wrote that liability for distributors "is merely a subset, or a species, of publisher liability, and is therefore also foreclosed by § 230."[45] This finding validates the argument that Bob Hamilton had been raising at conferences and in publications since his client prevailed in *Cubby v. CompuServe*: publishers and distributors are not separate creatures under defamation law. Zeran's negligence lawsuit against America Online, Wilkinson reasoned, is "indistinguishable from a garden variety defamation action."[46]

When an online service like America Online received a complaint about possible defamation, Wilkinson wrote, the company was "thrust into the role of a traditional publisher." This means that the online service "must decide whether to publish, edit, or withdraw the posting," Wilkinson concluded.[47] Wilkinson also recognized the practical difficulties of holding online services responsible for all defamatory posts after they received a complaint. "If computer service providers were subject to distributor liability, they would face potential liability each time they receive notice of a potentially defamatory statement—from any party, concerning any message," Wilkinson wrote. "Each notification would require a careful yet rapid investigation of the circumstances surrounding the posted information, a legal judgment concerning the information's defamatory character, and an on-the-spot editorial decision whether to risk liability by allowing the continued publication of that information."[48] Kayser's interpretation of Section 230, Wilkinson reasoned, would allow one angry person to censor online speech merely by lodging a complaint with a service provider. "Whenever one was displeased with the speech of another party conducted over an interactive computer service, the offended party could simply 'notify' the relevant service provider, claiming the information to be legally defamatory," he wrote. "In light of the vast amount of speech communicated through interactive computer services, these notices could produce an impossible burden for service providers, who would be faced with ceaseless choices of suppressing controversial speech of sustaining prohibitive liability."[49]

Wilkinson's approach parallels that of Justice Black in the latter's 1959 dismissal of the farmers' union's claims against WDAY, discussed in chapter 1. Like Wilkinson, Black was interpreting a statute—in Black's case, the Communications Act's equal time requirement. Yet Black recognized that the plaintiff's interpretation of the equal time statute would cause the television station to fear lawsuits and be more selective about the broadcasts that it aired. This caution, Black reasoned, would reduce the amount of political speeches on the airwaves. Likewise, at the heart of Wilkinson's opinion was a concern that Kayser's narrow reading of Section 230 would lead to online services' censoring users or prohibiting them from posting online. Neither Black nor Wilkinson was considering a claim involving the First Amendment; both cases required them to interpret statutes that Congress had passed. Yet their concerns about free speech guided their interpretations of those laws.

It is difficult to overstate the significance of Wilkinson's ruling. Had Wilkinson agreed with Kayser that Section 230 merely immunized online services until they received complaints or other notice about third-party content, then the legal landscape for platforms in the United States would look like the laws in much of the rest of the Western world. This would allow any person or company who is unhappy with user content to bully a service provider into taking down the content, lest the provider face significant legal exposure. But Wilkinson disagreed with Kayser. He concluded that Section 230 immunizes online platforms from virtually all suits arising from third-party content. This would forever change the course of Internet law in the United States.

When Congress passed Section 230, did it intend to create the sweeping immunity that Wilkinson provided in *Zeran*? Absolutely, Wyden told me in 2017. "We said very bluntly that we thought it would freeze innovation if somebody who owned a website could be personally liable," Wyden said. "There was not a lot of rocket science there."[50]

Zeran requested that all the judges on the Fourth Circuit—rather than just a panel of three—rehear the case, but the Fourth Circuit denied the request. He then asked the United States Supreme Court to rehear the case, but in June 1998 it refused to do so. He was stuck with Judge Wilkinson's ruling that he could not sue America Online over the anonymous user's posts. Wilkinson's interpretation of Section 230 was so broad that it exceeded the standard First Amendment protections afforded to publishers. *Zeran* turned Section 230 into a nearly impenetrable super–First Amendment for online companies.

Since his old college friend issued the opinion, Kayser said, he has seen Wilkinson at social events. But as of 2017, Kayser said, they had not discussed the *Zeran* case. Kayser remains certain that Wilkinson was flat-out wrong in his interpretation of Section 230. He continues to believe that Section 230 was merely intended to ensure that online services face the same standard of liability that Judge Leisure applied in *Cubby*: they are distributors who become responsible for user content only after they are put on notice. "America Online interposed the CDA [Communications Decency Act] as a defense for their responsibility, which to me was not intended to do that," Kayser said. Kayser believes that Wilkinson's decision is in line with a judicial philosophy of protecting companies from lawsuits. "Jay Wilkinson is a very conservative fellow," Kayser said. "He made a policy decision, I'm sure, simply to insulate these companies on the Internet from liability come hell or high water."[51] But the result in *Zeran* was not merely a matter of a judge's conservative or liberal viewpoint. Interpreting brand-new statutes, with no guidance from other courts, often does not lead to a clear-cut result. Wilkinson could have reasonably adopted Kayser's narrow reading of Section 230. But he did not. He was guided not only by Carome's persuasive arguments about Congress's intent but also by an unspoken but strong underlying belief in Internet exceptionalism. Congress passed Section 230, Wilkinson wrote, "in part, to maintain the robust nature of

Internet communication and, accordingly, to keep government interference in the medium to a minimum."

Wilkinson's interpretation of Section 230 is best summarized in four words: the Internet is different. Because the Internet is different, it needs to operate under different rules. Internet exceptionalism loomed over the drafting and passage of Section 230. And it certainly was at the very heart of the first appellate court interpretation of Section 230. Internet exceptionalism also meant that sympathetic plaintiffs, like Zeran, may be left with no remedies. Zeran's defamation lawsuit against the Oklahoma City radio station also failed. The Oklahoma district court dismissed the case, and the United States Court of Appeals for the Tenth Circuit affirmed, concluding that he had failed to prove that the broadcast injured his reputation. Zeran was unsuccessful in his attempt to demonstrate that the angry callers knew his last name, and thus he had not demonstrated that "any person thinks less of him, Kenneth Zeran, as a result of the broadcast," Judge Dale A. Kimball wrote.[52]

Zeran rarely discusses the outcome of his litigation against America Online in public or in the media, and I was unable to reach him for this book. But in 2011, he delivered a thirty-eight-minute address at a Santa Clara University School of Law symposium marking the fifteenth anniversary of Section 230. Surprisingly, Zeran did not reject the notion that the Internet is inherently different. He reflected on his time working at *CBS News* in the early 1970s, when television news changed the way that Americans received information. For Zeran, the question was not whether the Internet was exceptional. He was more concerned about whether the ground rules for this new technology were fair. "I believe the challenge of Section 230 is, Does it effectively provide for that ideal with constitutional protections in the medium of computer communication?" Zeran said. "I believe it is wanting."

More than any other court opinion, *Zeran* charted the way for an expansive view of Section 230 that has shaped the Internet as we know it today, as I will describe in chapter 6 of this book. Had Carome not been confident enough to rely entirely on this new, obscure, and untested statute, the history of Section 230—and the Internet—would look quite different.

Because Virginia's Rocket Docket decides cases so quickly, Zeran's case resulted in the first district court and appellate court opinions to interpret

Section 230. Even judges not bound by Ellis's and Wilkinson's opinions could not overlook two court rulings that broadly interpreted Section 230's immunity. Hundreds of court opinions construing Section 230 have since cited *Zeran*. Imagine what would have happened if the first court to interpret Section 230 had adopted Leo Kayser's narrower reading of the immunity: allowing courts to hold platforms liable if they knew or should have known of illegal third-party content. Such an opinion could have set a tone for judges around the nation to deny online services Section 230 immunity. As many litigators know, the facts of a case can determine a case's outcome as much as the legal rules. When a legal rule (such as the scope of a new statute) is not yet clear, the facts of the first case to interpret the rule are particularly important. Without a doubt, Kenneth Zeran's story is compelling and sympathetic. But another lawsuit against AOL—filed in Florida state court a month before Judge Ellis ruled against Zeran—involved even more tragic circumstances.

The mother of a boy who was eleven years old in 1994 alleged that Richard Lee Russell had recorded and photographed her son and two other minors in sex acts and that he had marketed the images and videos through AOL chat rooms. In a complaint filed on January 23, 1997, against Russell and America Online, the boy's mother (identified pseudonymously as Jane Doe) alleged that America Online violated child pornography laws and was negligent in allowing Russell to use its services to distribute child pornography. America Online had been "on notice" about the use of its services for marketing child pornography and had received complaints about Russell but failed to ban him from using its services, the plaintiff alleged in the lawsuit.[53] On June 26, 1997—about three months after Judge Ellis had dismissed Zeran's case, but three months before the Fourth Circuit heard oral arguments in Zeran's appeal—Florida trial court judge James T. Carlisle dismissed Jane Doe's claims against America Online. Relying largely on Judge Ellis's opinion in *Zeran*, Judge Carlisle reasoned that the lawsuit sought to hold America Online accountable as the "publisher or speaker" of Russell's chats—something that Section 230 prohibits.[54] Jane Doe appealed the dismissal to Florida's Fourth District Court of Appeal. On October 14, 1998, the three-judge panel unanimously affirmed the decision. By this point, the federal Fourth Circuit had issued its opinion in *Zeran*. The Florida appellate court relied largely on the Fourth Circuit's reasoning in reaching this conclusion. Yet the court found the scope of Section 230 "to be of great public importance," and it asked the Florida Supreme Court to review its decision.[55]

On March 8, 2001, the Florida Supreme Court issued a 4–3 ruling in favor of America Online. The majority opinion, written by Chief Justice Charles T. Wells, adopted the Fourth Circuit's broad reading of Section 230's immunity. In fact, most of the majority opinion consisted of large block quotes from the *Zeran* opinion. "It is precisely the liability based upon negligent failure to control the content of users' publishing of allegedly illegal postings on the Internet that is the gravamen of Doe's alleged cause of action," Wells wrote. "Such publication of obscene literature or computer pornography is analogous to the defamatory publication at issue in the *Zeran* decisions."[56] Only four of the seven justices on the Florida Supreme Court believed that the Fourth Circuit had gotten it right in *Zeran*. Three justices dissented, writing that the Fourth Circuit had issued a "totally unacceptable interpretation" of Section 230.

Writing for the dissent, Justice R. Fred Lewis concluded that Congress passed Section 230 only to protect online services from claims arising from their "implementation of a good-faith monitoring program whose goal is to preclude dissemination of illicit and improper materials through the ISP's electronic medium."[57] Section 230 did not, according to Lewis, allow online services to dodge all legal responsibility for third-party content. "Through the majority's interpretation, the so-called 'Decency Act' has, contrary to well-established legal principles, been transformed from an appropriate shield into a sword of harm and extreme danger which places technology buzz words and economic considerations above the safety and general welfare of our people," he wrote. The "fatal flaw" in the *Zeran* opinion, according to Lewis, was the categorization of distributors as a subset of "publishers." Section 230 prevents interactive computers service providers only from being treated as the *publishers or speakers* of third-party content, he noted. Liability for distributing content, he reasoned, simply is different from publishing. He noted that the plaintiff claimed that "AOL actually knew of the illicit character of the material which it was transmitting over its Internet service."[58] The ruling against Jane Doe "flies in the face" of Congress's reason for enacting the Communications Decency Act. "What conceivable good could a statute purporting to promote ISP self-policing efforts do if, by virtue of the courts' interpretation of that statute, an ISP which is specifically made aware of child pornography being distributed by an identified customer through solicitation occurring on its service may, with impunity, do absolutely nothing, and reap the economic benefits flowing from the activity?" Lewis wrote.[59]

Had Judge Ellis and the Fourth Circuit not ruled in Zeran's case before the Florida courts issued their opinions, the Florida courts probably would not have had guidance from such an expansive reading of Section 230. Without the *Zeran* opinion, there is a reasonable chance that a fourth Florida Supreme Court justice would have agreed with Lewis. And Section 230 would forever have looked different.

The quick and powerful effect of Judge Wilkinson's opinion could be seen in a much higher-profile case, playing out in a courthouse across the Potomac River from Alexandria. The plaintiffs in this District of Columbia case had far more power and resources than a photographer from Seattle. Sidney Blumenthal was a top White House adviser to President Clinton and a former political journalist for the *New Yorker* and the *New Republic*. His wife, Jacqueline Jordan Blumenthal, was President Clinton's director of White House fellowships. They were the quintessential Washington power couple. Matt Drudge had founded the *Drudge Report,* one of the earliest news gossip websites. He was well-known to have a conservative bias and an interest in digging up dirt about the Clinton White House.

On August 10, 1997, a headline blared across the top of Drudge's website: "CHARGE: NEW WHITE HOUSE RECRUIT SIDNEY BLUMENTHAL HAS SPOUSAL ABUSE PAST." The article quoted an anonymous "influential Republican" who claimed that there were "court records of Blumenthal's violence against his wife."[60] The following day, the Blumenthals' lawyer, William Alden McDaniel Jr., sent a stern letter to Drudge, flatly denying the allegations of spousal abuse. "No such records exist, in court or anywhere else," McDaniel wrote. "No such violence ever occurred. Mr. Blumenthal has no 'spousal abuse past.' No such story has been in circulation. No cover-up ever occurred."[61] McDaniel asserted that Drudge knew that these allegations were false yet published them anyway—an act that could increase the chances of a public figure such as Blumenthal winning a defamation lawsuit against Drudge. "You took no steps to verify your allegations: even the most rudimentary check by you would have revealed that no court records exist which document your accusations," McDaniel wrote.[62]

Drudge's report about the Blumenthals ran not only on his website but also on America Online, which offered the *Drudge Report* to its subscribers. Although Americans' ability to access the public Internet was increasing, many people still received their news and information from online services such as AOL and Prodigy. And AOL was quickly eclipsing its rivals as the dominant online service. The deal between Drudge and AOL markedly increased Drudge's audience; the AOL press release announcing the partnership estimated that the deal would give Drudge the ability "to reach a potential audience that is 160 times bigger than he has drawn to his web site."[63]

The Drudge story immediately spread around the nation. The day after Drudge posted it, *Washington Post* media columnist Howard Kurtz reported that Drudge said he was retracting the story. "Someone was trying to get me to go after [the story] and I probably fell for it a little too hard," Drudge told the *Post*. "I can't prove it. This is a case of using me to broadcast dirty laundry. I think I've been had."[64] Despite Drudge's public mea culpa, Sidney and Jacqueline Blumenthal filed a 137-page lawsuit against both Drudge and America Online seventeen days after Drudge posted the story. The lawsuit, filed in District of Columbia federal district court, lists twenty-one claims for defamation, invasion of privacy, and intentional infliction of emotional distress. For each claim, they sought thirty million dollars in compensatory and punitive damages, plus costs of the lawsuit.[65]

Two months later, America Online asked the court to dismiss the Blumenthals' claims against the company. Patrick Carome once again represented America Online. He largely presented the same interpretation of Section 230 that he had developed in Zeran's case. But there was another wrinkle for Carome to address. The Blumenthals' complaint alleged that Drudge was an employee or agent of America Online. Section 230's immunity applies only to information that is provided by "another information content provider." If Drudge was an employee or agent of America Online, then he might not qualify as "another" content provider, and Section 230 would not immunize America Online. America Online had a closer relationship with Drudge than it did with the anonymous user who posted Zeran's phone number. America Online had signed a contract with Drudge and paid him money for the newsletter. Yet Carome asserted that America Online had no control over Drudge's writing: "He is his own boss. He alone determines which stories to write, which sources to rely on, and when to publish any given story or edition."[66] The Blumenthals argued that even under the broad *Zeran* interpretation, Section 230 did not immunize America Online for publishing the defamatory words of a paid contractor. *Zeran* did not involve "a situation where the interactive computer service supplied the sole source of income to the person who provided the materials disseminated, and had a contractual relationship with that person giving the interactive service extensive control over the content of what the service sent out," McDaniel wrote in his brief opposing America Online's motion.[67]

The case was assigned to Judge Paul Friedman, a former federal prosecutor and corporate law firm partner whom President Clinton had appointed to the bench four years earlier.[68] On April 22, 1998, Friedman dismissed the Blumenthals' claims against America Online. Friedman's opinion quoted heavily from *Zeran*, concluding that Wilkinson's opinion had "provided a complete answer" to the Blumenthals' main argument. America Online's business relationship with Drudge, Friedman said, did not change his conclusion that Section 230 immunized the company.

America Online not only paid for Drudge's columns but also, in a press release, boasted that it had hired the "maverick gossip columnist," Friedman observed. "Because it has the right to exercise editorial control over those with whom it contracts and whose words it disseminates, it would seem only fair to hold AOL to the liability standards applied to a publisher or, at least, like a book store owner or library, to the liability standards applied to a distributor," Friedman wrote. "But Congress has made a different policy choice by providing immunity even where the interactive service provider has an active, even aggressive role in making available content prepared by others."[69] Friedman appeared somewhat baffled by Congress's policy choice. "In some sort of tacit *quid pro quo* arrangement with the service provider community, Congress has conferred immunity from tort liability as an incentive to Internet service providers to self-police the Internet for obscenity and other offensive material, even where the self-policing is unsuccessful or not even attempted," he wrote.[70] Friedman even got in a dig at America Online, writing that it had "taken advantage of all the benefits conferred by Congress in the Communications Decency Act, and then some, without accepting any of the burdens that Congress intended."[71] Yet Friedman's hands were tied. The text of Section 230 was "clear," and he had no option but to dismiss the Blumenthals' claims against America Online.

Friedman's opinion required more than just a quick glance at the twenty-six words in Section 230. He could have concluded that Drudge was not "another information content provider" and that the Blumenthals could sue America Online. Like Wilkinson, Friedman recognized that Congress believed the Internet needed a different playing field. No matter how unfair or illogical.

The Internet is different.

"The near instantaneous possibilities for the dissemination of information by millions of different information providers around the world to those with access to computers and thus to the Internet," Friedman wrote, "have created ever-increasing opportunities for the exchange of information and ideas in 'cyberspace.' "[72]

If Wilkinson's opinion served as a warning to plaintiffs that Section 230 created a new playing field for the Internet, Friedman's opinion was a four-alarm fire. The Blumenthals' case against America Online appeared to be the perfect storm for the dismantling of Section 230. The plaintiffs were one of Washington's best-connected power couples. The author was a notorious gossipmonger who trafficked in politically loaded rumors. The defendant was a large technology company that paid for those rumors and even touted Drudge in an effort to attract customers. And the judge questioned Congress's wisdom in passing Section 230 in the first place. Yet Judge Friedman still dismissed the case. In Section 230's earliest days, it seemed as though the statute was an impenetrable shield for Internet companies. Internet exceptionalism was winning.

5

Himmler's Granddaughter and the Bajoran Dabo Girl

During Section 230's early years, other courts across the country broadly interpreted the statute's immunity, following Judge Wilkinson's lead. But the United States Court of Appeals for the Ninth Circuit did not weigh in on Section 230 until more than seven years after Congress had passed the law. The court's silence on Section 230 left a question mark for technology companies, which carefully watch how the Ninth Circuit interprets technology laws. The United States is divided into twelve regional judicial "circuits," and each circuit has its own appellate court. When an appellate court interprets a law, all federal courts within that circuit must follow it. The Ninth Circuit covers the western United States: Alaska, Arizona, California, Hawaii, Idaho, Montana, Nevada, Oregon, and Washington State. Because of its size, the Ninth Circuit has the largest caseload of any federal appellate court. The court has about forty judges, although some have taken "senior status" and hear reduced caseloads.

By the early 2000s, many of the top Internet companies were based in California or Washington State, among them Yahoo, Google, eBay,

Microsoft, and Amazon. These tech companies are bound by the Ninth Circuit's rulings on Internet transactions, online copyright, and other technology issues. A single ruling from the Ninth Circuit could make or break a company's business model. Only the United States Supreme Court's interpretation of Section 230 would matter more, as it would set national precedent. (As of 2018, the Supreme Court had heard no cases that required it to apply Section 230.)

The Ninth Circuit has its share of critics. Over time, it gained a reputation for liberal rulings, with some outspoken Democrat-appointed judges. The Ninth Circuit has been reversed by the U.S. Supreme Court more than many other circuit courts. Judge Stephen Reinhardt, who was appointed by President Carter in 1980 and continued to hear a full load of cases until he died in 2018, infamously stated that the Supreme Court "can't catch 'em all."[1] During his 2012 presidential campaign, former House Speaker Newt Gingrich called for the abolition of the Ninth Circuit.[2] However, the Ninth Circuit's reversal rate is not far out of line with the rates of other circuits, and most of President Barack Obama's appointees were former prosecutors or corporate law firm partners, holding generally more moderate philosophies than those of Clinton and Carter appointees.[3]

The Ninth Circuit first applied Section 230 in two opinions that it issued in the summer of 2003. Ruling against the plaintiffs in both cases, the court applied the same general reasoning that the Fourth Circuit had adopted in *Zeran*. But the plaintiffs' stories were perhaps more shocking than Kenneth Zeran's or even Sidney Blumenthal's, and the defendants' actions were more controversial than America Online's. These two opinions further strengthened Section 230's immunity, in the circuit where it matters most. But the rulings also drew new attention to the law and to questions about its fairness.

Chris Cox is proud to have written Section 230. But his enthusiasm is a bit tempered. He believes that some judges have gone too far, immunizing defendants whom he did not intend to benefit from the law. There has been "an exceptional amount of embroidery on the statute," he says. When asked for an example of this embroidery, he immediately responds with one word: "Batzel."[4]

Ellen Batzel is an Ivy-educated lawyer who practices transactional law in southern California. In the 1980s and 1990s, she represented major businesses and entertainment personalities. By the early 1990s, she was outside counsel for a California hazardous waste management company. She joined the company and worked her way up in management. She bought a second home near Asheville, North Carolina, where she built the company's southeastern operations. Commuting between California and North Carolina, she eventually rose through the ranks to be president and chief executive officer. Batzel received repeated requests to speak to the media, she recalls; in the early 1990s, it was rare for a woman to run a publicly traded company. But she says she refused. That sort of publicity just wasn't attractive to her. She says that she wanted to focus on doing her job, not on claiming the limelight: "I protected my privacy."[5]

She saw an even greater need to protect her privacy in the mid-1990s, after the company's business turned south and it filed for bankruptcy protection. She believed the mob might be after her—it was, after all, a waste management business—so she relocated to Asheville full-time while continuing to own her home in California. She became a North Carolina bar member and slowly rebuilt her law practice, representing art galleries, artists, production companies, and antique dealers across the nation. She served on the board of the local museum.[6] In the summer of 1999, she hired general contractor Robert Smith to work on her house, after one of her clients had referred Smith to her. In addition to being a handyman, Smith was an aspiring screenwriter. Smith asked Batzel to pass along one of his scripts to her clients. She refused, and later said that Smith was angry. Batzel and Smith also disagreed about the amount of money that she owed him for his work.[7]

On September 10, 1999, Smith emailed the Museum Security Network (MSN), a Netherlands-based nonprofit that operates a website and email Listserv newsletter that publishes news about stolen art and other security topics of interest to museum managers. Ton Cremers, then the security director of Amsterdam's Rijksmuseum, published MSN, which contained both articles that he chose and user submissions.

Smith's email, sent from his Earthlink account, was titled "Stolen Art." Smith wrote:

> Hi there,
>   I am a building contractor in Asheville, North Carolina, USA. A month ago, I did a remodeling job for a woman, Ellen L. Batzel who bragged to me

about being the grand daughter [*sic*] of "one of Adolph Hitler's right-hand men." At the time, I was concentrating on performing my tasks, but upon reflection, I believe she said she was the descendant of Heinrich Himmler.

Ellen Batzel has hundreds of older European paintings on her walls, all with heavy carved wooden frames. She told me she inherited them.

I believe these paintings were looted during WWII and are the rightful legacy of the Jewish people. Her address is [redacted].

I also believe that the descendants of criminals should not be persecuted for the crimes of the [*sic*] fathers, nor should they benefit.

I do not know who to contact about this, so I start with your organization. Please contact me via email: [redacted] or phone [redacted] if you would like to discuss this matter.

Bob.[8]

Soon after receiving the email, Cremers made slight editorial changes and posted it on the MSN Listserv and MSN's website. Listserv subscribers took notice and complained to Cremers, who published their complaints on the Listserv. "Mr. Smith is completely out of line for suggesting that some woman with old paintings in her home has amassed a collection of paintings from Nazi war booty," a Boston museum employee wrote. "His claims, evidence, and assumptions were ridiculous, and he was very disrespectful of this woman's privacy in offering this woman's address."[9] Another admonished Cremers that "at the very least, you owe this woman an apology; at worst, you may end up owing her much of what you personally own."[10] After Cremers posted the email, Smith sent a message to Jonathan Sazonoff, a U.S.-based contributing editor of the site, apparently confused that his email had become public: "I [was] trying to figure out how in blazes I could have posted me [*sic*] email to [the Network] bulletin board. I came into MSN through the back door, directed by a search engine, and never got the big picture. I don't remember reading anything about a message board either so I am a bit confused over how it could happen. Every message board to which I have ever subscribed required application, a password, and/or registration, and the instructions explained this is necessary to keep out the advertisers, cranks, and bumbling idiots like me."[11]

After receiving the complaints, Cremers removed Batzel's personally identifiable information from the site's archives and emailed the Listserv about the lessons he learned from the experience. "All of you should realize that many messages remain off list and are answered privately," he assured them. "Looking back I am convinced that this message too should have remained off list and only forwarded to the kind of organizations [another subscriber] suggests. . . . I really do hope that finally nobody is or will be harmed."[12] Cremers said that he received an email informing him that the FBI was aware of Smith's email. He sent a message to the MSN Listserv:

> This mailing list message has two more postings on the Nazi art theft message in which the full name and address of a woman accused of possessing looted art was posted. I suppose all that could be said has been said by now.
>
> Jonathan Sazonoff, the MSM [*sic*] USA contributing editor, has been in touch with several people that might be of importance regarding this issue. He also has been in touch with the original sender.
>
> The FBI has been informed about the contents of the original message.
>
> I will keep all of you informed about future developments in this case.
>
> Ton Cremers.[13]

Batzel says she had no clue about the Listserv posting for more than three months. She had Internet access and email, but she says that she wasn't the type to self-Google. So she could not explain why odd things started to happen to her. Her clients, who were in the arts and entertainment industries, started to pull their business with her without giving any explanation.[14] Two days after the turn of the century, Batzel says, she received an anonymous letter in the mail, with a printout of the initial MSN message.[15] She was stunned. She says that she never claimed to be related to Nazis. And the paintings in her home did not even come from any of her relatives, she said; she purchased all her artwork from her clients.

Suddenly, the events of the past few months did not seem so odd to Batzel. "I had lost almost all of my clients, and now I knew why," she said. She contacted the local district attorney's office, who advised that she hire a bodyguard and move out of North Carolina.[16] The following day, Batzel wrote an email to Cremers:

> My name is Ellen Batzel. I am a lawyer in Asheville, N.C. . . .
>
> I am shocked and appalled by this outrageous slander, this malicious slander. I am outraged that you would print my name, address and phone number, putting me and my property at risk.

What do you want to do about this malicious slander? What do you want to do about the harm that you have caused and are causing to me? The risk you have caused and are causing me.

Oh, yes, I represent artists, art galleries, and antique dealers in Los Angeles. (In fact, all of the art and antiques that I own were bought from my clients, or at public auction) . . .

I am VERY UPSET about this. VERY UPSET.[17]

This began a back-and-forth, hostile email exchange between Batzel and Cremers. Cremers invited Batzel to send her "contrary opinion" to be published on MSN. "If you are interested to have this matter solved," Cremers wrote, "do speak out!" Cremers's offer to publish a "contrary opinion" did not satisfy Batzel. "Given your organization's relationship with Mr. Sazanoff, you probably have already done a search on my bona fides, and know that I am an attorney, that I represent persons and organizations of repute in the art world, and that I am not a relative of any of the Hitler gang, including but not limited to H. Himmler," Batzel emailed to Cremers. "You probably also know that the art-work, which I have collected, was all purchased after 1984, from art dealers in Los Angeles, and that very little of it is 'European.'"[18]

Batzel complained to Mosler, a sponsor of MSN. Batzel also contacted the museum where Cremers worked, and he soon was fired. Batzel alleged that Cremers had investigated her background.[19]

The emails and rumors continued to circulate, making it impossible for Batzel to find clients, she says. She had been rebuilding her life in North Carolina after the rocky collapse of the hazardous waste company, and suddenly she was branded a Nazi descendant. "I was representing entertainment clients again, business clients," Batzel said. "Things were picking up again. Then this hit. It totally ruined my life. It effectively bankrupted me."[20]

Batzel eventually sold her Asheville home, shut down her North Carolina law practice, and moved back to California full-time. Her reputation was beyond repair, she believed. She recalls receiving a call from one of Oprah Winfrey's producers, inviting her on the show. "'I'm not Himmler's granddaughter. Do you still want me on the show?'" Batzel recalls telling the producer. "They said, 'Never mind.'"[21]

Batzel's friends encouraged her to sue. They knew that the claims were false and had ruined her reputation and business. If anyone had a solid defamation case, they said, it was Batzel. But Batzel hesitated. The damage to her reputation was already done, and she questioned whether she'd succeed. "I didn't want to sue anybody," Batzel said. "I didn't see any upside. Courts do not like lawyers as plaintiffs. We're not supposed to pee in our own sandbox."[22] She did not have much time to decide. The statute of limitations for defamation lawsuits is one year in California. On September 7, 2000, she took her friends' advice, and her lawyer, Howard Fredman, sued Smith, Cremers, the Netherlands Museum Association, and Mosler in Los Angeles federal court for libel, invasion of privacy, and intentional infliction of emotional distress. She filed the lawsuit not for money, but to clear her name, she said. "I said to myself, 'I'm either going to be famous for being Himmler's granddaughter or famous for not being his granddaughter.' "[23]

Cremers asked district court judge Stephen V. Wilson to dismiss the case on a few grounds, including Section 230. Wilson found little merit in this argument, brushing it aside in little more than a page in a June 5, 2001, written opinion refusing to dismiss the case. Section 230, he wrote, applies to only "interactive computer services" such as America Online. The Museum Security Network, he wrote, "is clearly not an internet service provider, as it has no capability to provide internet access." Instead, he wrote, the site "is plainly an 'information content provider' within the meaning of the Act." Wilson raised a valid distinction between companies such as America Online and newsletters such as Museum Security Network. But that distinction did not "clearly" disqualify Museum Security Network from Section 230 protection. Wilson implied that "true Internet Service Providers"—companies that connect people to the Internet—are the only companies that receive Section 230 immunity. Section 230's text does not support that reading. Section 230 applies to a broader category of providers *and users* of "interactive computer services," which includes Internet service providers (ISPs) but also any other information service that provides or enables many users to access a computer server. Wilson should have asked whether the Museum Security Network fell within this broader category of a provider or user of interactive computer services. And if it did, the tougher question is whether the posts about Batzel were caused by another information content provider or by Cremers, who edited the Smith email and posted his own message.

Cremers appealed Wilson's rulings against him to the Ninth Circuit. Cremers's lawyers, from Latham & Watkins, one of the largest global law firms, argued that Congress intended to immunize more than just ISPs. Smith provided the content and was therefore the "information content provider," they wrote, and Cremers and his Museum Security Network provided the interactive computer service. "Immunity under Section 230 is straightforward and simple," his lawyers wrote. "Even if they moderate or manage content generated by third parties, internet site administrators cannot be held liable for defamatory statements they do not author."[24]

Batzel argued to the Ninth Circuit that Judge Wilson was correct to conclude that Section 230 did not immunize Cremers. Section 230 did not cover Cremers's contributions to the defamatory claims—such as new headings—Fredman wrote in Batzel's brief. Nor did Cremers act as a "mere conduit" for Smith's email, Fredman wrote; rather, he had made the conscious choice to publish the email on the Listserv and website.[25] "Cremers is being sued, personally," Fredman wrote in the brief, "for his own volitional acts in publishing and republishing false and uncorroborated defamatory content about Batzel which he plucked from his email in-box, and refusing to print a retraction or correction."[26]

Because this was the first time that the Ninth Circuit would interpret Section 230, the case attracted national attention, and not just from the technology industry. Public Citizen, the Ralph Nader–founded consumer advocacy group, filed a brief in the case. Public Citizen typically represents individuals against large corporate interests; by defending Section 230, the group aligned with some of the largest technology companies in the United States. In its brief, Public Citizen made clear that it sought to promote individual free speech rights. "In recent years, Public Citizen has watched with dismay as an increasing number of companies have used litigation to prevent ordinary citizens from using the Internet to express their views about how companies conduct their affairs," Public Citizen attorney Paul Alan Levy wrote.[27]

Levy focused much of his argument on a procedural issue: whether Cremers could appeal Wilson's denial of his motion at an early stage in the case. But Levy also argued that Wilson incorrectly concluded that Congress intended to immunize only ISPs and that Listservs, like websites, could qualify for Section 230 immunity. Levy did not go as far as Cremers, who asked the Ninth Circuit to dismiss the case entirely. Instead,

Levy urged the Ninth Circuit to send the case back to Judge Wilson to determine whether Section 230 protected Cremers. This would require a more in-depth look at exactly how he operated the Listserv, Levy wrote: "At one extreme, listservs may be generally open to any member of the public who sends a 'subscribe' message to the server; at the other extreme, only members of pre-determined groups may be permitted to join. Between those extremes are listservs whose operator may reserve the right to approve individual subscriptions to the list."[28]

Three Ninth Circuit judges heard oral arguments on November 4, 2002. Judges Marsha Berzon, Ronald Gould, and William Canby were assigned to the case. As in *Zeran*, it was difficult to predict how the judges would rule. Although Democrats had appointed the three judges (Berzon and Gould were appointed by Clinton, and Canby by Carter), their judicial philosophies differed. Berzon and Canby are fairly liberal, while Gould had staked out a reputation as a moderate. And as the *Zeran* opinion demonstrated, a judge's political leanings need not correlate with the judge's views on the new world of online speech.

More than seven months after argument, the judges issued a divided opinion. Berzon, joined by Canby, sent the case back to Judge Wilson. The first sentence of Berzon's opinion questioned the wisdom and fairness of Section 230 and Internet exceptionalism: "There is no reason inherent in the technological features of cyberspace why First Amendment and defamation law should apply differently in cyberspace than in the brick and mortar world."[29] But Congress chose to make the distinction, Berzon observed. Reviewing the history of Section 230, she concluded that Congress "sought to further First Amendment and e-commerce interests on the Internet while also promoting the protection of minors."[30] By linking Section 230 directly to the First Amendment, she was setting the stage for a broad reading of its immunity. Berzon wrote that Wilson was incorrect to rule that the Museum Security Network was not an "interactive computer service" under Section 230. She stressed that Section 230 applied both to providers *and* users of interactive computer services. "There is no dispute that the Network uses interactive computer services to distribute its online mailing and to post the listserv on its website," she wrote. "Indeed, to make its website available and to mail out the listserv, the Network *must* access the Internet through some form of 'interactive computer service.' Thus, both the Network website and the listserv are potentially immune under § 230."[31] This conclusion was noteworthy because most Section 230 cases focus on whether a defendant was the *provider* of interactive computer services. Immunizing a *user* of an interactive computer service could further expand the reach of Section 230.

But that wasn't the end of Berzon's analysis. Even if a defendant was a user or provider of an interactive computer service, it did not necessarily qualify for Section 230 immunity. It must also show that it is being sued over information provided by *another* information content provider. In some cases, this is easy to establish. The posts about Zeran, for instance, were written, developed, and posted by actors other than America Online. Batzel's case was tougher. Smith wrote the emails, but Cremers distributed them *and* made some minor editorial changes. Berzon wrote that Cremers's modest edits to Smith's emails did not eliminate the possibility of Section 230 immunity. Such a holding, she wrote, would contradict one of the main goals of Section 230: to protect online platforms that moderate or edit user content. "The 'development of information' therefore means something more substantial than merely editing portions of an e-mail and selecting material for publication," she wrote.[32] Nor did Berzon believe that the Museum Security Network became an information content provider because Cremers chose to include Smith's message on the site and Listserv. She asserted, "The scope of the immunity cannot turn on whether the publisher approaches the selection process as one of inclusion or removal, as the difference is one of method or degree, not substance."[33]

One remaining issue prevented Berzon and Canby from fully immunizing Cremers and dismissing the lawsuit altogether: Smith said that when he sent the email to Cremers, he did not anticipate that it would be published on MSN. Section 230 immunizes defendants only for claims stemming from information that is *provided* by another information content provider. So the question for Berzon was this: did Smith *provide* the email to be published online? "As we have seen, the section is concerned with providing special immunity for individuals who would otherwise be publishers or speakers, because of Congress's concern with assuring a free market in ideas and information on the Internet," Berzon wrote.[34]

Berzon sent the case back for Judge Wilson to gather more facts and determine whether it was reasonable for Cremers to believe that Smith had sent him the information to publish on MSN. "If Cremers should have reasonably concluded, for example, that because Smith's e-mail arrived via a different e-mail address it was not provided to him for possible posting on the listserv, then Cremers cannot take advantage of the § 230(c) immunities," Berzon wrote. "Under that circumstance, the posted information was not 'provided' by another 'information content provider' within the meaning of § 230."[35]

Judge Gould partly dissented from Berzon's ruling. He believed that her reading of Section 230 was far too generous to defendants and that the statute should apply only if the defendant "took no active role" in choosing third-party content. Berzon's interpretation of Section 230 "licenses professional rumor-mongers and gossip-hounds to spread false and hurtful information with impunity," Gould wrote.[36] "So long as the defamatory information was written by a person who wanted the information to be spread on the Internet (in other words, a person with an axe to grind), the rumormonger's injurious conduct is beyond legal redress," Gould stated. "Nothing in the CDA's text or legislative history suggests that Congress intended CDA immunity to extend so far."[37] The Ninth Circuit denied Batzel's request for a rehearing by a panel of eleven Ninth Circuit judges. Judge Gould dissented from the rehearing denial, writing that "the panel majority coldly goes where no circuit court has gone before, reaching further and providing broader automatic immunity of the most callous and damaging defamation that anyone might maliciously post on the Internet."[38]

The case went back to Judge Wilson. If he determined that Cremers acted reasonably in the belief that Smith intended to publish his message on the Museum Security Network, then Section 230 would immunize Cremers. But Wilson never ruled on that question. In 2005 he dismissed the lawsuit on unrelated procedural grounds: on the same day that she filed her lawsuit in California, Batzel had filed the same lawsuit in North Carolina federal court, and the court dismissed the case for failure to prosecute. Under civil procedure rules, once a court decides a case on the merits, the parties cannot relitigate it in another court. The five-year litigation ended with a whimper. But Judge Berzon's opinion has remained on the books as the first binding interpretation of Section 230 in the part of the country where it mattered most—that covered by the Ninth Circuit. Her opinion made clear that Judge Wilkinson's ruling in *Zeran* was not a fluke: Section 230's immunity really is that strong.

The opinion attracted national attention. *PC Magazine* wrote that the opinion "clears the way for content on the Internet to be treated as dialogue, and not necessarily set-in-stone fact."[39] The Associated Press reported that the Ninth Circuit ruled that "online publishers can post material generated by others without liability for its content—unlike traditional news media, which are held responsible for such information."[40] Although the reporting on the case did not capture all the nuances of Section 230, the media were correct to note the significance of the ruling. Judge Berzon's reading of Section 230 was even more expansive than Judge Wilkinson's. *Zeran* involved America Online, an online service that was precisely the kind of company that Cox and Wyden discussed when they drafted and advocated for Section 230. America Online passively trafficked in millions of user messages, emails, and posts each day. The Museum Security Network, on the other hand, had about one thousand members, and Cremers handpicked the messages on the Listserv and website.

Should the size and traffic volume of an online service determine whether it receives immunity under Section 230? Berzon said no. However, Chris Cox said yes. He said that when he wrote Section 230, he intended to protect companies such as America Online, Prodigy, CompuServe, and other services that handle large volumes of traffic and allow users to post content. The Museum Security Network, he said, is not what he had in mind: "This is a bilateral situation where there's a stranger who wrote to the operator of a website. It's got defamatory stuff in there and he makes the decision to publish it. He puts it up and even adds to it. If that's not a guy creating content, what the hell is that?" Cox said that he was troubled by a handful of court opinions such as *Batzel,* which he believes have granted immunity to websites and other online services that played a role in creating the harmful content. But he believes that platforms he intended to protect, such as Google and Yelp, depend on Section 230 immunity. So he does not believe that even the *Batzel* opinion is cause for Congress to amend Section 230: "Because all the anomalies people complain about are the artifacts of judge made law, the far easier remedy is to sand the rough edges of judge-made case law."[41]

Batzel continues to live and work in California, but the fallout from the posting—and her lawsuit—remain online. Batzel said that the lingering associations between her and Nazi art have harmed her business, and casual acquaintances still ask her about it. Batzel said that she does not believe that Congress intended for Section 230 to immunize defendants such as Cremers. And she disagrees with the entire premise of Internet exceptionalism. "Why should the Internet have any different kind of protection than TV or books?" Batzel asked. "Why should people not be held to a standard of care? You know what's right or wrong." One of Batzel's complaints about Judge Berzon's opinion, though, had nothing to do with the scope of Section 230. Berzon referred to Himmler—one of the most powerful military commanders during the Holocaust—as a "Nazi politician." That sort of description minimizes the devastation and death that Himmler caused and reflects little attention to the facts, Batzel said. "I've heard Himmler called many things in my life, but never a Nazi politician."[42]

Reflecting on the case more than a decade after its dismissal, Batzel does not blame Section 230 for the damage to her reputation. She doubts that Cremers, living in the Netherlands, had analyzed Section 230 when determining whether to post Smith's message on his Listserv. Even if she had won the case, Batzel said, the damage to her reputation still would have been permanent. "My loss happened before I filed the lawsuit," Batzel declared. "The lawsuit was meaningless. People are going to be assholes. So I get a judgment. What do I achieve?"[43]

Less than two months after it ruled against Batzel, the Ninth Circuit would rule against another woman who was the victim of a vicious online attack, and in doing so reinforce the strength of Section 230 throughout the West. The second case received even more attention than Batzel's because the plaintiff was already a celebrity.

Christianne Carafano is an actress who is better known by her screen name, Chase Masterson. Her most prominent role was on *Star Trek: Deep Space Nine,* where she played Leeta, a Bajoran Dabo girl, from 1995 to 1999. As with everything *Star Trek,* the television show and its actors had devoted fans. By the late 1990s, photographs of Carafano appeared on many *Star Trek* websites. In October 1999, Carafano discovered two messages on her home voicemail laced with obscenity. When she returned to her Los Angeles home, where she lived alone with her teenage son, she checked her home fax machine and discovered a note:

CHASE, GOOD NEWS HORNY BITCH! I WILL GIVE YOU THE FUCK OF YOUR LIFE! BUT FIRST I WILL ELIMINATE YOUR CHILD THAT

GETS YOUR WET PUSSY IN HEAT. I KNOW WHERE YOU ARE. I'LL
FIND YOU. IF YOU TRY TO ESCAPE. A PERSON LIKE YOU IS EASY
PREY FOR ME. TODAY TOMORROW OR SOME DAY SOON I'M
ABLE TO WAIT FOR THE RIGHT MOMENT AND PLACE. IT'S HUNT
SEASON![44]

She received more messages from men who said they saw her profile
on Matchmaker.com.[45] Matchmaker.com is a dating website that allows
users to create ads in response to multiple-choice and essay questions. At
the time, Carafano had never heard of the site. The messages alarmed
Carafano to the point that she took her son to a friend's house, where
they spent the night. Her friend's boyfriend responded to one of the vulgar
calls, and the caller said that he was responding to a listing from "Chase
Masterson on Matchmaker.com."[46]

The following day, Carafano drove to the police station to file a report
but was so distraught that she needed to find a police officer to accompany
her to the station. Once at the station, Carafano and a detective found the
"Chase Masterson" profile on Matchmaker.com. She saw not only her
name and public photographs but also her home address, filmography,
and other personal information, including that she lived with her child.[47]

The profiles also included a "Q&A" with Carafano:

Q: Have you had, or would you consider having a homosexual experience?
A: I might be persuaded to have a homosexual experience.
Q: [W]hy did you call [Matchmaker.com]?
A: Looking for a one-night stand.
Q: What is your main source for current events?
A: Playboy/Playgirl
Q: Try to describe the type of person you might be interested in meeting?
A: Hard and dominant in more ways than one. Must have strong sexual appetite.
Q: Describe your personality type? What type are you attracted to?
A: I like sort of being controlled by a man in and out of bed.[48]

The profile was created under the account name "Chase 529," by an
unknown user who apparently had connected to the Internet from Europe,
according to Matchmaker's access logs.[49] Emails sent to the address in the
Chase 529 profile returned auto-responses stating, "You think you're the
one. Proof it!!" The automatic responses also included Carafano's home

address and phone number.[50] By the time Carafano saw this profile, hundreds of people already had viewed it. Through word of mouth, some of her fans had heard about the profile and alerted her about it.[51] Carafano's assistant called Matchmaker.com and requested deletion of the profile. Matchmaker.com's director of operations told Carafano's assistant that the company could not remove the post because Carafano was not the author of the post. Matchmaker eventually removed the post in November.[52] Even after Matchmaker.com removed the profile, people continued to call Carafano and threaten her. Eventually, she and her son temporarily fled the Los Angeles area and lived in hotels and with friends.[53]

Carafano sued Matchmaker's owner, Metrosplash, and Metrosplash's parent company, Lycos Inc., in Los Angeles state court on October 27, 2000. She also sued a man who she at first believed to have posted the fake profile, but she later dropped him from the lawsuit. Carafano sued not only for defamation but also for invasion of privacy, negligence, and misappropriation of right of publicity (alleging that the site used her picture and screen name for commercial purposes without her permission). Metrosplash moved the case from state court to Los Angeles federal court. The judge denied Metrosplash's initial motion to dismiss, allowing both parties to conduct discovery to develop the facts of the case. Metrosplash then requested that Judge Dickran M. Tevrizian grant summary judgment in its favor and dismiss the case.

Metrosplash raised two primary arguments. It claimed that Section 230 immunized Metrosplash from the lawsuit. And even if Section 230 did not apply, Metrosplash argued, Carafano's claims were barred by the First Amendment because she was a public figure and thus had to meet a high First Amendment standard for privacy and defamation lawsuits. Under the First Amendment, a public figure who sues for defamation must demonstrate that the defendant published a false and injurious statement with "actual malice," which means knowledge that the statement is false or recklessly disregarding whether it is true or false.

Judge Tevrizian ruled on March 11, 2002, that Section 230 did not immunize Metrosplash from the lawsuit. He agreed with the company that Matchmaker was an interactive computer service that was covered by the statute. But Section 230 did not protect the site, he ruled, because it also was an "information content provider" that was partially responsible for the content of the profiles.[54] "The users of the Matchmaker website do not simply post whatever information they desire," Tevrizian wrote. "Rather, a profile for each user is created from the questions asked by Matchmaker and the answers provided."[55] Although Judge Tevrizian disagreed with Metrosplash's Section 230 argument, he granted the company's motion for summary judgment and dismissed the case because he agreed with its alternative argument: that the First Amendment prevented a visible public figure such as Carafano from successfully suing over the fake profile.[56]

Carafano appealed the dismissal to the Ninth Circuit, arguing that she had presented enough facts to allow the privacy, defamation, and negligence claims to proceed to trial. Matchmaker, Metrosplash, and Lycos were represented by Timothy Alger, a leading Internet lawyer who would rise to be deputy general counsel of Google. Alger told the Ninth Circuit that Tevrizian was correct to dismiss all the claims because Carafano did not meet the necessary legal standards. He also argued that Section 230 immunized his client. Alger asserted that Matchmaker's use of multiple-choice and essay questions did not disqualify it from Section 230's protections. "The Matchmaker questionnaire facilitates the creation by members of profiles that can be readily retrieved from a database and viewed by other members," Alger wrote. "The questionnaire is simply a method of collecting information for a searchable database. The District Court's view, if accepted by the Court, would strip interactive computer services of immunity under the CDA whenever they use prompts, questions, or categories."[57]

The Ninth Circuit held oral arguments on June 2, 2003. The panel consisted of two Clinton appointees to the Ninth Circuit—Judges Sidney Thomas and Richard Paez—and Judge Edward C. Reed Jr., a Nevada district court judge whom Jimmy Carter appointed. On August 13, 2003—fifty days after the Ninth Circuit ruled against Ellen Batzel—the court also ruled against Christianne Carafano. Rather than merely agreeing with the district court that Carafano's case was not strong enough to move to trial because of the First Amendment issue, the Ninth Circuit concluded that Section 230 immunized Metrosplash and Lycos. Writing for the unanimous three-judge panel, Judge Thomas relied on Judge Berzon's broad interpretation of Section 230. Matchmaker's use of the prepopulated questionnaire did not prevent Thomas from ruling in favor of the defendants. "Doubtless, the questionnaire facilitated the expression of information by individual users," Thomas wrote. "However, the selection of the content was left exclusively to the user. The actual profile 'information' consisted of the particular options chosen and the additional essay answers provided. Matchmaker was not responsible, even in part, for associating certain multiple choice responses with a set of physical characteristics, a group of essay answers, and a photograph."[58] Judge Thomas made clear that he was sympathetic to Carafano's plight. Indeed, he began the opinion by describing her case as one that involves "a cruel and sadistic identity theft." But he wrote that "despite the serious and utterly deplorable consequences that occurred in this case, we conclude that Congress intended that service providers such as Matchmaker be afforded immunity from suit."[59]

By the end of the summer of 2003, Section 230 appeared to be kryptonite to any plaintiffs who were considering a lawsuit against a website or Internet service provider. Throughout California, Washington State, and the rest of the western United States, judges were bound by the Ninth Circuit's broad reading of Section 230. Both opinions reverberated beyond the Ninth Circuit. Each case appeared to be the perfect storm that would limit the reach of Section 230. Batzel's career was ruined by claims that she was a Nazi heiress, and the defendant made a conscious choice to broadcast those rumors to the world. Carafano and her child received vulgar threats and fled town in fear of their safety.

If Ellen Batzel and Christianne Carafano could not overcome Section 230, who could?

The pair of rulings provided U.S. technology companies with strong confidence that they could provide third-party content to the world and avoid liability, even if the content pushed the limits of decency and legality. Business models would soon develop around this principle.

6

THE FLOWER CHILD AND
A TRILLION-DOLLAR INDUSTRY

The early Section 230 court opinions could not have come at a better time for Silicon Valley. As the industry was slowly recovering from the dot-com implosion of 2000 and 2001, entrepreneurs were retrenching and developing new business models. Fueled by a deep talent pool of engineers and computer scientists and renewed interest from venture capitalists, technology companies began developing new services. The resulting round of Internet innovations became truly two-way experiences. Rather than just deliver words and images to users, these new websites and online services allowed users to share their own content. Even the more traditional websites became more interactive. News sites allowed comments underneath their stories. E-commerce sites encouraged users to post honest reviews of their products.

Some websites—in particular, online consumer review sites, Wikipedia, social media, and search engines—built their operations around third-party content. Consumer review sites provided once-voiceless consumers with a megaphone to warn others against companies' scams and broken promises. Wikipedia revolutionized how Americans receive information. Social media sites created billions of dollars in wealth and thousands of jobs. Search engines began to serve as the gateway to the Internet. These sites turned the Internet into a seemingly infinite town square.

To be sure, residents in many countries with intermediary protections far weaker than Section 230 have access to social media and other interactive services. However, the most successful of such enterprises were born in the United States. The technology industry has long said that Section 230 has played a key role in fostering this competitive advantage. A 2017 economic study commissioned by the Internet Association, a trade group, found that of the twenty-one largest digital companies, thirteen are based in the United States. Excluding China (which closes off much of its Internet access to outside companies), thirteen of the largest sixteen Internet companies are based in the United States. This disproportionate success is at least partly attributable to Section 230 and the Digital Millennium Copyright Act, which requires online services to receive a notice and opportunity to take down user content that infringes copyright before they can be sued, economist Christian M. Dippon wrote in the study: "The effects of the greater certainty, among other reasons, contributed to the business success of U.S.-based Internet intermediaries. A number of the U.S. Internet participants are among the most successful and innovative firms in the world."[1]

Dippon's study estimated that the United States would lose forty-four billion dollars in gross domestic product annually and 425,000 jobs if Congress or the U.S. courts were to weaken legal protections for intermediaries.[2]

Without Section 230, each user who posted a comment, photo, or video on a website would represent another small but real risk that the website could be sued out of existence. When you multiply that small risk by billions of user contributions, businesses start to pay attention. As Anupam Chander wrote, Section 230 "proved central to the rise of the new breed of Silicon Valley enterprise":

> What risks did such firms face? By offering platforms for users across the world, Internet enterprises faced the hazard that some users would use these platforms in ways that violated the law, bringing with it the possibility of liability for aiding and abetting that illegal activity. Consider a sampling of

the array of claims that might lie against these platforms for the behavior of their users. Yahoo might be liable if someone uses Yahoo Finance to circulate a false rumor about a public company. Match.com could face liability if a conniving user posted defamatory information about another individual. Craigslist might be liable under fair housing statutes if a landlord put up a listing stating that he preferred to rent to people of a particular race. Amazon and Yelp might be liable for defamatory comments written by a few of their legions of reviewers.[3]

The mere passage of Section 230 was not enough to pave the way for these new models of websites. Had the Fourth and Ninth Circuits read Section 230's immunity more narrowly, the websites could not have existed, at least not in their current forms. The broad *Zeran* interpretation of Section 230 was a catalyst for the success of these interactive websites. If there was even a chance that the websites could be successfully sued for user posts, their business models simply could not exist. The sites could not review the millions of words, pictures, and videos that were uploaded. And if they did not screen every bit of third-party content in advance, they could be liable for existential amounts of damages. Had courts adopted a more limited reading of Section 230, the websites could not exist in their current form. Consider Leo Kayser's narrower interpretation of Section 230—that websites and other online services could be liable as soon as they received notice of possibly harmful content. That would allow any person or business that was upset about a user post to send a removal request to the website, and if the website did not immediately remove the post, it could face a costly lawsuit. If a restaurant with a one-star review notified the site that the review was false and defamatory, and the site did not remove the posting, then Section 230 would not protect the website in a defamation lawsuit over the review. These sites have faced many potentially devastating lawsuits because of user content, and Section 230 has provided nearly bulletproof protection.

No single defendant has been the subject of more Section 230 court opinions than Ripoff Report. As its name suggests, the website contains more than two million postings (often called "reports") about businesses, many of these reports alleging that the businesses failed to deliver on their promises to consumers. All the site's reports are written by customers and posted to the site after moderators conduct a short review for clearly prohibited content. The site's motto, across the top of the website, is "Don't let them get away with it! Let the truth be known!" The site's home page warns its visitors of the unmoderated nature of the site: "While we encourage and even require authors to only file truthful reports, Ripoff Report does not guarantee that all reports are authentic or accurate. Be an educated consumer."[4]

The reports often are among the first search results for a company's name on Google, and from the site's founding through 2017, it had received nearly nine billion visits.[5] Consider a July 2017 review of a medical supplement vendor. The user, named "Richard," stated that the company "rips you off. That is their business. They help no one except themselves." When provided the opportunity to list the category of business, Richard chose "ORGANIZED CRIME."[6] Ripoff Report embodies an absolutist view of free online speech: the good, the bad, and the bizarre. To understand the personality of Ripoff Report, it is necessary to understand its founder, Ed Magedson.

A two-hour phone conversation with Ed Magedson is not a linear experience. It is a tiring journey across the figure eights of Magedson's personality. The call starts out with his rant about the businesses that sue his company despite Section 230's protections and about personal attacks on some of the unsuccessful lawyers. We briefly talk about why he started the company. Then he pauses to answer questions from workers who are putting up curtains in his Arizona home, blocking gorgeous views. "People say, 'What, are you paranoid?'" Magedson says. "I say, 'No, I'm in my business.'" That gets him talking about the time when someone burned down another one of his homes in 2007. And the hundreds of threat letters that he has received. And the Russian hackers who attack Ripoff Report. Then he gets a call from a woman he is seeing, and he talks about how she had been his girlfriend decades ago in high school. Please interrupt me if I go off track, he says halfway through the conversation.[7] (It seems impossible to interrupt him.)

Distilling the barrage of facts from the phone call and publicly available documents and news reports, this is a brief, chronological story of Ripoff Report: Ed Magedson grew up on Long Island in the 1960s, and in his early twenties, he founded the Flower Children, a business that employed hippies, students, and senior citizens who sold flowers on street corners across the nation. In 1973 the *Tampa Tribune* ran a long profile on his growing business, with the headline "The Head Flower Child Is Bullish on Capitalism." Despite the free-love vibe of his business, Magedson was a tough customer for flower vendors. "I learned this from my dad—he was a savvy consumer and he never took crap," Magedson stated. "He brought stuff back to the store if it was wrong. He didn't mind saying anything." In some cities, zoning inspectors and other government officials issued citations, claiming that the street sales violated local zoning regulations. Magedson's fights with the local governments attracted media attention.[8] Magedson next went into the real estate development business in New York, and he believes that as he tried to create low-income housing, he ran into anti-Semitism from local government officials.

In the 1990s, Magedson moved to Mesa, Arizona, to care for his elderly parents. He operated indoor swap meets and believed that local government officials were preventing him from acquiring the necessary real estate for his business. Once again, Magedson was furious. He was convinced that his problems traced back to corrupt government officials. He even considered purchasing a local radio or television station so that he could tell his side of the story. Then one of his customers suggested that he start a website. At the time, Magedson did not even have an email address. "I said, 'I'm too old for that,'" Magedson recalled. "I can't get into the Internet."[9] But he heeded the advice and in 1997 started the site mesaazcorruptionreport.com (Mesa, AZ, Corruption Report). He posted his own stories and allowed users to contribute as well.

The Mesa website quickly gained visibility, and Magedson soon saw the power of the Internet. He had worked with the Better Business Bureau while running the indoor swap meet and questioned whether it truly helped to educate consumers. Throughout his time working in low-income housing, he had helped to advocate for people against businesses that had mistreated them. After his experience with the Mesa corruption site, Magedson saw the power of the Internet to help provide customers with a voice. So later in 1997, he started a "Bad Business Bureau" website, allowing customers to post complaints about businesses. He said that soon attracted a trademark infringement threat from the Better Business Bureau, so in 1998 he created Ripoff Report at www.ripoffreport.com. Magedson discusses Ripoff Report's mission with a fervent passion that is uncommon even for the most ambitious technology companies: "It used to be just buyer beware in the twentieth century. Today, it's more seller beware. Everyone's a critic. Bashful people wouldn't say anything. Now they're sitting at a computer and you're getting to know how they feel." Even though the Fourth Circuit had handed down the *Zeran* opinion only months before Magedson founded Ripoff Report, he said the two events were unrelated. At the time, he said, he did not know what Section 230 was. He had no idea about technology law. Or, for that matter, technology. "I didn't understand the Internet," he said. "I was still learning how to move the damn mouse."[10]

The site's popularity spread by word of mouth throughout the late 1990s. America Online featured Ripoff Report as one of the top consumer websites. The *Arizona Republic* ran a feature on Magedson's site. As Google developed its sophisticated search algorithm, posts on Ripoff Report became one of the first things that consumers would see when researching some businesses online. Magedson first understood the impact of his website when he received a request from a large car transmission company to remove a consumer review. The company offered him fifty thousand dollars. He declined. Since Magedson had founded the site, he maintained a general policy against removing an entire user post. In some cases, such as an apparent harassment campaign, the site may redact personal information or other highly objectionable or dangerous content in the reports or comments.[11] That is not to say that Ripoff Report simply ignores complaints from angry businesses. All businesses have the opportunity to publish, at no cost, a rebuttal on the site. The website also offers a Corporate Advocacy Program. For a fee, a business that is unhappy with a review on Ripoff Report can join the program. Ripoff Report contacts the author who complained about the business, providing an opportunity for the business to resolve the complaint. Ripoff Report will update the review's headline and might add the business's story of how it addressed the complaint. This often improves the company's Google results.

Ripoff Report also offers a VIP Arbitration Program, which connects complainants with independent and neutral arbitrators who will investigate claims of false statements in reviews. If, after gathering evidence, an arbitrator determines that a factual claim in a review is false, Ripoff Report will redact the falsehood as identified by the arbitrator and state in the title that the post had been redacted through Ripoff Report's arbitration process. But Ripoff Report will not delete the entire post. The site's general no-removal policy applies even if a consumer posts a review and then later asks Ripoff Report to delete the post. It often receives such requests, and it refuses, fearing that the consumer was asking for the removal after receiving a threat from the company that was reviewed. Consumers can update the reports by adding new comments—such as a story about how the company resolved the complaint—but they cannot delete what they had already posted.[12] Magedson has prepared a stock email that he uses, nearly three thousand words long, to respond to such requests from consumers who have posted reviews on the site. The email reminds the customers that before they submitted the review, they had checked a box agreeing that it would be permanently posted on a public website. "Our policy never to remove any report protects consumers," the email explains. "It doesn't do any good for a company to harass the consumer who posted a report—we never take the report down. If businesses thought they could get reports removed by putting pressure on consumers, some of them would just put heavy pressure on the consumer through lawsuits or harassment. But, suing or harassing the consumer won't do any good, because it won't change the report."[13]

As Ripoff Report drew more reviewers and readers, it also drew the anger of businesses. Unlike the transmission company that believed it could make its Ripoff Report problems disappear with a bribe offer, many companies believed that they could sue—or threaten lawsuits—to bully Ripoff Report into deleting negative reviews. Those who thought that such threats would work have not spent much time talking to Magedson. He laughs as he recounts the countless threats that he has received. Ripoff Report attracts so many formal complaints that it does not even maintain an official count of the number of lawsuits and litigation threats it has received over the past two decades. As of 2017, Magedson estimated that the company had spent more than seven million dollars on legal costs.[14] As of mid-2017, Ripoff Report had not lost a single lawsuit in a U.S. court arising from a user review, even though the site has lost a few preliminary rulings. Section 230 is largely responsible for the site's ultimate victory in the cases. When asked if Ripoff Report could operate without Section 230 on the books, Magedson quickly responds, "Of course not." He says, "I would have been out of business," adding, "Half the stuff on the Internet wouldn't even exist because everyone claims it's false."[15]

For instance, on March 27, 2006, Tennessee resident Spencer Sullivan posted a review on Ripoff Report about Global Royalties Inc., an

Ontario-based company that brokers investments in gemstones. Sullivan's review, signed under the name "Liam," alleged that Global Royalties was a "scam." Sullivan placed the review under a category labeled "Con Artists."[16] About two months later, Sullivan added an update to his post on Ripoff Report, stating that Global Royalties had threatened him with litigation and that, in response, "I am stating that I have no information that would indicate that Global Royalties is following anything but the best of business practices." But he noted that his experience with "two individuals involved with Global Royalties . . . [had] been less than honourable."[17] About a week later, Sullivan again updated his review to report that he had been threatened by the company's lawyer, and warned anyone considering investments with Global Royalties to first contact the Royal Canadian Mounted Police: "I would think that any upstanding commercial operation could bear the scrutiny of a crime unit without any issue."[18] Global Royalties claimed that after it explained to Sullivan that the post was "based on misunderstandings," Sullivan requested that Ripoff Report delete the posts, but Ripoff Report declined.[19]

Global Royalties and its principal, Brandon Hall, filed a defamation suit against Ripoff Report's parent company, Xcentric Ventures LLC, and Magedson in Arizona federal court. Judge Frederick Martone at first dismissed the lawsuit for a failure to allege sufficient facts but allowed the plaintiffs to amend the complaint.[20] In the amended complaint, Global Royalties claimed that Xcentric and Magedson were "solely responsible" for creating and developing the "defamatory portion" of Sullivan's first post, noting that the site provided "Con Artists" as a category for reports. Global Royalties also claimed that Xcentric and Magedson used the complaints about the reviews "as leverage to coerce businesses and individuals to pay for Xcentric's Corporate Advocacy Program, which purports to provide assistance in investigating and resolving the posted complaints."[21]

Ripoff Report moved to dismiss the amended complaint, pointing to the Ninth Circuit's rulings in *Batzel* and *Carafano* (Arizona is in the Ninth Circuit, so the court there is bound by those rulings). "Because Mr. Sullivan's report(s) (whether one or three or more) contained no content until Mr. Sullivan created them, the CDA applies in full to any and all claims based on *that content* and although Mr. Sullivan might be, Defendants simply are not responsible for the accuracy of this third-party content," Ripoff Report's lawyers wrote.[22] Global Royalties argued that *Batzel* supported its position that Section 230 did not immunize Ripoff Report. "In

Batzel, the third party (Smith) provided the content, but allegedly never meant for it to be published on the defendant's website," Global Royalties wrote. "In our case, the third party (Spencer) originally provided the content for publication, but later directed that it be taken down and published no more. Defendants refused."[23]

Martone dismissed the lawsuit, finding a big difference between Sullivan's posting and Smith's email in *Batzel*. According to Martone, even if Sullivan later asked Ripoff Report to remove the post, he had already uploaded the review onto Ripoff Report, intending that it would be published to the public. "Sullivan obviously meant his messages to appear on the website," he wrote. "Whether website operators have a duty to withdraw content when an author later changes his mind is another question—one that is not addressed by *Batzel*."[24] Martone acknowledged that Ripoff Report might encourage defamatory content. But merely encouraging defamatory posts, he wrote, did not cause Section 230's protections to evaporate: "After all, plaintiffs have not alleged that defendants solicited Sullivan's postings in particular, or that they specifically solicited any postings targeting Global. Nor have they alleged that defendants altered Sullivan's comments, or had any more than the most passive involvement (providing a list of possible titles) in composing them. Unless Congress amends the statute, it is legally (although perhaps not ethically) beside the point whether defendants refuse to remove the material, or how they might use it to their advantage."[25]

The *Global Royalties* case represents a common outcome in a lawsuit against Ripoff Report. A plaintiff's lawyer tries to creatively argue that Ripoff Report somehow contributed to the user review and thus is not entitled to Section 230. Ripoff Report asks the court to dismiss the case, pointing to a growing body of similar suits in which other judges have held that Section 230 protects sites like Ripoff Report. The judge grudgingly agrees with Ripoff Report and dismisses the case. Despite Ripoff Report's success record in courts, companies continue to threaten the site with lawsuits. Anette Beebe, Ripoff Report's lawyer, receives the brunt of these threats and complaints. Beebe's outgoing and helpful demeanor makes her the ideal foil for furious businesses that call or write her to demand removal. Before going to law school, Beebe was a paralegal at a law firm that Ripoff Report had retained in its early years, although she had been doing work unrelated to Ripoff Report at the time. Beebe continued to work for the firm during law school. By the time she had graduated and was studying for the bar, Magedson engaged her services for some smaller projects and quickly hired her to work at the company in-house.[26]

When she receives calls or letters from angry businesses—or their lawyers—she views herself as an educator. She calmly explains Section 230 to people, who often have never heard of it before. "When I tell them about Section 230, they typically don't like it," Beebe said.[27] Beebe often points people to what is called the "Legal Issues" page on Ripoff Report's website, which includes a section that explains how Section 230 protects the site from lawsuits based on user reviews and provides examples of Section 230 cases. Much of this is based on an eighty-three-hundred-word article on the site that explains how Section 230 protects the site from any lawsuits based on user reviews. The page's title: "Want to Sue Ripoff Report?" The page explains its absolutist stance against removing a user post: "For any website that allows user-generated comments, investigating and verifying every posting would be economically and practically impossible, so the law (at least here in the United States) does not hold website operators responsible for the accuracy of material posted by a user." Ripoff Report then explains Section 230 and provides a detailed review of the cases against Ripoff Report and other sites that have resulted in dismissal of the claims. "So, why should you care about the CDA?" the webpage asks. "Well, it's simple—if someone posts false information about you on the Ripoff Report, the CDA prohibits you from holding us liable for the statements which others have written. You can always sue the author if you want, but you can't sue Ripoff Report just because we provide a forum for speech."

Ripoff Report has grown to about fourteen employees, plus independent contractors. The site supports itself through the Corporate Advocacy Program and similar offerings. Because of the legal fees, Magedson said, he does not earn much net income from the site. ("I swear on my dog's life, and I don't usually even do that.") Magedson says that he runs the website because he is gratified when he learns that he has helped customers avoid scams and rip-offs, but the barrage of legal threats, lawsuits, and nasty emails has taken a toll on him.[28] "I'm sixty-five," Magedson lamented. "I can't deal with it. I'm gaining weight and I'm killing myself."[29]

Ripoff Report pioneered the practice of unvarnished online consumer reviews, but it has remained a relatively small business. Yelp, on the other hand, has perfected the commercialization of online user reviews and turned it into a multibillion-dollar business with thousands of employees. Although Yelp's reviews are not always as sharp edged as many posts on Ripoff Report, Yelp's business model also could not exist without Section 230.

In 2004, Russel Simmons and Jeremy Stoppelman founded Yelp as a side project after Stoppelman had trouble finding useful online reviews while looking for medical care. After some initial iterations of the site, they settled on a format that allowed users to rate restaurants and other local businesses on a scale of one to five stars.[30] This exclusive focus on user ratings differentiated Yelp from its competitors. Other sites had long allowed user reviews of businesses, but those user reviews typically were comments underneath professional reviews. As the *New York Times* observed in 2008, Yelp set itself apart by "attracting a small group of fanatic reviewers."[31] Yelp is a truly interactive experience for its reviewers, allowing visitors to the site to rate whether the review was helpful. In 2006 Yelp created an "Elite Squad" for its top reviewers, offering them a prestigious designation on their Yelp profiles and inviting them to events.[32]

Because of Yelp's increasing importance, businesses—and their competitors—have tried to game the system by posting fake reviews that purport to come from customers. Like Ripoff Report, Yelp will not remove a user review simply because the subject of the review is upset. But unlike Ripoff Report, Yelp allows users to delete reviews that they have posted. Yelp does not have the staff to sift through the millions of reviews and verify their accuracy before they are posted. So it has developed an algorithm to assess the quality of the review to determine whether to include the review on the business's main page or to banish it to a separate page of "reviews that are not currently recommended."[33]

Yelp's geographic coverage and readership expanded as it attracted venture capital investments.[34] In 2009 Yelp rejected Google's offer to acquire the company for about $550 million.[35] Rather than looking for another large company to acquire it, Yelp operated independently and continued to expand to markets around the world, attracting millions of users and reviewers. It also developed an app for smartphones, integrating geolocation features to allow users to find businesses around them. Yelp went public in March 2012. When the stock closed after its first day of trading, the company was valued at $1.47 billion.[36] As of March 2018, Yelp had accumulated 155 million user reviews worldwide. The company had $214 million in advertising revenues during the first three months of 2018, up 20 percent from a year ago, and more than four thousand employees.[37] As Yelp became one of the most visited sites and apps on the Internet, even a slight change in the average user rating could determine a local business's fate. A study of the site's restaurant data concluded that "moving from 3 to 3.5 stars is associated with being 21 percentage points more likely to have sold out all 7:00 PM tables and moving from 3.5 to 4 stars makes restaurants an additional 19 percentage points more likely to have sold out all tables."[38]

Because Yelp can make or break a business, it has received many legal threats claiming that user reviews were inaccurate. To defend itself, the company has long relied on Section 230, just as Ripoff Report does. At a 2011 conference about Section 230, Yelp general counsel Laurence Wilson said the company receives hundreds—or sometimes thousands—of complaints each day, and it relies on Section 230: "By and large we're more likely to keep a review up instead of take it down because we're not in a position to make factual determinations about whether the radiator in your car was properly fixed by your mechanic or not."[39]

Despite Section 230's broad protections, some angry businesses still sue Yelp, claiming that negative consumer reviews harmed their business. For instance, in September 2011, "Sarah K" posted a one-star Yelp review of a Washington State locksmith business owned by Douglas Kimzey:

THIS WAS BY FAR THE WORST EXPERIENCE I HAVE EVER EN-COUNTERED WITH A LOCKSMITH. DO NOT GO THROUGH THIS COMPANY. I had just flew [sic] back from a long business trip with absolutely no sleep, had to drive into work right after getting off the plane. I was so tired that I locked my keys in the car. So when I realized what happened I called Redmond Mobile. The gentlemen [sic] on the phone told me that a technician would be out ASAP and quoted me $50 for the service, which seemed reasonable. $35 for the service call and $15 for the lock. The technician called and said he'd be at my office in 30 min., an hour goes by and nothing. Call the company back to ask about the ETA and was greeted rudely by the person I had spoken to earlier. He took no responsibility. After the technician finally showed up, he was trying to charge me $35 for the service call and $175 for the lock. I got 20% off after trying to argue with him about being late and the incorrect quote. Supposedly, the lock is $15 and up. Bullshit. CALL THIS BUSINESS AT YOUR OWN RISK. I didn't even need new keys. I just needed my car unlocked.[40]

About a year after Sarah K. posted the review, "D.K. of Redmond Mobile Locksmith" responded to the review on Yelp, writing that "Yelp has Posted a Fraudulent review on our Business."[41] Sarah K responded:

I was just informed recently by a friend that this business has been trying to contact others on my friends list asking about my original review. A year ago, I had also received similar msgs from this business and also yelp requesting authentication of the review and the business directly asking me to take down the review because I must have gotten the company incorrect. So let me clarify, I do not work for a competitor of this business nor do I appreciate this type of harassment. I've already confirmed to Yelp that indeed this review was meant for Redmond Mobile Locksmith and I have the receipt to prove it. I will be issuing an official complaint to Yelp about this now.[42]

Kimzey, the business owner, sued Yelp in Washington State federal court—without help from a lawyer—for defamation and violations of the Washington State Consumer Protection Act and the federal Racketeer Influenced and Corrupt Organizations Act. In the complaint, he argued that Section 230 "is completely inapplicable" because he "is not suing Yelp for statements made by a third party." Instead, Kimzey wrote, "Yelp's statements are actionable as they convey statements of fact and not statements made by a third party information content provider."[43] Apparently trying to get around Section 230, Kimzey alleged that Yelp "republishes" the review on Google.

District Judge Richard A. Jones disagreed. He dismissed the case in a five-page order, concluding that Section 230 immunized Yelp and that Kimzey "has not alleged non-conclusory factual content that is plausibly suggestive of a claim entitling him to relief."[44] Kimzey appealed to the Ninth Circuit, which affirmed the district court's dismissal without holding oral arguments. Like the district court, the Ninth Circuit swiftly dismissed Kimzey's attempts to circumvent Section 230. "Simply put, proliferation and dissemination of content does not equal creation or development of content," Judge Margaret McKeown wrote for a unanimous three-judge panel.[45] McKeown wrote that Kimzey failed to explain how Yelp "created" the review and wrote that "the immunity in the CDA is broad enough to require plaintiffs alleging such a theory to state the facts plausibly suggesting the defendant fabricated content under a third party's identity."[46] McKeown also rejected Kimzey's assertion that Yelp's five-star rating structure helped to create the content of user reviews and thus rendered Section 230 inapplicable, as well as his claim that Yelp "republished" the statements by making them available to search engines. "These characterizations have superficial appeal, but they extend the concept of an 'information content provider' too far and would render the CDA's immunity provisions meaningless," McKeown explained.[47] Perhaps frustrated with Kimzey's arguments, McKeown noted in her opinion that the lawsuit "pushes the envelope of creative pleading in an effort to work around § 230."[48]

Although Kimzey's unsuccessful lawsuit was far from the most sophisticated attempt to circumvent Section 230's immunity, it was useful because it resulted in a binding opinion in which the Ninth Circuit held that Section 230 applied to the central features of Yelp. Consider how Yelp would operate without Section 230. Under the First Amendment protections of *Smith v. California* and *Cubby v. CompuServe*, an online platform like Yelp might become liable for its users' defamatory comments once it knows or should have known that users posted defamatory content. In the best-case scenario for Yelp, this would mean that as soon as the company received a complaint from the subject of a review, the site would have two choices: remove the review immediately or take a chance and spend large sums on legal fees defending a defamation suit in court. This could amount to a heckler's veto for anyone who was not happy with their reviews and ratings on Yelp, and it would undercut the ability of consumers to turn to Yelp for comprehensive reports on businesses. And there is an even bleaker outcome for Yelp in a non–Section 230 world. Courts could find that because Yelp is known to contain negative and false reviews, the company should have known of any defamatory user posts. This reading of *Smith v. California* would mean that Yelp becomes liable for defamatory reviews as soon as they are posted, so removing them after getting a complaint would not absolve the company of liability. Yelp could avoid liability by prescreening and vetting every user post for defamation, but the costs of this screening would be astronomical. Yelp's only other option would be to entirely ban user reviews, but that would defeat the entire purpose of Yelp. What is Yelp without user reviews?

Just as Ripoff Report and Yelp changed consumer awareness, Wikipedia forever altered the world of reference information, providing free, crowd-sourced encyclopedia entries about nearly every imaginable topic (and if an imaginable topic has no Wikipedia entry, it can be created by Wikipedia users). By 2017, the English version of Wikipedia had more than five million articles[49] and was the fifth-most-visited site on the Internet.[50] Wikipedia epitomizes the two-way nature of the Internet. Rather than presenting a static article about a subject, Wikipedia allows any user with an Internet connection to edit, update, and improve upon the entry, and it allows others to review that work. Few sites have benefited more from on-line crowd collaboration than Wikipedia.

The concept of "wikis"—which allow communities of users to collaborate on a work product—originated more than five years before Wikipedia was founded. The creator of wikis, Ward Cunningham, proudly states that he was never much into reading or writing.[51] In the summer of 1994, Cunningham, a Portland-based software programmer, organized a conference at the University of Illinois. He convened about one hundred programmers to develop pattern languages, a new method of developing software programs to solve problems. The participants presented works in progress and offered suggestions to improve one another's work. After the conference, Cunningham was talking with a University of Illinois graduate student who showed him something called the World Wide Web. Cunningham was intrigued about the possibility to use the Web to collaborate on pattern languages, and when he got home to Portland, he met with a former colleague who had founded a Portland Internet service provider. His friend set him up with a computer and a dial-up Internet connection, and Cunningham was on the Web with his own site, c2.com.[52]

Cunningham posted about five software patterns on a c2.com pattern repository for the roughly five hundred members of his developer community to view. But it was a static experience: visitors could view the patterns and email Cunningham, but they could not edit the patterns or create their own. So Cunningham began tinkering with his website's programming and created a form that allowed users to automatically post their own patterns—and edit the patterns that others had posted. Cunningham was amazed at the speed of collaboration. He contemplated calling the new tool QuickWeb, but chose WikiWikiWeb instead (WikiWiki is "very fast" in Hawaiian). The name was soon shortened to "wiki."[53]

"This is a public space," Cunningham recalled later. "You can enter this space like going to the park. Just out of respect for each other, you like the park and want to make the campground better than it was before."[54]

The wiki caught on immediately within the pattern language community, and every day, the small group of programmers would post dozens of new pages on the wiki. For about five years, the "wiki" concept was limited to this small group of techies. Until Jimmy Wales and Larry Sanger came along. Jimmy Wales, the research director at a Chicago futures trading firm, and Larry Sanger, a philosophy graduate student, had been operating Nupedia, a peer-reviewed online encyclopedia. The peer review process, which Sanger managed as the site's editor in chief, was toilsome, resulting in few new Nupedia articles.[55] In early 2001, Sanger learned about the concept of wikis from a friend in Cunningham's pattern language community. This seemed to Sanger like good way to increase the amount of articles on Nupedia. He emailed Nupedia's mailing list with the headline "Let's make a wiki," proposing to create a wiki side project: "As to Nupedia's use of a wiki, this is the ULTIMATE 'open' and simple format for developing content. We have occasionally bandied about ideas for simpler, more open projects to either replace or supplement Nupedia. It seems to me wikis can be implemented practically instantly, need very little maintenance, and in general are very low-risk. They're also a potentially great source for content. So there's little downside, as far as I can determine."[56]

The small group that ran Nupedia registered Wikipedia.com on January 15, 2001. Wikipedia used another programmer's version of Cunningham's code for its initial wiki.[57] Cunningham says that he was fine with Wikipedia's using a version of his code, but at the time he questioned how useful a crowd-sourced encyclopedia would be, at least compared with the new pattern literature his wikis had created. When he was growing up, he had a set of World Book encyclopedias that he found to be of limited use. "I'd just read two paragraphs in an article and be on to the next one," he remembered.[58]

In less than a month, users had posted one thousand articles on Wikipedia. The site first gained widespread fame on September 20, 2001, when the *New York Times* ran a long feature on it, marveling at the communal nature of the site and observing that Wikipedia's accomplishments suggested "that the Web can be a fertile environment in which people work side by side and get along with one another."[59] Sanger left the site in late 2002. Wales, who continued his leadership role, wanted to prevent the site from becoming commercialized or institutionally edited. He helped it become a self-governing organization under a nonprofit, the Wikimedia Foundation. By the end of 2004, the site had more than one million articles, and that number would multiply by more than five times in the following fourteen years.[60] The Wikipedia community has developed an intricate set of content policies and guidelines that cover several areas, including requiring a neutral point of view and prohibiting harassment. The other users/editors enforce the policies, and for serious violations, an editor can be banned from editing the site. Such decisions are made by administrators, volunteers who typically are frequent Wikipedia contributors who have been selected by other Wikipedia editors. The site has created other safeguards, such as an arbitration committee that resolves disputes between editors.[61] This comprehensive and responsible set of procedures sounds similar to the self-regulation that Cox and Wyden sought as they wrote Section 230.

Despite the intricate self-governing mechanisms that the Wikipedia community has adopted, the editors and administrators cannot immediately detect every bit of false information across the millions of entries. The first high-profile failure of its editing system came in 2005. John Seigenthaler Sr., the founding editorial director of *USA Today*, learned that a Wikipedia entry about him, created four months earlier, contained the following claim:

> John Seigenthaler Sr. was the assistant to Attorney General Robert Kennedy in the early 1960s. For a short time, he was thought to have been directly involved in the Kennedy assassinations of both John, and his brother, Bobby. Nothing was ever proven.
>
> John Seigenthaler moved to the Soviet Union in 1972, and returned to the United States in 1984.
>
> He started one of the country's largest public relations firms shortly thereafter.[62]

Seigenthaler had served as Robert Kennedy's administrative assistant in the 1960s. He also was a pallbearer at Kennedy's funeral. He had never, in any way, been implicated in the assassinations of Robert or John Kennedy. A Wikipedia editor removed the claims after Seigenthaler complained, but Seigenthaler was still furious. In November 2005 he wrote a furious op-ed for *USA Today,* in which he criticized Wikipedia as being "populated by volunteer vandals with poison-pen intellects."[63] Seigenthaler took aim at Section 230 for enabling sites like Wikipedia to transmit such rumors:

> Federal law also protects online corporations—BellSouth, AOL, MCI Wikipedia, etc.—from libel lawsuits. Section 230 of the Communications Decency Act, passed in 1996, specifically states that "no provider or user of an interactive computer service shall be treated as the publisher or speaker." That legalese means that, unlike print and broadcast companies, online service providers cannot be sued for disseminating defamatory attacks on citizens posted by others.
>
> Recent low-profile court decisions document that Congress effectively has barred defamation in cyberspace. Wikipedia's website acknowledges that it is not responsible for inaccurate information, but Wales, in a recent C-Span interview with Brian Lamb, insisted that his website is accountable and that his community of thousands of volunteer editors (he said he has only one paid employee) corrects mistakes within minutes.
>
> My experience refutes that. My "biography" was posted May 26. On May 29, one of Wales' volunteers "edited" it only by correcting the misspelling of the word "early." For four months, Wikipedia depicted me as a suspected assassin before Wales erased it from his website's history Oct. 5.[64]

Wikipedia does not require editors to use their real names, but it does log and publish the IP addresses of editors. Seigenthaler acknowledged that he could have filed a defamation lawsuit against the anonymous poster and subpoenaed the Internet service provider for the name of the subscriber of that IP address. He did not do so.[65] Instead, the operator of an anti-Wikipedia website tracked down the anonymous poster based on the IP address and publicly identified him. The poster sent a handwritten apology letter to Seigenthaler, and Seigenthaler did not sue him.[66] Seigenthaler had cleared his reputation, but his *USA Today* column highlighted the flaws in Wikipedia's editing system. The column also marked one of the first mainstream criticisms of Section 230.

Seigenthaler was correct that Section 230 provides strong protection for Wikipedia. It is difficult to imagine how Wikipedia could operate if it would be held liable for the vast amount of content provided by its millions of user-editors. Consider the case of Barbara Bauer, a New Jersey–based literary agent. She was upset about many online statements about her business, and she sued more than twenty defendants, including the Wikimedia Foundation. Among the forty-two counts in her second amended complaint were two claims against the Wikimedia Foundation for defamation and tortious interference with prospective economic advantage. She claimed that Wikipedia published a statement that she was "the Dumbest of the Twenty Worst" literary agents and that she had "no documented sales at all."[67] The Wikimedia Foundation asked the New Jersey trial court to dismiss the claims against it. The Wikimedia Foundation told the court that no version of the Wikipedia article about Bauer described her as the dumbest. But a mid-2006 version of the Wikipedia entry stated that her agency "was listed by Writer Beware (part of the Science Fiction and Fantasy Writers of America writers' organisation) as one of the twenty worst literary agencies—the agencies that they receive the most complaints about."[68] In its motion to dismiss, the Wikimedia Foundation argued that Section 230 barred Bauer's claims against it. "Plaintiffs do not assert that Wikimedia created or developed those statements, in whole or in part," the foundation wrote. "Such an allegation would be inconsistent with the basic nature of the Wikipedia online encyclopedia, which . . . is written and edited by its users."[69]

Bauer's attorney, Dan Martin, opposed the motion. Martin wrote that there "is no question" that Section 230 "prohibits the imposition of liability on any user or provider of an interactive computer service, such as Wikipedia, for publishing content provided by another." But the entry by Bauer was created by a Wikipedia user whose name was on a list of Wikipedia administrators, Martin wrote, and thus the article was not provided "by another."[70] The Wikimedia Foundation responded that although a Wikimedia administrator had revised the entry, Bauer had failed to prove that the administrator "was responsible for creating or adding any statement" that served as the basis for the lawsuit. And even if an administrator had created the allegedly defamatory content, Wikimedia argued, the plaintiffs "offer no evidence whatsoever" that administrators were employees or agents of the Wikimedia Foundation rather than "simply a class of users of the Wikipedia website."[71] Judge Jamie S. Perri agreed with the Wikimedia Foundation. In a two-page order, Perri dismissed the claims against the Wikimedia Foundation, writing that it was a provider and user of an interactive computer service and thus immune under Section 230.

As seen in Bauer's failed lawsuit against the Wikimedia Foundation, Wikipedia relies heavily on Section 230 because all its content is provided by millions of users around the world. Some of those users are administrators with special privileges. Without Section 230, Wikipedia could be exposed to liability for all these users' article creations and edits. Even if the First Amendment ultimately would protect Wikipedia, the site would be forced to spend massive amounts on legal fees to convince a court why the First Amendment applied. Section 230 provides a bright-line rule that shields potential plaintiffs from even trying to sue sites like Wikipedia.

Mike Godwin, the Wikimedia Foundation's former general counsel, claimed that without the protections of Section 230 and the Digital Millennium Copyright Act, Wikipedia and other interactive online services probably could not exist, concluding that "these laws are essential to making today's robust online public squares possible, and they will likely be essential for the next generation of online entrepreneurs."[72]

Wikipedia has had a remarkable influence on human knowledge, but the nonprofit site never was intended to become a booming business. Perhaps the greatest economic impact of Section 230 can be seen in the social media sector. Of the twenty most visited websites in the United States as of July 2017, four were social media sites: Facebook, Instagram, Twitter, and LinkedIn (others in the top twenty, such as Reddit, Imgur, and Tumblr, have social media features). U.S.-based social media platforms have become a utility for people around the world. As of mid-2017, Facebook had more than 2 billion users, Instagram had more than 700 million, LinkedIn had more than 500 million, Twitter had more than 300 million, and Snapchat had more than 160 million.[73]

Social media companies have become massive business successes as they have gained users. By July 2017, Facebook (which also owns Instagram), Twitter, LinkedIn, and Snap (which owns Snapchat) employed more than twenty-five thousand people.[74] The combined market value of their stock exceeded $550 billion. For comparison, the combined market value of the stock of Ford and General Motors at that time was about $100 billion. As of mid-2018, Twitter users sent 6,000 tweets every *second*, or two hundred billion every year.[75] Every minute, Facebook handles more than three million user posts and Instagram displays more than sixty thousand new photos.[76] It is difficult to imagine how Facebook, Twitter, and Instagram (all of which are based in the United States) could function without Section 230. "You absolutely need to have Section 230 to have a Facebook," said Chris Cox, Section 230's coauthor. At the 2011 Santa Clara Law School conference about Section 230, Twitter's then–general counsel, Alex Macgillivray, said that Section 230, as well as U.S. copyright laws, had helped the United States lead the development of new Internet companies that rely on third-party content: "Legislation has really fostered a tremendous amount of growth in U.S. competitiveness."

Over the past decade, courts have ruled that social media services are interactive computer services that are entitled to Section 230's immunity. One of the most influential court opinions to apply Section 230 to social media involved not Facebook or Twitter, but MySpace, which was founded in 2003 and was one of the earliest social media success stories. Rupert Murdoch's media conglomerate, News Corp, purchased MySpace for more than five hundred million dollars in 2005. In the mid-2000s, MySpace was particularly popular among teenagers (its policy was that users must be at least fourteen years old). In 2006 MySpace reported that about 22 percent of its users were minors.[77] Sexual predators took advantage of MySpace's popularity with young people. State law enforcement officials nationwide urged the service to bar users under sixteen years old and take other steps to protect minors. "I am increasingly concerned by reports that young children using MySpace.com have been victims of harassment, sexual solicitation, and even sexual assault," Jim Petro, then the attorney general of Ohio, wrote to the MySpace CEO, Chris DeWolfe, in 2006.[78]

One such victim was a teenage girl in Travis County, Texas. In 2005, when she was thirteen years old, she created a MySpace account, even though the site's policies required users to be fourteen. When she was fourteen, a nineteen-year-old man named Pete I. Solis reached out to her on MySpace, and they began sending messages to one another on the service.[79] She gave him her phone number. They eventually met in person, and Solis sexually assaulted the girl.[80] The girl told her mother, who reported the assault to the police. Solis was arrested for second-degree felony sexual assault.[81] The girl's mother sued Solis, MySpace, and News Corporation on behalf of the girl (who was given the pseudonym Julie

Doe in the court papers). The litigation began in federal and state courts in Texas and New York, and finally ended up in Texas federal court, before Judge Sam Sparks. MySpace asked Sparks to dismiss the case, arguing that Section 230 immunized it from the lawsuit. Julie's lawyers argued that Section 230 did not apply because they sought to hold MySpace liable for failing to protect children from predators, not for its publication of third-party content. For instance, even though Julie was not yet fourteen, she could create a MySpace profile. "Defendants undisputedly knew that sexual predators used their 'cyber-premises' to communicate with minors," they wrote. "They took no reasonable measures to prevent such communication."[82]

At a hearing on the motion to dismiss, Judge Sparks appeared to have trouble accepting the argument that MySpace should be liable for the girl's sexual assault. "I want to get this straight," Sparks said to the lawyer for the girl and her mother, Jason A. Itkin. "You have a 13-year-old girl who lies, disobeys all of the instructions, later on disobeys the warning not to give personal information, obviously, [and] does not communicate with the parent. More important, the parent does not exercise the parental control over the minor. The minor gets sexually abused, and you want somebody else to pay for it? This is the lawsuit that you filed?"[83] Itkin noted that MySpace could have adopted simple safeguards, such as verifying the ages of users. "Pete Solis is liable for an assault," he said. "But what we're trying to hold MySpace liable for isn't the publishing of a phone number but, rather, we're trying to hold MySpace responsible for not putting in the safety precautions to keep the two of them separated."[84]

Judge Sparks still was not convinced. Less than two weeks after the hearing, he dismissed the case, concluding that Section 230 shielded MySpace from the lawsuit. MySpace, he wrote, is "a company that functions as an intermediary by providing a forum for the exchange of information between third party users."[85] Just as Kenneth Zeran could not successfully sue America Online for failing to promptly delete the Oklahoma City posts, Judge Sparks wrote, Julie Doe could not sue MySpace for failing to protect her from sexual predators.[86] Sparks wrote that it was "disingenuous" for Julie Doe's lawyers to try to circumvent Section 230 by claiming that the lawsuit did not treat MySpace as a publisher: "It is quite obvious the underlying basis of Plaintiffs' claims is that, through postings on MySpace, Pete Solis and Julie Doe met and exchanged personal information which eventually led to an in-person meeting and the sexual assault of Julie Doe. If MySpace had not published communications between Julie Doe and Solis, including personal contact information, Plaintiffs assert they never would have met and the sexual assault never would have occurred."[87]

Julie Doe's lawyers appealed to the United States Court of Appeals for the Fifth Circuit. The randomly chosen panel of three judges was about as conservative as it could get. Judge William Garwood, a Reagan appointee, in 1993 had struck down a law that banned the possession of guns near schools. Judge Edith Brown Clement was George W. Bush's first appointee to the Fifth Circuit, and she was rumored to be a frontrunner for the U.S. Supreme Court seats that eventually went to John Roberts and Samuel Alito.[88] Judge Jennifer Elrod had just been appointed to the Fifth Circuit in October 2007 by Bush, at age forty-one.

The three judges unanimously agreed with Sparks: Section 230 protected MySpace from all of Julie Doe's claims. "Their claims are barred by the CDA, notwithstanding their assertion that they only seek to hold MySpace liable for its failure to implement measures that would have prevented Julie Doe from communicating with Solis," Clement wrote for the panel. "Their allegations are merely another way of claiming that MySpace was liable for publishing the communications and they speak to MySpace's role as a publisher of online third-party-generated content."[89] Clement's decision helped the nascent social media industry, a fraction of its current size when she wrote the opinion in 2008. Her ruling provided a binding, federal appellate opinion which clarified that Section 230 applied to social media companies. Other courts around the nation would later cite her opinion when immunizing other social media companies, such as Facebook and Twitter. The opinion also was important to Section 230's development because it expanded the scope of cases to which Section 230 applies. The typical Section 230 claim involves a defamatory comment posted by a user. But nothing about Section 230 limits its application to defamation cases.

Julie Doe's case was more troubling than the garden-variety defamation case. This was not just about damage to a plaintiff's reputation. A teenage girl was sexually assaulted. And she claimed that MySpace failed to adopt even the most basic safety precautions for her and millions of other minors. Bad facts can change the outcome of a case. And these were bad facts. A sympathetic judge might have adopted the arguments of Julie Doe's lawyers—that MySpace did not provide adequate security for minors and that this failure had nothing to do with the publication of third-party content. Had Judge Clement and her colleagues taken such a position, social media companies across the United States would have faced a legal duty to protect their customers from the billions of users who would soon frequent their sites. Meeting this obligation is unimaginable. Social media is about more than just words and images; it is about connections between people. Those connections can occur online or offline. The broad interpretation of Section 230 was essential to the development of social media.

Just as Yelp could not exist in its current form without Section 230, neither could social media. Imagine if Facebook or Twitter were forced to defend any user content once it was on notice that someone believed that the content was defamatory or otherwise illegal. This would allow anyone who was upset about a Facebook post or tweet to send a letter to the social media company demanding its removal. If the social media provider did not remove the material, then it would have to defend the user content to a court. Such a prospect likely would cause the social media provider to err on the side of removing any content after receiving a demand letter, for fear of spending huge amounts of money in court or suffering a large judgment.

Google is the most visited website in the world, and it is difficult to imagine how it could have developed in its current form had Congress not passed Section 230. Larry Page and Sergey Brin began developing the search engine as a research project as Stanford graduate students in January 1996, a month before President Clinton signed Section 230 into law. Google went public in 2004,[90] and it has expanded its business far beyond the search engine. As of mid-2017, the market value of Google's parent company exceeded six hundred billion dollars,[91] more than ten times the value of General Motors. Searches continue to be essential to Google's operations, even though the company has expanded into many other lines of business, and it continues to dominate the online search market. In 2017 Google's share of the global online search market exceeded 80 percent, as it fulfilled more than 1.2 trillion searches a year.[92] Google represents the modern Internet company—its unparalleled success has resulted not from content that the company has created, but from how it has been able to connect its users with the content of third parties. Courts have held that Section 230 covers the search results that Google and its competitors provide. This allows Google to serve as the gateway to the Internet, and it prevents people who are unhappy about the search results from bullying the company into blocking certain sites.

For instance, Beatrice Fakhrian was angry about a consumer review of her talent agency. Unsurprisingly, the review was posted on Ripoff Report, by a user named "Hg." The December 29, 2008, posting stated, "Mega Artist Talent Agency—New World Management—Beatrice Fakhrian Not a real agency, a Fake management firm, Steals money and lies, criminal. Beverly Hills California."[93] Fakhrian sued Google for defamation, claiming that by distributing the Ripoff Report to its users, the search engine had "destroyed" her business. The California state trial court dismissed her lawsuit, and the California Court of Appeal affirmed, noting that courts "have repeatedly held that Google meets the definition of a protected interactive computer service."[94] Even if Fakhrian had notified Google that the search result was defamatory and Google failed to remove it, the court wrote, Section 230 still would have blocked her lawsuit. "If computer service providers were subject to distributor liability, they would face potential liability each time they receive notice of a potentially defamatory statement—from any party, concerning any message," Associate Justice John L. Segal wrote, quoting a California Supreme Court ruling that quoted *Zeran*. "Each notification would require a careful yet rapid investigation of the circumstances surrounding the posted information, a legal judgment concerning the information's defamatory character, and an on-the-spot editorial decision whether to risk liability by allowing the continued publication of that information."[95]

Imagine a world in which Google were held legally responsible for the seemingly infinite number of websites that are indexed in its search engine. It's not difficult to imagine that world, as that is the case across most of the rest of the globe. We need look only to Europe to see how Google and other online services operate in a world without Section 230.

7

AMERICAN EXCEPTIONALISM

As United States courts continued to adopt expansive readings of Section 230, a new U.S. industry based on third-party content emerged, largely in Silicon Valley. Section 230 was the catalyst for this U.S.-centric growth. To be sure, it is impossible to attribute the success of an entire sector to one factor. But after reviewing the laws in other countries, it becomes clear that an industry based on unfettered third-party content was possible only in the United States. As Jack Balkin observed, an "early version of Google or Facebook might not have survived a series of defamation lawsuits if either had been treated as the publisher of the countless links, blogs, posts, comments, and updates that appear on their facilities."[1]

Section 230 is a uniquely American law. Although other countries provide a limited amount of protection for online intermediaries, few are as sweeping or as firm as Section 230. The U.S. inclination toward nearly absolute free speech rights traces back to the nation's founding, out of an understandable concern that free speech and press are a necessary check on government power. In 1774 the First Continental Congress captured this sentiment in the famous Letter to the Inhabitants of Quebec:

> The last right we shall mention, regards the freedom of the press. The importance of this consists, besides the advancement of truth, science, morality, and arts in general, in its diffusion of liberal sentiments on the administration of Government, its ready communication of thoughts between subjects, and its consequential promotion of union among them, whereby oppressive officers are shamed or intimidated, into more honourable and just modes of conducting affairs.[2]

Section 230 reflects this strong U.S. bias toward free speech ahead of other values, such as privacy. This value is unique to the United States, as Noah Feldman wrote in 2017:

> Hate speech can only be banned in the U.S. if it is intended to incite imminent violence and is actually likely to do so. This permissive U.S. attitude is highly unusual. Europeans don't consider hate speech to be valuable public discourse, and reserve the right to ban it. They consider hate speech to degrade from equal citizenship and participation. Racism isn't an idea; it's a form of discrimination. The underlying philosophical difference here is about the right of the individual to self-expression. Americans value that classic liberal right very highly—so highly that we tolerate speech that might make others less equal. Europeans value the democratic collective and the capacity of all citizens to participate fully in it—so much that they are willing to limit individual rights.[3]

To be sure, consumers can post their thoughts and creations on websites around the world. But these sites face far greater legal risk for lawsuits, and they thus must exercise more control over user content to avoid being sued. In the United States, online intermediaries have robust liberty to transmit user content and determine if—and how—to moderate that content. So not surprisingly, many of the leading platforms that rely on user-generated content—such as Google, Facebook, Yelp, Wikipedia, and Twitter—all are based in the United States. Facebook and other user content-focused companies serve the residents of many other nations, even those with far weaker legal protections for platforms than the United States. But it is difficult to conceive of these businesses being created and headquartered anywhere but the United States. When these companies were starting out, they simply did not have the resources to litigate disputes over user content in Europe, Canada, and elsewhere. Section 230 acted as an incubator, allowing them to develop business models based on user content without the fear of lawsuits and regulation.

Section 230's extraordinary immunity in the United States stands in stark contrast to the more limited—or nonexistent—protections that intermediaries face in other nations. The result has been that websites and other services in these jurisdictions must be more careful about user content, and they often face no choice but to prescreen and block content or immediately remove any word or image after receiving a complaint. Even websites that are exceedingly careful to moderate third-party content can be held liable if their governments have not adopted protections like Section 230. Not surprisingly, governments that do not share Western democratic values are likely to impose liability on online intermediaries for any illegal user content. For instance, Article 21 of Iran's Computer Crime Law imposes severe criminal penalties on Internet service providers that fail to block user content that "generates crime."[4] Turkish courts have repeatedly blocked YouTube because user videos criticize Ataturk.[5] Russian law requires search engines to block links to "untrustworthy" or "irrelevant" results.[6] Consider China, which has shut down websites and platforms when regulators object to content. In April 2018, for instance, Chinese regulators ordered the closure of social media platform Neihan Duanzi. The next day, the CEO of the platform's parent company issued an apology: "Our product took the wrong path, and content appeared that was incommensurate with socialist core values."[7] In a June 2018 report, free speech advocacy group PEN America described the "Great Firewall" that China's laws and censorship technology created for social media: "China's legal system conscripts domestic social media companies to be active participants in the monitoring and censorship of their own users. Chinese companies have no choice but to operate in accordance with the government's demands."[8]

Imagine the chief executives of Facebook or Twitter apologizing merely because a user angered a U.S. government official. Such a blatant assault on free speech is unfathomable in the United States, not only because of Section 230 but also given the First Amendment's free speech guarantees. But even jurisdictions that generally share the democratic values of the United States—such as the European Union, Canada, and Australia—do not go as far to immunize online intermediaries as the United States has with Section 230.

Delfi is one of the largest websites in Estonia. Like many news sites, it allows users to post comments below articles. Most users have posted these comments under pseudonyms.[9] Recognizing that some comments might be objectionable or illegal, Delfi developed a system that allowed a reader to designate a user comment as *leim* (Estonian for "mocking"), and Delfi would quickly remove the comment. Delfi's software also automatically removed posts containing words that the company had designated as obscene. And Delfi promptly removed defamatory comments at the subjects' request.[10] Delfi's website advised readers that each user was "liable for his or her comment" and that Delfi barred comments that did not "comply with good practice," such as threats, insults, hostility, and incitement of violence or other illegality.[11]

Delfi published an article, titled "SLK Destroyed Planned Ice Road" on January 24, 2006. (Ice roads connect Estonian islands to the mainland, and SLK is an Estonian ferry provider.) Over the next two days, readers wrote 185 posts below the article. About twenty comments were threatening or offensive and involved someone identified in court documents only as "L," the sole or majority shareholder of SLK. Among the comments were "burn in your own ship, sick Jew!" and "I pee into [L's] ear and then I also shit onto his head."[12] About six weeks later, L's lawyers demanded that Delfi delete the twenty comments and sought about thirty-two thousand euros in damages. Delfi removed the comments as soon as it received the demand, but it refused to compensate L.[13]

L sued Delfi a few weeks later in Harju County Court in Estonia. If this dispute had occurred in the United States, there is little doubt that L would have lost. Delfi operated an interactive computer service, and L was suing Delfi for content created by others. As a result, Section 230 would have blocked the lawsuit, even if Delfi had refused to delete the comments after receiving the demand. If sites like Ripoff Report could receive Section 230 immunity, there is no reason Delfi wouldn't. But because this dispute played out in Estonian court, under Estonian law, Section 230 did not apply. The closest thing to Section 230 that Estonia has is its Information Society Services Act, based on the European Union's 2000 Electronic Commerce Directive.

The directive, which sets a required framework for national laws about Internet commerce, states that an information service provider that is a "mere conduit" cannot be held liable for information transmitted over its services. A service qualifies as a mere conduit if it does not "initiate the transmission," "select the receiver of the transmission," and "select or modify the information contained in the transmission."[14] The directive also provides more limited protection to "hosting," stating that providers cannot be liable for storing user content if either "the provider does not have actual knowledge of illegal activity or information and, as regards claims for damages, is not aware of facts or circumstances from which the illegal activity or information is apparent" or "the provider, upon obtaining such knowledge or awareness, acts expeditiously to remove or to disable access to the information."[15] Thus, the directive provides some protections for intermediaries. Truly neutral conduits are not liable for the transmission of user content. But services that host and store user content can become liable if they obtain "actual knowledge" of the illegal content and do not quickly remove it. But as with Section 230, the actual effect of these protections depends on how courts interpret them.

The county court at first dismissed the lawsuit, concluding that the Information Society Services Act and the EU directive immunized Delfi.[16] But the Tallinn Court of Appeal bounced the case back to the county court, ruling that the county court had misinterpreted the directive.[17] The county court reconsidered the case and concluded that removing the comments after receiving notice was "insufficient" protection for L. The court awarded L about 320 euros.[18] Delfi appealed. Both the Tallinn Court of Appeal and the Estonia Supreme Court affirmed the ruling against Delfi. The Supreme Court reasoned that Delfi's comment system was not "merely of a technical, automatic, and passive nature" because, among other reasons, the comments were "integrated" into Delfi's news stories.[19] Delfi appealed the ruling to the European Court of Human Rights, which determines whether EU national court rulings comply with the European Convention on Human Rights. Delfi argued that the court's decision violated Article 10 of the convention, which provides a right to free expression.

The European approach to freedom of speech and expression is more limited than that of the United States. The First Amendment of the U.S. Constitution succinctly states, "Congress shall make no law respecting an establishment of religion, or prohibiting the free exercise thereof; or abridging the freedom of speech, or of the press; or the right of the people peaceably to assemble, and to petition the Government for a redress of grievances." In forty-five words, the Founders established the right to free religion, speech, press, assembly, and petitioning.

Article 10 of the European Convention, in contrast, is about three times as long, mainly because of the many qualifications. Article 10 begins by providing Europeans with a right to free expression, but it states that this freedom is subject to "formalities, conditions, restrictions or penalties as are prescribed by law and are necessary in a democratic society, in the interests of national security, territorial integrity or public safety, for the prevention of disorder or crime, for the protection of health or morals, for the protection of the reputation or rights of others, for preventing the disclosure of information received in confidence, or for maintaining the authority and impartiality of the judiciary." Although the U.S. courts have issued opinions that provide for some comparable exceptions to the First Amendment, it is telling that the text of Article 10 reads as much like a fine-print contract as it does a statement of human rights.

A group of seven judges of the European Court (known as the Chamber) dismissed the appeal and agreed with Estonia's Supreme Court. The judges ruled that the European Convention on Human Rights did not protect Delfi in part because it was a "professional publisher" that should have been able to anticipate the potential liability that arises from operating an open commenting system.[20] Article 10 of the European Convention did not protect Delfi, they reasoned, because there was a "legitimate aim of protecting the reputation and rights of others."[21] Delfi appealed the verdict again to all seventeen judges on the European Court of Human Rights. The full court (the Grand Chamber) hears only cases of exceptional legal importance, much like the United States Supreme Court. And the Grand Chamber agreed to hear Delfi's case. Once the Grand Chamber agreed to hear it, the case became more than a dispute between a news site and a corporate executive. It turned into a test of how far the European Convention's free expression rights extended in the Internet age.

A coalition of twenty-eight media organizations and companies filed comments with the Grand Chamber, stressing the importance of strong and clear protections for online intermediaries. The media groups and companies focused on the increasingly important roles that online platforms played in fostering free expression. "User comments have become an integral part of online media," the media coalition wrote. "Whereas a traditional newspaper might devote one or two pages per issue to readers' letters, with a small sample of letters being selected for publication from the hundreds that they might receive, online media allow their readers to publish comments and remarks below most stories. Thousands of comments appear on news websites every day, providing space to readers to voice their opinions and spark debate on all manner of issues. This has turned the media from a space where the news is 'merely' reported to an online community where the news is reported and discussed."[22] The media companies pointed to the U.S. experience with Section 230 as a success story that Europe should emulate. "This clear approach has encouraged investment in the technology industry and has created a vibrant marketplace of ideas in online media," the companies wrote. "Technology industry observers credit Section 230 for fostering the environment for companies such as Facebook, Twitter, YouTube, TripAdvisor and others."[23]

Despite the media coalition's advocacy for Section 230-like protections, the Grand Chamber concluded that Article 10 did not prevent Delfi from being held liable for the user comments. Fifteen of the seventeen judges voted to uphold the Estonian Supreme Court's ruling against Delfi. To determine whether the ruling against Delfi complied with the charter, the Grand Chamber looked at the "context" in which the anonymous posters made the comments, the steps that Delfi took to block the defamation, whether the pseudonymous authors of the comments could be liable in place of Delfi, and the impact of the judgment on Delfi.[24] Although the Grand Chamber believed that the news article was a "balanced one," it concluded that because Delfi "actively called for comments" and set rules for user comments, Delfi "must be considered to have exercised a substantial degree of control" over user comments, and its role "went beyond that of a passive, purely technical service provider."[25] Identifying the authors of the post requires measures of "uncertain effectiveness," the judges noted, making it difficult for L to sue the anonymous posters.[26]

In the starkest contrast with U.S. courts, the Grand Chamber ruled that Delfi had a responsibility not only to remove defamatory comments after receiving complaints but *also* to have adopted safeguards to ensure removal of the comments without delay. The judges acknowledged that Delfi had not "wholly neglected its duty to avoid causing harm to third parties," but those measures fell short of Delfi's legal obligations.[27]

Key to the Grand Chamber's ruling was Delfi's status as a major news organization, which the Grand Chamber believed created an obligation for Delfi to "take effective measures to limit the dissemination of hate speech and speech inciting violence."[28] The Grand Chamber did not specify the exact steps that Delfi should have taken, but wrote that Delfi's notice-and-take-down process should have been "accompanied by effective procedures allowing for rapid response."[29] The judges noted that EU member states still could pass additional protections for online intermediaries, but the Grand Chamber's role was limited to "determining whether the methods adopted and the effects they entail are in conformity with the Convention."[30]

The two dissenting judges wrote that by expecting websites to find and delete certain user content, the majority opinion threatened to chill online speech. "The consequences are easy to foresee," the dissenting judges wrote. "For the sake of preventing defamation of all kinds, and perhaps all 'illegal' activities, all comments will have to be monitored from the moment they are posted. As a consequence, active intermediaries and blog operators will have considerable incentives to discontinue offering a comments feature, and the fear of liability may lead to additional self-censorship by operators."[31] The two dissenting judges cited Balkin's warning that imposing legal liability on platforms could lead to "collateral censorship" of user speech. "Governments may not always be directly censoring expression, but by putting pressure and imposing liability on those who control the technological infrastructure (ISPs, etc.), they create an environment in which collateral or private-party censorship is the inevitable result," the dissenting judges wrote.[32] The Grand Chamber's ruling made international headlines, and some observers criticized the decision as promoting such "collateral censorship." Access, a global digital rights group, immediately criticized the Grand Chamber's ruling as a "worrying precedent that could force websites to censor content."[33]

The Grand Chamber's *Delfi* ruling shows the very different approaches that the U.S. and EU legal systems take to intermediary liability. The European Union lacks the strong protections of Section 230. At best, its liability standard is much like the *Cubby v. CompuServe* First Amendment protections, which hold an online platform liable if it knows or should have known of the illegal content. The "should have known" aspect of *Delfi* is perhaps the most troubling part of the ruling for free speech advocates. Delfi is not another Ripoff Report, refusing to remove entire posts and only editing content modestly in rare situations; Delfi makes it a policy to immediately remove user content if it believes that the content is illegal or harmful. It established policies for user contributions and even automatically screened for some words. Yet even with these safeguards in place, Delfi did not do enough to satisfy the Grand Chamber's expectations. The entire implication of the ruling was that Delfi somehow should have known at least of the possibility for users to post hate speech, and that because it is a large company, it should have removed those comments "without delay."

Imagine how a site like Ripoff Report could function if it were based in Europe. It couldn't. The general premise of Ripoff Report—with "Don't let them get away with it" at the top of the website—could not function. Any business that is unhappy about being listed on Ripoff Report (which likely is most of the businesses listed on the site) could immediately request its removal. The platform would face serious legal risk for not complying.

Trustpilot, a Denmark-based company, is among the most popular online consumer review sites in Europe. Trustpilot allows reviewed businesses to report reviews that violate Trustpilot's policies. Among the reviews that are permissible to report are those that contain "offensive language that is accusatory, defamatory, violent, coarse, sexist or racist." If a business reports a review, Trustpilot automatically hides it temporarily as Trustpilot's compliance staff reviews the complaint. If the compliance staff determines that the complaint is invalid, it makes the review publicly accessible again. If the staff determines that there is "no way to address the problem(s)" with the review, they will permanently remove the post. Or they will continue to investigate and ask the reviewer for documentation.[34] Such moderation is not unheard of in the United States. In fact, many sites have large teams that explore complaints about user content. But in Trustpilot's case, it has no other viable option because of the European legal system's presumption that online platforms like Trustpilot are responsible for their users' posts. What is particularly unique—and from a free speech perspective troubling—about Trustpilot's system is the automatic temporary removal of a review after the site receives a complaint.

This reflects the *Delfi* court's focus on the need for online platforms to promptly address even the possibility of harmful or illegal user content.

Privacy and free speech often conflict. Even if a website contains information that is true—and thus not defamatory—it still may infringe on an individual's privacy. Whereas Europe's freedom of expression protections are weaker than those in the United States Constitution, its privacy protections are far more explicit. The United States Constitution does not explicitly state that individuals have a right to privacy, although courts have found privacy rights in, among other provisions, the Fourth Amendment's prohibition of unreasonable searches and seizures and the Fourteenth Amendment's Due Process Clause. In contrast, Article 8 of the European Charter of Fundamental Rights—which is based on the values of the European Convention on Human Rights and enforced by the Court of Justice of the European Union—states that everyone "has the right to the protection of personal data concerning him or her" and that the data "must be processed fairly for specified purposes and on the basis of the consent of the person concerned or some other legitimate basis laid down by law."[35]

Europe has codified those values in its data protection legislation. A Europe-wide directive passed in 1995 restricted the ability of companies to collect, use, and share personal information, and provided individuals the ability to request the erasure or blocking of data that violates privacy rights. Each member state passed privacy laws that are based on the EU directive, and the state's data protection regulators enforced the law. Europe's strong belief that privacy is a fundamental human right often conflicts with its citizens' free expression rights. The conflict between privacy and free speech became international news on May 13, 2014, when the Court of Justice of the European Union issued its ruling in *Google Spain v. Costeja Gonzalez*,[36] better known as the "Right to Be Forgotten" case.

In 2010 Mario Costeja Gonzalez was upset that a Google search of his name would find two 1998 articles in *La Vanguardia* newspaper about attachment proceedings connected to social security debts. Gonzalez, who lived in Spain, asked the country's data protection regulator to order the newspaper to make technical changes so that the articles do not appear in search results, or to delete the article entirely. He also asked the regulator to prohibit Google from including the articles in its search results for his name.[37]

The regulator refused to order the newspaper to delete or change the articles. But the regulator concluded that the data protection directive allowed it to order Google to deindex pages that violate individuals' "dignity" and general rights to privacy. Google appealed through Spain's court system, and the case was sent to the Court of Justice of the European Union, which has the final say in interpreting European laws such as the Privacy Directive (the European Court of Human Rights, which ruled on the Delfi case, has the final say on the European Convention on Human Rights).[38] The Court of Justice recognized the need to balance the ability of search engines to make information public with the individual rights to privacy. The balance between those two interests, the court wrote, depends "on the nature of the information in question and its sensitivity for the data subject's private life and on the interest of the public in having that information, an interest which may vary, in particular, according to the role played by the data subject in public life."[39] In other words, privacy regulators could, under certain circumstances, order a search engine to deindex certain pages so that they did not appear in the search results for an individual's name. But the obligation to deindex is not absolute and could be outweighed if there was a strong public interest in keeping the material accessible via a search engine. The Court of Justice did not provide much concrete guidance about when the privacy interests should require deindexing. The court suggested a case-by-case examination. Deindexing may be appropriate, the court wrote, if the information is "inadequate, irrelevant or no longer relevant, or excessive in relation to the purposes of the processing at issue carried out by the operator of the search engine."[40] There are cases in which the individual's privacy rights may not require removal, the court ruled, such as if it appeared that the privacy violation is justified "by the preponderant interest of the general public in having, on account of inclusion in the list of results, access to the information in question."[41]

Few court rulings globally had as much immediate impact on the Internet as this opinion. Search engines needed to develop processes to receive and evaluate requests to deindex pages from the search engines. Google developed an online form, titled "Request Removal of Content Indexed on Google Search Based on Data Protection Law in Europe," that allows people to request the removal of some pages from searches of their names. As of 2017, Google stated that it informs the requesters that it "will balance the privacy rights of the individual with the public's interest to know and the right to distribute information." In conducting this balancing test, Google will consider "whether the results include outdated information about you, as well as whether there's a public interest in the information— for example, we may decline to remove certain information about financial scams, professional malpractice, criminal convictions, or public conduct of government officials."

Although this process has become known as the "right to be forgotten," the information is not entirely deleted. Even if a request is successful, it remains on the website; the only changes are to the search results. Still, the ruling has created a huge amount of work for search engines operating in Europe. A year and a half after the European court's ruling, Google reported that it received nearly 350,000 requests to deindex more than 1.2 million web pages. Of the requests fully processed at the time, about 42 percent were deindexed.[42] For instance, Google granted a request from a Finnish widow to deindex a claim that her late husband had committed sex crimes. Google also deindexed a news article about an Ireland citizen's acquittal on domestic violence charges. Google denied a request to delist news articles about a cybersecurity firm employee's exit from the company, concluding that "the information closely relates to his current professional role in public life."[43]

Search engines' deindexing decisions immediately received criticism. For instance, Google deindexed a BBC blog post about former Merrill Lynch CEO Stan O'Neal's role in the bank's financial problems. The *Independent* newspaper cited this deindexing as confirmation of "fears that the EU's ruling can be used by the rich and powerful to airbrush their reputations online despite assurances from EU lawmakers that no information of 'public interest' would be affected."[44] In an article published about two years before the *Google Spain* decision was issued, Jeffrey Rosen characterized the "chilling effect" that the right to be forgotten would have on online speech by imposing massive potential liability on platforms: "I can demand takedown and the burden, once again, is on the third party to prove that it falls within the exception for journalistic, artistic, or literary exception. This could transform Google, for example, into a censor-in-chief for the European Union, rather than a neutral platform. And because this is a role Google won't want to play, it may instead produce blank pages whenever a European user types in the name of someone who has objected to a nasty blog post or status update."[45]

Despite the criticism, European Union officials have largely embraced the right to be forgotten. In 2016 the European Parliament enacted the General Data Protection Regulation, which replaced the 1995 privacy directive and went into effect in 2018. The new regulation explicitly provides for a right to be forgotten, or "right to erasure," requiring businesses that control European residents' information to delete it upon request in certain circumstances. Although this new regulation contains some exceptions, such as "for exercising the right of freedom of expression and information,"[46] overall it greatly expands the right to be forgotten far beyond search engine indexes.

In a 2012 speech in Munich, as European legislators were beginning their work on the new privacy regulation, EU justice commissioner Viviane Reding attempted to minimize concerns about the impact of the right to be forgotten on access to information and freedom of expression. "The right to be forgotten is of course not an absolute right," Reding said. "There are cases where there is a legitimate and legally justified interest to keep data in a data base. The archives of a newspaper are a good example. It is clear that the right to be forgotten cannot amount to a right of the total erasure of history. Neither must the right to be forgotten take precedence over freedom of expression or freedom of the media."[47] Although it is encouraging to know that the European regulators at least considered free expression while developing the new privacy rules, the final regulation poses substantial threats to free online speech. The regulation begins with a baseline assumption that data controllers must delete personal data upon request *unless* an exception applies.

Daphne Keller of Stanford University, a former Google lawyer and one of the foremost experts on global intermediary liability law, wrote that the new European data protection regulation "unintentionally but seriously disrupts" the balance between privacy and information rights. "The result is a powerful new tool for abusive claimants to hide information from the public," she continued. "Bloggers documenting misuse of power can be silenced, and small businesses can lose access to customers, all through secret accusations sent to private technology companies."[48] The regulation's exception for "the right of freedom of expression and information" was problematic for many reasons, Keller felt, including the lack of clarity that it provides to online platforms. "A tweet about a dishonest car mechanic, a Yelp review of a botched medical procedure, or a post criticizing an individual Etsy or Amazon vendor may not be covered," she noted. "Neither might a personal blog post recounting domestic abuse."[49]

Just as Section 230 is a uniquely American law, the right to be forgotten is a uniquely European law. When there is tension between privacy and free expression, Europe is more likely than the United States to adopt a privacy-centric policy. That is precisely what the right to be forgotten is. It curtails the free expression rights of individuals by regulating Google and other intermediaries, with the ultimate goal of protecting individuals whose lives are haunted by online artifacts such as news articles of decades-old arrests. But the right to be forgotten comes with costs. And understanding these costs helps to illuminate the unique role that Section 230 has played in shaping the Internet in the United States, where courts have long held that Google and other search engines are interactive computer services that receive Section 230 immunity for third-party content. Section 230 prohibits a court from directing Google to deindex search results, unless the content violates intellectual property law (such as copyright infringement) or federal criminal laws (such as child pornography).

In the United States, it is comparatively difficult to get Google to deindex search results. Google states that it will remove illegal content: child sexual abuse imagery and copyright violations. It also reserves the right to remove "sensitive personal information" such as Social Security numbers, bank account numbers, images of signatures, and nonconsensually shared nude or sexually explicit images. But these are narrow exceptions to Google's standard U.S. rule that it wants "to organize the world's information and make it universally accessible and useful."[50] Without Section 230, Google simply could not take such a bold stance to removal requests. Rather than relying on only its own judgment and values to determine whether to deindex search results, Google would need to look to any requirements set by legislatures or courts.

In practice, this means that more information is available through Google—and other search engines—in the United States than in Europe. Let's say that a job candidate is in the final stages of interviews for a job. That candidate had been convicted of embezzling from a former employer fifteen years ago, and a newspaper article about the conviction remained online. For the job applicant, the European approach is superior. In Europe the applicant might be able to persuade Google to remove the request under the right to be forgotten, arguing that the violation of his or her privacy by posting a fifteen-year-old newspaper article far outweighs any benefits of keeping the article online. But if Google granted the request, the potential employer would be deprived of what is perhaps useful information for determining whom to hire. Imagine that the employer is considering two people of roughly equal qualifications. The conviction of one of those people for embezzlement might tip the scale to the other candidate. Even if the conviction occurred fifteen years ago, it still weighs on the overall character of the job applicant.

It is impossible to reconcile the values and effects of Europe's right to be forgotten with the United States' Section 230. The stark contrast in outcomes shows the different prioritization of individual privacy versus free expression and information flow.

Increased legal obligations for online intermediaries are not merely quirks of the European legal system. Other jurisdictions that generally share Western democratic values—such as Canada and Australia—have no equivalent of Section 230. The Canadian Charter of Rights and Freedoms—Canada's equivalent of the U.S. Constitution's Bill of Rights—guarantees "fundamental freedoms," among them the "freedom of thought, belief, opinion and expression, including freedom of the press and other media of communication." But just above this guarantee is an important qualifier: these rights are "subject only to such reasonable limits prescribed by law as can be demonstrably justified in a free and democratic society." Such qualification is not extraordinary or particularly controversial. Although the First Amendment to the U.S. Constitution does not contain an explicit exception, U.S. courts have found many exceptions and limits to First Amendment free speech rights, such as for obscenity and incitement of imminent violence. But Canada's explicit statement—like that in the European Convention on Human Rights—that free speech can be limited sets the general tone for an environment in which courts agree with plaintiffs who seek to hold online services accountable for the speech of third parties.

These principles became clear in a lawsuit against the British Columbia Federation of Foster Parents Associations. The federation works to improve foster care in British Columbia, and it operates an online forum.[51] In February 2000 a federation forum member with the pseudonym "Dberlane" posted a comment about Liza Carter, a former president of the federation. Although the Canadian court opinion does not state what Dberlane posted, it described it as "arguably defamatory." The comment was harmful enough for Carter to demand that the foundation close the online forum.[52] A federation board member says that soon after, he asked the forum host to temporarily shut down the forum. Rather than shut down the online forum, the host converted it to a read-only board so that users could no longer post new comments. Yet the comments that already had been posted—including those about Carter—were not deleted. About two years later, Carter learned that Dberlane's post was still online. She filed a defamation suit against the federation as well as other defendants, for both the Dberlane comment and a post on another Internet forum. The trial court judge dismissed Carter's claims against the federation, concluding, besides offering other reasons, that the post was "innocent and unintentional."[53] But a three-judge panel of the Court of Appeal for British Columbia, deciding that it was possible to hold the federation liable, unanimously sent the case back to the trial court for further fact-finding on key issues.

The appeals court wrote that it was "difficult to see" how the "continuing publication" of the comment for more than two years after notice was not caused, at least partly, by the federation's negligence. After all, the board member had been notified of the post and tried to fix the situation. "Here the Federation did not take effective steps to remove the offending comment and there seems to have been no proper follow up to see that necessary action had been taken," Justice John E. Hall wrote.[54] The Federation lost the appeal because it had been placed on notice yet failed to take appropriate actions. Sound familiar? The British Columbia court's logic follows that of Judge Leisure's ruling in *Cubby*. The online service receives limited protection from lawsuits that arise from third-party content, but it loses that protection if the provider knows or has reason to know of the allegedly harmful content. The protection for online platforms in Canada, therefore, bears a closer resemblance to pre–Section 230 American law.

Courts in other countries also impose the rule of *Stratton Oakmont*: holding a website responsible just because it had the ability to moderate third-party content. As in the pre–Section 230 United States, this rule provides websites with an incentive to take a hands-off approach to third-party content.

For instance, there is the case of Anthony Scott Brisciani, who ran ZGeek, an Australian online discussion forum. In 2005 Brisciani, using the pseudonym "Pirate," wrote a post on ZGeek about Gabriella Piscioneri, a lawyer who provided an Australian court with information about juror misconduct that helped set aside the convictions of two brothers for a rape of a sixteen-year-old girl. The post, under the heading "Tool of the Week," stated, "Gabriella Piscioneri you're a big tool and you should practice the mantra of 'Shut the Fuck Up.'"[55] That day, Brisciani started another thread, titled "Bitching and Rants," that also badmouthed Piscioneri and prompted additional user commentary about her.[56]

Below the articles were comments from pseudonymous users about Piscioneri, with some criticizing her and branding her with vulgar names. Piscioneri discovered the posts about four years later and wrote to Brisciani requesting an apology and the removal of the posts. Brisciani removed the 2005 posts,[57] but in 2010 he posted about her legal threats to him without identifying her by name. That began another round of nasty comments about Piscioneri. "Yep, the levels of retard just went off the scale," a user with the pseudonym "RedMaN" wrote. "Seriously, no one gives a shit about this person. Maybe they should crawl back into the hole they came out of."[58] Piscioneri sued Brisciani for defamation, not only for the posts that he wrote as "Pirate," but also for the other users' posts.

Justice John Burns of the Supreme Court of the Australian Capital Territory wrote that Australian law allowed Brisciani to be liable not only for the posts that he wrote, but also for the other ZGeek users' posts: "Internet content hosts can, in some circumstances, be vicariously liable for matter published by others, by virtue of the failure to remove from public display defamatory material published by the third party. In order to be vicariously liable, the host must have failed to remove the material after being notified of its existence, and the host must be a publisher, as opposed to a mere passive facilitator of the material."[59] Burns concluded that Brisciani was a publisher—and not a merely passive conduit, observing that—"his own post titled 'Tool of the Week' initiated the discussion of the plaintiff, he actively engaged in the ongoing discussion and he had the ability to remove the posts from ZGeek at any time."[60] After analyzing the defamatory nature of the posts and the harm caused to Piscioneri,

Burns awarded her eighty-two thousand dollars. The Supreme Court of the Australian Capital Territory Court of Appeal affirmed the judgment in 2016.[61]

Like the result in the British Columbia case, the Australian ruling against Brisciani—at least for the other users' posts—simply would not have been possible in the United States. Section 230 would have undoubtedly shielded him from being held legally responsible for any of the other users' posts.

The United States is not the only government in the world that protects online intermediaries. Throughout the West, websites and other online service providers receive some immunity from claims arising from user-generated content. What is unique about the United States is the strength of the immunity that these companies receive. Many jurisdictions, such as the European Union, Canada, and Australia, will protect online intermediaries that were entirely unaware of the harmful user content. But as soon as they receive notice (or, in some cases, should have been aware), they can be on the hook for defamation claims and even criminal charges. Section 230 is radically different in its indifference to whether the intermediaries knew or should have known what its users were posting. This extraordinary protection provides online services with breathing room to allow others to create content on their services, without fear of a company-ending court ruling five years later.

Congress recognized this disparity in 2010, when it passed the Securing the Protection of our Enduring and Established Constitutional Heritage Act (known as the SPEECH Act). Congress wrote the law to address "libel tourism," the practice of filing a defamation lawsuit against a U.S. defendant in countries with relatively weak protections for defamation defendants (such as the United Kingdom) and then asking a U.S. court to enforce that judgment. The SPEECH Act prohibits U.S. courts from enabling plaintiffs to collect U.S. assets based on foreign defamation judgments that failed to provide "at least as much protection for freedom of speech and press" as the defendants would receive under the First Amendment.[62] The SPEECH Act also explicitly prohibits U.S. courts from enforcing defamation judgments against interactive computer services unless the court determines the judgment is "consistent" with Section 230. "The purpose of this provision is to ensure that libel tourists do not attempt to chill speech by suing a third-party interactive computer service, rather than the actual author of the offending statement. In such circumstances, the service provider would likely take down the allegedly offending material rather than face a lawsuit," the bill's sponsor, Representative Steve Cohen, said on the House floor before its passage. "Providing immunity removes this unhealthy incentive to take down material under improper pressure." The SPEECH Act provided a huge shield for U.S. online platforms that increasingly have customers abroad. Plaintiffs could still avoid Section 230 by asking courts to seize the defendants' foreign assets, the plaintiffs could not touch any money or other assets located in the United States if Section 230 blocked their claims.

Although the disparity between the United States and the rest of the world was accepted in the early years of the modern Internet, by 2008, U.S. courts began to question exactly how exceptional the Internet should be.

Part III

The Gradual Erosion of Section 230

During the first decade of Section 230, the section evolved from an obscure sliver of a massive telecommunications law to one of the most fundamental protections for online speech and online innovation. But Section 230 also began to draw critics. With each victory for an online platform—and a loss for a sympathetic victim—judges were raising questions about the wisdom of providing such sweeping and unprecedented protection for websites. With dozens of state and federal courts around the country adopting the Fourth Circuit's *Zeran* ruling, judges largely were boxed in and stuck with an expansive interpretation of Section 230's protection. The U.S. Supreme Court had never taken a case that required it to interpret Section 230, so *Zeran* effectively was the law of the land. Still, there were two key ambiguities in Section 230 that allowed judges to begin to chip away at the edges of its immunity. To understand these ambiguities, consider again the twenty-six words of Section 230: "No provider or user of an interactive computer service shall be treated as the publisher or speaker of any information provided by another information content provider."

First, the platforms are immune only from information that is "provided by another information content provider." If a plaintiff can show that the website, in fact, was an information content provider, then the website would not receive Section 230 immunity. Second, even if a third party was responsible for creating all the content that was the subject of the lawsuit, Section 230 prevents courts only from treating the platform as a "publisher or speaker." If the plaintiff can demonstrate that the lawsuit stemmed from an action of the defendant other than publishing or speaking—such as breaking a promise or failing to warn of danger—then a court might decide that Section 230 did not block the lawsuit.

The following two chapters explain how courts have seized on both rationales and denied immunity to many platforms. If the first decade of Section 230 represented an expansion of the section's reach, its second decade represented a slow but steady erosion.

8

A LAWLESS NO-MAN'S LAND?

Section 230's simplicity is one of its greatest strengths. Other U.S. laws—often far less potent than Section 230—occupy hundreds of pages in the United States Code and require teams of highly specialized lawyers to parse. Section 230, on the other hand, packs most of its punch in twenty-six words and contains few exceptions or caveats. But its brevity also has left room for some courts to set important limits on the scope of its immunity. Perhaps the most vexing omission in Section 230 is its lack of a definition of the words *development* and *responsible*. The immunity applies only if an interactive computer service is being treated as the publisher or speaker of information that has been "provided by another information content provider." Section 230 defines *information content provider* as anyone who is "responsible, in whole or in part, for the creation or development" of information. Is a platform "responsible" for the "development" of content only when it creates and uploads it to its services? Or is a platform responsible merely by encouraging third parties to create the content? What if the platform structures its site to require third parties to post illegal words or images? The text of Section 230 does not provide many answers. Courts are left to rely on competing dictionary definitions and commonsense interpretations of the words *responsible* and *development.*

For the first decade of Section 230's history, courts were reluctant to conclude that an interactive computer service acted as a developer of third-party content. Even the Museum Security Network, whose moderator modestly edited and distributed the email about Ellen Batzel, as discussed in chapter 5, received some Section 230 protection. This began to change in 2008 and 2009, when two federal appellate courts issued opinions that adopted broader readings of the terms *responsible* and *development,* and thus narrowed the scope of Section 230 immunity.

"I am seeking a single Asian Male or Female student or working professionals."

"This is a Christian home and we are looking for a Christian female to rent a downstairs room."

"looking for ASIAN FEMALE OR EURO GIRL."

"I am NOT looking for black muslims."

"looking for gay white or latin guy who is responsible"[1]

These were among the advertisements that appeared in November 2003 on Roommates.com (also known as Roommate.com), a popular roommate-matching website. Disputes stemming from such Roommates.com listings would lead to a court opinion that some legal scholars predicted would be the death of Section 230. It wasn't, but the disputes were the first significant demonstration that Section 230 is not, in fact, bulletproof immunity for websites.

In addition to asking posters to describe the type of roommates they are looking for in their ads (in an open-ended "Additional Comments" section), the website had asked new users specific questions about categories such as gender, sexual orientation, and age, and also asked users to provide "details regarding your lifestyle." The site also allowed users to declare the preferred sex, sexual orientation, and familial status of their roommates.[2] The Fair Housing Council of San Fernando Valley and Fair Housing Council of San Diego, nonprofits that fight housing discrimination, claimed in a 2003 federal lawsuit that Roommates.com was violating federal and California housing discrimination laws. The federal Fair Housing Act prohibits housing sale or rental advertisements that indicate a "preference, limitation, or discrimination" based on, among other characteristics, race, sex, familial status, or religion. The councils claimed that Roommates.com violated the California Fair Employment and Housing Act, which also prohibits discrimination based on sexual orientation. Further, the lawsuit included more general claims for unfair business practices and negligence.[3]

The case was assigned to Judge Percy Anderson, a former law firm partner whom George W. Bush had appointed to the Los Angeles federal court two years earlier.[4] The councils asked Judge Anderson to grant a preliminary injunction, prohibiting the site from transmitting discriminatory advertisements. In their motion, the councils argued that the site's discriminatory questions received no additional legal protection than questions being asked by an in-person rental agent. "Defendant is taking money in order to provide the service that many property managers provide in Los Angeles and San Diego," they wrote. "They are screening the renters. The renter has to answer a lot of questions about themselves before they can post their notice of interest. The questions are written by the defendant. No third party is involved."[5] Section 230, the councils argued, provided absolutely no protection to a site such as Roommates.com: "Congress never intended for the Internet to be a place where housing providers and their advertisers and agents could sneak back to the early part of the last century and begin posting 'signs' that state 'Whitehme' or 'White males only' or 'Asian Preferred' or 'I prefer a Christian male, no women allowed in home' that so obviously offend, alienate and humiliate persons who are just looking for a place to live in cities where it is already very difficult to find homes. The CDA is not about free speech, and it does not trump the civil rights laws."[6]

Timothy Alger, the Internet lawyer who had successfully defended Metrosplash and Lycos against Carafano's lawsuit, discussed in chapter 5, represented Roommates.com. In August 2004, Alger moved for summary judgment, asking Anderson to dismiss the complaint. Alger characterized the Roommates.com ads as the run-of-the mill user-generated content that is covered by Section 230. "It is the users who create the profiles and select the information in the profiles," he wrote. "Plaintiffs identify no statement of *Roommate* that indicates a preference. The site's questionnaire is simply a method of collecting standardized information for a convenient, searchable database."[7]

On September 13, 2004, Judge Anderson held a hearing on Alger's motion in the judge's Los Angeles courtroom. Gary W. Rhoades, the lawyer for the councils, began the hearing by highlighting the illegal preferences presented in many ads.

"But the third party is making the choice," Judge Anderson said.[8]

"They're making the choice," Rhoades responded. "But they would, you know, when they make that choice, they are ignoring the fair housing laws. And I think they're being encouraged, you know, if not really forced to make those choices. And the defendant is setting them up for this. The defendant has no information on the Website about the fair housing laws. They just say, in rather mandatory language, 'Select your preferences.'"[9]

And that was the core of Rhoades's key argument: even though Roommates.com did not actually draft the discriminatory advertisements, the site's design and questions *encouraged* the creation of illegal content. That encouragement, Rhoades argued, meant that the ads were not provided by another information content provider and thus did not qualify for Section 230 immunity. To rebut this argument, Alger relied on the Ninth Circuit's ruling for his client in Christianne Carafano's lawsuit; because Los Angeles is located within the Ninth Circuit, the Ninth Circuit's interpretation of Section 230 bound Judge Anderson's decision. "*Carafano* was a remarkably similar situation, where there were multiple-choice questions, the users would select from those multiple-choice questions, hit a submit button, and a profile that would be created that would be on a search database," Alger said.[10] Alger's argument appeared to give Anderson pause, and the judge asked Rhoades to distinguish this lawsuit from *Carafano*. "It was for a dating service," Rhoades said. "It wasn't involving housing, and the drop-down—the formatting that was created—that's created by these defendants contain discriminatory statements in them."[11]

Apparently, this distinction was not persuasive for Anderson. At the end of the hearing, he said he had "tentatively" concluded that Section 230 shielded Roommates.com from all claims.[12] Later that month, he issued a nine-page order granting Alger's motion for summary judgment. To Anderson, this was a simple application of Section 230's core protections. Roommates.com was an interactive computer service. The councils were suing Roommates.com for publishing ads that were created entirely by third parties: the posters. The fact that some of this illegal content was in response to a questionnaire, Anderson wrote, was immaterial. He pointed to the Ninth Circuit's ruling against Christianne Carafano, despite the fact that Matchmaker's ads used a questionnaire. "The Ninth Circuit's decision in *Carafano* compels the conclusion that Roommate cannot be liable for violating the [Fair Housing Act] arising out of the nicknames chosen by its users, the free-form comments provided by the users, or the users' responses to the multiple choice questionnaire," he noted.[13] Even though the plaintiffs could not recover damages from the website for violating the fair housing laws, Anderson reasoned, they still could sue the people who created the allegedly discriminatory ads.

The councils appealed Anderson's ruling to the Ninth Circuit. In 2006 the appeal was randomly assigned to a panel of three Ninth Circuit judges. The senior judge on the panel was Stephen Reinhardt, the liberal Carter appointee mentioned in chapter 5. Also on the panel was Alex Kozinski. Born in Romania to Holocaust survivors, Kozinski worked in the Reagan White House, and in 1985 Reagan appointed him, at age thirty-five, to the Ninth Circuit.[14] The final judge on the panel was Sandra Segal Ikuta, a former law clerk to Kozinski whom George W. Bush had appointed to the Ninth Circuit earlier in 2006.[15]

In some cases that went to the Ninth Circuit, it was relatively easy to predict the outcome based on the three judges on the panel. In criminal cases, for example, Judge Reinhardt and his similarly minded liberal colleagues were likely to recognize expansive civil rights for defendants, while conservatives such as Ikuta were more likely to agree with the government. The Ninth Circuit also had some less predictable judges—like Kozinski. Although he is a Republican appointee who often adheres to conservative principles, he does not hesitate to criticize the government when he believes it has overreached or to develop his own unique solutions that are not easily pigeonholed by partisan or political philosophy. For instance, in an opinion involving the constitutionality of lethal injection, Kozinski advocated a return to the guillotine, electric chair, or firing squad. "Sure, firing squads can be messy, but if we are willing to carry out executions, we should not shield ourselves from the reality that we are shedding human blood," he announced. "If we, as a society, cannot stomach the splatter from an execution carried out by firing squad, then we shouldn't be carrying out executions at all."[16] Kozinski would resign from the Ninth Circuit in December 2017, soon after former law clerks publicly accused him of sexual misconduct.[17]

The Roommates.com litigation wasn't the type of case in which an observer could easily predict the outcome based on the panel. One might expect a liberal judge to allow plaintiffs to sue for housing discrimination. But a liberal judge is also likely to support free speech protections. And it is even harder to guess the inclinations of a judge such as Kozinski, a Republican appointee who takes libertarian positions so extreme that they sometimes align him with the court's most liberal judges.

Kozinski acknowledged in a 2017 interview that the outcome of the case was not immediately apparent to him after he was named to the panel. He related that he had to think carefully about the scope of Section 230's immunity and how it applied to Roommates.com's conduct. As Kozinski reviewed Section 230's history and the dispute over Roommates.com, it eventually became clear to him that some of Roommates.com's behavior fell outside the scope of what Congress had intended when it enacted Section 230. "It seemed to me that Roommates was doing enough where they were different from a passive Internet service provider running a bulletin board," Kozinski remarked. "The hard part, or the part that really required careful thought, was how to express it in an opinion in such a way that it will create liability for the things that should be covered and at the same time not create a risk of liability for things that should be immune under 230."[18] Ikuta wanted to limit the website's liability for user content entirely, and Reinhardt sought to hold the site accountable for any discriminatory posts by its users. Kozinski was in the center, and he would write an opinion that compromised between those two extreme positions.

On May 15, 2007, about five months after it heard oral arguments, the three-judge panel issued its opinion, partly reversing the district court. Each judge wrote a separate opinion, but the controlling opinion—written by Kozinski—concluded that Section 230 would not shield Roommates.com from liability for asking questions that specifically invited users to violate fair housing laws, or for publishing that information and allowing users to search through it to discriminate.[19] "Imagine, for example, www.harrassthem.com with the slogan 'Don't Get Mad, Get Even.' A visitor to this website would be encouraged to provide private, sensitive and/or defamatory information about others—all to be posted online for a fee," Kozinski wrote in the panel's majority opinion. "To post the information, the individual would be invited to answer questions about the target's name, addresses, phone numbers, social security number, credit cards, bank accounts, mother's maiden name, sexual orientation, drinking habits and the like. In addition, the website would encourage the poster to provide dirt on the victim, with instructions that the information need not be confirmed, but could be based on rumor, conjecture or fabrication."[20] Unlike Matchmaker.com, which Section 230 protected from Carafano's lawsuit, www.harassthem.com would specifically request the illegal user content, Kozinski wrote. As a result, he concluded, holding Roommates.com liable for asking illegal questions and publishing the responses to those questions was not necessarily inconsistent with its ruling against Carafano a few years earlier: "*Carafano* did not consider whether the CDA protected such websites, and we do not read that opinion as granting CDA immunity to those who actively encourage, solicit and profit from the tortious and unlawful communications of others."[21]

Kozinski, however, did not believe that the website should be liable for all the allegedly discriminatory advertising content. The website did not create the statements in the "Additional Comments" section, he wrote. The site solicited no specific type of content. Instead, it told users that "we strongly recommend taking a moment to personalize your profile by writing a paragraph or two describing yourself and what you are looking for in a roommate."[22] Although these free-form responses tended to contain some of the most objectionable portions of the ads (such as a desire to avoid "psychos or anyone on mental medication"), Kozinski concluded that the site's involvement with these ads was "insufficient" to hold it liable.[23] "Roommate's open-ended question suggests no particular information that is to be provided by members; Roommate certainly does not prompt, encourage or solicit any of the inflammatory information provided by some of its members," Kozinski wrote. "Nor does Roommate use the information in the 'Additional Comments' section to limit or channel access to listings."[24]

Ikuta agreed with Kozinski that Section 230 immunized Roommates.com for liability arising from the "Additional Comments" section, so Kozinski's ruling became the opinion of the panel. But Reinhardt disagreed with the ruling on "Additional Comments," and in a partial dissent argued that Section 230 should not immunize Roommates.com for *any* portion of the advertisements. Roommates.com synthesized all the content from the

"Additional Comments" section along with the sections about household profiles and preferences into a single ad, Reinhardt reasoned. So the site should be held responsible for all the content. "There is no justification for slicing and dicing into separate parts the material that Roommate elicits and then channels as an integral part of one package of information to the particular customers to whom it selectively distributes that package," Reinhardt wrote.[25] Judge Ikuta, on the other hand, warned that Kozinski's opinion risked limiting Section 230's immunity and conflicting with the Ninth Circuit's earlier opinions, such as *Carafano*. The Ninth Circuit, she noted, had already held that "a website operator does not become an information content provider by soliciting a particular type of information or by selecting, editing, or republishing such information."[26]

The three opinions represented three very different takes on the scope of Section 230 immunity. Judge Ikuta's opinion represented the Ninth Circuit's status quo: broad immunity for websites for claims arising from third-party content. Judge Reinhardt's opinion called for a radical shift, imposing liability on sites that have virtually any connection to the users' decision to post illegal content. Judge Kozinski's compromise—the controlling opinion—allowed the website to be responsible for any content that it specifically elicited through its questions. Even that middle ground was dubbed in national media coverage to be a "fundamental shift" in Section 230 case law.[27] With its rulings against Ellen Batzel and Christianne Carafano, the Ninth Circuit had appeared to recognize expansive protections for websites. The Roommates.com ruling directly contradicted that interpretation of Section 230, calling into question the scope of the immunity in the western United States, home to many of the largest online intermediaries.

Roommates.com could have asked the United States Supreme Court to review the panel's opinion, but the chances of success would have been tiny. The Supreme Court receives thousands of such requests each year, and it grants fewer than one hundred. Instead, the website filed a petition for rehearing en banc. If a majority of nonrecused active Ninth Circuit judges votes to grant an en banc rehearing, the three-judge panel's ruling is vacated as though it had never happened. An en banc panel of eleven Ninth Circuit judges hears the appeal and issues a new opinion.[28] Recognizing the importance of maintaining strong protections for intermediaries in the Ninth Circuit, the Electronic Frontier Foundation urged the judges to hear the case en banc. In its brief, EFF wrote that Kozinski's opinion was not a clear reading of Section 230 but rather a "policy disagreement" with Congress: "As the statutory language and legislative history makes clear, CDA 230 was explicitly passed to immunize interactive computer services from liability for exercising the type of editorial control that publishers ordinarily make. Far from an attempt to retain liability for hosts of Internet-based information, CDA 230 was intended to codify a broad-based anti-regulatory approach that would encourage the development of innovative technologies online."[29]

The Ninth Circuit granted the en banc rehearing request. Unlike a three-judge panel, an en banc panel in a circuit court is not bound by previous rulings by that circuit. That means that the eleven judges did not have to follow the broad interpretations of Section 230 in the *Carafano* and *Batzel* cases. If the en banc panel decided that these decisions were too defendant friendly, it could merely overrule them.

As with the three-judge panel, the eleven judges on the en banc panel came from a diverse cross-section of political backgrounds. The panel included Kozinski (who by then was chief judge and therefore sat on every en banc panel) and Reinhardt, but not Ikuta. Other judges included conservatives such as Carlos T. Bea, Pamela Rymer, and N. Randy Smith; liberals such as William Fletcher and Richard Paez; and moderates such as Milan D. Smith Jr. and Barry G. Silverman. Also on the panel was M. Margaret McKeown, a Clinton appointee who had founded the intellectual property practice at a large Seattle law firm; her clients included Nintendo and Amazon.[30] The en banc panel held oral arguments on December 12, 2007. About four months later, it issued its opinion.

Kozinski again wrote the majority opinion, joined by seven of the remaining ten judges. Kozinski's en banc opinion reached the same ultimate conclusion as that of his earlier opinion—that Roommates.com was liable for asking allegedly discriminatory questions, requiring subscribers to answer those questions to use its services, and displaying those answers to those questions, but not for the "Additional Comments" portion. Section 230, Kozinski declared in one of the most-quoted passages from the opinion, "was not meant to create a lawless no-man's land on the Internet."

Roommates.com, Kozinski concluded, was at least partly "responsible" for the "development" of the allegedly discriminatory advertisements as a result of asking the questions, requiring subscribers to answer the questions, and making the advertisements searchable to users. Section 230 does not define the word *development*. Kozinski wrote that a website "develops" content—and thus is not protected by Section 230 immunity—if it "contributes materially to the alleged illegality of the conduct."[31]

Also central to Kozinski's ruling was his broad interpretation of the word *responsible*. Roommates.com argued that because the users ultimately wrote and transmitted the discriminatory advertisements, only the users should be held responsible. Kozinski disagreed. "The projectionist in the theater may push the last button before a film is displayed on the screen, but surely this doesn't make him the sole producer of the movie," Kozinski wrote. "By any reasonable use of the English language, Roommate is 'responsible' at least 'in part' for each subscriber's profile page, because every such page is a collaborative effort between Roommate and the subscriber."[32] Therefore, Kozinski wrote, the questions and responses at issue in the councils' lawsuit were not entirely provided by "another information content provider," and Roommates.com could not claim Section 230 protection from these claims: "By requiring subscribers to provide the information as a condition of accessing its service, and by providing a limited set of pre-populated answers, Roommate becomes much more than a passive transmitter of information provided by others; it becomes the developer, at least in part, of that information. And section 230 provides immunity only if the interactive computer service does not 'creat[e] or develop' the information 'in whole or in part.' "[33] A real estate broker, Kozinski analogized, "may not inquire as to the race of a prospective buyer, and an employer may not inquire as to the religion of a prospective employee. If such questions are unlawful when posed face-to-face or by telephone, they don't magically become lawful when asked electronically online."[34]

As in his earlier opinion in the case, Kozinski separately considered whether Section 230 applies to three claims against Roommates.com: (1) asking the allegedly discriminatory questions, (2) developing and displaying the allegedly discriminatory preferences, and (3) allegedly discriminatory statements in the "Additional Comments" section. His conclusions on all three issues were unchanged.

Section 230 did not protect Roommates.com from claims arising from its requirement that customers respond to those questions upon registration, Kozinski wrote: "The CDA does not grant immunity for inducing third parties to express illegal preferences. Roommate's own acts—posting the questionnaire and requiring answers to it—are entirely its doing and thus section 230 does not apply to them."[35]

Likewise, Kozinski wrote, Roommates.com could not claim Section 230 protection from claims arising from its development and display of preferences. He noted that the site mandated that users list characteristics that they sought in a roommate, such as gender, sexual orientation, and whether the potential roommate would have children in the home. "Roommate then displays these answers, along with other information, on the subscriber's profile page," Kozinski wrote. "This information is obviously included to help subscribers decide which housing opportunities to pursue and which to bypass. In addition, Roommate itself uses this information to channel subscribers away from listings where the individual offering housing has expressed preferences that aren't compatible with the subscriber's answers."[36] Kozinski implied that the Ninth Circuit's earlier ruling against Carafano was not entirely consistent with the court's conclusion that Roommates.com might be liable for user ads. After all, the Ninth Circuit had concluded in *Carafano* that no dating profile "has any content until a user actively creates it."[37] Kozinski reasoned that the court's ruling against Carafano ultimately was correct but that it was unnecessary for the court to make such a broad statement about Section 230 immunity. Because the court was sitting en banc, Kozinski was free to revise the rationale of the three-judge panel in *Carafano*. "We believe a more plausible rationale for the unquestionably correct result in *Carafano* is this: The allegedly libelous content there—the false implication that Carafano was unchaste—was created and developed entirely by the malevolent user, without prompting or help from the website operator," he wrote.[38] In contrast to the dating website in Carafano's lawsuit, Kozinski observed, Roommates.com invited users to post the allegedly discriminatory advertisements and made "aggressive use" of them. "Roommate does not merely provide a framework that could be utilized for proper or improper purposes," Kozinski wrote, "rather, Roommate's work in developing the discriminatory questions, discriminatory answers and discriminatory search mechanism is directly related to the alleged illegality of the site."[39]

As in his original opinion, Kozinski continued to conclude that Section 230 protected Roommates.com from liability for claims arising from the free-form "Additional Comments" section: "Roommate publishes these comments as written. It does not provide any specific guidance as to what the essay should contain, nor does it urge subscribers to input discriminatory preferences."[40]

Reinhardt, who had earlier argued that Roommates.com should be held liable for the material in the "Additional Comments" section was one of the seven judges who signed on in full to Kozinski's en banc opinion. Reinhardt wrote no separate concurrence or dissent arguing to hold Roommates.com liable for these free-form comment fields. However, three judges did not agree with Kozinski. McKeown, the former technology lawyer, wrote a separate opinion, partly dissenting and arguing that Section 230 should shield Roommates.com from liability for user content. Bea and Rymer joined McKeown's dissent. Kozinski's opinion, McKeown wrote, could "chill the robust development of the Internet," contrary to Congress's intent when it passed Section 230. "My concern is not an empty Chicken Little 'sky is falling' alert," she added. "By exposing every interactive service provider to liability for sorting, searching, and utilizing the all too familiar drop-down menus, the majority has dramatically altered the landscape of Internet liability. Instead of the 'robust' liability envisioned by Congress, interactive service providers are left scratching their heads and wondering where immunity ends and liability begins."[41] Roommates.com, according to McKeown, did not "create" or "develop" the allegedly discriminatory advertisements. "All Roommate does is to provide a form with options for standardized answers," she wrote. "Listing categories such as geographic location, cleanliness, gender, and number of occupants, and transmitting to users profiles of other users whose expressed information matches their expressed preferences, can hardly be said to be creating or developing information. Even adding standardized options does not 'develop' information."[42]

Kozinski agreed with McKeown that the subscribers were information content providers. But Roommates.com, he reasoned, *also* was an information content provider and thus should not receive Section 230 protection. McKeown's dissent, Kozinski argued, failed to acknowledge the very real role that Roommates.com played in developing the allegedly illegal information. "The FHA makes it unlawful to ask certain discriminatory questions for a very good reason: Unlawful questions solicit (a.k.a. 'develop') unlawful answers," Kozinski wrote in response to McKeown's dissent. "Not only does Roommate ask these questions, Roommate makes answering the discriminatory questions a condition of doing business. This is no different from a real estate broker in real life saying, 'Tell me whether you're Jewish or you can find yourself another broker.' When a business enterprise extracts such information from potential customers as a condition of accepting them as clients, it is no stretch to say that the enterprise is responsible, at least in part, for developing that information."[43]

The case went back to the district court and came back to the Ninth Circuit a third time, this time to resolve the narrower issue of whether the website's questions, display, and search functions actually violated federal and state housing laws. Kozinski, Reinhardt, and Ikuta agreed that even though Section 230 did not protect Roommates.com from liability, the site did not commit illegal discrimination because the housing laws did not apply to roommate selection. Therefore, the case ended with a whimper, and Roommates.com ultimately was not liable.[44] Still, the nearly decade-long litigation left an indelible mark on Section 230 in the judicial circuit that is home to the most technology companies.

Not surprisingly the *Roommates.com* opinion received tremendous attention and to some signaled a nationwide shift toward a narrower reading of Section 230. A case note published in the influential *Berkeley Technology Law Journal* shortly after the opinion suggested that the opinion marked the decline of Internet exceptionalism: "These changes to section 230 case law are a direct consequence of the Ninth Circuit's view on the Internet and the Internet age. The *Roommates.com* majority no longer sees fit to extend the notion of *cyber exceptionalism*. Instead, it considers the Internet as just another medium of communication, no more special than any other, despite the fact section 230 uses the term 'unique' in describing the opportunities that the Internet creates."[45]

When asked if his opinion had been a turning point for Section 230, Kozinski paused and said, "I think it was," though he cautioned that judges have "a tendency to view [their] own work as being more pivotal than other people think it is."[46] However, he scoffed at the notion that his opinion caused any harm to free online speech: "The views were that if you allow this lawsuit, online businesses will be sunk by the litigation costs and this will bring down the Internet. *Roommates* showed you can have a limited basis for liability and not really affect online commerce any more than you affect any other kind of commerce. The aftermath of *Roommates* hasn't really caused any serious problems."[47]

Online platforms might differ with that characterization. Ever since the 2008 ruling, plaintiffs seeking to circumvent Section 230 in their lawsuits against platforms routinely cite *Roommates.com*, to varying degrees of success. Orly Lobel, in a 2016 article for the *Minnesota Law Review,* articulated how Kozinski's analysis might harm platforms that are more interactive in nature than traditional websites such as Craigslist, which often used Section 230 immunity to avoid liability in lawsuits arising from user ads:

> Under this newer analysis, an interactive platform company may not be as fortunate as Craigslist, but rather is more closely characterized to Room-mates.com, and certainly may be liable for any illegal behavior if prose-cutors bring criminal charges. There are fine lines separating conduct that would fall within the exceptions. If the service provider puts branding on elicited content; supplies the user with tools of the trade, such as GPS de-vices or equipment to process transactions; or sets the pricing and the trans-actional conditions, then it is unclear if the service provider is still a pure publisher. Still, the CDA has largely acted as a liability shield from civil liti-gation, and it is likely that, for the most part, platform companies will con-tinue to enjoy at least partial immunity under the Act.[48]

Reflecting nearly ten years after his *Roommates.com* decision and twenty years after the passage of Section 230, Kozinski said that in pass-ing Section 230, Congress may have overreacted to *Stratton Oakmont*. The Internet today, he said, might be better equipped to handle some de-gree of regulation and liability than it was in 1996 or 2008.[49] Section 230, Kozinski noted, may no longer be justified. Yet he cautioned that the stat-ute is such an engrained part of Internet business and culture that repeal-ing it would "cause a lot of disruption." And he questioned the political reality of making such a drastic change to a law that is so cherished by the technology sector. "Congress has done what it's done," he admitted. "I don't think there is any way in the world that they can get the votes together to repeal it."[50] Kozinski is correct that the *Roommates.com* opin-ion did not cause Section 230 immunity to disappear, nor did it lead to the elimination of all user-generated content. But the opinion marked the beginning of a gradually growing reluctance among judges to grant Sec-tion 230 immunity. This reluctance began with Kozinski's *Roommates. com* opinion, and it increased a year later, when the federal appellate court to the east of the Ninth Circuit issued another opinion that questioned the scope of Section 230.

Wyoming-based Accusearch operated Abika.com, which offered customers access to a wide swath of information that one would expect to be private: GPS location information of specific cell phones, telephone call records (the numbers that a phone has dialed or received calls from), Social Security numbers, and Department of Motor Vehicle records.[51] Abika.com did not maintain its own database of this information. Instead, it connected customers to third-party researchers who obtained the information, which consumers accessed on Abika.com or via email. Abika.com's website touted the ability of consumers to purchase "details of incoming or outgoing calls from any phone number, prepaid calling card or Internet phone."[52] The website advertised the following service:

MONTHLY REPORT OF CALL ACTIVITY FOR CELL PHONE NUMBERS

Lookup detailed outgoing calls from the most recent billing statement (or statement month requested). Most call activities include the date, time and duration of the calls. You may request target dates or target numbers that fall within each statement cycle along with the statement cycle dates. You can usually search statements that are 1–24 months old. . . .

MONTHLY LOCAL OR TOLL CALL ACTIVITY OF LANDLINE PHONE NUMBER

Lookup outgoing local, long distance or local toll calls made from any landline phone number during a billing period. List includes the date, phone numbers called and may include the duration of calls.[53]

Federal privacy laws protect the confidentiality of such records and require a third party to obtain the customer's consent before obtaining the information. The Federal Trade Commission (FTC), which regulates privacy and data security, was concerned about the types of information available through Abika.com. Accusearch described Abika.com as an "interactive person to person search engine that connects persons seeking information (searchers) to independent researchers who state that they can search that information for a fee." Accusearch said that it received "an administrative search fee" only when customers use the site.[54] The FTC had a different view of the role that Accusearch and Abika.com played in the transactions. On May 1, 2006, the FTC sued Accusearch and its owner and president, Jay Patel, for violating a federal law that prohibits unfair trade practices. The FTC characterized Accusearch as far more than a passive intermediary. The FTC alleged that the site "used, or caused others to use, false pretenses, fraudulent statements, fraudulent or stolen documents or other misrepresentations, including posing as a customer of a telecommunications carrier, to induce officers, employees, or agents of telecommunications carriers to disclose confidential customer phone records."[55] The FTC did not necessarily claim that Accusearch or its employees were the ones to gather the information illegally. Instead, the FTC alleged that the site "used, or *caused others to use*" illegal means. This does not necessarily contradict Accusearch's claim that independent researchers gathered the personal information.

The FTC moved for summary judgment and asked the federal court to grant an injunction restricting the company's sale of personal information. Accusearch filed its own motion for summary judgment, asking the court to dismiss the lawsuit. The company argued that it was merely an interactive computer service and that the independent researchers were entirely responsible for developing the investigative reports. Thus, under Section 230, it contended, it should be immune from any claims arising from the actions of the researchers. Accusearch said that its website did not create the research reports. "Instead, Abika.com is a home-based website that hosts an interactive person to person search engine that connects persons seeking information (searchers) to independent researchers who state that they can search that information for a fee," the company's lawyers wrote in its court filings.[56] The FTC, Accusearch maintained, sought to penalize the company for third-party content that the company did not create or develop. Congress passed Section 230 to prevent precisely this form of liability, Accusearch claimed: "Abika.com has allowed independent researchers to advertise that they can provide searches of phone records and have allowed searchers to request such data through its website, as long as the researcher has verified that it can obtain such information lawfully, but Abika.com has not personally obtained any phone information from anyone except the researchers and merely charges an administrative search fee for the use of its website and search engine."[57]

Accusearch presented a seemingly straightforward argument in favor of Section 230 immunity. But it relied on many cases that were somewhat different from its dispute. For instance, Accusearch repeatedly cited the Ninth Circuit's ruling against Christianne Carafano. But the defendant in that case operated a dating website, and an anonymous person misused the service by posting a false profile of Carafano. The dating website was more passive than Accusearch, which connected its consumers with the researchers.

The case was assigned to Judge William F. Downes, a former Marine captain whom President Clinton appointed to the Wyoming federal court in 1994.[58] In September 2007, after hearing oral arguments, Downes rejected Accusearch's attempts to claim Section 230 immunity. Although Downes wrote that he was "skeptical" of Accusearch's claims that it was an "interactive computer service" as defined in Section 230, he ultimately concluded that the definition was "broad enough" to include websites such as Abika.com. Yet Downes held that Section 230 did not immunize Accusearch because the FTC did not seek to "treat" the company as the publisher of content. As he described it, "Defendants advertised the availability of phone records, solicited orders, purchased the records from third-party sources for a fee, and then resold them to the end-consumers."[59] Even if the FTC's complaint had "treated" Accusearch as a publisher, Downes reasoned, the company *still* would not be immune under Section 230, because it took part in the development of the phone records: "Where a defendant contributes to and shapes the content of the information at issue, there is no immunity under the CDA."[60] Downes also concluded that Section 230 was never intended to protect sites such as Abika.com, which provide information that may be useful to stalkers: "It is ironic that a law intended to reflect a policy aimed at deterring 'stalking and harassment by means of computer' is now being urged as a basis for immunizing the sale of phone records used for exactly these purposes."[61]

Not only did Downes deny Accusearch's summary judgment motion, but he also granted the FTC's summary judgment motion and later issued an injunction that restricted Accusearch's ability to sell products and services based on personal information. Accusearch appealed Downes's rulings to the United States Court of Appeals for the Tenth Circuit. In its appeal the company stressed that the independent researchers were entirely responsible for conducting the searches and compiling the reports. The company portrayed itself as a neutral intermediary with no actual control over the researchers' actions. If the researchers had violated privacy laws, Accusearch reasoned, they could be held accountable in court. But Congress had passed Section 230 to shield mere conduits such as Accusearch. "Ultimately, it appears that the District Court based its decision upon the discomfort it feels with having phone records published," the company wrote in its brief to the Tenth Circuit. "The District Court went to any length to achieve its desired result, including ignoring case law and imposing additional statutory language. There are other cases in the CDA world where the information that was disseminated was offensive, sexist, racist, and oftentimes illegal. Nonetheless, Congress chose to immunize users and providers from civil liability for information they did not create or develop."[62]

The FTC urged the Tenth Circuit to affirm the district court's denial of Section 230 immunity, arguing in its brief that the agency did not seek to treat Accusearch as liable for communicating any third-party information through publishing or speaking, but instead it challenged "Accusearch's business of procuring and selling confidential telephone records without consumers' knowledge or consent."[63]

The outcome of this case was unpredictable because it was unlike the standard Section 230 case that U.S. courts had confronted dozens of times in the decade since the Fourth Circuit ruled against Kenneth Zeran. In the standard case, the website or service provider passively transmitted third-party content through a service such as a bulletin board or comments section. Accusearch's Abika.com *connected* users with third-party information providers and received an administrative fee. No court had dealt with a Section 230 case quite like this, and both sides struggled to come up with analogies, albeit imperfect, to cases that involved very different online services. In his summary judgment order, Judge Downes acknowledged that "application of the CDA to the facts of this case do not fit neatly within any existing case law." The case also was unpredictable—and unusually high profile—because it involved allegedly egregious privacy violations. Abika.com promised not only standard phone directory information but also details of *incoming and outgoing phone calls*, information that traditionally was considered private and protected by law. The ultimate outcome of the case could send a signal to the world about whether U.S. companies could traffic in such highly sensitive data.

The privacy stakes were so high here that the privacy commissioner of Canada, Jennifer Stoddart, retained Sidley Austin, one of the largest U.S. law firms, to file an amicus brief in the Tenth Circuit. Stoddart urged the Tenth Circuit to uphold the district court's rulings against Accusearch. "A judgment of this Court confirming that United States organizations cannot freely trade in personal information without consent will substantially strengthen privacy protection in the United States," she wrote. "It will also provide Canadian-based organizations with the level of assurance they need to continue to outsource operations to, and otherwise conduct business with, United States organizations."[64]

On November 17, 2008, the Tenth Circuit held oral arguments. The case was assigned to three judges whom George W. Bush had appointed to the Tenth Circuit: Harris Hartz, Jerome Holmes, and Timothy Tymkovich. In an opinion released the following June, the panel affirmed Judge Downes's ruling that Section 230 did not shield Accusearch from the FTC's complaint, but their reasoning was somewhat different. Judge Downes had concluded that there were two separate reasons that Section 230 did not immunize Accusearch: first, the FTC's complaint did not treat Accusearch as a publisher, and, second, even if the complaint treated Accusearch as a publisher, Accusearch participated in the development of the reports.

Two of the three Tenth Circuit judges declined to rely on Judge Downes's first reason. Judge Hartz, for himself and Judge Holmes, wrote in the majority opinion that the only way Accusearch could have violated privacy laws would have been by publishing the private data on its website. "It would seem to be irrelevant that Accusearch *could have* operated the same business model without use of the Internet," Hartz wrote.[65] Even though Hartz disagreed with Downes's first conclusion, he agreed with Downes's alternative reason to hold that Section 230 did not apply: Accusearch helped to develop the reports. Hartz's ruling hinged on the same question that had caused Kozinski to rule against Roommates.com: what is the definition of *development*? Accusearch had urged the Tenth Circuit to adopt a narrow definition of the term. The company pointed to dictionary definitions that defined *develop* as "make something new" and "come into existence." The information originated from telephone companies, Accusearch explained, so the company did not make anything new or bring anything into existence.

Accusearch's narrow definition, however, did not satisfy Judge Hartz. He noted that Section 230 defines an information content provider as anyone who is responsible for the "*creation or* development" of information. Accusearch essentially proposed to equate development with the creation of content. Under that interpretation, Hartz reasoned, it would be unnecessary to even include the term *development* in the statute, as Congress had already included *creation*. Courts try to read statutes to give effect to every word.

Hartz conducted his own research into the history of the word *develop*. He traced the word back to the Old French *desveloper*, which he loosely translated as "to unwrap." (*Veloper* means "to wrap up," and *des* is a negative prefix.) He pointed to other dictionary definitions of *develop* that "revolve around the act of drawing something out, making it 'visible,' 'active,' or 'usable.' "[66] "Thus, a photograph is developed by chemical processes exposing a latent image," Hartz explained. "Land is developed by harnessing its untapped potential for building or for extracting resources. Likewise, when confidential telephone information was exposed to public view through Abika.com, that information was 'developed.' "[67] Although Hartz concluded that the website had "developed" the allegedly illegal information, he still had to determine whether the site's parent company, Accusearch, was "responsible" for that development. If the company was at least partly responsible, then Section 230 would not apply.

Because Section 230 does not define *responsible*, Hartz again looked to the dictionary, which defined the term as "morally accountable for one's actions." Therefore, Hartz concluded, to be at least partly "responsible" for content development, "one must be more than a neutral conduit for that content." A platform, he wrote, is "responsible" for developing offensive content "only if it in some way specifically encourages development of what is offensive about the content."[68] A standard online bulletin board, Hartz reasoned, would not typically be "responsible" for offensive third-party content. For example, "we would not ordinarily say that one who builds a highway is 'responsible' for the use of that highway by a fleeing bank robber, even though the culprit's escape was facilitated by the availability of the highway."[69] But Accusearch differed from "neutral conduits" such as highways or online bulletin boards, noted Hartz. The company sought consumer requests and coordinated with researchers: "By paying its researchers to acquire telephone records, knowing that the confidentiality of the records was protected by law, it contributed mightily to the unlawful conduct of its researchers."[70]

The Ninth Circuit had issued its en banc opinion in the *Roommates. com* case mere months before Hartz filed his opinion. Hartz relied heavily on Kozinski's reasoning and ultimately concluded that Accusearch's responsibility for content was even "more pronounced than that of Roommates.com." He asserted, "Roommates.com may have encouraged users to post offending content, but the offensive postings were Accusearch's *raison d'etre* and it affirmatively solicited them."[71]

Judge Tymkovich agreed that Accusearch should not receive Section 230 immunity, but he disagreed with Hartz's reasoning. Rather than determining whether Accusearch was responsible for developing the reports, he wrote, the Court should deny Section 230's immunity because the FTC's complaint did not treat Accusearch as the publisher of information. The complaint sought to penalize Accusearch for its "*conduct* rather than for the *content* of the information it was offering," and thus Section 230 does not apply: "The CDA says nothing about immunizing publishers or speakers for their own conduct in *acquiring* the information. Indeed, other courts have explicitly recognized this distinction."[72] Tymkovich worried that Hartz's intent-based approach required a court to get inside the mind of a computer service. "Under this definition, the line between passive posting of tortious or unlawful commentary, news articles, or other previously unpublished information and content development depends on an amorphous analysis of the motivations of the content provider in soliciting or acquiring that information," he wrote.[73] His concurrence highlighted why Hartz's opinion was so different from previous interpretations of Section 230. By concluding that Accusearch was responsible for the development of the reports, Hartz concluded that a website that *specifically encourages* illegal content is not entitled to Section 230 protection.

No federal appellate court had ever imposed such an explicit limit on Section 230. Even Kozinski concluded that Roommates.com's "weak encouragement" of discriminatory preferences was not enough to render the site responsible for discriminatory advertisements in the free-form "Additional Comments" sections. What should have been equally concerning to online services across the United States was Judge Hartz's inquiry into the intent of websites. This subjective exercise can produce great uncertainty, particularly because most defendants claiming Section 230 immunity are companies and not people. What was the intent of Accusearch, Room-mates.com, or any other company that operates a website? Most likely, the end goal was to make a profit (indeed, if the company is publicly traded, its management is obligated to have that goal). But the Tenth Circuit now *required* courts to conduct this inquiry into the minds of corporate defendants to determine whether they were entitled to Section 230's protections.

Commentators took notice of the Tenth Circuit's new, remarkable limits on Section 230 immunity. In the *Tulane Journal of Technology and Intellectual Property*, Santa Clara University professor Eric Goldman listed the *Accusearch* case fifth among "the ten most important Section 230 rulings," claiming that the opinion "has emerged as perhaps the most significant remaining incursion into *Zeran's* defense-favorable immunity."[74] Indeed, state and federal courts across the country have relied on the Tenth Circuit's ruling to hold that a website was liable just because it encouraged user-generated content. Taken together, the rulings by the Ninth and Tenth Circuits sent a clear signal to website operators: the Internet might not be all that exceptional. The Ninth Circuit created—and the Tenth Circuit adopted—a new rule holding that if a website "materially contributes" to the illegality of user material, it may not receive Section 230 immunity. This would open a new question for courts: what does it mean to "materially contribute" to the illegality of third-party content? Courts continue to struggle with this question.

By 2009, the Internet was no longer a nascent technology. User content–focused platforms such as Facebook and Yelp had evolved from start-ups into large businesses. More and more people—including judges—were starting to question why twenty-six words in the United States Code afforded extraordinary benefits to this specific category of thriving business. This skepticism underlies the rulings in the *Roommates.com* and *Accusearch* cases. To be sure, both cases were outliers and did not involve the standard user content defamation claims often seen in Section 230 cases. But the courts went to great lengths to interpret *development* and *responsible* in manners that would restrict Section 230 in many cases for more than a decade. As platforms increasingly develop more sophisticated algorithm-based technology to process user data, it remains to be seen whether courts will conclude that they are "responsible" for the "development" of illegal content. For example, if a social media site allows companies to target their job advertisements to users under forty, could the site be liable for "developing" ads that violate employment discrimination laws? At least under an expansive interpretation of *Roommates. com* and *Accusearch,* such liability is possible, though far from certain.

In addition to these newly restrictive definitions, online intermediaries faced a separate threat to Section 230: courts' concluding that the type of claim or underlying conduct simply did not fall within the scope of Section 230's protections.

9

Hacking 230

The rulings against Roommates.com and Accusearch received significant attention among media lawyers and academics as the first federal appellate court rulings to narrow the scope of Section 230 immunity. The Ninth and Tenth Circuits took a similar approach to reach the ultimate conclusion that Section 230 did not shield the websites: the courts concluded that the sites were at least partly responsible for developing allegedly discriminatory ads or research reports that allegedly violated privacy law. The *Roommates.com/Accusearch* approach—finding a defendant "responsible" for content development—is one of the two primary ways for courts to get around Section 230. The other common rationale focuses on a separate limitation of Section 230: the plaintiff seeks to hold the websites accountable for something other than publication or speech. Think back to the twenty-six words in Section 230. They do not provide complete immunity to websites from all types of lawsuits; instead, the statute holds that interactive computer service providers will not be "treated as the publisher or speaker" of information provided by another party.

Among the most common cases in which Section 230 is successfully invoked involve defamation claims; by definition, those suits usually seek to treat the websites as publishers or speakers of false and harmful claims made by third parties. For more than a decade, courts routinely relied on Judge Wilkinson's decision in *Zeran* and quickly dismissed defamation lawsuits against online intermediaries. This caused plaintiffs' lawyers eventually to devise creative new claims that went beyond defamation and other suits typically filed against publishers. By targeting conduct rather than speech, the plaintiffs argue, they are not asking the court to treat the websites as the speakers or publishers of third-party content. Instead, they target specific acts or omissions, such as failing to warn of dangers, breaking a promise to remove harmful user conduct, and engaging in improper business deals with third parties. Sometimes these claims are thinly veiled attempts to dodge Section 230's immunity. If the central claim in a lawsuit against a website arises from user content, then it is difficult to rationalize how Section 230 would not apply. After all, one of the main goals of Section 230 was to prevent platforms from fearing liability arising from user content.

Even so, courts have been open to some creative attempts to avoid Section 230. In many cases, it is easier to convince a court that a lawsuit targets something other than a website's speech than it is to show that the website was responsible for the development of the content. As with many developments in Section 230 law, this trend started in the Ninth Circuit, in a case decided just months after *Roommates.com*.

In December 2004, Cecilia Barnes received a number of phone calls and emails at work. There were graphic phone calls from men she didn't know, requesting sex. Such men began showing up at her workplace. Barnes learned that the men had seen a profile posted on Yahoo, containing nude pictures of her taken without her consent and also her work contact information. Her ex-boyfriend had created this profile, and he also impersonated Barnes in Yahoo chat rooms and directed men to these profiles.[1]

Yahoo's website told visitors that if they wished to complain about an unauthorized profile, they should send to Yahoo by snail mail a signed statement in which they attested that they did not create the profile, along with a copy of photo identification. Barnes did so immediately, and Yahoo did not respond.[2] Men continued to visit, call, and email Barnes in February. She again mailed a request to Yahoo to remove the profiles, and still she received no response. She mailed another request in March. Radio silence. The profiles remained online, and the harassment continued.[3] Barnes spoke with a local Portland television station, which planned to run segments about her troubles with Yahoo on March 30 and 31. On March 29, Barnes says, she finally heard from the Yahoo director of communications, Mary Osako, who asked Barnes to fax the requests to Yahoo. Barnes claims that Osako assured Barnes that Osako "would personally walk the statements over to the division responsible for stopping unauthorized profiles and they would take care of it." With this assurance, Barnes took no further steps to try to delete the profiles, and she called the television reporter to tell him that Yahoo had promised to remove the profiles.[4]

The profile remained on Yahoo for about two months. Barnes sued Yahoo in Oregon state court. The four-page complaint recounted Barnes's troubles with Yahoo, but it was not entirely clear about what her legal basis for suing Yahoo was. The lawsuit could best be distilled into two separate claims: first, Barnes alleged that Yahoo was negligent in undertaking but failing to remove the profiles; second, Barnes appeared to assert that she detrimentally relied on Yahoo's promise to remove the profiles and that Yahoo failed to do so (a quasi-contract-type claim known as promissory estoppel, though the complaint does not use that term).[5] Yahoo removed the case from state court to Oregon federal court and hired Pat Carome to represent it against Barnes. Carome moved to dismiss the entire lawsuit, arguing that all of Barnes's claims arose from posts that Yahoo did not develop. "Yahoo! indisputably had no role in creating or developing any of the online profiles or the chat room conversations about which she complains," Carome wrote in Yahoo's court filing. "Instead, Yahoo!'s involvement in this case stems from the fact that the ex-boyfriend allegedly used Yahoo!'s Internet-based services to post the profiles and engage in the chat room conversations."[6]

Oregon federal Judge Ann Aiken agreed with Carome. In a ten-page opinion issued on November 8, 2005, Aiken dismissed the entire lawsuit. Although Barnes had argued that her lawsuit arose from Yahoo's failure to abide by its promises—and not from third-party content—Aiken found the distinction to be immaterial. Section 230, she ruled, barred all of Barnes's claims. "Plaintiff alleges she was harmed by third-party content, and that the service provider (defendant) allegedly breached a common law or statutory duty to block, screen, remove, or otherwise edit that content," Aiken pronounced. "Any such claim by plaintiff necessarily treats the service provider as 'publisher' of the content and is therefore barred by § 230."[7]

Barnes appealed the dismissal to the Ninth Circuit. The case was assigned to three judges who were not necessarily predisposed to rule in favor of plaintiffs: Judge Diarmuid O'Scannlain, a Reagan appointee and one of the most conservative judges on the Ninth Circuit;[8] Susan Graber, a moderate Clinton appointee;[9] and Consuelo Callahan, a conservative former prosecutor who was appointed by George W. Bush.[10] By Ninth Circuit standards, this was a relatively conservative panel of judges. It would not have been surprising for them quickly to affirm Aiken's dismissal of the lawsuit.

But they did not do that. Although the judges agreed with Aiken that Section 230 immunized Yahoo from Barnes's negligence claim, the three judges unanimously reversed Aiken's dismissal of Barnes's claim arising from Yahoo's promise to remove the post, which the Ninth Circuit concluded could be "recast" as promissory estoppel.

Promissory estoppel claims share some similarities with standard breach-of-contract lawsuits, although there are important differences. Contracts are reached through a bargained-for exchange, and promissory estoppel claims are based on a mere promise. Promissory estoppel claims require evidence that the plaintiff relied on the defendant's promise to the plaintiff's detriment and that the reliance was reasonably foreseeable. Barnes appeared to claim that because Yahoo promised to remove the profiles, she relied on the promise and took no further steps to counter the harmful information.

Writing the opinion for the panel, Judge O'Scannlain observed that Barnes "does not seek to hold Yahoo liable as a publisher or speaker of third-party content, but rather as the counter-party to a contract, as a promisor who has breached."[11] O'Scannlain observed that the promissory estoppel claim arose from the promise to delete the profile, which he acknowledged was "quintessential publisher conduct."[12] But the promissory estoppel claim stemmed not from the actual publishing (or removal) of the profiles but from a promise. "Promising is different because it is not synonymous with the performance of the action promised," O'Scannlain explained. "That is, whereas one cannot undertake to do something without simultaneously doing it, one can, and often does, promise to do something without actually doing it at the same time."[13]

O'Scannlain did not rule on whether Yahoo actually had broken a promise to Barnes that gave rise to a legitimate promissory estoppel claim. Instead, he sent the case back to the district court for Judge Aiken to determine whether Barnes had a sufficient promissory estoppel claim. On December 8, 2009, Aiken refused to dismiss the case, concluding that Barnes's complaint alleged a plausible promissory estoppel case against Yahoo. Aiken wrote that it was reasonable to infer that Barnes "relied on defendant's promise by calling the reporter and informing him that there was no longer a news story worthy to air."[14] The Ninth Circuit never had the opportunity to determine whether Aiken's decision was correct, because a few months later, Barnes voluntarily dismissed the lawsuit.

Although Barnes's case never went to trial, the impact on Section 230 was perhaps as great as that of the suits against Roommates.com and Accusearch. Just as the rulings in those cases narrowed Section 230 immunity by clarifying when a website site helps to "develop" information, Judge O'Scannlain's ruling gave courts reason to question whether Section 230 even applies. By holding that Barnes's lawsuit did not treat Yahoo as a publisher or speaker of third-party content, O'Scannlain developed a new tool to get around an immunity that until recently had appeared to be impenetrable. Of course, Barnes's case was relatively uncommon in that the online platform allegedly made a specific promise to her, caused her to rely on that promise, and then broke the promise. Nonetheless, in the following decade, dozens of court opinions would cite the *Barnes* ruling for the proposition that Section 230 immunity is not absolute, and many plaintiffs would try to use the opinion to dissuade judges from dismissing their claims against online platforms.

Some legal observers welcomed the *Barnes* opinion. Daniel Solove wrote that O'Scannlain drew the correct distinction in his opinion: "Promissory estoppel and contract claims differ from tort claims such as negligence, defamation, or invasion of privacy. Indeed, such claims are treated very differently under the First Amendment, with tort claims receiving full scrutiny and contract/promissory estoppel claims receiving virtually no scrutiny."[15] Despite his overall support for the Ninth Circuit's ruling, Solove noted a troubling side effect: by holding websites responsible for their promises—and exempting those promises from Section 230 immunity—courts may discourage websites from moderating their content and making guarantees to users, just as the *Stratton Oakmont* decision had done in 1995. "This isn't the fault of the Ninth Circuit's holding, which strikes me as quite valid," Solove wrote. "Rather, it is due to the perverse implications of the overreaching interpretations of CDA immunity that most courts have now adopted, making such immunity near absolute for tort claims."[16]

Indeed, this paradox reveals the trade-offs that arise whenever a court narrows the scope of Section 230 immunity. By allowing plaintiffs such as Barnes to sue online platforms by carving out exceptions to Section 230, courts often discourage platforms from taking affirmative steps to prevent offensive online content. Had Yahoo simply ignored Barnes's repeated requests for help in removing the profiles and not made any promises, the Ninth Circuit probably would have affirmed the dismissal of the entire lawsuit. Barnes's only claim against Yahoo would have been that it negligently published the harmful ads, and Section 230 easily shields Yahoo from such claims, as they treat the company as the publisher or speaker. But Yahoo faced liability—and ultimately had to settle the lawsuit—because one of its employees promised to address Barnes's concerns. Of course, Yahoo also could have avoided liability by following through on its promise and removing the advertisements. Yet the safest bet for Yahoo would have been simply to have never made a promise to remove the content in the first place. Any lawsuit that Barnes would have brought would have treated Yahoo as the publisher of the profiles, and Yahoo could have been protected.

Under *Barnes*, service providers are rewarded if they do not assure customers that they will remove objectionable content; had Yahoo not responded to Barnes in the first place, she would not have had a valid promissory estoppel claim. Even though platforms do not lose their immunity for merely editing content in good faith—Section 230 explicitly says as much—any outreach to customers are actions that go beyond mere editing and could place the platforms outside Section 230's protections.

Like many aspiring models, Jane (not her real name) advertised online, with the hope of being found by a talent agent or scout. Among the sites that she used was ModelMayhem.com. In February 2011, Jane received a message from someone claiming to be a talent scout. At the time, a California media company, Internet Brands, owned ModelMayhem.com and more than one hundred other websites. The site connected models with potential employers.[17] The purported talent scout invited Jane to "audition" for a modeling contract in Florida. Jane traveled from Brooklyn to Florida. But what she arrived to, she says, was not an audition. Lavont Flanders Jr. and Emerson Callum drugged her. Callum raped her, she alleged in a court complaint, and Flanders and Callum made a video recording of the assault.[18]

Jane recalled waking up the next morning in a hotel, feeling "disoriented, sick, and confused," and "noticed that her mouth was swollen and that there was blood in her vaginal and anal area, as well as blood in the bathtub," according to the complaint.[19] She called the police and was taken to the hospital, where exams and tests concluded that she had been given benzodiazepine, a date rape drug.[20]

A bit of research revealed that Internet Brands was aware not only that ModelMayhem.com had been used in at least five previous sexual assaults but also that Flanders was the perpetrator of the earlier assaults. Internet Brands had purchased ModelMayhem.com from Donald Waitt and Tyler Waitt on May 13, 2008. The Waitts sued Internet Brands in April 2010, claiming that the company did not fully pay them the agreed-upon amount for the site. In August 2010—about a half year before Jane was attacked—Internet Brands filed a counterclaim to the Waitts' lawsuit. The company alleged that the Waitts failed to inform them that on July 13, 2007, the Miami Police Department had arrested Flanders for drugging at least five women whom he met through ModelMayhem.com and raping them in a warehouse. "The charges against Flanders and his alleged use of the website to lure his victims to the warehouse, as well as the contentions made by his victims with regard to his use of the website, were all known by [the Waitts] in July, 2007, nearly one year before they entered into the Agreement," Internet Brands' lawyers wrote in their brief.[21] From that brief, there is no dispute that Internet Brands had known about Flanders's use of the site months before the attack on Jane. Internet Brands could not argue in Jane's case that it was unaware that Flanders used the website to commit crimes; it stated as much in court filings.

In April 2012, Jane filed a negligence lawsuit against Internet Brands in Los Angeles federal court, alleging that the company knew that Flanders and Callum were using ModelMayhem.com to lure, drug, and rape women. The company, Jane claimed, had a duty to warn users of the dangers of sexual predators but failed to do so. Internet Brands filed a seven-page motion to dismiss, relying exclusively on Section 230. The company pointed to the Fifth Circuit's 2008 ruling in favor of MySpace, discussed in chapter 6, in the case arising from the sexual assault of the thirteen-year-old girl. Just as the Fifth Circuit concluded that Section 230 immunized MySpace from a duty to adopt basic user safety protections, the company argued, Internet Brands had no duty to warn users about Flanders. "The law is well-settled and unanimous; the CDA provides immunity to web-based service providers for common law torts committed by website users," Internet Brands' lawyer wrote.[22]

In a brief order issued in August 16, 2012, Judge John F. Walter agreed with Internet Brands and dismissed the case. He wrote that Jane's lawsuit would require Internet Brands "to advise its users of known risks associated with content provided by third parties on its website" and that any such duty would arise from Internet Brands' role as a third-party content publisher. Therefore, such a claim falls within the immunity of Section 230, he maintained.[23] Judge Walter's ruling hinged on his determination that Jane's lawsuit held Internet Brands accountable as a publisher or speaker of third-party content, just as Judge Wilkinson had decided that Kenneth Zeran's lawsuit treated America Online as a speaker or publisher of the Oklahoma City advertisements. But Jane's claims differed from Zeran's. Zeran sued America Online for words that appeared on its services. Jane sued Internet Brands for words that did *not* appear on ModelMayhem.com: a warning. And that warning did not necessarily need to be drafted by a third party; in fact, Jane claimed that Internet Brands itself should have been the one to warn the site.

Jane's lawyers seized on this distinction when they appealed Judge Walter's dismissal to the Ninth Circuit. "Internet Brands' status as an internet services provider publishing content from its members is entirely peripheral to Jane Doe's claim that Internet Brands failed to warn its vulnerable members of modelmayhem.com that they were targets of a rape scam," Jane's lawyers wrote, arguing that Section 230 simply did not apply. Jane's lawyers said that her failure-to-warn claim was much like Cecilia Barnes's promissory estoppel lawsuit against Yahoo: "This failure to warn in the face of superior information posing a grave danger to modelmayhem.com members is not a publishing decision regarding third party content, nor does it implicate any such publishing decision."[24] In a succinct response, Internet Brands' lawyers appeared confident that the Ninth Circuit would easily agree with Judge Walter's dismissal. They pointed to what they called "well-settled authority" that online platforms have no duty to warn, so the site was "absolutely immune" from Jane's lawsuit.[25] The Ninth Circuit's ruling in favor of Barnes did not help Jane, Internet Brands argued, because the lawsuit did not allege that Internet Brands made any promises to Jane.

The case was assigned to Mary Schroeder, who was appointed to the Ninth Circuit by President Carter, and Richard Clifton, a George W. Bush appointee. Brian M. Cogan, a federal district judge from Brooklyn, was the third judge on the panel, sitting by designation. (Because the Ninth Circuit has the largest caseload in the United States, it often relies on federal judges across the country to visit for a week to sit on oral argument panels and help to decide cases.)

The oral argument took place on February 7, 2014. Jeffrey Herman, who represented Jane throughout the case, presented the oral argument. Wendy E. Giberti, a lawyer with a small Beverly Hills firm that represented Internet Brands in several cases, argued for the company.

Jane Doe's complaint alleged that Flanders and Callum contacted Jane "through Model Mayhem." But at oral argument, Herman stated that they contacted Jane "outside the website."[26] The way they contacted Jane could be important to resolving the Section 230 issue, as it relates to whether ModelMayhem.com acted as an intermediary for third-party content. About seven months later, the panel issued a short, unanimous opinion ruling in favor of Jane Doe, reversing Judge Walter's dismissal of the case. Writing for the Ninth Circuit panel, Judge Clifton reasoned that Section 230 prevents websites only from being held liable for third-party content. If Internet Brands were to be required to warn users of predators, Clifton concluded, the warning would be entirely created by Internet Brands, and not by a third party.[27] That content would fall outside the scope of Section 230's immunity, he wrote. Clifton noted that Section 230(c)—which contains the statute's core immunity—is titled "Protection for 'Good Samaritan' Blocking and Screening of Offensive Material." A key purpose of the immunity, he believed, is to allow platforms to "self-regulate offensive third party content."[28] Jane Doe's lawsuit, he reasoned, did not involve the self-regulation of third-party content: "The theory is that Internet Brands should be held liable, based on its knowledge of the rape scheme and its 'special relationship' with users like Jane Doe, for failing to generate its own warning. Liability would not discourage 'Good Samaritan' filtering of third party content."[29]

Clifton noted the second primary goal of Section 230: immunizing platforms to avoid a "chilling effect" on online speech. He acknowledged that imposing liability on Internet Brands might chill speech, although he swiftly dismissed the argument that this broad goal justified immunizing Internet Brands from a failure-to-warn claim. "Congress has not provided an all purpose get-out-of-jail-free card for businesses that publish user content on the Internet, though any claims might have a marginal chilling effect on internet publishing businesses," he wrote.[30]

A particularly noteworthy—and logically troubling—part of Clifton's ruling was his dismissal of the free speech implications of requiring an online platform to warn users about dangerous third parties. He recognized that such liability could lead some platforms to reduce avenues for online user speech. But he implied that there was some sort of sliding scale for free speech reduction and that a marginal reduction in online speech was acceptable under Section 230. To the contrary, Section 230 provides binary, absolute immunity, regardless of the degree of harm that liability might impose. Either a site qualifies for the immunity or it does not. That is precisely why Section 230 has been so successful in fostering the growth of online platforms over more than two decades, even though such success has resulted in some severe inequities to plaintiffs.

Clifton's more compelling line of reasoning was that Jane wanted Internet Brands to create a warning, and that warning would be created by Internet Brands and not a third party. That reasoning also isn't entirely satisfactory because, as Clifton acknowledged in his opinion, ModelMayhem.com acted as an intermediary between Jane and the predators and transmitted information created by Jane. Without that third-party information exchange, Jane never would have been injured. The real question for the Ninth Circuit—which Clifton's opinion addressed in only a perfunctory manner—was whether the duty to warn users of predatory third parties was separate from any third-party content posted by Jane or her attackers. Cecilia Barnes's case was somewhat more clear-cut, as Yahoo took an independent action—making a promise—that led to her lawsuit. In contrast, Jane's claim arose from what she believed was an *omission* on the part of Internet Brands.

The technology industry quickly recognized the implications of Clifton's opinion. Within a few days of the Ninth Circuit's ruling, Internet Brands retained Munger, Tolles, & Olson, one of California's top law firms (President Obama appointed three Munger lawyers to be Ninth Circuit judges). Daniel Collins, a Munger partner who has argued dozens of cases in the Ninth Circuit, led the Internet Brands team.[31]

Collins petitioned the Ninth Circuit to rehear the case. He had two main arguments. First, he claimed that the panel should not have allowed Herman to state at oral argument that Flanders and Callum had contacted Jane Doe outside Model Mayhem, when the complaint stated that they contacted her "through" the site. Changing a position on such a key fact, Collins wrote, would require Jane Doe to file a new complaint. Second, Collins argued that the Ninth Circuit simply misinterpreted Section 230 and that, no matter how it was framed, Doe's lawsuit stemmed from third-party content. The Ninth Circuit's narrow interpretation of Section 230 immunity, Collins claimed, "threatens to chill the free exchange of information on the Internet and could significantly increase potential liabilities and burdens for a wide range of website operators."[32]

Pat Carome filed an amicus brief in support of Internet Brands' rehearing petition on behalf of a coalition of technology companies and groups, including Craigslist, Facebook, and Tumblr. Carome, who had persuaded the Fourth Circuit to issue the first broad immunity in Kenneth Zeran's case, stressed the harm that the Ninth Circuit's interpretation would cause for online speech. "The panel's reasoning could allow suits against online service providers in a wide range of circumstances in which they merely intermediated third-party content that somehow resulted in harm to a user. The specter of such tort litigation and liability would undermine the very growth and development that Congress enacted Section 230 to promote," Carome wrote. "It also would discourage companies from responsible self-policing, even though elimination of exactly such disincentives was another of the statute's core purposes."[33]

The arguments apparently were convincing enough for the panel to withdraw its opinion and schedule a new round of oral arguments for April 2015 in the Ninth Circuit's San Francisco courthouse. Judge Cogan appeared by videoconference from Brooklyn.[34] Jane Doe's lawyer, Jeffrey

Herman, who had initially convinced the panel that Section 230 did not immunize Internet Brands, argued first. "The CDA is what it is," Herman said. "It's a limited liability that was created to protect Internet service providers from activity that would hold them as a publisher for third-party content. What it's not is blanket immunity." But, asked Clifton, did Jane Doe have any relationship with Model Mayhem besides the site's publication of content? No, Herman responded, but Internet Brands had a specific duty to warn Jane Doe because the company had "superior information" about the risk posed by Flanders and Callum. Judge Cogan noted that Internet providers usually will have "superior information," such as their legal department's files on misuse of services. He questioned whether service providers would always need to review confidential user files and warn others of potential harm.

Collins had an equally difficult time persuading the panel to rule in Internet Brands' favor. Jane Doe's claim, he argued, would treat the website as the speaker of third-party content. Cogan appeared unpersuaded. "You're saying that everything related in any way to publication or speaking that your client does cannot give rise to liability," he countered. "And if Congress wanted to give that kind of blanket immunity, why couldn't it simply say 'the provider shall be immune from every act arising from or relating to its publishing activity?' They didn't say that. There must be something that's not covered." Clifton similarly seemed to believe that his initial ruling against Internet Brands was correct. Section 230, he said, simply did not apply to a claim such as Jane Doe's: "The whole point of the CDA appears to be that you shouldn't be treated as a speaker of what somebody else has put up because you can't necessarily control what somebody else put up." Jane's claim against Internet Brands, Clifton said, is "an entirely different context."

Carome faced similar resistance as he argued that a ruling for Jane Doe could chill online speech, asserting, "Today's Internet services are platforms for a torrent of communications flowing back and forth between users of websites."

"I think your policy argument is really strong," Cogan said, "and if I were sitting in Congress, I might write a broader immunity provision than is currently in the statute." But Cogan is a judge who can interpret laws only as Congress passed them. And he had trouble seeing how Section 230, as drafted by Congress, prevented Jane Doe's lawsuit.

Clifton also struggled to adopt Carome's interpretation. "I have trouble looking at the statute seeing how a provision that's entitled—now let's actually get its title," Clifton said as he flipped through his materials for the text of Section 230. "'Protection for Good Samaritan Blocking and screening of offensive material' gets turned into a hall pass, a get-out-of-jail-free card when it has something to do with the Internet."

The judges did not appear to be more sympathetic to Internet Brands than when they had first heard oral arguments in the case more than a year earlier. Yet the panel voluntarily withdrew its opinion to hear additional arguments. And during the second arguments, Internet Brands was represented by one of the top appellate lawyers on the West Coast. So it was difficult to predict how the Ninth Circuit would rule.

The technology community waited.

On May 31, 2016, more than a year after the second oral argument, the three judges again unanimously ruled in favor of Jane Doe, reversing Judge Walter's dismissal of the lawsuit. The Ninth Circuit's second opinion was much like its first, with most of the paragraphs either identical or nearly the same. Judge Clifton expanded on the unique circumstances of the case and clarified some important details, such as the fact that Flanders and Callum did not post profiles on ModelMayhem.com. Clifton also added a footnote to clarify that whether Flanders and Callum contacted Jane Doe through the website or outside it was immaterial to its decision in the case. The panel's overall reasoning remained largely unchanged.[35]

The case went back to Judge Walter for a determination of whether Internet Brands actually breached a duty to warn Jane Doe; the Ninth Circuit's opinion addressed only whether Internet Brands was immune under Section 230. In November 2016, Judge Walter again dismissed the lawsuit, this time because he concluded that, regardless of Section 230, the company had no obligation to warn Jane Doe of Flanders and Callum. "Although it may have been foreseeable that Flanders and Callum would strike again, Internet Brands only had knowledge of a threat to its member base at large, not to a specific member," Walter wrote. "Imposing a duty to warn under these circumstances would, in the Court's opinion, only minimally increase the precautions already taken by website users, and would also likely cause website operators to inundate and overwhelm their users with warnings, ultimately diluting the effectiveness of such warnings."[36]

Jane Doe again appealed to the Ninth Circuit. The Ninth Circuit sent both sides to mediation, and before either party filed a brief in the new appeal, Jane Doe voluntarily dismissed the case without explanation.

Despite the quiet end to the case, the litigation had a lasting effect: in the Ninth Circuit, Section 230 does not protect websites from lawsuits arising from their failure to warn, even though that failure might be related entirely to user-generated content. Combined with the *Barnes* opinion, the case makes it harder for websites to claim immunity from lawsuits outside the traditional publication-related claims, such as defamation.

If Section 230's first decade was marked by a rapid expansion of immunity for websites, the second decade saw a gradual—but real—erosion of Section 230 immunity as I documented in a 2017 article in the *Columbia Science and Technology Law Review*. In 2001 and 2002, U.S. courts issued written opinions in ten cases in which online intermediaries claimed Section 230 immunity. Of those ten cases, the courts concluded that eight intermediaries were immune. The remaining two cases involved intellectual property claims, which are explicitly exempt from Section 230. In contrast, a review of all written court opinions involving Section 230 issued between July 1, 2015, and June 30, 2016, found that in fourteen of the twenty-seven cases, the courts refused to provide intermediaries with full immunity.[37] The courts' refusals to immunize the sites stemmed largely from two theories: the *Roommates.com/Accusearch* rationale that the sites somehow contributed to the illegal content, and the *Barnes/Internet Brands* argument that the sites were sued for activities other than publishing and speaking.

These four landmark cases from the second decade involved victims of serious harms: tenants who were discriminated against, consumers whose private information was trafficked, a woman whose boyfriend posted pictures without her knowledge, and, most troubling, a rape victim. But difficult cases did not suddenly emerge around 2005. Ever since Section 230 was enacted, online platforms had claimed immunity against lawsuits from victims who were harmed, often with devastating circumstances. Think back to the second Section 230 case ever decided: *Doe v. America Online*. The victim in that case was an eleven-year-old boy who was sexually assaulted and had his images trafficked on

America Online in child pornography videos. Or Ellen Batzel, whose career was ruined. Or Christianne Carafano, who was forced to leave her home. Section 230 cases often come with a tough set of facts that make it tempting to carve out an exception to the broad immunity and allow victims to recover damages from large online providers. Difficult cases are not new. What is new is that courts have become increasingly likely to abrogate Section 230's immunity.

This trend represents a significant contraction of the Internet exceptionalism that marked the first decade of Section 230. The statute was passed during the infancy of the modern, commercial Internet. By the beginning of Section 230's second decade, several mammoth Internet service providers, websites, and other platforms were benefiting greatly from Section 230's immunity. Many scholars and jurists questioned whether the Internet needed special legal protections such as Section 230. These views were articulately expressed in a 2009 essay titled "A Declaration of the Dependence of Cyberspace":

> It has been fifteen years since America Online unleashed its hordes of home computing modem-owners on e-mail and the Internet and fifteen years since the release of the Mosaic Web browser. After all that time, we have today relatively few legal rules that apply only to the Internet. Using the Internet, people buy stocks, advertise used goods and apply for jobs. All of those transactions are governed by the exact same laws as would govern them if they were done offline.
>
> Those who claim the Internet requires special rules to deal with these ordinary controversies have trouble explaining this history. Despite this dearth of Internet-specific law, the Internet is doing wonderfully. It has survived speculative booms and busts, made millionaires out of many and, unfortunately, rude bloggers out of more than a few. The lack of a special Internet civil code has not hurt its development.[38]

Its authors were Josh Goldfoot, a U.S. Justice Department computer crimes attorney, and the Ninth Circuit judge for whom Goldfoot had clerked: Alex Kozinski, who penned both *Roommates.com* majority opinions. Indeed, no opinions better encapsulated the anti-exceptionalism philosophy than those of *Roommates.com*. Goldfoot and Kozinski make an interesting argument against special rules for the Internet. By 2009, the Internet was one of the American economy's greatest success stories.

However, their argument overlooks one critical fact: the Internet was *not* governed by the exact same laws as those of the brick-and-mortar world. The Internet had the benefit of Section 230, which provided an absolute immunity rarely seen in U.S. law. It is impossible to divorce the success of the U.S. technology sector from the significant benefits of Section 230.

Part IV

The Future of Section 230

Just as the courts issued the *Roommates.com, Accusearch, Barnes,* and *Internet Brands* opinions, I graduated from law school and began writing articles that largely defended Section 230. I also soon started practicing media law, and I frequently invoked Section 230 on behalf of corporate clients who received complaints about user-generated content on their websites. I was fully on board with the benefits of Section 230. I was troubled by the slow erosion of Section 230 immunity because I saw first-hand the vibrant and open Internet that Section 230 had allowed. Without the immunity, there is no way that my clients could have allowed users to speak freely, openly, and loudly. I also helped clients develop user content policies that were driven by user demand. Some news websites, for example, received floods of complaints about nasty online comments underneath stories, so many of them began requiring users to post under their real name, via their Facebook logins.

Section 230, I believed, was fulfilling the twin goals of Cox and Wyden: it fostered open forums for online speech, while allowing users—and not courts—to dictate any restrictions on that speech.

As I moved from law practice to academia in 2015, I continued to write and speak about Section 230 and have been invited to speak with members of Congress and their staff about the equities of this immunity. The challenges that I began exploring in depth were much more complex, troubling, and, in many cases, damaging than those that had existed two decades earlier when Cox and Wyden first began drafting Section 230. In its infancy, Section 230 created cases raised by individualized harms, such as that caused by the anonymous user who posted Kenneth Zeran's phone number on America Online. The more recent objections to Section 230 involved more than just individual instances of defamation. These were systemic problems that affected thousands or millions: trolling and revenge pornography, terrorist recruitment via social media, and the pervasive use of classified websites by sex traffickers. In part IV, I describe why I find that these problems raise some of the most compelling arguments against Section 230. In one case, I even concede that Section 230 requires a modest amendment to address a particularly egregious flaw. I also examine how websites have voluntarily adopted moderation practices and suggest where they could improve.

But as I explain in this section, I believe that we should preserve the core Section 230 immunity because the overall benefits of an open Internet outweigh the harms. This was not an easy conclusion to reach, but Section 230 has become so intertwined with our fundamental conceptions of the Internet that any wholesale reductions to the immunity could irreparably destroy the free speech that has shaped our society in the twenty-first century.

10

SARAH VERSUS THE DIRTY ARMY

The plaintiffs in many of the most troubling Section 230 cases were women: Cecilia Barnes, Jane Doe, Ellen Batzel, and Christianne Carafano, to name a few. One of the strongest and most pervasive criticisms of Section 230 is that by protecting *all* speech, it encourages some of the most vile, sexist, and oppressive words and images. By targeting women, racial minorities, and other groups, these attacks both harm them *and* further weaken their voices. In my review for this book of the hundreds of published court opinions addressing Section 230 immunity, women were disproportionately the plaintiffs in the cases with the most disturbing sets of facts. Women are the targets of revenge pornography, as was Cecilia Barnes; computer-assisted crime, as was Jane Doe; and, perhaps most commonly, just outright and persistent harassment. Men can be the victims of revenge pornography, but such cases are not nearly as common as those involving female victims such as Barnes. Had *Ethan* Batzel, rather than *Ellen* Batzel, gotten into a dispute with a contractor, I'm not sure if Ethan would have faced the same vitriol on Museum Security Network as did Ellen.

Those of us who have supported Section 230—and the companies that benefit greatly from it—must take a hard look at the flip side of this statutory subsidy for free speech. For every well-meaning Yelp reviewer or Wikipedia-based amateur journalist, there is a troll lurking in the background, ready to use free speech as a weapon.

Andrea Dworkin—whose court battle against Larry Flynt was discussed in chapter 1—helped set the stage for many of the most compelling critiques of Section 230. Although her writings did not focus on Section 230 or on-line speech (she died in 2005), the works of Dworkin and her contemporary Catharine MacKinnon focused on the harms that free speech causes to women. Their particular focus was pornography, which throughout the 1970s saw reduced regulation and which gradually expanded. The Supreme Court had held that only *obscene* pornography fell outside the First Amendment's free speech protections, and it was difficult to establish that mainstream pornography was so offensive to contemporary standards that it was obscene. Dworkin argued that by degrading women, pornography suppressed their ability to speak freely, as she wrote in her 1981 book, *Pornography: Men Possessing Women*: "By definition the First Amendment protects only those who can exercise the rights it protects. Pornography by definition—'the graphic depiction of whores'—is trade in a class of persons who have been systematically denied the rights protected by the First Amendment and the rest of the Bill of Rights. The question this book raises is not whether the First Amendment protects pornography or should, but whether pornography keeps women from exercising the rights protected by the First Amendment."[1]

To Dworkin and MacKinnon, pornography was not speech. It suppressed speech. It violated the civil rights of women. In 1993, MacKinnon published *Only Words*, a book in which she argued that broad First Amendment rights protect more than just words; the First Amendment also guards against harmful acts that effectively suppress the voices of specific groups. Pornography, MacKinnon argued, epitomized this tension: "Protecting pornography means protecting sexual abuse *as* speech, at the same time that both pornography and its protection have deprived women *of* speech, especially speech against sexual abuse. There is a connection between the silence enforced on women, in which we are seen to love and choose our chains because they have been sexualized, and the noise of pornography that surrounds us, passing for discourse (ours, even) and parading under constitutional protection."[2]

Dworkin and MacKinnon applied this theory by devising a local ordinance that broadly prohibited trafficking in many types of pornography. Rather than target only obscene materials, the ordinance prohibited many types of pornography that contains "graphic sexually explicit subordination of women." The Indianapolis City Council adopted the ordinance in 1984, and the U.S. Court of Appeals for the Seventh Circuit struck it down the following year, concluding that it violated the First Amendment by discriminating against certain speech. Judge Frank Easterbrook rejected Dworkin and MacKinnon's arguments that pornography is not speech. "Racial bigotry, anti-semitism, violence on television, reporters' biases—these and many more influence the culture and shape our socialization. None is directly answerable by more speech, unless that speech too finds its place in the popular culture," he wrote. "Yet all is protected as speech, however insidious. Any other answer leaves the government in control of all of the institutions of culture, the great censor and director of which thoughts are good for us."[3] To MacKinnon and Dworkin, Easterbrook was allowing the First Amendment's free speech protections to protect abusive acts that actually suppressed speech. "Behind his First Amendment façade, women were being transformed into ideas, sexual traffic in whom was protected as if it were a discussion, the men uninhibited and robust, the women wide-open," MacKinnon wrote.[4]

The Supreme Court summarily affirmed Easterbrook's ruling,[5] but his opinion continued to attract great criticism for its minimization of the harms that speech can cause to women. Pornography had been weaponized and, as Dworkin and MacKinnon persuasively showed, led to violence against women. And that violence leads to silence and inequality. Although MacKinnon and Dworkin were ultimately unsuccessful in making the legal case for prohibitions on oppressive pornography, their advocacy and writing showed the true harms that some speech can have, going far beyond the standard types of defamation cases that are often at the center of free speech disputes.

The tension between free speech and real-world harm that MacKinnon and Dworkin documented would reappear in some of the toughest Section 230 cases.

Congress passed Section 230 more than a decade after Easterbrook struck down the Indianapolis ordinance. Yet many of the same arguments that surrounded his disagreement with Dworkin and MacKinnon live on in the debate about Section 230. In a *Fordham Law Review* article, Danielle Keats Citron and Benjamin Wittes question whether, on balance, Section 230 actually promotes free speech: "We are skeptical that Section 230, as currently interpreted, is really optimizing free speech. It gives an irrational degree of free speech benefit to harassers and scofflaws, but ignores important free speech costs to victims. Individuals have difficulty expressing themselves in the face of online assaults."[6]

Section 230, to be sure, is a statutory protection that Congress is free to amend or eliminate at any time, while Easterbrook's ruling was grounded in the First Amendment. Section 230 is the First Amendment on steroids, for the Internet age. By broadly immunizing websites and other online intermediaries, Section 230 allows unfettered speech, ranging from valuable political discourse to vile content, often attacking women.

Ann Bartow argues that Section 230 not only allows such harmful content but also incentivizes online platforms to attract it: "Under Section 230 the financial incentives for ISPs all fall in favor of ignoring internet harassment. Controversial news reports, gossip blogs and sexy intriguing dating profiles, even when false, generate logons, eyeballs, and browser clicks, all the things that lead to revenue streams. Section 230 enables large ISPs to disclaim any legal or moral responsibility for the harms that online speech can inflict all the way to the bank."[7] Indeed, lascivious content generates clicks, and clicks generate revenue. Although Bartow is correct that Section 230 *allows* platforms to disclaim responsibility for user content, platforms increasingly have adopted policies and procedures to moderate content, albeit imperfectly. As I describe in chapter 12, large platforms have done so in response to consumer demand, although their solutions have been far from perfect. Still, some platforms are not as responsible. And some sites even encourage user content that degrades women. That makes it harder to defend Section 230.

Sites like TheDirty.com.

TheDirty.com is a gossip news site. Hooman Karamian—who goes by the name Nik Richie—launched the site's earlier incarnation, DirtyScottsdale.com, in 2007. At first, Richie created most of the site's content. That soon changed, and by 2009, he was allowing his site users to upload text, pictures, and videos. The site instructed users to "tell us what's happening. Remember to tell us who, what, when, where, why."[8] Unlike other sites, TheDirty.com was curated. Richie and his staff published between 150 and 200 of the thousands of daily submissions that users uploaded. Richie sometimes edited parts of posts to remove content such as obscenity but usually did not materially edit the posts. He did, however, often add his own snarky editorial comments at the end of the post, signed "—nik." All users are identified by the same pseudonym, "The Dirty Army."[9]

Even with Section 230's immunity, Richie was liable for any comments that he added. But Section 230 broadly protects websites from claims that arise from user-created content, even if the site operators delete parts of the posts or affirmatively decide whether to publish only certain user content. In other words, the site appeared to be designed with Section 230 in mind. In fact, the website's "Legal FAQs" section begins with "Can I Sue TheDirty For Publishing False Information?" The answer: "In a word— NO. Under a federal law known as the Communications Decency Act or 'CDA,' website operators like TheDirty are generally not liable for 'publishing' content from third party users. This does NOT mean you are helpless if someone has posted false information about you. You can always sue the author. You just can't sue us for running an online forum that someone else misused."[10] To support this bold claim, TheDirty links to a federal appellate court decision in a lawsuit that Sarah Jones, then a high school teacher and Cincinnati Ben-Gals cheerleader, filed against Richie and the website's parent company.

Jones's dispute with TheDirty began with an October 27, 2009, user submission of two photographs of Jones and a male, with the following comment from a member of the Dirty Army: "Nik, this is Sara J, Cincinnati Bengal Cheerleader. She's been spotted around town lately with the infamous Shayne Graham. She has also slept with every other Bengal Football player. This girl is a teacher too!! You would think with Graham's paycheck he could attract something a little easier on the eyes Nik!"[11] Richie published the post, adding the following comment: "Everyone in Cincinnati knows this kicker is a Sex Addict. It is no secret . . . he can't even keep relationships because his Red Rocket has freckles that need to be touched constantly.—nik" Graham called Jones to alert her about the post, according to a narrative statement that Jones would later submit to the court.[12] The gossip began to spread quickly around the high school where Jones taught, and Jones found it "humiliating." The students were sharing the article in school so much that the county board of education eventually blocked the site from school computers. Jones said that she emailed Richie asking him to remove the post, and although he had initially agreed to do so, he said he decided to keep the post online because "Shayne pissed me off."[13]

Two months after the initial post, Jones was the subject of another user submission on TheDirty.com, titled "The Dirty Bengals Cheerleader," containing a picture of Jones with the following comment: "Nik, here we have Sarah J, captain cheerleader of the playoff bound cinci bengals . . . Most ppl see Sarah has a gorgeous cheerleader AND highschool teacher . . . yes she's also a teacher . . . but what most of you don't know is . . . Her ex Nate . . . cheated on her with over 50 girls in 4 years . . . in that time he tested positive for Chlamydia Infection and Gonorrhea . . . so im sure Sarah also has both . . . whats worse is he brags about doing sarah in the gym . . . football field . . . her class room at the school she teaches at DIXIE Heights."[14] Richie posted the "article" and added "Why are all high school teachers freaks in the sack?—nik."

Two days later, another picture of Jones, with a man, appeared on TheDirty.com, titled "Bengals Cheerleader Boyfriend." The text accompanying the picture read, "Nik, ok you all seen the past posting of the dirty Bengals cheerleader/teacher . . . well here is her main man Nate. Posted a few pics of the infected couple. Oh an for everyone saying sarah is so gorgeous check her out in these nonphotoshopped pics."[15] Richie wrote below the post, "Cool tribal tat man. For a second yesterday I was jealous of those high school kids for having a cheerleader teacher, but not anymore.—nik."[16]

Jones told the court that her cheerleading director called to tell her of the third post. Jones said that the humiliation from that incident caused her to miss school the next day. When she returned to the school, students asked her about the post. School administrators investigated the claims that she had had sex on school property, reviewing security video footage. At cheerleading practice, she spent most of the time explaining why the posts were false.[17] Jones said she emailed Richie at least twenty-seven times, begging him to remove the post. Jones's father also emailed him. She retained a lawyer, who sent Richie an email demanding removal of the posts. Richie did not remove the posts, and on December 24, 2009, Jones filed a defamation lawsuit in Kentucky federal court against Dirty World Entertainment Recordings LLC.[18]

The lawsuit received national attention. Four days after Jones sued, TheDirty.com carried this comment from a member of the Dirty Army:

> Nik, I'm a lawyer who does a lot of internet work and I just saw the news story on the Huffington Post about you getting sued in Kentucky bysome [sic] airhead cheerleader. I know you have a kick-ass legal team already, but I just wanted you to know the law in this area is 100% on your side and is so clear I think you have a decent chance of getting all of your attorney's fees awarded as a sanction for this girl filing a frivolous action against you. Love the site and don't let anyone push you around. I know a lot of lawyers who love the site and I personally would be happy to represent you if you ever need it at no charge. Good luck and keep us posted on what happens.
>
> P.S.—I looked up her profile on their website and she is grossssss!!![19]

Richie added the following commentary:

> I am all good in the legal department. I have Cochran Kardashian (that is what I call him to his face) representing my ass. This is just a desperate attempt for attention by some no name DreamKiller
>
> According to my lawyer CK, "I just checked the court docket for all federal courts in Kentucky, and there's no record of this case being filed."
>
> Let's see how the media and every other blogger that hates me tries to spin this in her favor.—nik[20]

The following day, TheDirty.com posted two more user-written articles, claiming that the Bengals cheerleaders were unattractive. "I love how the DIRTY Army has a war mentality," Richie wrote below one of the user posts. "Why go after one ugly cheerleader when you can go after all the brown baggers. (Sorry Cleveland Browns, that was not a stab at your girls.)"[21]

In court filings, Jones recounted the embarrassment of facing her students after winter break: "In each class, I had to tell my 15 year old students that I didn't have two STD's and that I was still a role model for them. In each class, I sobbed uncontrollably, letting them see a side of me that no student should see."[22] Some students posted comments in her defense on the website. Another poster, purporting to be a student, wrote that she never could learn from a "slut" like Jones again. "This was the most devastating to me," Jones wrote. "I love my job more than anything in the world."[23] When the new school year began that August, several students asked Jones about the postings. "I have worked too hard and had to push this issue to show that people shouldn't get treated like this," Jones wrote. "Nik Richie, the owner of thedirty.com, has pushed me over my emotional limit. He has ruined a part of my life that I can't get back and it will forever be with me."[24]

Because the initial lawsuit was filed against Dirty World Entertainment Recordings LLC, which was not Richie's company, Jones had to amend her complaint, and the case dragged on through 2010 and into 2011. Richie and the companies asked Judge William Bertelsman to dismiss the case, claiming that Section 230 immunized them from claims stemming from user content. On January 21, 2011, Bertelsman denied the motion, concluding that discovery was necessary to determine whether the website at least partly developed the postings. That allowed both sides to gather all sorts of materials through document requests and depositions, no matter how embarrassing.

That April, Alexis Mattingly, a lawyer for Richie and TheDirty, deposed Jones. The 175-page transcript is full of questions about Jones's medical history, career, and sex life. For instance, Mattingly asked Jones what was defamatory about the first post about Jones.

Jones: That I slept with every other Bengals football player. I mean, I'm pretty confident in the fact that if somebody would say something negative about me, specifically, I take that, I have thick skin, I teach 15 year olds, but it was the part that said I had had sex with other football players.

Mattingly: So is that false?

Jones: Absolutely.

Mattingly: Have you had sex with any Bengals football—

Jones: No.

Mattingly: —players?[25]

After lawyers questioned Jones about some of her most intimate details, the defendants moved for summary judgment dismissal of the case, arguing that based on the facts gathered in discovery, TheDirty.com was an interactive computer service that was immune from her lawsuit under Section 230.

In January 2012, Judge Bertelsman denied the request to toss the case out. He concluded that Section 230 did not apply because of Richie's encouragement of the allegedly defamatory user posts. Bertelsman noted that Richie published only a "small percentage" of user contributions and that he wrote editorial comments and appended them underneath many posts: "One could hardly be more encouraging of the posting of such content than by saying to one's fans (known not coincidentally as 'the Dirty Army'): 'I love how the Dirty Army has war mentality.' "[26] Bertelsman relied heavily on the reasoning of the Ninth Circuit in *Roommates.com* and the Tenth Circuit in *Accusearch* to conclude that specific encouragement of illegal content causes a platform to lose Section 230 immunity. The site was titled TheDirty, he noted, and it invited users to post "dirt." And Richie's inflammatory comments—while not in and of themselves defamatory—could prompt some users to participate in the public reputational flogging that Jones experienced. But unlike Roommates.com, TheDirty did not *require* users to answer questions that could be used to create illegal content. And unlike Accusearch, TheDirty did not connect users with third parties that violated the law. Because TheDirty was different from Roommates.com or Accusearch, Bertelsman's ruling could not rest entirely on the Ninth and Tenth Circuit's decisions. The nature of the site—and Richie's comments—apparently offended Bertelsman. "Richie's goal in establishing the site was to bring reality TV to the Internet," Bertelsman wrote, citing Richie's deposition. "He wants everybody to log on to 'the dirty.com' and check it out. In his opinion, 'you can say whatever you want on the internet.' "[27]

Because Bertelsman denied the summary judgment motion, the case proceeded to a three-day jury trial in January 2013. Both Richie and Jones testified. During Richie's testimony, Jones's attorney, Eric Deters, focused on the gossipy nature of the site that had troubled Bertelsman. Deters asked Richie whether he truly believed that Jones had slept with every Bengals player. Richie admitted that the claim was an "exaggeration."

"So you think she slept with one?" Deters asked

"I couldn't tell you," Richie replied. "You know, after—to this day, if you ask me now, I would say probably. She lies a lot."

Deters asked why Richie did not delete the post after receiving Jones's email requests.

"If someone sends me evidence that it's false, which Sarah never did, then I would remove it," Richie responded.

"How do you prove you didn't have sex with every Bengal football player?" Deters asked.

"I don't know," Richie replied.[28]

Deters asked Richie if the millions of visitors to TheDirty.com saw the claim that Jones had STDs. Richie estimated that based on the time that the post was on the site's main page, about fifty thousand people saw the post, and three hundred were in Cincinnati.

"Don't you think that's 50,000 and 300 too many?" Deters asked.

"It's the Internet," Richie responded. "It's like going on YouTube and Facebook. It's the same thing."

"Is it your position that with the Internet, that you are allowed to post things that you know are not true about another person because it's the Internet?" Deters asked. "Is that your position?"

"My position's freedom of speech, and people are entitled to their own opinions," Richie said. "This is America."[29]

Richie's testimony probably did not make him seem like a terribly sympathetic defendant to the jury. But Jones's testimony did not help her case.

Jones had had a sexual relationship with Cody York, who then was a seventeen-year-old student at her high school. Jones said the sexual relationship began in October 2011—nearly two years after she sued TheDirty.com and Richie. Jones pleaded guilty to a sexual misconduct misdemeanor and resigned from her teaching job. Jones and York have since married.[30]

The posts on TheDirty.com did not allege that Jones had been sleeping with students. Still, her criminal case had made national news. And she fielded many questions about the relationship during her jury testimony. For instance, Alexis Mattingly, the lawyer for TheDirty and Richie, questioned Jones in detail about the timing of the relationship, reading text messages that Jones had sent to York in which Jones claimed to have fallen in love with York years earlier, when he was a high school freshman. And even though the website posts did not allege that Jones was having an affair with a student, Mattingly used Jones's criminal conviction to bolster the general claims that Jones's sexual behavior was inappropriate.

"Now, despite all of that talk about your ministry and wanting respect from the students, you chose to engage in a romantic and sexual relationship with a student, correct?" Mattingly asked.

"Yes, ma'am," Jones said.

"Okay," Mattingly said, "but do you believe that rumors that you slept with Bengals players, have STDs, and have sex with your fiancé at school are more harmful to your profession, your ministry, as you call it, than the truth you were having sex with a student?"

"No, ma'am," Jones replied.[31]

On the second day of jury deliberations, the jurors sent a note to Judge Bertelsman: "We the jury have deliberated for 4 hours yesterday and another 4 hours today and we are at an impasse. We cannot agree and are a hung jury."[32]

The judge declared a mistrial, and Judge Bertelsman presided over a new trial in July 2013. This time, the jury ruled in favor of Jones and awarded her a total of $338,000 in damages. Richie and the company promptly appealed to the United States Court of Appeals for the Sixth Circuit, which hears appeals from federal courts in Kentucky, Michigan, Ohio, and Tennessee. Unlike the technology-heavy Ninth Circuit, the Sixth Circuit hears few cutting-edge cyberlaw disputes. In fact, this was the first time that the Sixth Circuit would interpret the full scope of Section 230.

The Sixth Circuit held oral arguments in May 2014, and less than two months later, it issued a unanimous opinion reversing Judge Bertelsman's conclusion that Section 230 did not apply. In the opinion, written by Judge Julia Smith Gibbons, the Sixth Circuit ruled that Richie and TheDirty.com were immune from Jones's lawsuit. Central to the Sixth Circuit's reversal was its conclusion that Bertelsman had incorrectly reasoned that a website "develops" content—and is therefore not eligible for Section 230 immunity—if it intentionally encourages that user content. Judge Gibbons wrote that the correct test, following the Ninth Circuit's *Roommates.com* opinion, is whether the website "materially contributed" to the illegality of the user content: "The district court elided the crucial distinction between, on the one hand, taking actions (traditional to publishers) that are necessary to the display of unwelcome and actionable content and, on the other hand, responsibility for what makes the displayed content illegal or actionable."[33]

Denying Section 230 immunity to sites that "encourage" user content, Gibbons noted, would harm not only gossip websites but also consumer review sites and sites that allow users to warn of consumer fraud. A consumer review site, for example, could be seen as "encouraging" negative consumer reviews, only because it provides a platform with a one-to-five-star rating. "Under an encouragement test of development, these websites would lose the immunity under the CDA and be subject to hecklers' suits aimed at the publisher," she wrote.[34] Applying the *Roommates.com* material contribution test to TheDirty.com, Gibbons concluded that the site (and Richie) was not responsible for the development of the user posts. TheDirty.com, unlike Roommates.com, did not require its visitors to upload defamatory comments, she reasoned, and the content submission form merely directs users to describe "what's happening" and is "neutral." Gibbons recognized that Richie's additional editorial comments were "absurd" and "ludicrous," but those comments did not "materially contribute" to the alleged defamation of the user comments, which were written *before* Richie added his commentary. "It would break the concepts of responsibility and material contribution to hold Richie responsible for the defamatory content of speech because he later commented on that speech," Gibbons wrote.[35]

The decision sparked more national attention and controversy than a typical Section 230 ruling, in part because of the high profile of the plaintiff (her relationship with and marriage to a student received national media coverage) and in part because of the vile nature of the comments about her and Richie's apparent encouragement of the attacks.

In their *Fordham Law Review* article, Citron and Wittes cite Jones's case in support of their argument that Congress should narrow the scope of Section 230's immunity. "The site should not be protected from liability since it is designed for the express purpose of hosting defamation and privacy invasions," they wrote. "To immunize it would turn the notion of the Good Samaritan on its head since its interests are aligned with the abusers. Enjoying section 230 would be a windfall for the site operator who gives lip service to preventing defamation in this site's terms of service but encourages his 'Dirty Army' to email him 'dirt' and chooses which gossip to post."[36] Although TheDirty is anything but a sympathetic defendant, it is difficult to envision precisely how a court would apply the rule that Citron and Wittes propose. Would Yelp be liable for all defamatory business reviews because it is designed for (and encourages) customers to post reviews? Of course, Yelp does not encourage its users to share "the dirt," but TheDirty does not explicitly ask its users to post defamation and lies. How would Congress—or the courts—draw a line that distinguishes TheDirty from Yelp? Would that line be clear enough to provide certainty to companies that are building new businesses that are based on third-party content?

Perhaps because of the troubling nature of this case, Gibbons included a paragraph at the end of the opinion to point out another avenue for Jones to recover for reputational harm: suing the anonymous people who posted about her in the first place. Section 230 provides them with no protection from lawsuit. "We note that the broad immunity furnished by the CDA does not necessarily leave persons who are the objects of anonymously posted, online, defamatory content without a remedy," Gibbons stated. "In this case, Jones conceded that she did not attempt to recover from the person(s) whose comments Richie elected to publish."[37] Gibbons is correct, although she does not address the difficulty of bringing such a lawsuit. TheDirty did not require users to post under their real identities; indeed, every user post was under the name "The Dirty Army." To sue the posters, Jones first would need to unmask them.

Unmasking anonymous online posters requires a few steps—and often does not succeed. First, the plaintiff sues the anonymous defendant, typically naming the defendant as John Doe or Jane Doe. As part of that lawsuit, the plaintiff issues a subpoena to the website that hosted the defamatory post, requesting all data about the poster. Many websites do not require posters to provide their real names or email addresses. Most (but not all) maintain logs of Internet Protocol (IP) addresses, unique sets of numbers that identify a user's Internet connection. If the plaintiff obtains the IP address, the plaintiff then must subpoena the Internet service provider that hosts that IP address and request the name of the subscriber to that Internet connection.

Plaintiffs face a few significant hurdles with this process. First, not all websites keep logs of IP addresses, and some sites that host particularly controversial user content have been known to avoid recording this data. Second, if a website, ISP, or anonymous user challenges a subpoena for identifying information, courts apply complex First Amendment balancing tests to determine whether they should enforce the subpoena. And third, even if a court enforces the subpoenas, the plaintiff will have only the name and contact information of the subscriber to the Internet connection from where the post originated. If, for instance, the user posted from a library or coffee shop, this information will be of little use in identifying the poster. Given the uncertainty of the unmasking process, it is disingenuous to simply dismiss the harms suffered by plaintiffs such as Jones because they did not sue the posters. There is a very real chance that they never will be able to identify those posters. Section 230 means that in many cases, women and others who have been the victims of systematic harassment may be unable to recover any damages, even if the website encouraged users to harass. This is a cold fact that even the most ardent Section 230 supporters should not avoid.

Because of Section 230, a woman—and, yes, the victims of the most vile online harassment campaigns are often women—may be left unable to successfully sue a site, even if that site encourages anonymous users to post defamatory rumors about their sex lives or revenge pornography. Such user posts can destroy a woman's reputation, and, as Dworkin and MacKinnon argued in their critiques of pornography, this hateful speech can silence woman. Indeed, the same concerns that Dworkin and MacKinnon raised about First Amendment protections for pornography could apply to Section 230's protections for online platforms.

Among the most persuasive critiques of Section 230 is that it allows the harassment of women and other groups. This may actually suppress their voices. Mary Anne Franks has argued that Section 230 removes any incentive for sites to block harmful content: "Today, the Internet is awash in threats, harassment, defamation, revenge porn, propaganda, misinformation, and conspiracy theories, which disproportionately burden vulnerable private citizens including women, racial and religious minorities, and the LGBT community. They are the ones who suffer while the websites, platforms, and ISPs that make it possible for these abuses to flourish are protected from harm."[38]

Indeed, without Section 230, it is difficult to imagine how TheDirty.com could operate, at least with the procedures that allowed the posts about Jones to appear. Had the posts not appeared on the website, Jones never would have sued, and she never would have faced hours of questioning in deposition and at trial about her moral character, sex life, medical history, and other deeply personal information.

This criticism of Section 230 is compelling, but we must consider another key point: without Section 230, the traditional media would have even more power over speech and expression. And those power structures could be even more stacked against the disenfranchised.

Although eliminating Section 230 might result in fewer comments such as TheDirty.com posts about Jones, such a move also could result in a net reduction in free speech for everyone, including communities whose voices are historically underrepresented. Unfortunately, that also results in the protection of speech that some might not value as much. During his testimony in the first trial, Richie said he believes in "freedom of speech" and declared "I'm supposed to be protected under the Communications Decency Act."[39]

As I read the Sixth Circuit's opinion and the hundreds of pages of documents in the case file, I could not help but think of an 1890 *Harvard Law Review* article, "The Right to Privacy." Written by Samuel D. Warren and the future Supreme Court justice Louis D. Brandeis, the article is among the most cited law review pieces in U.S. history, and it has been cited by courts to provide plaintiffs with causes of action to sue for invasion of privacy. In the article, Warren and Brandeis articulate a "right to be let alone." The news media and their new technologies—such as "instantaneous photographs and newspaper enterprise"—threatened this privacy right more than ever before:

> Of the desirability—indeed of the necessity—of some such protection, there can, it is believed, be no doubt. The press is overstepping in every direction the obvious bounds of propriety and of decency. Gossip is no longer the resource of the idle and of the vicious, but has become a trade, which is pursued with industry as well as effrontery. To satisfy a prurient taste the details of sexual relations are spread broadcast in the columns of the daily papers. To occupy the indolent, column upon column is filled with idle gossip, which can only be procured by intrusion upon the domestic circle.[40]

Scholars long have hypothesized that this argument may have grown out of Warren's disgust for invasive coverage of his family's personal affairs, including gossipy newspaper articles about his marriage to the daughter of a U.S. senator. "Indeed, if Samuel D. Warren had not married a United States Senator's daughter, *The Right to Privacy* would very likely never have been written," Amy Gajda concluded after an exhaustive review of newspaper coverage of the Warren family.[41] By modern standards, the coverage of Warren's wedding was not anywhere near as repulsive or shocking as the anonymous rumors about Sarah Jones. But it arose from a similar concern: robust freedom of speech can harm those who are the subjects of that speech, particularly in light of unpredictable new technology. It was true in 1890, and it is true in the Section 230 world.

So do cases like Jones's mean that Section 230 actually reduces freedom of speech, at least for some?

There is no way to provide a precise, quantitative answer to that question, as the modern Internet in the United States always has operated under the protections of Section 230. But just as the Dworkin-MacKinnon view reveals some of the key failings of Section 230, another free speech concept highlights some of Section 230's benefits. That concept is known as "self-help."

In the landmark 1964 case *New York Times v. Sullivan*, the U.S. Supreme Court held that if the plaintiff in a defamation lawsuit is a public official, the First Amendment requires that the public official establish that the defendant made the defamatory statement with actual malice—knowledge of falsity or reckless disregard of the falsity.[42] The actual malice requirement imposed a substantial barrier to many such suits, as proving actual malice is difficult. Three years later, the Supreme Court extended this protection to public figures—people who were in the spotlight but not necessarily "officials." But in 1974, in *Gertz v. Robert Welch,* the court declined to impose the actual malice requirement on private figures. One of its key reasons for this distinction was that private figures do not have access to "self-help," which it defined as "using available opportunities to contradict the lie or correct the error and thereby to minimize its adverse impact on reputation."[43] Justice Lewis Powell noted that not every person has the same access to self-help: "Public officials and public figures usually enjoy significantly greater access to the channels of effective communication and hence have a more realistic opportunity to counteract false statements than private individuals normally enjoy. Private individuals are therefore more vulnerable to injury, and the state interest in protecting them is correspondingly greater."[44]

That remained true for about thirty years after the *Gertz* opinion. Only the powerful had access to the newspaper ink and broadcast airwaves, allowing them to tell their stories. The rest of the United States remained largely voiceless, except those who received the support of an established organization that had power. A citizen who was concerned about congressional corruption could write a letter to the editor but had no power unless the newspaper editor decided to publish it. A customer who was upset about a deceptive car dealer could call the local television station's consumer reporter but could expose the dealer only if the reporter considered the story worthy of an on-air report. Most individuals did not control their self-help; they relied on powerful institutions such as the news media.

That all changed soon after the turn of the twenty-first century. The commercial Internet slowly evolved from merely the electronic version of newspapers and other traditional media to a two-way, interactive experience. The angry citizen could publish opinions about the government in an instant, on a host of online political forums. The disgruntled consumer could write scathing reviews of the car dealer on Yelp, Ripoff Report, or other consumer sites. The Internet became a tool for self-help, and not just to correct defamatory statements—although it certainly allows individuals to do that. It allows anyone with a computer or other device and an Internet connection to have a voice against even the most powerful. Section 230 is a catalyst for this self-help. Without Section 230, platforms might remove users' posts as soon as they receive a complaint, lest they face a company-ending lawsuit. Or they would entirely prohibit automatic posts by their users. The average person would have a much quieter microphone. Or no microphone at all.

Perhaps the most successful example of self-help emerged in the early days of social media but came to international prominence in 2017, as I wrote this book. It is the #MeToo movement.

Activist Tarana Burke worked with a teenage girl at a youth camp in Alabama. The girl was a survivor of sexual abuse, but she was unable to share her story. That led Burke to wonder, "Why couldn't you just say 'me too?' "[45] In 2006 Burke created a "Me Too" page on MySpace, which then was one of the top social media sites in the world. The page served as a forum to encourage women to share their stories. More than a decade later, "Me Too" resurfaced, this time on Twitter. After the *New*

York Times reported in October 2017 about the movie producer Harvey Weinstein's sexual abuse and harassment, actress Alyssa Milano posted on Twitter the following note: "If all the women who have been sexually harassed or assaulted wrote 'Me too' as a status, we might give people a sense of the magnitude of the problem."[46] Within a week, more than 1.7 million tweets included #MeToo as a hashtag.[47] Women around the world shared their personal stories. Some named names. Others described their experiences. But they had a voice. This collective scream was part of a movement that prompted new allegations seemingly every day about male journalists, politicians, corporate executives, and others in power.

I'm not suggesting that Section 230 is single-handedly responsible for the #MeToo movement; that was caused by several factors, including long-standing egregious behavior by predators and harassers, women who had reached a breaking point after years of mistreatment and abuse, media coverage of high-profile cases such as the allegations against Harvey Weinstein, and celebrities such as Milano who encouraged women to speak up. The #MeToo movement was a collective form of self-help. It allowed thousands and thousands of women to have a voice. The most powerful tool of the #MeToo movement was social media. Twitter not only gave women a megaphone; it also amplified those voices into a loud roar that created an entire movement. If Congress had never passed Section 230, the #MeToo movement probably would not have spread so rapidly. Social media sites like Twitter and Facebook would be far more restrictive of user content, and at the very least they would temporarily remove posts after receiving a takedown demand.

When I look at Section 230, I closely examine the individual harm suffered by people like Jones and the many other victims of online bullying, revenge pornography, and other forms of systematic harassment. These stories give me real pause and cause me to question whether Section 230 causes more harm than good. But then I look at the robust and open online discourse about some of the most critical social and political issues. I see once-voiceless people now able to speak truth to power. I doubt that online platforms could be so open without Section 230's broad protections. The ability of an average person to exercise self-help would not be nearly as strong. Unfortunately, the debates about Section 230 tend to focus only on one side. Section 230 either is responsible for every bit of online harassment or it is the most essential free speech law since the First

Amendment. Both are partly true. And an examination of Section 230 requires a clearheaded examination of its weaknesses and strengths. And that story is more complicated.

There is no way to quantify whether the harms to individuals such as Jones outweigh the benefits of Section 230, such as the #MeToo movement. An individual's position on Section 230 depends on how that person prioritizes values such as free speech and privacy. I have a bias toward free speech, and I believe that the self-help that Section 230 enables is worth the risk of facilitating abhorrent behavior, such as the user posts on TheDirty.com. But I understand the compelling argument that the harms to thousands of women like Jones are not worth the additional free speech.

There is not a right answer, but there is a right way to ask the question.

11

KILL. KILL. KILL. KILL.

When protesters, the media, whistleblowers, and others can speak freely, that speech may harm U.S. security interests. The First Amendment prohibits Congress from abridging freedom of speech and of the press, though courts have held that right is not absolute. Congress can—and has—passed laws, for instance, that prohibit the disclosure of classified information or making death threats to U.S. officials. Despite the tension between national security and free speech, U.S. courts generally are loath to abridge free speech unless the national security interests are overwhelming.

Perhaps the most prominent example of this tension was the U.S. Supreme Court's 1971 refusal to prevent the *New York Times* and *Washington Post* from publishing the Pentagon Papers, the classified report that exposed the fatal flaws in the U.S. military strategy in Vietnam. "The word 'security' is a broad, vague generality whose contours should not be invoked to abrogate the fundamental law embodied in the First Amendment," Justice Hugo Black, perhaps the most adamant free speech advocate ever to sit on the Supreme Court, wrote in a concurring statement accompanying the court's opinion. "The guarding of military and diplomatic secrets at the expense of informed representative government provides no real security for our Republic. The Framers of the First Amendment, fully aware of both the need to defend a new nation and the abuses of the English and Colonial governments, sought to give this new society strength and security by providing that freedom of speech, press, religion, and assembly should not be abridged."[1]

And therein lies the tension between security and free speech. Critics of free speech protections are correct that some seek to exploit these protections to harm others, not only through defamation but also by distributing information that harms individuals or the nation as a whole. Yet free speech advocates say that *security* often is a nebulous term, that it offers a pretext for preventing the expression of unpopular ideas. Just as the First Amendment has been at the center of these debates, so too have the free speech protections of Section 230. Terrorists use social media to recruit new followers. The Russians used social media to spread propaganda and fake news during the 2016 presidential election. And Section 230 protects the social media providers from liability for much of this third-party content. So social media companies and other online platforms fail to block these harmful posts, and critics point their fingers at Section 230. By protecting platforms, they argue, the statute reduces the incentive for them to screen proactively for harmful user content.

On June 12, 2015, Lloyd Fields Jr. traveled to Jordan for what was intended to be a two-week work trip. He would not return alive. And Section 230 was at the center of a legal dispute following his death.

Known to his family and friends as Carl, the former Louisiana police officer was a government contractor for DynCorp International, helping to train police officers in the Middle East at the International Police Training Center in Amman.[2] Fields had advised police departments in Iraq and Afghanistan, and he believed the Jordan assignment to be relatively safe; in fact, he did not carry a gun or any other weapon.[3] Among the students at the training center was a twenty-eight-year-old police captain from Jordan, Anwar Abu Zaid. On November 9, 2015, Abu Zaid opened fire in the center, killing five people, including Fields. Soon after the attack, a foundation associated with the terrorist group ISIS, or the so-called Islamic State, issued a statement in which ISIS took responsibility for the murders: "Yes . . . we kill the Americans in Amman. Do not provoke the Muslims more than this, especially recruited and supporters of the Islamic State. The more your aggression against the Muslims, the more our determination and revenge . . . time will turn thousands of supporters of the caliphate on Twitter and others to wolves."[4]

Abu Zaid appeared to be a "lone wolf," like many ISIS-inspired attackers. His brother publicly stated that Abu Zaid had been "very moved" by the ISIS execution of Maaz al-Kassabeh, a Jordanian pilot, earlier that year.[5] After ISIS captured al-Kassabeh, the group went to its Twitter followers for suggestions on al-Kassabeh's execution, with the hashtags #SuggestAWayToKillTheJordanianPilotPig and #WeAllWantToSlaughter Moaz. Soon after those campaigns, ISIS set al-Kassabeh on fire and brutally executed him. ISIS tweeted links to the twenty-two-minute film of his death, titled *Healing the Believers' Chests*.[6] (There is no definitive evidence that Abu Zaid actually viewed the video.)

This murder was not the only time that ISIS used Twitter to carry out its terror. Such propaganda allowed the group to raise money and recruit followers, who would later become attackers. However, there is no public evidence that ISIS used Twitter to recruit Abu Zaid. The group's reliance on Twitter is summarized in a sixty-five-page report from Brookings, in which its authors estimate that between September and December 2014, ISIS supporters used at least forty-six thousand Twitter accounts, most commonly based in Syria or Iraq, and claim that the vast propaganda network could inspire people who were already predisposed to carry out terrorism. "Regardless of where on the spectrum such individuals lie, research indicates that mental illness plays a significant role in lone-actor terrorism," they note, "and ISIS's ultraviolent propaganda provides an unusually high level of stimulation to those who might already be prone to violence."[7]

In 2015 testimony to the Senate Judiciary Committee, then–FBI director James Comey described how ISIS recruits followers. "They are pushing this through Twitter," he said. "So it's no longer the case that someone who is troubled needs to go find this propaganda and this motivation. It buzzes in their pocket. There is a device—almost a devil on their shoulder—all day long, saying 'Kill. Kill. Kill. Kill.' "[8] Once ISIS organizers begin a conversation with a potential recruit, Comey said, they move the discussion to encrypted communications apps, potentially putting their discussions out of the reach of law enforcement and intelligence agencies. "With the widespread horizontal distribution of social media, terrorists can spot, assess, recruit, and radicalize vulnerable individuals of all ages in the United States either to travel or to conduct a homeland attack," he told the House Judiciary Committee in 2016. "As a result, foreign terrorist organizations now have direct access into the United States like never before."[9]

Through 2014, Twitter had touted a largely hands-off approach to terrorist content on its site. The company saw the open platform as essential for free speech. "If you want to create a platform that allows for the freedom of expression for hundreds of millions of people around the world, you really have to take the good with the bad," Biz Stone, a cofounder of Twitter, told CNN in June 2014.[10] Tamara Fields, Carl's widow, apparently was not satisfied with Twitter's position regarding ISIS's use of its platform. Along with the widow of James Damon Creach, another American victim of the Jordan shooting, she sued Twitter in California federal court for violating the federal Anti-Terrorism Act, which allows a victim or the victim's estate to sue if the victim was "injured in his or her person, property, or business by reason of an act of international terrorism."[11] In their lawsuit, Fields and Creach alleged that Twitter's social network constituted "material support" that "has been instrumental to the rise of ISIS and has enabled it to carry out numerous terrorist attacks," including the shooting that killed their husbands.[12]

Twitter quickly moved to dismiss the lawsuit, claiming that the suit arose from user content, and thus Section 230 protected Twitter from the suit. Pat Carome and his colleagues represented Twitter. In their request to dismiss the case, Twitter's lawyers wrote that even if Abu Zaid had been inspired by ISIS to shoot the five people, Twitter was not responsible for the "heinous crime." "Not even the thinnest of reeds connects Twitter to this terrible event, and Twitter's alleged conduct is immune from liability under federal law," they wrote.[13] The plaintiffs argued that their claims did not arise from the actual content of any ISIS tweets but merely from Twitter's provision of accounts to ISIS and supporters. Additionally, they argued that Twitter's direct messaging functions—in which users can send private messages to one another—did not involve making information available to the public, and thus Section 230 did not protect Twitter.[14]

The case was assigned to Judge William Orrick, a former Obama Justice Department official whom Obama had appointed to the San Francisco federal court in 2013. On June 15, 2016, Orrick held a hearing on Twitter's motion to dismiss the lawsuit. Arguing for Twitter was Carome's law firm colleague, Seth P. Waxman, who as U.S. solicitor general in the Clinton administration was the federal government's top lawyer before the U.S. Supreme Court; he has argued before the Supreme Court seventy-five times. This was not just a standard Section 230 motion in a defamation case. This involved the deaths of Americans at the hands of terrorists. It would be a tough defense. Twitter apparently recognized this, bringing in one of the nation's most skilled legal advocates.

But Waxman needed to say only one sentence—introducing himself—before Judge Orrick cut him off and said that he was "inclined" to grant Twitter's motion to dismiss. He made it clear from the start of the hearing that he found neither of the plaintiffs' arguments compelling. Although the plaintiffs argued that the lawsuit was based on Twitter's provision of accounts to ISIS and not the content of the tweets, Orrick had trouble divorcing these claims from the content of the ISIS tweets: "All the allegations seem content based, to me, and that the essence of the complaint seems to be that Twitter permits ISIS to spread its propaganda, raise funds and attract new recruits. It's all content based." Orrick also rejected the plaintiffs' argument that Section 230 did not immunize Twitter for claims stemming from its direct messaging capability: "Just because it's private messaging, I think, doesn't put this beyond the Communications Decency Act's reach."

The plaintiffs' lawyer, Joshua David Arisohn, spent much of the hearing trying to explain why the lawsuit did not treat Twitter as the publisher or speaker of user content. He compared the case to two cases in which the Ninth Circuit found that Section 230 did not apply: Cecilia Barnes's promissory estoppel case against Yahoo for breaking its promise to remove the revenge pornography and Jane Doe's lawsuit against Internet Brands, the owner of ModelMayhem.com, which allegedly failed to warn of the sex predators on its site. Orrick did not seem persuaded. "Don't you see a distinction?" he asked Arisohn. "*Barnes* was a promissory estoppel case. The *Internet Brands* case is a failure to warn case. Don't you see a difference between those cases and yours?"

Recognizing that the judge agreed with him, Waxman said he would not give his "stump speech" but instead described his experience opening a Twitter account the previous weekend. Without posting a single tweet, uploading his picture, or following anyone, Waxman said, he soon received many followers. "I'm not leading, but people are following me on Twitter because of the content that I have posted simply by the act of opening an account," Waxman said.

"Just because of your name?" Orrick asked. "Is that—what is the content that you posted that people were following?"

"I posted, yes, my name," Waxman said. "I mean, I also had to post my email. I had to provide my email address and a telephone number. And Twitter of course doesn't check on whether it is actually really my name or really my email address or really my telephone number. But I mean I'm feeling some pressure to say something. But the point is that the act of opening an account is an act of providing content." Even if simply writing a name does not constitute the publication of content, Waxman said, the decision to grant or block someone from the Twitter platform is a "publishing decision."

"If I decide I have a mimeograph machine—I'm dating myself," Waxman said. "I had a mimeograph machine—"

"That's the last piece of technology that I knew how to operate," Orrick joked.

"I'm not sure I actually ever really did know how to operate it," Waxman said. "But if I send out an announcement saying, 'I have a printing press' or 'I have a mimeograph machine,' and it's either available to anybody who wants to use it or it's available if I decide to let you use it or not, that is a consummate publishing decision, that is who to allow access to the publishing medium or not."

At the end of the hearing, Orrick said that he would issue an opinion fairly soon and that he was "very much inclined" to dismiss the complaint. But he said that he would give the plaintiffs "one more shot" to amend the complaint before permanently dismissing the suit.[15] "As horrific as these deaths were," Orrick wrote in an order two months later, "under the CDA Twitter cannot be treated as a publisher or speaker of ISIS's hateful rhetoric and is not liable under the facts alleged."[16]

The plaintiffs filed another complaint, this time focusing more specifically on Twitter's provision of accounts to ISIS and avoiding generalized claims about content posted by ISIS members or supporters: "For years, Twitter knowingly and recklessly provided ISIS with accounts on its social network. Through this provision of material support, Twitter enabled

ISIS to acquire the resources needed to carry out numerous terrorist at-tacks."[17] Waxman and Carome moved to dismiss the new complaint, and Judge Orrick held a second hearing, on November 9, 2016. Orrick kicked off the second hearing much as he had the first: telling Arisohn that the new complaint suffered from the same flaws as the first. Even with the more detailed allegations, Orrick said, the plaintiffs couldn't get around Section 230. He also questioned whether Twitter caused the shooting. "I feel for your clients," Orrick confessed. "And it's a tragic situation and ISIS is a horrible terrorist group, but that doesn't mean that Twitter was responsible for the death of Mr. Fields or Mr. Creach."[18] Arisohn tried to sway Orrick, but it was clear that the latter was not going to change course. Less than two weeks after the hearing, Orrick issued an opinion dismissing the lawsuit. This time, the plaintiffs did not receive another opportunity to reframe their suit. No matter how the lawyers drafted the complaint, Orrick wrote, Section 230 prohibited the suit against Twitter: "No amount of careful pleading can change the fact that, in substance, plaintiffs aim to hold Twitter liable as a publisher or speaker of ISIS's hateful rhetoric, and that such liability is barred by the CDA." Orrick also concluded that the plaintiffs failed to adequately allege that Twitter caused the harms.[19] The plaintiffs quickly appealed, arguing that Orrick had misinterpreted Section 230. "Deciding whether someone can sign up for a Twitter account is not the same thing as deciding what content can be published," they wrote in their brief to the Ninth Circuit; "handing someone a tool is not the same thing as supervising the use of that tool."[20]

The case was assigned to Ninth Circuit judges Sandra Ikuta and Milan D. Smith Jr. and to Steven McAuliffe, a New Hampshire federal district court judge who heard Ninth Circuit cases by designation. Ikuta is a con-servative judge. She sat on the initial three-judge panel that heard the Roommates.com case and had wanted to provide greater immunity to the website than Kozinski's opinion ultimately did. Smith, who like Ikuta is a Bush appointee, has a reputation as a moderate conservative judge. (Full disclosure: I clerked for Smith from 2011 to 2012. I consider him a friend and mentor. We never discussed this case, which was filed years after I clerked for him.) George H. W. Bush appointed McAuliffe to the New Hampshire court in 1992. At a hearing in December 2017 in the Ninth Circuit's majestic San Francisco courthouse, Arisohn tried to con-vince the three judges that Section 230 did not immunize Twitter. But about a minute into his argument, Smith suggested that allowing users to establish accounts is a "publishing" activity that Section 230 immunizes.

"The question is whether the very establishment of an account and giving somebody a handle is in and of itself a publishing decision," Smith said.

"I don't think it is a publishing decision, because handing someone a tool that can be used to create content is not the same as disseminating content," Arisohn responded. "If you give someone a typewriter, that's not the same thing as saying, well, now you could publish an op-ed piece in my newspaper. These are really separate and distinct activities."

"Do you have any case law that says that?" Smith asked.

"I do think this is an issue of first impression on that, so there aren't really any cases to point to either way on that," Arisohn said. In other words, he had no court opinions to support his narrow reading of Section 230. He was asking the Ninth Circuit to be the first court in the United States to create another barrier to Section 230.

Smith pointed out another flaw in Arisohn's argument: to overcome Section 230, Arisohn had to establish that his clients were not seeking to hold Twitter liable as a content publisher. Yet the gist of his claim was that the harmful ISIS posts caused the shooting.

"Your whole theory doesn't survive if it's tied to content, right?" Smith asked.

Arisohn replied, "Well, we certainly rely on content for purposes of causation. I'm happy to get into that, but the breach of the duty—"

"You have to, because that's your problem," Smith interrupted. "You're hoisted up on your own petard, because if there is no content, then how do you get to the foreseeability? How do you get to the causation?"

Smith and Ikuta continued to press Arisohn for a link between Twitter and the Jordan attack. Twitter, Arisohn said, was "instrumental" in the rise of ISIS by providing a platform for fund-raising and propaganda.

"But then you're getting to content," Smith said. "If you're saying that just establishing the account is enough, then you get to the question that the district judge wrestled with. But once you get to content, then you're saying that Twitter permitted them to put certain content there, then they're a publisher. That's really clear under almost any caselaw."

Waxman's argument went more smoothly, and he faced fewer questions and interruptions. He explained why Section 230 prevented all the claims in the lawsuit.

The judges suggested that they might be able to avoid the Section 230 issue altogether and instead dismiss the lawsuit, because there was no link—or "proximate cause"—between Twitter's conduct and the shooting, Orrick's other reason for dismissal. Rather than simply agreeing with that approach, Waxman took the bold move of urging the judges to issue a binding decision that directly addressed the Section 230 issue. For Twitter, the Ninth Circuit's decision would affect not just the Tamara Fields lawsuit. After she sued Twitter, terrorism victims filed similar suits against Twitter and other social media providers in courts across the country. That might explain why Twitter invested in the services of one of the top appellate litigators in the United States. "This was the very first one of these cases brought against Twitter, Google, or Facebook, but it has generated many, many copycat cases," Waxman told the judges. "It is very important for this court to speak clearly and I think quite emphatically on the Section 230 grounds. Otherwise we are going to be eaten to death by ten thousand duck bites."[21]

The three judges disagreed. Although they ruled in favor of Twitter, they did not do so because of Section 230. Instead, they determined that there was not proximate cause: there was not a sufficient claim that they were injured *by reason of* international terrorism. In an opinion for the unanimous panel, Smith wrote that the statute's "by reason of" requirement means that "a plaintiff must show at least some direct relationship between the injuries that he or she suffered and the defendant's acts." He noted that the plaintiffs failed to plead that Twitter's provision of accounts and direct messaging to ISIS had a "direct relationship" with the deaths.[22] Because the Ninth Circuit affirmed the dismissal based on lack of proximate cause, it did not rule on whether Section 230 immunized Twitter. So as of January 2018, no federal appellate court had ever determined whether social media sites were immune under Section 230 from terrorism injury and death cases. But at least four district courts had ruled that Section 230 immunized them in those claims, and none had ruled that Section 230 did not apply.

Even though Twitter won the case, Smith's opinion represented a potential setback for social media sites. By declining to address Section 230, he left open the possibility that Twitter could have been liable had the plaintiffs established a direct relationship between Twitter's conduct and the deaths. The link between Twitter and the shooting was relatively weak.

But imagine a case in which a terrorist was directly recruited on Twitter. Or if two terrorists used Twitter's direct messaging system to privately communicate. It would be more difficult for Twitter to argue that there was not a direct relationship between the terrorist attack and Twitter. If Twitter could not convince the court on that point, then its only fallback would be Section 230. And the Ninth Circuit declined to tell us whether Section 230 would immunize Twitter.

Lawsuits aren't the only source of pressure for platforms to do a better job in preventing terrorist content. Legislators—who could amend or repeal Section 230 at any time—are increasingly vocal about the failures of social media. In January 2018, just weeks before the Ninth Circuit issued its opinion ruling against Fields, the Senate Commerce Committee held a hearing titled "Terrorism and Social Media: #IsBigTechDoingEnough?" Senators grilled executives from Facebook, YouTube, and Twitter about their efforts to keep ISIS and other groups off their platforms. Although Section 230 was not the primary topic of discussion, lawmakers noted that social media companies faced little regulation. At the hearing, Senator John Thune, the South Dakota Republican who chaired the committee, examined how terrorism and social media are linked. The Orlando nightclub shooter who killed forty-nine and injured fifty-three was reported to be inspired by content he viewed on social media. YouTube hosted hundreds of videos from Al Qaeda recruiter Anwar al-Awlaki. "YouTube, Facebook, and Twitter, among others, help to connect people around the world, give voice to those oppressed by totalitarian regimes, and provide a forum for discussions of every political, social, scientific, and cultural stripe," Thune stated. "These services have thrived online because of the freedom made possible by the uniquely American guarantee of free speech, and by a light touch regulatory policy. But, as is so often the case, enemies of our way of life have sought to take advantage of our freedoms to advance hateful causes."[23]

Although the national security–based criticism of Twitter and other social media platforms has merit, so does the counterargument: social media often is public facing, giving law enforcement and intelligence agencies a clear view into users' communications. Once those communications move to email or private communications, the government must obtain warrants or other legal process. And if the communications are encrypted, the government may be entirely unable to access their contents.

To be sure, none of the large platforms wants to be known as the forum of choice for ISIS and other terrorists. But because Internet companies are immunized for user content, the platforms are free to set their own rules for when to edit or block not only terrorist communications but also other user content that offends or harms general society, such as hate speech and advocacy of violence. Thus an analysis of Section 230's overall efficacy depends, in part, on an evaluation of the steps that platforms are voluntarily taking to moderate such harmful content.

12

MODERATION INC.

Section 230 has rightly earned a reputation as a kind of super–First Amendment, providing remarkably robust online speech protections unseen anywhere else in the world. That is part of the story. But the paradox of Section 230 is that it also encourages online services to moderate user content as they see fit. Chris Cox and Ron Wyden made it clear in the brief text of Section 230. The law states that one of its goals is "to remove disincentives for the development and utilization of blocking and filtering technologies that empower parents to restrict their children's access to objectionable or inappropriate online material."[1] And while the twenty-six words that immunize platforms have received the most public attention, the law contains a less-noted provision that prevents platforms from being liable for "good faith" actions to block "obscene, lewd, lascivious, filthy, excessively violent, harassing, or otherwise objectionable" material.[2]

Indeed, even with Section 230's unprecedented immunity, online platforms have adopted their own policies for user content and put in place innovative procedures and technologies to enforce those policies. But these companies are fallible. Sometimes, the failures to moderate are shocking, and they cause critics to question whether a statute can *both* function as an exceptionalist free speech protection *and* encourage responsible moderation of content.

Like other disputes surrounding Section 230, the criticism of Twitter for allowing ISIS content begs a question: is Section 230 encouraging responsible moderation practices, as Cox and Wyden intended? As with all questions surrounding Section 230, the answer is complicated.

The experiences of Ellen Batzel, Christianne Carafano, Kenneth Zeran, and others are troubling, particularly for those of us who support Section 230. Yet Tamara Fields's lawsuit is among the most agonizing Section 230 cases that I reviewed for this book. Her lawsuit was not about a ruined reputation or invasion of privacy. Her husband died. And she believes that Twitter was responsible.

We'll never know for sure whether ISIS's use of Twitter was directly linked to the shooting in Jordan. Fields's attorneys did not produce sufficient evidence directly linking her husband's shooter to ISIS's Twitter posts. But there is at least a possibility that Twitter played a role in recruiting ISIS's supporters and building the organization's financial resources. As the 2015 Brookings report concluded, ISIS "has exploited social media, most notoriously Twitter, to send its propaganda and messaging out to the world and to draw in people vulnerable to radicalization."[3] Even the most ardent supporters of social media companies must acknowledge that terrorists and other evildoers use the services to spread propaganda and recruit. To deny this is to be willfully ignorant. Experts are more divided, however, about whether social media and the Internet *cause* terrorist radicalization. An extensive literature review on terrorism and Internet use found that "the Internet alone is not a cause of radicalisation, but a facilitator and a catalyser of an individual's trajectory towards violent political acts."[4]

Section 230 typically will bar lawsuits that stem from social media services' alleged failure to edit or delete user posts. That is not a surprising result; in fact, it is a fairly basic application of Section 230. But that alone does not explain whether Section 230 enables terrorists' use of social media. Determining that would require evidence that social media companies avoid moderating such harmful content because they know that they probably will not be liable for it. And such concrete proof would be hard to come by. The best we can do is look at how social media providers and other online platforms currently moderate content and whether they could be doing more. Even that is a tough task, for online platforms do not always publicly disclose all the ways that they moderate content. Based on what the platforms have revealed, it is reasonable to conclude that the companies often could do more to block harmful user content. But that is only part of the story. Online services have received an increasing amount of pressure from the media, consumers, and lawmakers; in response, they have voluntarily adopted content moderation policies and procedures that they believe best serve their users.

For instance, the Brookings report found that in September 2014, after ISIS supporters tweeted pictures and videos of hostage beheadings, Twitter "began to aggressively suspend" ISIS accounts.[5] In February 2016, Twitter announced that since mid-2015, it had suspended more than 125,000 accounts "for threatening or promoting terrorist acts, primarily related to ISIS" and that it hired more employees to manually review potential terrorist accounts. "As an open platform for expression, we have always sought to strike a balance between the enforcement of our own Twitter Rules covering prohibited behaviors, the legitimate needs of law enforcement, and the ability of users to share their views freely—including views that some people may disagree with or find offensive," the company wrote in a blog post.[6] This was a marked shift from the hands-off approach that Twitter cofounder Biz Stone had touted in the CNN interview in 2014.

What had changed in those intervening months? Perhaps it was the torrent of negative publicity that Twitter received, followed by high-profile congressional hearings about terrorists' use of the Internet. Although Twitter is not legally obligated to block or delete ISIS posts, it did so voluntarily. To claim further ignorance would risk ruining the company's reputation with customers—and source of revenues.

Twitter is not the only platform to voluntarily develop standards for user content. Facebook, YouTube, and most other large online services have written user content policies that they believe strike a balance between protecting users' speech and promoting public safety. And these policies go far beyond terrorist content; they prohibit and reserve the right to delete many categories of harmful online content.

In an article that I published in a technology law journal, I found that of the twenty-five most popular U.S. websites, eighteen allowed public user content. All those sites had adopted user content policies that addressed, at minimum, illegal activities, hate speech, harassment, bullying, distribution of personal information, nudity or pornography, and violent content.[7]

Policies may exist, but what do the sites *actually* do to moderate the content? Do they merely have policies on the books, or do they actively enforce those policies? For example, Google's user content policy states that after it receives a notice, it may "review the content and take action, including restricting access to the content, removing the content, refusing to print the content and limiting or terminating a user's access to Google products."[8] In general, platforms have been notoriously tight-lipped about their specific moderation and removal practices. This began to change in 2017 and 2018, as sites faced more criticism for allowing illegal user content. At a conference at Santa Clara University in February 2018, representatives of many of the largest platforms discussed their moderation practices. This was perhaps the most in-depth view that these companies had ever provided into their moderation practices. They shared statistics and specific stories about how they addressed real concerns about harmful or illegal user content.

Google lawyer Nora Puckett explained how Google's moderation team of ten thousand employees worldwide divides tasks to ensure compliance both with local laws and with Google's content policies.[9] The employees who review Google's legal removal requests to delete content have backgrounds in journalism, hard sciences, and other fields and can think critically about Google's legal obligations as well as other interests such as free speech. They can "escalate" particularly difficult problems to lawyers, product specialists, and other experts at Google. The company also has a separate team of moderators who determine whether user content violates Google's content policies, all of which are publicly available on its website.[10]

Companies also are increasingly developing thoughtful moderation procedures to address particularly concerning problems on their platforms. For instance, Pinterest, the social media site, was concerned that its "image-heavy" platform might contribute to eating disorders. So it worked with the National Eating Disorder Association (NEDA) to compile a list of keywords related to the problem. "We limit the search results we show when people seek out content using these queries, and also use these terms as a guide for Pinterest's operational teams to decide if any given piece of self-harm-related content should be removed or hidden from public areas of the service," Adelin Cai, of Pinterest's policy team, wrote in an essay for the conference. "The subject matter experts at NEDA generously agreed to review our list to see if our bar for problematic terms was consistent with their expert knowledge, and they provided us with the feedback we needed to ensure we were aligned. We were relieved to hear that our list was fairly comprehensive, and that our struggle with grey area queries and terms was not unique."[11] Pinterest's approach to a sensitive and serious issue such as eating disorders is not mandated by any particular law; rather, it is the product of a socially responsible platform that is unconstrained by legal requirements and free to develop a creative solution.

Patreon, which provides a platform for creators such as podcast hosts to sell content directly to their fans, in a paper for the conference explained that it sets a "higher bar for moderation." As described by its author, Colin Sullivan, the head of the company's legal section, if Patreon learns of noncompliant user content, it first emails the poster "to establish a line of communication, educate the creator on guidelines that they may not have known about, and give them a sense of agency in dealing with our guidelines."[12] In most cases, the posters agree to a "mutually beneficial outcome" after receiving the email, Sullivan attested. If they cannot, the user's account is suspended, making the page inaccessible to the public and preventing further payment processing. Yet the users still can edit their pages to address the compliance concerns. "By disabling public access to the page we remove the risk the content poses to Patreon, and then allow the creators to control the moderation and removal process," Sullivan explained. "We can be clear with creators what steps they need to take for the suspension to be lifted, but allow the creator to retain their agency."[13] In the most "egregious" situations, Patreon deletes an entire webpage. "Even in these situations, we provide a path forward for the creator by allowing them to create a new page," Sullivan elaborated. "We give the creator a list of their patrons' emails and offer them the opportunity to start fresh. This gives creators the opportunity to create a page within our guidelines, but resets their page and their relationship with patrons."[14] Patreon permanently bans users only in "extreme situations where the creator's past behavior is a permanent risk, such as creators convicted of serious crimes."[15]

Like Pinterest's efforts to combat eating disorders, Patreon's multistep moderation process is the type of nuanced moderation system that Section 230 allows. Patreon recognizes the need to keep its services free of truly objectionable content, but it also provides creators with multiple opportunities to fix problems. This grows out of a recognition that it is best for Patreon's business model to retain as many users as possible. Its procedures preserve open communication and expression, while ridding the site of the truly objectionable and sometimes illegal content.

The Santa Clara conference—and a second moderation conference three months later in Washington, D.C.—began to pull back the curtain on the opaque world of content moderation. Academic research also is beginning to provide transparency, as revealed by Kate Klonick, who conducted interviews and reviewed publicly available information to provide insight into the moderation practices. Klonick described the portion of Facebook's moderation procedures that rely on user reports, stating that each day, Facebook's users identify more than a million pieces of objectionable content. As of 2016, they flagged the content in categories such as "hate speech" or "violence or harmful behavior." This allows Facebook to determine how urgent it is to review content. Then a moderator examines the flagged content, and depending on the difficulty of the issue, the review could be escalated up three "tiers" of moderators. Moderators in the initial tier are in call centers, usually outside the United States in countries such as the Philippines, Ireland, or India. The highest tier are lawyers or policy makers in Facebook's headquarters.[16]

Facebook moderators receive extensive training on the company's content rules, Klonick found. These rules, known as "Abuse Standards," are quite detailed and draw on U.S. free speech legal norms:

> In "Graphic Content," listed violations include any "[p]oaching of animals" as well as "[p]hotos and digital images showing internal organs, bone, muscle, tendons, etc.," while "[c]rushed heads, limbs, etc. are ok as long as no insides are showing." Likewise, "mere depiction" of some types of content— "hate symbols" like swastikas, or depictions of Hitler or Bin Laden—are automatic violations, "unless the caption (or other relevant content) suggests that the user is not promoting, encouraging or glorifying the [symbol]."

Some more complicated types of speech borrow from American jurisprudence for the structure of their rules. Under "Hate Content," a chart provides examples of "Protected Categories" and counsels moderators to mark "content that degrades individuals based on the . . . protected categories" as a violation. A second chart on the page demonstrates how the identification of the type of person—ordinary persons, public figures, law enforcement officers, and heads of state—as well as their membership in a protected group will factor into the permissibility of the content. All credible threats are to be escalated regardless of the "type of person." These examples demonstrate the influence of American jurisprudence on the development of these rules. Reference to "Protected Categories" is similar to the protected classes of the Civil Rights Act of 1964. The distinction between public and private figures is reminiscent of First Amendment, defamation, and invasion of privacy law. The emphasis on credibility of threats harkens to the balance between free speech and criminal law.[17]

Relying on humans to moderate content is costly; they receive paychecks and require their own computers and workspace. Platforms have shifted some of the moderation burden to automated systems that rely on artificial intelligence. Although artificial intelligence has improved, it is not a substitute for human moderation. As Tarleton Gillespie aptly wrote in a 2018 book about platform moderation, *Custodians of the Internet,* artificial intelligence–based moderation is "just not very good yet":

> Automated detection is just not an easy task—arguably it's an impossible one, given that offense depends so critically on both interpretation and context. State-of-the-art detection algorithms have a difficult time discerning offensive content or behavior even when they know precisely what they are looking for, when they can compare an image to a database of known violations or can scan for specific profanities or racial slurs. But detection grows vastly more complicated when platforms are trying to identify whether something is pornography or hate speech, without being able to match it to a corpus of examples.[18]

Even as automated moderation technology and artificial intelligence have improved, purely technical approaches to moderation have their limits. Many platforms are integrating technological developments *and* human review to optimize content moderation. For instance, in 2017

YouTube faced a flood of criticism for allowing users to upload videos containing terrorist propaganda, hate speech, and content harmful to children, and in response to this criticism, YouTube's parent company, Google, announced that it would expand the number of its moderators to more than ten thousand the following year. "Human reviewers remain essential to both removing content and training machine learning systems because human judgment is critical to making contextualized decisions on content," YouTube's chief executive, Susan Wojcicki, wrote in a blog post.[19]

At the January 2018 Senate hearing on social media and terrorism, mentioned in chapter 11, Juniper Downs, YouTube's director of public policy and government relations, told the senators that YouTube uses machine learning to automatically identify extremist videos and supplement the teams of moderators who manually review videos for violating YouTube policies. As of the time of Downs's testimony, machine learning had increased the amount of video removals fivefold. Downs estimated that the algorithms allowed YouTube to remove nearly 70 percent of content that qualifies as "violent extremism" within eight hours after it was uploaded.[20] "We are deeply committed to working with law enforcement, government, others in the tech industry, and the NGO community to protect our services from being exploited by bad actors," she told the senators. "We will only make progress by working together to address these complex issues at their root."[21]

Many of the largest platforms also have been leaders in the fight against child pornography. Because child pornography is a federal crime, it is exempt from Section 230's immunity. But federal law requires platforms to report child pornography to the National Center for Missing and Exploited Children only if the platforms have "actual knowledge" of a user's apparent violation of child pornography laws.[22] The law states that service providers have no obligation to proactively monitor for child pornography.[23] Even so, Microsoft, America Online, and other service providers voluntarily use technology that scans cloud content and emails for known child pornography images.[24] If the companies detect a match, they then have a legal duty to report the images, because they have "actual knowledge." Because the companies face no legal requirements to scan, a hands-off approach might reduce administrative and legal costs for the companies. Yet they do so anyway because it is in their business interests. During a criminal prosecution that relied on evidence detected by AOL, an AOL representative testified that the company scanned partly in response to complaints about "objectionable content" and that AOL "would like to actually keep the members who complain about it and have a countermeasure against those who do it."[25]

Online platforms often react to criticism after their failure to moderate has caused substantial harm. For instance, in September 2017, Facebook acknowledged that Russians had used "inauthentic accounts" to purchase about three thousand advertisements on Facebook in an effort to affect U.S. politics. "We know we have to stay vigilant to keep ahead of people who try to misuse our platform. We believe in protecting the integrity of civic discourse, and require advertisers on our platform to follow both our policies and all applicable laws," Alex Stamos, then Facebook's Chief Security Officer, wrote in a blog post. "We also care deeply about the authenticity of the connections people make on our platform."[26] Yet later that month, the media reported that advertisers could target groups based on topics such as "Ku-Klux-Klan" and "Jew hater."[27] Facebook responded to that report by announcing that it was "removing these self-reported targeting fields until we have the right processes in place to help prevent this issue."[28] In the face of the massive wave of negative publicity, Facebook announced it would add one thousand more advertisement moderators and that it would deploy more machine learning to "better understand when to flag and take down ads."[29]

More than any other time in the history of the Internet, 2017–2018 was the era when online platforms began to take concrete steps to reduce the harm of user content and to add some transparency to the process. They did so not necessarily in response to the fear of company-ending lawsuits but as a reaction to public criticism and consumer demands. When the average customer visits YouTube, he or she wants to see cute cat videos or concert footage, not terrorist propaganda. If YouTube—or any other platform—developed a reputation for hateful or savage user content, a competitor could emerge and steal its customers. So YouTube adjusted its policies and procedures and made significant investments in human and machine review. The increased drumbeat of criticism in the media and halls of Congress certainly also played a role in platforms' unprecedented focus on responsibility.

In May 2018 the organizers of the Santa Clara conference followed up with a packed content moderation conference in Washington, D.C., where platforms continued to explain how they moderated user content at great scale. The companies stressed the need to involve their users in the development of moderation policies. Tal Niv, the vice president of law and policy at the software development platform Github, said that the open source collaboration that its users employ for code sharing extends to its policies: "We have to rely on the governance decisions of our community and not supersede it with our own." Sean McGilvray, director of legal affairs and trust and safety at the video-sharing site Vimeo, said that "to a certain degree, they'll tell us what our platform is."

User empowerment is one of the goals that Chris Cox and Ron Wyden articulated more than twenty years ago when they wrote Section 230. "We want to encourage people like Prodigy, like CompuServe, like America Online, like the new Microsoft network, to do everything possible for us, the customer, to help us control, at the portals of our computer, at the front door of our house, what comes in and what our children see," Cox said during the 1995 congressional floor discussion of the bill that would become Section 230.[30]

The Russian interference, racist ads, ISIS propaganda, and misogynistic rants show that this system is far from perfect; it does not screen every bit of content that might be harmful. And increased moderation is not necessarily in line with security interests. When ISIS and other terrorist groups communicate on social media or other public forums, they provide a window into their operations not only for potential followers but also for law enforcement. If platforms overfilter such content—either voluntarily or because they are legally required to do so—they can disrupt law enforcement or intelligence surveillance operations.

Section 230 also has empowered companies—rather than the government—to act as censors. By preventing legislatures and courts from requiring particular forms of moderation or filtering, Section 230 gave the online service providers a tremendous amount of power: they could choose to block—or allow—whatever speech they considered appropriate for their customers. In her article, Klonick concluded that platforms are the "New Governors" of speech: "These New Governors play an essential new role in freedom of expression. The platforms are the products of a self-regulated and open internet, but they are only as democratic as the democratic culture and democratic participation reflected in them."[31]

Is it better for online speech to be determined by these new governors or by courts and legislators? Neither is perfect, as it concentrates power in the hands of someone other than the speaker. For instance, Alex Jones's Infowars site long received criticism for trafficking in conspiracy theories, such as claiming that the 2012 Sandy Hook Elementary School shooting was a hoax. In August 2018, Facebook, YouTube, and Apple banned much of his content for violations of their policies covering hate speech or harassment, effectively silencing Jones on their platforms.[32] The platforms received praise from those who argue that hate speech and conspiracies harm our democracy, but Jones and his defenders argued that the moves amounted to corporate censorship of conservative views.

On balance, however, platforms—and not the government—are better suited to be the gatekeepers of online speech. A company is responsive to customers. If a platform fails to meet customer demands, it likely will struggle to stay in business. Facebook and Twitter may be among the most popular social media sites in 2018, but they were not the first social media sites. Friendster, MySpace, and others once were dominant, but they failed to maintain their market share. So too would platforms that do not respond to the prevailing customer demand for user content standards. Courts are not as directly responsible to the public. Federal judges are life tenured. If they impose significant liability on a platform for user content, they face little pushback from the platforms' users. And lawmakers are equally ill-suited to make judgments about editorial standards, for they could favor rules that are more likely to help them succeed in elections.

A company's decision to censor content affects only the company's own platform. Let's say that Twitter automatically blocked any tweet that mentioned "ISIS" or "terrorism," in an effort to prevent ISIS from using Twitter to recruit. Such a decision likely would block not only ISIS propaganda but also speech that most would consider legitimate and valuable, such as news reports. But Twitter's decision would not apply to other social media platforms, such as Facebook. They would be free to continue to provide news reports and other legal content. In contrast, a court ruling or statute that restricted user content would apply across the board, preventing customers from choosing the platform that best reflected their expectations. Moderation by platforms is more targeted and does not have the same society-wide chilling effect as government regulation.

More than twenty years after Congress passed Section 230, companies have adopted their own moderation policies and procedures, as Cox and Wyden intended. However, those procedures are far from perfect.

Platforms do not always catch harmful content before it is posted to the public. And that can lead not only to ruined reputations but also to the rise of terrorist groups such as ISIS. As Klonick correctly described them, platforms indeed have become the new governors of online speech. Still, companies' moderation policies require more scrutiny than they have received in the past. As Russians continue to set up fake Twitter accounts and spread propaganda, Twitter could do more to verify the identities of posters and cut down on abuse. Of course, this moderation should not over-censor legitimate speech. But Twitter has a social responsibility to do so.

Section 230 is not a birthright for online platforms. The Constitution does not require Section 230. It is a policy choice that Congress made in 1996 as it sought to balance the need for online innovation, free speech, and responsible content moderation. Section 230 reflects an implicit contract between Congress and the technology community: if online platforms develop responsible and reasonable moderation procedures, Congress will grant them extraordinary legal immunity. Although platforms have taken significant steps to meet their obligations under that social contract, they can and should do more. Technology companies too often forget that one of the main reasons Congress passed Section 230 was to eliminate the *Stratton Oakmont/Cubby* dichotomy that created an incentive for companies to take a completely hands-off approach to user content. Twitter's early response to the criticism of its practices is precisely the type of response that threatens Section 230's future.

One benefit of having the government—rather than private companies— set the rules for the Internet is that the government's rules must be public. Private companies, by contrast, do not face those transparency requirements. This chapter relies heavily on essays and talks from the 2018 content moderation conferences in Santa Clara and Washington, D.C., because they were rare instances of platform transparency about how they actually moderate content. For Section 230 to survive future challenges, platforms must not only improve their moderation practices but also publicly explain how they have done so.

Sen. Ron Wyden is among Internet platforms' greatest allies in Washington. In addition to coauthoring Section 230, he is one of the most ardent proponents of net neutrality and the fiercest opponents of government surveillance. So when he presented opening remarks at the 2018

Santa Clara content moderation conference via prerecorded video, one might have expected it to be a love fest. It was anything but.

In his brief remarks, Wyden took the large platforms to task for allowing Russian trolls to influence the 2016 election. Wyden said he still believed that technology companies—and not the government—were best suited to set the rules for the Internet. But he warned that it is difficult to maintain public faith in online platforms unless they do a better job at moderation. "I've written laws to keep the old rules off your back," Wyden told the audience, which consisted of legal and policy executives at most of the large U.S. platforms. "And I did it under the idea that it was possible for technology leaders to do better. I'm concerned that your employers are now proving me wrong, and time is running out."

Even Jerry Berman, the former head of the Center for Democracy and Technology and one of the key architects of Section 230, now expresses concerns about platforms' lack of responsible moderation. "I'm a big 230 fan," Berman said in 2018, "but I really believe that there is a responsibility by industry to recommit themselves to the Good Samaritan side."[33]

Section 230 is a product of Congress, which is a product of the public. If technology companies fail to show how Section 230 continues to benefit the public (and I believe that it does), then Section 230 will eventually disappear. This became abundantly clear to me in the fall of 2017, during the greatest threat ever to Section 230's existence.

13

Exceptional Exceptions

In early October 2017, I sat at the witness table in an intimidating hearing room in the Rayburn House Office Building. To my right was Chris Cox. We stared across at some of the lions of the House Judiciary Committee, which was holding a subcommittee hearing about Section 230. After Cox discussed the origins and intent of Section 230, I described what I had found as I researched this book. I talked about the unprecedented free speech protections, the massive user content industry, and the growing reluctance of many courts to grant Section 230 immunity. Then I did something that I never thought I would do before I began researching this book. I told Congress that it would be OK to amend Section 230 in a narrow and focused manner, to address a particular problem: online sex trafficking. "Changing Section 230 would not cause the Internet to disappear," I told the members of Congress.

If you've read the first twelve chapters of this book, my testimony might surprise you. I remain convinced that the massive industry, social change, and free speech that we have seen since 1996 would not have been possible without Section 230. Then why would I tell Congress that it could change Section 230? As in many issues emanating from Section 230, to understand my answer, you have to look at the terrible facts of a single court case.

At first glance, Backpage.com was an online classified website that appeared much like Craigslist. Users could post ads for clothing, event tickets, furniture, and other products, as well as services. Until early 2017, Backpage had an "Adult Entertainment" section, and a subcategory, "Escorts," in which people often offered sexual services. A Senate Permanent Investigations Subcommittee report on Backpage found that the platform was the source of more than 80 percent of all U.S. commercial sex advertising revenue.[1]

Commercial sex advertising, however, is a term that is too sanitized. Some advertisements on Backpage were related to sex trafficking. Forced prostitution. According to the Senate report, the National Center for Missing and Exploited Children stated that Backpage was linked to more than 70 percent of the reports it received about suspected child sex trafficking.[2]

Officials had long complained about Backpage's link to forced child prostitution. In a letter to the company, forty-five state attorneys general wrote that they had tracked more than fifty cases over three years in which prosecutors filed charges against people who trafficked or tried to traffic children on Backpage. They wrote of charges against a Massachusetts man who allegedly forced a teenage girl to have sex with men whom he solicited on Backpage. The man charged $100 to $150 an hour, and law enforcement found that he had nineteen thousand dollars in cash.[3] "These cases often involve runaways ensnared by adults seeking to make money by sexually exploiting them," the attorneys general wrote. "In some cases, minors are pictured in advertisements. In others, adults are pictured but minors are substituted at the 'point of sale' in a grossly illegal transaction."[4]

Backpage had assured state officials that it had "strict content policies to prevent illegal activity" and that it removed "inappropriate" content. But the attorneys general argued that Backpage simply was not doing enough: "We believe Backpage.com sets a minimal bar for content review in an effort to temper public condemnation, while ensuring that the revenue spigot provided by prostitution advertising remains intact."[5] They recognized that as a "practical matter," Backpage might not be able to determine whether a sex advertisement featured a minor.[6] The only way to have any certainty that sex advertisements did not promote children was to stop running sex advertisements, they wrote. That is exactly what Craigslist did in September 2010; the Senate investigators wrote in their report that Backpage saw Craigslist's closing of its adult section as an "opportunity." Backpage had briefly increased the number of terms that caused an advertisement to be deleted, but it soon walked back that policy. Rather than blocking an entire advertisement because it appeared to advertise child prostitution, Backpage removed the objectionable content and ran the rest of the ad.[7]

The investigators had obtained an email in which Backpage's chief executive, Carl Ferrer, explained the company's decision: "We are in the process of removing ads and pissing off a lot of users who will migrate elsewhere. I would like to go back to having our moderators remove bad content in a post and then locking the post from being edited."[8] Backpage's new technique, known as "Strip Term From Ad," automatically filtered out a series of prohibited words *before* Backpage.com published the ads rather than blocking the ad altogether. The Senate investigators reported that among the words and phrases that would be filtered from the ads were *lolita, teenage, rape, young, amber alert, little girl, teen, fresh, innocent,* and *school girl*.[9] If an ad contained any of these, Backpage's software would automatically delete them, and a moderator would review the remainder of the ad before publication. But the Senate report concluded that moderators rejected only ads that were "(at most) egregious, literal sex-for-money offers."[10] Rather than deleting or blocking ads, Backpage moderators often focused on further removing words that might attract law enforcement attention. In October 2010, Andrew Padilla, who ran Backpage's content moderation department, emailed an employee with instructions to stop "failing" ads and to start "editing."[11] "As long as your crew is editing and not removing the ad entirely, we shouldn't upset too many users," Padilla explained in the email, with the subject line "your crew can edit," according to the Senate report. "Your crew has permission to edit out text violations and images and then approve the ad." Among the terms that moderators routinely removed: *bang for your buck, all access,* and *yung*.[12]

Adam Padilla, Andrew's brother and a former Backpage moderator, testified in a 2016 deposition that it was understood that even after the removal of objectionable language, the advertiser still was trying to illegally sell sex: "[I]t would be pretty much common knowledge that it's still going to run. So a person is still going to . . . do what they wanted to do, regardless." He agreed that his job was to "sanitize" prostitution ads.[13] Despite the content moderation policies that purported to crack down on illegal ads, the Senate investigators concluded that Backpage "guided its users on how to easily circumvent those measures and post 'clean' ads." For instance, a user who posted a sex ad containing the word *teen* would receive an error prompt: "Sorry, 'teen' is a banned term." The user could then repost the ad without *teen*.[14]

While developing these moderation tools and policies, the investigators concluded, Backpage was "acutely aware that its website facilitates prostitution and child sex trafficking."[15] And executives admonished employees who acknowledged this awareness. For instance, a Backpage moderator placed a note in a user account that had repeatedly violated Backpage's terms. Andrew Padilla wrote to the employee that "leaving notes on our site that imply that we're aware of prostitution, or in any position to define it, is enough to lose your job over." Padilla wrote that the issue was not "open for discussion" and that if the employee disagreed, "you need to find another job."[16] Although Backpage claimed to work with law enforcement and the National Center for Missing and Exploited Children to identify child sex trafficking, the Senate report concluded that Backpage erred on the side of not reporting apparently illegal ads. "Young ads do not get deleted unless they are clearly a child," a Backpage supervisor emailed to moderators.[17]

On the day before the Senate was scheduled to hold a hearing on the report in January 2017, Backpage announced that it would shut down its adult entertainment advertisements section. However, media reports suggest that this did not end sex trafficking on the site. For instance, *Fox News* reported a few months later that the "dating" section of Backpage. com's Manhattan site included ads with phrases such as "2 Girl Special."[18] About six months after the blistering Senate report, the *Washington Post* reported that Backpage had hired a Philippines company to create fake ads on competing sites, with titles such as "Little angel seeks daddy" and then direct responders to actual ads on Backpage.[19] The media reports, combined with the Senate's thorough report, paint a picture of a website that was not a passive conduit for the appalling ads that it hosts. Viewing the reports in the most charitable light, it is clear that Backpage knew that its users were posting sex trafficking ads, yet it failed to take all possible steps to stop them. A more skeptical observer might say that Backpage not only knowingly ran illegal ads but also helped its posters break the law by deleting the suspicious words but allowing the ads to run. Pimps sold children for sex on Backpage.

Pimps sold children for sex on Backpage.

Read that sentence a few times. Let it sink in for a minute. This is radically different from any of the cases discussed earlier in this book. Even sites like TheDirty, which at least implicitly encouraged harmful user posts, did not cause physical harm to anyone, much less children. And while ISIS's use of Twitter helps the terrorist network build support, the link between Twitter and terrorist attacks is far more attenuated than that of Backpage and sex trafficking. Every case in this book carries a troubling set of circumstances, and often the victim of a serious wrong is unable to seek justice. But their stories pale in comparison to those of the Backpage victims.

The federal Trafficking Victims Protection Reauthorization Act (TVPRA) allows sex trafficking victims to sue their traffickers or anyone who "knowingly benefits, financially or by receiving anything of value from participation in a venture which that person knew or should have known" violated the TVPRA's criminal sex trafficking provisions.[20] In 2015 Congress amended the TVPRA to include "advertising" sex trafficking in the list of acts covered by the federal criminal statute. (Federal criminal laws always have been exempt from Section 230 immunity.) Many state trafficking laws provide similar remedies for victims. Based on the public information about Backpage, it seems that the site would be an easy target for such lawsuits. Yet Backpage often has managed to evade liability when sex trafficking victims have filed civil lawsuits in federal court. The reason? Section 230. Although Section 230 explicitly allowed federal prosecutors to bring federal criminal charges against online platforms, that explicit exception does not extend to *civil lawsuits* that are based on a violation of federal criminal law. Backpage's success in these lawsuits brought the once-obscure Section 230 into more national prominence—and criticism—than at any other time in its two-decade history.

The case that drew the most attention to Section 230 was a 2014 lawsuit filed by three anonymous plaintiffs in Boston federal court. The plaintiffs alleged that pimps sold them on Backpage when they were girls. Ropes & Gray, one of the largest law firms in Boston, represented the girls and some of their parents.

The plaintiffs are all over eighteen now; they alleged in their lawsuit that they were fifteen when they were first trafficked on Backpage. To maintain their anonymity, I'll briefly recount their stories, as alleged in their court complaint, using the pseudonyms under which they filed the lawsuit: Jane Doe No. 1, Jane Doe No. 2, and Jane Doe. No. 3. Jane Doe No. 1, like many sex trafficking victims, was a runaway. Her pimp said that by using Backpage rather than other sites, they would "avoid getting caught" and that it was "the most popular with customers," according to the court complaint. "The pimp required Jane Doe No. 1 to 'repost' or 're-fresh' her ads a few times per day," Doe's lawyers wrote in the complaint against Backpage. "This would involve posting an ad again so it would show at the top of the page when new customers visited the 'Escorts' section. Jane Doe No. 1 posted around three ads per day to maximize exposure to customers and maximize her pimp's profits." At one point, he sold her for sex on Backpage on average between ten and twelve times a day. She estimates that over eighteen months, men raped her more than one thousand times.[21]

Jane Doe No. 2 met her pimp after she left a residential program in 2010. She was sold on Backpage to between five and fifteen men a day, for a total of more than nine hundred times between June 2010 and September 2012. The pimp "would typically keep his group of girls in one location for one to seven days, depending on how secure he felt at a particular location, before moving to a new location, where Jane Doe No. 2 would be raped again by those who had seen and responded to her Backpage.com advertisements," according to the complaint. Her pimp told her that he used Backpage because it was "fast," which she believed meant that the site "easily and quickly connected sellers and buyers of sex," her lawyers wrote in the complaint.[22]

Jane Doe No. 3 met her pimps at a friend's house. They took her to an apartment in Boston and advertised her on Backpage (paying the site with a prepaid debit card, which allowed them to mask their identities). The advertisement titles included words such as *playful* and *sweet*. According to the complaint, the advertisements included photos that "omitted or obscured her face, but they displayed her shoulders, legs, buttocks, and/or breasts." She was later raped in a hotel. Her parents learned that their daughter was advertised on Backpage, and they discovered her ads online. They demanded that Backpage take the ads offline, according to the complaint. When Jane Doe No. 3 returned home, they took her to a hospital and enrolled her in outpatient treatment. Yet Jane Doe No. 3's ads remained on Backpage a week after she was raped.[23]

The three victims and their parents sued Backpage and its parent company for violations of the federal sex trafficking law, the Massachusetts sex trafficking law, the Massachusetts consumer protection statute, unauthorized use of the plaintiffs' pictures, and copyright infringement.[24] The complaint focused on Backpage's moderation policies and practices, their lawyers wrote in the complaint, which served to "increase the revenues and market share of Backpage.com, increase the market demand for illegal sex with children, increase the number of child sex trafficking victims that are advertised for sale on Backpage.com, increase the number of times each particular victim is raped or otherwise sexually exploited, and impede law enforcement's ability to find and recover victims."[25] For instance, the complaint alleged, Backpage's software removed metadata from user photos before posting. That metadata included the time and location that the photo was taken. Backpage deleted this data, the plaintiffs alleged, "so that law enforcement cannot track the photo."[26] Perhaps anticipating that Backpage would claim Section 230 immunity, the plaintiffs wrote in the complaint that Section 230 did not apply because the lawsuit stemmed from Backpage's "own course of egregious conduct."[27]

Backpage retained two law firms—Prince Lobel Tye, a Boston firm, and Davis Wright Tremaine, a national firm with expertise in media defense. The company moved to dismiss the case. Because it sought dismissal at an early stage, Backpage had to convince the court that even if every fact in the complaint was true, the plaintiffs still did not have a valid legal claim. Not surprisingly, Backpage's argument relied primarily on Section 230. The lawsuit, Backpage wrote, failed to "distinguish this case from hundreds of others in which individuals claim third-party content posted on websites led to their injury."[28] Section 230's protection of websites for claims arising from third-party content is well-settled, Backpage argued. "Congress made a policy decision to hold websites immune from suits arising from such injuries. Plaintiffs may not like that policy, but they cannot override Section 230, and their claims must be dismissed."[29] To respond to Backpage's motion, the plaintiffs could have made two main arguments. First, they could have argued that their lawsuit did not hold Backpage responsible as the publisher or speaker of the illegal ads; instead, they sued Backpage as an active participant in the sex trafficking. This theory worked for Cecilia Barnes in her lawsuit against Yahoo and for Jane Doe's lawsuit against the owner of ModelMayhem, though their cases are not analogous to the claims against Backpage. Second, they could assert that Section 230 did not apply because Backpage partly developed illegal ads, and therefore the ads were not from "another information content provider." This is the argument that succeeded in the cases against Roommates.com and Accusearch.

The plaintiffs relied on the first argument. In a footnote in its response brief, the lawyers wrote that determining whether Backpage was an "information content provider" is a "fact-based inquiry" that first required discovery.[30] The Senate report and the *Washington Post* story about Backpage were not yet published, so the plaintiffs did not have the benefit of those facts to support a claim that Backpage helped create the ads. Other Backpage opponents appeared to disagree with this strategy. A coalition of six local governments, led by San Francisco, filed an amicus brief in support of the plaintiffs and argued that Backpage was an information content provider, as the Ninth Circuit did in its ruling against Roommates.com. "Backpage is an information content provider because it develops the content of illegal escort ads and adopts business practices that themselves convey information about the illegal nature of the Escorts marketplace," the local governments wrote.[31]

What matters most to a court, however, are the arguments that the *parties* make. And the plaintiffs chose not to argue that Backpage created the ads. So to avoid dismissal, the plaintiffs needed to convince a judge that it wasn't trying to hold Backpage accountable as a speaker or publisher. That was a tough task, as the lawsuit stemmed from sex ads that Backpage published on its site. And a Missouri federal judge had dismissed a similar lawsuit against Backpage in 2011, finding that he could not hold Backpage liable for a victim's "horrific" ordeal because "it nonetheless is a matter Congress has spoken on and is for Congress, not this Court, to revisit."[32]

If the lawsuit was not an attempt to hold Backpage responsible as a publisher, then what was it doing? According to the plaintiffs, the suit targeted Backpage's business conduct and not the precise content of the ads. Backpage would have violated the anti-trafficking laws even if it never posted the ads, the plaintiffs' lawyers wrote in the opposition brief. They acknowledged that "content is one link in the chain" connecting Backpage's actions and the harms that the girls suffered, but cautioned that this did not necessarily mean that the suit treated Backpage as a publisher or speaker: "To hold otherwise allows the presence of any third-party speech to insulate online service providers from liability for unlawful conduct that is separate from and independent of that speech."[33] Under the harsh simplicity of Section 230 judicial precedent, the outcome of this tragic and important case would turn on a technical legal question: did the lawsuit seek to hold Backpage responsible as a publisher or speaker of third-party content? Judge Richard G. Stearns, who had served on the Boston federal court since 1993, held a hearing to help him answer that question on April 15, 2015. "They contend their claims are wholly independent of the ads about them, and they say they would survive even if the ads had never been posted," James C. Grant, a Davis Wright Tremaine lawyer representing Backpage, told Judge Stearns. "So fundamentally, this is a generic and general attack on Backpage.com itself, on the entire website." But that argument required the plaintiffs also to "divorce their claims" from any of the ads' content, he said. That would make it impossible for them to show that Backpage caused them any harm. "You can't simply say that, 'A website exists, therefore I was harmed, and therefore, I am going to sue.'"

Sterns asked whether Europe had an equivalent of Section 230. It did not, Grant replied. He noted that in 2010, Congress passed the SPEECH Act, the law that prohibits U.S. courts from enforcing defamation judgments issued by foreign courts if those judgments are inconsistent with Section 230. "Congress has reiterated that our standard is, you cannot hold someone liable for third-party content posted on the Internet," Grant said. "In Europe, that is not always true." Judge Stearns had few other questions for Grant or the other lawyers representing Backpage.

John Montgomery, the Ropes & Gray lawyer representing the Jane Doe plaintiffs, faced more aggressive questioning. Grant's argument, Montgomery said, misinterpreted Section 230. "We think that it reflects a strategy to use Section 230 as a sword to affirmatively protect illegal conduct, rather than the shield that was intended by Congress," Montgomery stated.

"I understand you have a different view of 230," Stearns said, "but it is hard to find a court, of the many who have heard these cases, that agrees with that interpretation."

Montgomery said that Section 230 cases typically involved defamation or similar sorts of cases. His clients' lawsuit, he said, was more like Cecilia Barnes's claim: it involved conduct that was separate from the publication of speech. Judge Stearns seemed unconvinced that the lawsuit treated Backpage as anything other than a speaker or publisher. He shifted to the argument that the plaintiffs chose not to make, and he asked whether Backpage was an information content provider.

"I need to be careful here," Montgomery responded. "We believe that Backpage is a content provider, but it is not an aspect of the case upon which we are defending this motion to dismiss. We think the respects in which they are a content provider is something that ought to be developed on a full record." But Stearns could reject the Section 230 defense, Montgomery said, because the lawsuit did not hold Backpage responsible as the publisher or speaker. Backpage accepted "untraceable payment methods" such as Bitcoin and removed metadata from images so that police could not trace the location of the photo, he said. He accused Backpage of attempts to "thwart the interests of law enforcement." Backpage's overall business strategy, Montgomery added, has allowed the company to go "from a bit player in the online sex business to the gorilla of the online sex business."[34]

Despite Montgomery's best efforts, he could not persuade Stearns to allow the case to move forward. A month after the hearing, Stearns issued an opinion in which he concluded that Section 230 barred the sex trafficking and unfair business practice claims, and he dismissed the lawsuit. (He dismissed the intellectual property claims on other grounds.) Stearns emphasized his sympathy for the three plaintiffs and acknowledged that sex traffickers, drug dealers, and other criminals took full advantage of the Internet. Like many judges before him, Stearns strongly implied his disagreement with Congress's decision to pass Section 230. And like all these judges, he had no choice but to follow its harsh rule: "Whether one agrees with its stated policy or not (a policy driven not simply by economic concerns, but also by technological and constitutional considerations), Congress has made the determination that the balance between suppression of trafficking and freedom of expression should be struck in favor of the latter in so far as the Internet is concerned. Putting aside the moral judgment that one might pass on Backpage's business practices, this court has no choice but to adhere to the law that Congress has seen fit to enact." Stearns also rejected the local governments' argument that Backpage developed the third-party content, and the plaintiffs' argument that some of their civil claims were exempt from Section 230 because they incorporated standards from federal criminal law.[35]

The plaintiffs appealed. Because Stearns hears cases in Boston, the appeal went to the U.S. Court of Appeals for the First Circuit, which hears appeals from federal courts in Maine, Massachusetts, New Hampshire, Puerto Rico, and Rhode Island. With only six full-time active judges and three senior judges, the First Circuit is among the smallest appeals courts in the nation. The First Circuit had issued only one published opinion interpreting Section 230, and that 2007 case involved a straightforward defamation claim against an online message board. Unlike the much larger Ninth Circuit—home to some of the largest technology companies—the First Circuit had not yet interpreted many key provisions of Section 230. The First Circuit is bound by only its rulings and those of the Supreme Court, so it was free to adopt or reject any of the Ninth Circuit's readings of Section 230.

The three judges assigned to the case were David Barron, a former journalist and Harvard law professor appointed by President Obama; Bruce Selya, a senior First Circuit judge appointed by President Reagan; and retired U.S. Supreme Court justice David Souter, who grew up in Massachusetts and New Hampshire and often hears cases for the First Circuit. (Federal law allows retired Supreme Court justices to volunteer to hear appeals in circuit courts.) The judges heard oral argument in Boston in January 2016, and less than two months later, they unanimously voted to affirm Judge Stearns's dismissal. Like Stearns and many other judges who have granted Section 230 immunity to unsympathetic websites, the First Circuit judges seemed uncomfortable with the outcome of their ruling. Writing for the three judges, Selya declared in the opinion's first sentence that the lawsuit was a "hard case—hard not in the sense that the legal issues defy resolution, but hard in the sense that the law requires that we, like the court below, deny relief to plaintiffs whose circumstances evoke outrage."[36]

Yet like Stearns and so many judges before him, Selya acknowledged that he was bound by Section 230 and the court rulings that interpreted it broadly. The plaintiffs and their supporters had made a "persuasive" case that Backpage structured its site to enable sex trafficking, he noted. "But Congress did not sound an uncertain trumpet when it enacted the CDA, and it chose to grant broad protections to internet publishers," Selya went on. "Showing that a website operates through a meretricious business model is not enough to strip away those protections. If the evils that the appellants have identified are deemed to outweigh the First Amendment values that drive the CDA, the remedy is through legislation, not through litigation."[37]

In a footnote, Selya observed that the plaintiffs did not argue that Backpage developed the illegal ads. Some amicus briefs in support of the plaintiffs had made that argument, but Selya asserted that it was "clear beyond hope of contradiction that amici cannot interject into a case issues which the litigants, whatever their reasons might be, have chosen to ignore."[38] So the primary issue before the First Circuit was whether the lawsuit sought to hold Backpage responsible as a publisher or speaker. And Selya concluded that it did, so Section 230 shielded Backpage from any liability. "In this case, third-party content is like Banquo's ghost: it appears as an essential component of each and all of the appellants' TVPRA claims," he wrote. "Because the appellants' claims under the TVPRA necessarily treat Backpage as the publisher or speaker of content supplied by third parties, the district court did not err in dismissing those claims."[39]

The plaintiffs filed a petition to the Supreme Court, requesting a review of the decision. This received significant attention in the legal community because the Supreme Court had never interpreted Section 230. The Supreme Court is not bound by the rulings of any other federal court. So it could swiftly disregard the Fourth Circuit's interpretation in the *Zeran* case and adopt the far more limited interpretation of Section 230 that Leo Kayser advocated twenty years earlier. Other plaintiffs had attempted to get the Supreme Court to review their Section 230 losses, but all had failed. However, these plaintiffs had a particularly tragic story, and Backpage was an unsympathetic defendant. Nevertheless, in January 2017, the Supreme Court declined to take the case. That left the long line of cases based on *Zeran* untouched, and the Supreme Court's refusal to hear such a traffic case indicates that it might not be inclined to rule on Section 230 in the future. And it meant that the three Jane Does' lawsuits had come to an end.

Based on the information from the Senate investigative report, Backpage should not have received Section 230 immunity. Unfortunately for the victims, the Senate released its report after they filed their lawsuit, so the report was not part of the court record.

I believe there is another reason that Backpage managed to win this case. The plaintiffs' lawyers did not present the strongest possible defense of their lawsuit. They focused exclusively on the argument that their complaint was not treating Backpage like the publisher or speaker of third-party content. Of course it did. The entire lawsuit stemmed from ads that pimps posted on Backpage. That is quintessentially the *publication* of content. This simply was not like Cecilia Barnes's case, which arose from a promise that a Yahoo employee allegedly had made to her but failed to keep. As judges and the plaintiffs' supporters hinted throughout the case, the plaintiffs would have had a stronger argument that Backpage *contributed* to the content. Yet their lawyers said that they wanted to get more facts in the discovery process before making that argument.

Backpage continued to avoid liability in other venues. In 2017 a California state court judge dismissed sex trafficking charges against Backpage's CEO, Carl Ferrer, and its former controlling shareholders, Michael Lacey and James Larkin, though it did not dismiss money laundering charges.[40] Media reports had stated that the U.S. Justice Department was criminally investigating Lacey and Larkin under a 2015 federal criminal sex trafficking law, but by 2017, a grand jury had not issued any indictments.[41]

The public attention to Backpage continued to build. Months earlier, a documentary, *I Am Jane Doe,* was released. Narrated by Oscar nominee Jessica Chastain, it told the tragic stories of sex trafficking victims who had sued Backpage but had their cases dismissed because of Section 230. Suddenly, Section 230 was in the national spotlight more than it had ever been in its two-decade history. Responding to Backpage's ability to avoid criminal and civil liability, in 2017 members of Congress introduced bills in both the House and the Senate to create exceptions to Section 230 that would allow states to prosecute websites for sex trafficking and permit victims to sue. The House bill, as first introduced by Missouri Republican Representative Ann Wagner, would create a Section 230 exception to allow civil actions against websites under any federal or state law that provided causes of action for child sexual exploitation, child sex trafficking, or sex trafficking by "force, threats of force, fraud, or coercion" and also would allow criminal prosecution under such state laws.[42] The Senate bill, as first introduced by Senator Rob Portman, an Ohio Republican, was a bit narrower: it would create an exception to Section 230 to allow civil lawsuits against platforms only under the TVPRA and allow state prosecution or civil enforcement action for violation of federal sex trafficking laws.[43] Portman was quoted in a press release when he introduced the bill: "For too long, courts around the country have ruled that Backpage can continue to facilitate illegal sex trafficking online with no repercussions." He declared that "the Communications Decency Act is a well-intentioned law, but it was never intended to help protect sex traffickers who prey on the most innocent and vulnerable among us."[44] More than any time in the history of Section 230, it looked like Congress had the political will to amend the law.

The bills came at a tough political moment for platforms. Large technology companies—long the darling of lawmakers for their job creation and innovation—also had fallen out of favor with many members of Congress. They criticized Facebook for allowing Russians to run fake ads to influence the 2016 presidential election. They criticized YouTube for allowing terrorist propaganda videos to remain on the site. They criticized Twitter for failing to block hate speech. The long-standing goodwill toward technology platforms in Washington was running out. Quickly. And it's tough for a member of Congress to oppose a bill that cracks down on selling children for prostitution. So the bills became one of the few areas where members of both parties agreed. Portman's bill had more than sixty co-sponsors in the Senate. Nearly half the members of the House co-sponsored Wagner's bill.

The Senate Commerce Committee held a hearing on Portman's bill in September 2017, and it would set the stage for the rest of the debate over Section 230 and sex trafficking. The scheduled witnesses were California attorney general Xavier Becerra, who had attempted to prosecute Backpage under sex trafficking laws but was blocked by Section 230; Yiota Souras, the general counsel of the National Center for Missing and Exploited Children; Abigail Slater, the general counsel of the Internet Association, a trade group for large online platforms; and Eric Goldman, a Santa Clara University law professor and one of the foremost experts on Section 230. But before any of them spoke, the committee heard testimony from Yvonne Ambrose. She told the story of her daughter, Desiree Robinson, a sixteen-year-old high school student who had aspired to be an air force doctor. Desiree met a man on social media who sold her for sex on Backpage. On Christmas Eve 2016, a man raped and murdered Desiree. "The truth is Backpage.com and other sites are making millions of dollars by exploiting our children and allowing them to be taken advantage of by predators," Ambrose, in tears, told the senators.

The panelists then debated the technicalities of the Senate proposal. But it was difficult for observers to care much about the precise wording of a Section 230 exception after hearing Ambrose. Slater, the Internet Association general counsel, began her statement by conveying her "sympathy" to Ambrose but proceeded to spend much of her time distinguishing "legitimate Internet companies" from Backpage. Portman's proposal, she said, created "legal uncertainty and risk for legitimate actors." Slater raised valid points. But her concerns about the potential for "frivolous lawsuits" fell flat after Ambrose's powerful testimony.

Online platforms are not new to Washington. They had engaged in a decade-long fight with telecommunications carriers over "net neutrality," a prohibition on carriers' charging websites more money for prioritized access. And some platforms challenge the federal government's ability to monitor their customers' communications. To make their case, they often use apocalyptic language and rely a bit on Internet exceptionalism. Their arguments are typically along the lines of "If (insert whatever opponent wants) happens, the Internet as we know it will end. And (opponent) is greedy." That works well for issues like net neutrality—it's hard to have much sympathy for Comcast or AT&T. But the approach does not work well when the opponents are sex trafficking victims, minors who were sold for sex, families of children who were murdered. Consider the statement that the Internet Association chief executive Michael Beckerman released in response to Portman's introduction of his sex trafficking proposal. After recognizing that sex trafficking was "abhorrent and illegal," he cautioned that the bill was "overly broad" and "counterproductive": "While not the intention of the bill, it would create a new wave of frivolous and unpredictable actions against legitimate companies rather than addressing underlying criminal behavior."[45]

Such a statement might be appropriate for, say, data security legislation. But this is about children being raped and murdered. Not about greedy plaintiffs' lawyers. If a child was sold for sex on a website and that child sues the website, that is not a "frivolous" lawsuit. This isn't a lawsuit over a fender bender or a slip-and-fall accident in a grocery store.

Completely tone-deaf.

I understood—and agreed with—many of the concerns that the technology industry raised about the bills. Some of the proposals would allow lawsuits and state criminal prosecutions of websites that carried sex trafficking ads regardless of whether they intended to do so. Such a system might discourage platforms from allowing users to freely post, out of fear that they could be held liable. Even the bills that applied only to "knowingly" running sex trafficking ads were imprecise, as courts might interpret "knowingly" to mean not only that the site actually knew but also that it should have known. Further, the bills risked exposing platforms to a patchwork of legal requirements by subjecting the platforms to state laws regarding sex trafficking. Imagine if one state required websites to block ads with particular terms that are associated with sex trafficking, another state required sites to block ads based on a different list of keywords, and a third state allowed websites to run those ads but required the sites to report the ads to law enforcement to enable stings. Compliance with these requirements would be burdensome, particularly for small start-ups that were trying to become the next Facebook or Twitter. Depending on how the bills were written, companies might face liability for user content at the moment that it was posted, even if they had no reason to know of the posting. Platforms might respond by overmoderating legitimate speech or by blocking user-generated content altogether. Such responses could reduce the available venues for speech.

In addition, I worried that no matter what bill Congress passed to hold platforms accountable, online sex trafficking would continue on a part of the Internet known as the "dark web." The dark web is a loosely defined network of hidden platforms, and their users employ technology to mask their locations and identities and encrypt their communications to hide them from law enforcement. The dark web is a haven for terrorism, drug sales, sex trafficking, and other heinous crimes. Even if public sites such as Backpage were shut down, I have no doubt that the pimps would continue to shift to the darker corners of the web. But I was appalled by the technology companies' general approach to the issue. Other than beginning their statements with the obligatory affirmation that they opposed sex trafficking (not exactly a profile in courage) and that the lawmakers were well-intentioned, they immediately explained why the proposals were bad. They did not provide viable alternative solutions that would allow states to prosecute and victims to sue the websites that knew about, encouraged, or even participated in the sale of children for sex.

When I was invited to testify at the October 2017 House Judiciary Committee hearing about sex trafficking and Section 230, I wasn't sure exactly what I would say. But I knew what I wouldn't say. I would not approach the problem the same way that the technology companies did. I would not trivialize the concerns of victims and their families, nor would I merely criticize legislative solutions without offering concrete alternatives.

Chris Cox was the first to testify at the hearing. He was testifying not only as Section 230's coauthor but also as outside counsel to NetChoice, a technology industry association that opposed proposals to create exceptions to Section 230. Cox's five-minute oral statement focused primarily on the social benefits of Section 230. He brought up Wikipedia, for instance, which is operated by a small nonprofit despite its high visibility: "If it were subject to lawsuits for the contributions and comments of its volunteers and its users, it couldn't sustain itself, and it would cease to exist as a valuable, free resource for every American." Creating a Section 230 exception for sex trafficking, he claimed, would contradict the principles that led to Section 230's passage, and it might make it harder to bring prosecutions involving other sorts of illegal content. Congress did not intend to immunize websites that were even partly responsible for content creation, he said. In his written testimony for the hearing, Cox proposed that Congress enact a concurrent resolution "restating the clear intent of Section 230, and reemphasizing the plain meaning of its language that denies protection to internet platforms even partly complicit in the creation or development of illegal content."[46]

I testified after Cox. It felt surreal to speak about a law that the previous witness had written when I was in high school. And it felt even more surreal to present a somewhat different take on Section 230.

I explained the history of Section 230, and I told the committee that the twenty-six words in the statute were responsible for creating the Internet that we know today. I told the committee that Backpage never should have received Section 230 immunity. But I also recognized that we can't wait for the courts to get it right. "Our legal system must have strong criminal penalties and civil remedies to deter not only the act of sex trafficking, but also the knowing advertisement of sex trafficking by online platforms. Period," I told the committee. "I hope that Congress agrees on a solution that imposes severe penalties on bad actors—and we need to be clear, there are some very bad actors—without chilling legal online speech." I urged the members to draft a sex trafficking exception to Section 230 that applied a uniform nationwide standard, rather than subjecting platforms to fifty different state laws. And I encouraged them to apply the exception only to websites that had actual knowledge of sex trafficking ads.

I agree with Cox that some courts have misread Section 230 and immunized sites that played a role in content development. But the sex trafficking problem is so urgent and heartbreaking that we cannot wait years for the courts to get it right. This was not a theoretical technology policy debate involving economic studies and policy papers. This was a tragic issue that demanded immediate attention. I understand the criticism that if Congress were to create a sex trafficking exception to Section 230, that would set the precedent for additional exceptions: terrorist propaganda, revenge pornography, and so on. After a while, Section 230 would look like a piece of Swiss cheese and would provide little certainty for platforms. I share those concerns, but I believe they can best be addressed by narrowly tailoring the exceptions to the harms. So, for instance, rather than exposing platforms to any state civil law regarding "sex trafficking," Congress could create a Section 230 exception that mandated a single nationwide standard that applied to intentionally carrying sex trafficking ads. It would not apply to legitimate sites like large social media companies, but it arguably would apply to the truly bad actors. A focused exception would address the problem while preserving the core of Section 230's benefits to innovation and free speech.

In the months after the hearing, a number of hybrid versions of the House and Senate bills circulated, gained momentum, and stalled, until February 27, 2018, when the House passed a revised version of Wagner's bill in a 388–25 vote. Less than a month later, the Senate passed the bill in a 97–2 vote, with only Wyden and Kentucky Republican Rand Paul voting against it. President Trump signed the bill on April 11, 2018.

The final law is clearly the product of a number of compromises and changes, and the version that was signed is far more complex and burdensome than it needed to be. The bill, as passed, begins with a statement that Section 230 was "never intended to provide legal protection to websites that unlawfully promote and facilitate prostitution and websites that facilitate traffickers in advertising the sale of unlawful sex acts with sex trafficking victims."[47] This is perhaps the most straightforward—and least objectionable—part of the law.

The new law adds a new federal crime to the Mann Act, prohibiting interactive computer services from operating their services, conspiring, or attempting to conspire "with the intent to promote or facilitate the prostitution of another person."[48] The federal crime carries up to ten years in prison and a fine. The law also creates an aggravated offense, punishable by up to twenty-five years in prison, if the defendant promoted or facilitated the prostitution of five or more people or acted in "reckless disregard of the fact that such conduct contributed to sex trafficking."[49] Victims of the aggravated violation "may recover damages and reasonable attorneys' fees" in federal court, although the new law does not explicitly create an exemption from Section 230 for such civil recovery. The new law's most significant changes involve the TVPRA. The TVPRA allows federal criminal prosecutions of and lawsuits against someone who "knowingly benefits, financially or by receiving anything of value from participation in a venture which that person knew or should have known" violated federal criminal sex trafficking laws. The new law amends the federal TVPRA to define "participation in a venture" as "knowingly assisting, supporting, or facilitating a violation" of the TVPRA provision that prohibits advertising a person for sale. The law then clarifies that Section 230 does not immunize defendants from civil claims under the federal TVPRA, nor does it prohibit "any charge in a criminal prosecution brought under State law if the conduct underlying the charge would constitute a violation" of the Mann Act and the TVPRA provisions.[50]

The new law presents a number of important questions. What does it mean to knowingly assist, support, or facilitate a TVPRA violation? Would a classified advertising website need to have actual knowledge of a specific sex trafficking advertisement? Or would general awareness of the use of the site by sex traffickers be sufficient? The answers are not clear, but a rational platform would err on the side of caution, lest it risks facing civil lawsuits and prosecutions in every jurisdiction in the United States.

The impact was immediate. Two days after the Senate passed the bill, Craigslist entirely shut down its online personals site. "Any tool or service can be misused," Craigslist wrote in a message to users. "We can't take such risk without jeopardizing all our other services, so we are regretfully taking craigslist personals offline. Hopefully we can bring them back some day. To the millions of spouses, partners, and couples who met through craigslist, we wish you every happiness!"[51]

What impact, however, did the new law have on Backpage? None. On April 6, 2018, just five days *before* President Trump signed the bill into law, the FBI seized and shut down Backpage. Seven people associated with Backpage, including cofounders Michael Lacey and James Larkin, were indicted.[52] Again, this was *before* the new bill was signed into law, as the charges were permitted under the exception for federal criminal prosecutions that always has been part of Section 230. The former Backpage CEO Carl Ferrer pleaded guilty to conspiracy to facilitate prostitution and money laundering in three state courts on the day after the new bill was signed.[53]

But won't the new law help victims of sex trafficking bring civil lawsuits against online platforms that contributed to their exploitation? Perhaps, though a court ruling that was issued just days before the bill was signed into law suggests that such claims already were possible, if argued correctly. The law firm that represented the three "Jane Doe" victims who lost in the First Circuit in 2016 had filed a new case against Backpage, its CEO, and owners. This time, the lawyers argued that Backpage helped to develop the illegal ads. Backpage again moved to dismiss the lawsuit. On March 29, 2018, Judge Leo T. Sorokin dismissed the claims of two of the plaintiffs, but he allowed one of the plaintiff's claims to proceed. Her claim was different, Sorokin reasoned, because the complaint alleged that Backpage "redrafted the advertisement to suggest Jane Doe No. 3 was an adult."[54] Had the plaintiffs' lawyers presented such arguments in the first lawsuit, the First Circuit may never have issued its controversial ruling, and Congress may never have amended Section 230. It is impossible to predict with any degree of certainty exactly how this new exception will affect the Internet and whether its impacts will be limited to online personal ads, or have a broader reach.

Ultimately, the exception to Section 230 is not what I had hoped for when I testified in Congress. I continue to believe that Congress would not have done significant harm to online speech had it passed a law that narrowly targeted platforms that have actual knowledge of specific sex trafficking on their sites yet continue to encourage the behavior. But the bill that was signed into law is ambiguous and overbroad and leaves well-intentioned platforms with the choice of censoring legitimate speech or risking lawsuits and criminal prosecution. Santa Clara University law professor Eric Goldman, who closely followed the various bills on his blog, dubbed the final law the "Worst of Both Worlds" and was particularly concerned about the liability for platforms for "knowingly assisting, supporting, or facilitating" sex trafficking. "As a result, liability based on knowledge pushes Internet companies to adopt one of two extreme positions: moderate all content perfectly, and accept the legal risk for any errors; or don't moderate content at all as a way of negating 'knowledge,'" he wrote. "The Moderator's Dilemma is bad news because it encourages Internet companies to dial-down their content moderation efforts, potentially increasing the quantity of 'bad' content online—including, counter-productively, the quantity of now-unmoderated sex trafficking promotions."[55] An even more dangerous impact of the sex trafficking debate is that it has set a precedent for amending Section 230 to address a particular problem. Although such amendments may not necessarily destroy online free speech, they could gradually erode the ability of platforms to allow unfettered third-party content.

CONCLUSION

Are you out there? Can you hear this?
—DAR WILLIAMS

I wrote this book to document the history of Section 230 and how it shaped the Internet that we know today. By writing the biography of the statute, I sought to tell the broader story of Americans' relationship with free online speech. This history is necessary to inform the debate about the future of Section 230—and the future of the Internet. Beyond looking at how Section 230 has shaped the Internet we know today, I have examined the consequences of the law's broad immunity. Whether Section 230 is "good" or "bad" hinges largely on an individual's personal preferences and life experiences. So I cannot tell others whether their stances on Section 230 are correct. The best I can do is explain how I arrived at my opinion on Section 230 and describe how that opinion has evolved.

I was born in 1978, making me a few years too young for Generation X but a few years too old for the millennial generation. *Slate* magazine referred to my in-between generation as "Generation Catalano," named after Jordan Catalano, Jared Leto's character on *My So-Called Life*, a broody teenage drama from 1994. My generation has a unique relationship with the Internet—Generation Catalano was born into an Internet-free world, yet by our late teens and early twenties, many of us were online nonstop. By our late twenties, we had BlackBerries, and then iPhones.

I grew up in East Brunswick, New Jersey, an unremarkable suburb between New York City and Philadelphia that lacked a town square or much of an identity. As with most suburban teenagers at that time, my media diet consisted of a few dozen cable television channels, VHS rentals, and top-40 radio stations. On one clear night in the early 1990s, I tried to tune my FM radio to Z100, the most popular of the popular music stations. But my dial was off by a few stations, and I ended up at 99.5 instead. I was in a new world: WBAI. The far-left affiliate of the nonprofit Pacifica network caused me to question everything that I had learned in school and on the news. Was Bill Clinton a secret Republican? Did the U.S. government conspire to spread diseases in impoverished nations? Why should we celebrate Thanksgiving, which marks the misappropriation of a culture? WBAI's hosts raised many existential questions and fundamentally changed how I viewed the world—even though, in hindsight, many of those questions were off base and unnecessarily conspiratorial. WBAI was unpolished, and that drew me to it. The hosts stammered over their words and took minutes or hours to get to their points—something you would not see on the *CBS Evening News*. They invited people from all over the New York area to call in and share their own fringe views. While living in a bland suburb, I finally felt like I was in a community. It was the first time I experienced receiving information from actual people, not from large companies.

I had used computers in grade school to learn how to type and program in BASIC. But those computers were not connected to any other computers. To type my school papers at home, I used a word processor—a glorified typewriter that displayed a few lines of text on a black-and-white screen. The father of a middle school friend worked for a computer manufacturer, so my friend always had the greatest technology. One day, I was confused when my friend turned on the computer and clicked a few buttons, and the computer made beeps and buzzes for a few minutes. A window popped up on the screen:

Prodigy.

For hours upon hours, we saw the world. We read articles. We chatted with people across the country—I can't remember everything that we chatted about, but it was the mere fact that we were chatting that had me awestruck. It was the same feeling I had from listening to WBAI. But unlike with WBAI, I could participate in the discussion. WBAI allowed me to hear about the world. Prodigy allowed me to travel the world and live in it.

Throughout high school, Prodigy and then AOL were my gateway to the world. Like many 15-year-olds in 1994, I read about Kurt Cobain's death in the print edition *Rolling Stone*. And I spent hours on Prodigy, commiserating with like-minded Nirvana fans around the world. I left New Jersey for college at the University of Michigan in fall 1996, just months after Congress passed Section 230. I soon joined the daily student newspaper, and the first article I wrote, titled " 'U' Web Sites Visited 500,000 Times Each Day," explained that the "World Wide Web is becoming a necessity of University life." When I graduated from college, I moved to Portland, Oregon, to cover telecommunications and Internet companies for the *Oregonian* newspaper. I covered the tail end of the first dot-com boom, and the bust. I wrote about online communities and witnessed how global interactivity shaped lives and businesses.

So it is not a surprise that as I studied and practiced law, I appreciated the elegant efficacy of Section 230. This was a law that promoted the interactive, communitarian nature of the Internet I had appreciated since I had first accessed Prodigy. Section 230 helped to build so many communities I had witnessed for years. When I represented news organizations, I often received complaints about user comments. Because of Section 230, the news sites could exercise their own judgment about whether to edit or delete the comments. Had Congress not passed Section 230, or if the courts had adopted Leo Kayser's argument in *Zeran* that the statute no longer immunized websites after they received notice of illegal or harmful third-party content, then the Internet would look very different. Anyone who was angry about a user post could demand that the website remove it. And the website would have great incentive to comply, for fear of being sued out of oblivion.

I do not intend to trivialize the experiences of the many victims of cyberharassment, online bullying, and life-changing defamation. Some evil and twisted people use the Internet, and they take advantage of open communities to harm others. Section 230 did not motivate the people to write defamatory lies, invade privacy, or plan crimes. The root causes of these harms are greed, mental instability, malice, and other social ills. But I do not entirely dismiss Section 230 critics' arguments that the law may remove the incentives for some websites to take all possible measures to prevent these harms. My once-absolute enthusiasm for Section 230 waned a bit during the two years in which I researched this book, as I looked at Section 230 from every angle. This forced me to examine tough cases that challenged my fervent support of the law. I spent hours on the phone with Ellen Batzel and heard how her life collapsed after the single Listserv message. I reviewed so many documents from Kenneth Zeran's case against America Online that I could picture how the Oklahoma City posts shook his quiet Seattle life. I heard the agonizing stories of children who were sold on Backpage.

Still, I believe that Section 230 has produced, overall, more benefits than harms for U.S. society. The only way to prevent illegal third-party content with any certainty—and avoid being sued out of oblivion—is to turn the Internet into a closed, one-way street that looks more like a broadcaster or newspaper and less like the Internet we know today. And that is not a world to which I want to return. I had seen the world before and after the creation of the modern Internet, and I prefer the latter version. That view is colored by my personal experience with the Internet. Ellen Batzel or Ken Zeran have had very different experiences, and they understandably have different perspectives on Section 230. So when people ask me if Section 230 is "good" or "bad," my answer is not all that useful in informing the debate. I think that on balance, Section 230 has provided net benefits to society. But I also agree with nuanced criticisms of Section 230 that were not readily apparent to me before I began researching and writing this book. In the book, I have sought to go beyond the basic question of whether Section 230 is good. Instead, I have examined the section's *effect* on the Internet. And I can only conclude that the Internet as we know it today could not exist without Section 230: the good (#MeToo), the bad (Backpage), and everything in between.

As I have stressed throughout this book, Section 230 is a right that Congress conferred on technology companies more than twenty years ago. Although it overlaps with many First Amendment protections, the full benefits of Section 230 do not amount to a constitutional right.

Congress giveth Section 230, and Congress can taketh it away. Technology companies—the most direct beneficiaries of Section 230—have a responsibility to prove that they are using this extraordinary immunity to the benefit of society. As seen in the sex trafficking debate, they often take this awesome privilege for granted.

It is impossible to predict the criticisms—fair and unfair—that Section 230 will receive in the future. When I started writing this book in 2016, platforms were not in the national spotlight to the same degree that they were when I finished writing it in 2018. Election interference, discriminatory job postings, foreign propaganda, and advertisements that carry hateful speech are just some of the issues that arose as I began writing. And new challenges seem to emerge every day. For instance, increasingly sophisticated technology has allowed the creation of fake videos, images, and audio that appear authentic. The content, known as "deep fakes," could result in the destruction of an individual's reputation—imagine the impact on a person whose image is used in a fake pornographic video.[1] Deep fakes also could cause chaos for national security if an elected official's words are fabricated in a realistic manner. Such technological chaos was not conceivable in 1996; now it is available to wrongdoers with low costs and few barriers to entry.

Platforms also are exponentially more complex than they were in 1996, offering amazing new services but also raising significant questions about their obligations to society. In her article "Law of the Platform," Orly Lobel presciently summarized many of the important and unanswered questions that are raised by new business models for platforms:

> Are companies like Uber and Lyft digital clearinghouses connecting independent drivers-for-hire with customers, or rather are they employers violating wage-and-hour laws? Are zoning laws parsing parts of town for short-term rentals still relevant when residential property owners list their homes on Airbnb? Was Aereo, which went bankrupt following its recent Supreme Court defeat, a digital antenna rental company, or a service that streams broadcasted content, thereby infringing copyright? Is TaskRabbit just an app to connect people searching for odd jobs, or a manpower agency that should withhold taxes? Companies such as Uber, Lyft, Airbnb, Aereo, and TaskRabbit have been running against existing regulations and the legal battles often turn on how to define the platform business: Are these digital companies service providers or brokers of individualized exchanges?

Should they be viewed as merely enabling intermediaries or robust corporate infrastructures?[2]

There are no easy answers to these questions, either normatively or in the existing body of Section 230 opinions. I'm fairly certain that the list of questions will grow, and as it does, Section 230 will receive even more scrutiny, and attempts to amend or entirely eliminate it will continue to proliferate. In one example of an innovation that might attract attention, platforms are increasingly using artificial intelligence to process user data in ways that likely were not imagined in 1996. A solid history of Section 230—warts and all—is necessary as we determine how the Internet will look two decades from now. But now that we have that background, where should we go from here? Can—and should—Section 230 remain on the books for another twenty years? Or is it a relic of a simpler time in Internet history?

As I seek to answer those questions, I look down the street from my house in Arlington, Virginia. Developers built modest bungalows in my neighborhood nearly one hundred years ago. Over the past decade, as property values surged, developers have torn down those bungalows and built larger houses with smaller yards. The homes typically have at least four bedrooms and four bathrooms, with a rec room and guest suite in the basement. A few blocks away from my house, a developer tore down one of these bungalows nearly a decade ago. For reasons I still can't explain, the developer built the house without a basement, even though almost every other new home in the neighborhood has a furnished basement. The house sat on the market for years. Finally, the developer realized that a basement-less house would not sell. So a crew dug a basement underneath the house. The end result is a house that, from the outside, looks uneven and poorly constructed. I wouldn't feel comfortable visiting the house for five minutes, much less living in it. Not surprisingly, it is still vacant years later.

Scaling back or eliminating Section 230 more than twenty years after its passage is like digging the basement after building the house. The modern Internet in the United States is built on the foundation of Section 230. To eliminate Section 230 would require radical changes to the Internet. These changes could cause the Internet to collapse on itself. The Internet without

Section 230 would be an Internet in which litigation threats could silence the truth. If websites were liable for third-party content after receiving complaints, they probably would quickly remove the content. Some of this content has little social value. But much of it does. In an essay for the February 2018 content moderation conference at Santa Clara University, discussed in chapter 12, lawyers for Automattic, the company that operates the popular blogging service WordPress, explained the company's firm policy of removing allegedly defamatory posts only if it received a court order to do so. The lawyers described a sample of the "dubious" takedown demands they have received as follows:

> A multi-national defense contractor lodged numerous defamation complaints against a whistleblower who posted information about corruption to a WordPress.com blog.
> An international religious/charitable group brought defamation charges against a blogger who questioned the organization's leadership.
> A large European pharmaceutical firm sought, on defamation grounds, to disable a WordPress.com blog, which detailed negative experiences with the firm's products. A court later determined that this content was true.[3]

All these blog posts served a useful social purpose. This type of information exposes corporate malfeasance, and there is a strong public interest in allowing the public to see it—such truths are fundamental to our democracy. Because of Section 230, WordPress could decline the takedown demands and leave the posts online.

If Congress eliminated Section 230 tomorrow, I would advise any company with a website or app to be extremely cautious about any third-party content on its platform. Automated and manual moderation has improved greatly since Congress passed Section 230, but no moderation is 100 percent effective. The sites' only legal protections would be the bizarre First Amendment rule articulated in *Cubby* and *Stratton Oakmont,* in which moderating content might actually increase their liability. And today's websites process exponentially more third-party content than Prodigy and CompuServe did in the early 1990s, exposing them to more potential liability. Without Section 230, sites would either prohibit user content altogether or remove it as soon as they receive complaints. Either outcome would be a drastic departure from the free and open Internet entwined in everyday life. Rather than digging underneath the basement-less house, the developer should address the shortcomings by expanding outward or upward, or improving the interior.

Like the house's foundation, Section 230 is imperfect. We can—and should—fix the problems in a tailored and focused manner that minimizes damage. That is precisely why I supported a narrow exception to Section 230 for sex trafficking. Section 230 was protecting horrific sites like Backpage, and the courts were not solving the problem quickly enough. The Backpage cases demonstrated a flaw in the system, and Congress acted to solve that specific problem. That is precisely how the legislative process should work.

Congress passed Section 230 at the peak of the Internet exceptionalism era. Twenty years later, the Internet is less exceptional. It is not a cool new technology. The Internet has realized much of the potential that Cox and Wyden lauded in 1996, and Section 230 has been a catalyst. The Internet is not as exceptional as it was in 1996 because it is now woven into the fabric of nearly every aspect of life. It also is more complicated, with artificial intelligence and complex algorithms processing third-party content while employing power and capabilities that probably were not contemplated in 1996. But those are not reasons to eliminate Section 230. Instead, that is why we must preserve it; to eliminate Section 230 would remove the foundation from underneath the trillion-dollar industry that the section created. Instead, we should all work to understand how to improve Section 230. Platforms must do a better job at blocking illegal or harmful third-party content, and if they are not doing that, then Congress should consider narrow carve-outs to Section 230 that address those problems without compromising the entire structure that the section supports.

The modern Internet is the House That Is Built on Section 230. It isn't the nicest house on the block, but it's the house where we all live. We can't tear it down. We're stuck with it. So we must maintain our home and preserve it for the future.

Notes

Introduction

1. Glenn Kessler, *A Cautionary Tale for Politicians: Al Gore and the "Invention" of the Internet*, Wash. Post (Nov. 4, 2013).
2. 47 U.S.C. § 230(c)(1).
3. Interview with Ron Wyden (June 6, 2017).
4. Top Sites in United States, Alexa, *available at* https://www.alexa.com/topsites/countries/US.
5. Marvin Ammori, *The New York Times: Free Speech Lawyering in the Age of Google and Twitter*, 127 Harv. L. Rev. 2259, 2260 (2014).
6. *See* Kathleen Ann Ruane, Congressional Research Service, Freedom of Speech and Press, Exceptions to the First Amendment (Sept. 8, 2014).

Part I. The Creation of Section 230

1. Jack M. Balkin, *The Future of Free Expression in a Digital Age*, 36 Pepp. L. Rev. 427, 432 (2009).

Chapter 1. Eleazar Smith's Bookstore

1. *See* Arthur C. Townley, *Encyclopedia of the Great Plains*, *available at* http://plainshumanities.unl.edu/encyclopedia/doc/egp.pd.052.

2. Complaint, Farmers Educational and Cooperative Union of America, North Dakota Division v. Townley, District Court of Cass County, North Dakota (Jan. 14, 1957).

3. Farmers Educational & Cooperative Union of America, North Dakota Division v. WDAY, Inc., 360 U.S. 525, 526 (1959).

4. Clerk of the U.S. House of Representatives, Statistics of the Presidential and Congressional Election of November 6, 1956.

5. Complaint, Farmers Educational and Cooperative Union of America, North Dakota Division v. Townley, District Court of Cass County, North Dakota (Jan. 14, 1957).

6. Ibid.

7. Rulings on Demurrer, Farmers Educational and Cooperative Union of America, North Dakota Division v. Townley, District Court of Cass County, North Dakota (May 23, 1957).

8. Farmers Educational and Cooperative Union of America, North Dakota Division v. WDAY, 89 NW 2d 102, 110 (N.D. 1958).

9. Ibid. at 111–112 (Morris, J., dissenting).

10. The transcript and audio recording from the Supreme Court oral argument was obtained through the Oyez Project, *available at* https://www.oyez.org/cases/1958/248 (hereinafter "Oyez Farmers Educational Transcript"). Because there are not page numbers on the Oyez transcript, the specific quotes are not pin cited.

11. Oyez Farmers Educational Transcript.

12. Ibid.

13. Ibid.

14. Black, Hugo Lafayette (1886–1971), Biographical Directory of the United States Congress, *available at* http://bioguide.congress.gov/scripts/biodisplay.pl?index=B000499.

15. *See Reflections on Justice Black and Freedom of Speech,* 6 VAL. U. L. REV. 316 (1972) ("Truly, Justice Black always referred to the Bill of Rights as a code of 'absolutes'; more particularly, he continually stressed the propriety of a literal interpretation of the first amendment provision that 'Congress shall make no law . . . abridging the freedom of speech'").

16. Farmers Educational & Cooperative Union of America, North Dakota Division v. WDAY, Inc., 360 U.S. 525, 529–530 (1959).

17. Ibid. at 530.

18. Ibid.

19. Ibid.

20. Ibid. at 533.

21. Ibid. at 534.

22. Ibid. at 536 (Frankfurter, J., dissenting).

23. Ibid. at 542.

24. Ibid. at 541.

25. The Reporter's transcript from Smith's Los Angeles Municipal Court trial on September 23–24, 1957, as quoted in this book (hereinafter "Smith Trial Transcript"), was attached to the case record that Smith filed with the United States Supreme Court on November 14, 1958. Specific citations to the trial transcript refer to the page number in the Supreme Court record.

26. Smith v. California, 361 US 147, 172 n.1 (1959).

27. Declaration of Intention, Eleazar Smith, August 26, 1936.

28. Roth v. United States, 354 U.S. 476 (1957).

29. Ibid. at 481.

30. Ibid. at 489.

31. Smith Trial Transcript.

32. Mark Tryon, SWEETER THAN LIFE.

33. Smith Trial Transcript at 91.

34. Ibid. at 81.

35. Ibid. at 43–46.

36. Ibid. at 91.

37. Ibid. at 35.

38. Ibid. at 38–39.

39. Ibid. at 41.

40. Ibid. at 92.

41. State v. Smith, Superior Court No. CR A 3792, Trial Court No. 57898 (Cal. Ct. App. June 23, 1958).

42. Ibid.

43. Ibid. (Swain, J., dissenting).

44. Jurisdictional Statement, Smith v. California, Supreme Court of the United States (1958) at 16.

45. Ibid.

46. Edward de Grazia, *I'm Just Going to Feed Adolphe,* 3 CARDOZO STUDIES IN LAW AND LITERATURE 127, 145–146 (1991).

47. The transcript and audio recording from the Supreme Court oral argument was obtained through the Oyez Project, *available at* https://www.oyez.org/cases/1959/9 (hereinafter "Oyez Smith Transcript"). Because there are not page numbers on the Oyez transcript, the specific quotes are not pin cited.

48. Oyez Smith Transcript.

49. Ibid.

50. Jacobellis v. Ohio, 378 U.S. 184, 197 (1964) (Potter, J., concurring).

51. Oyez Smith Transcript. Unless otherwise indicated, quotations are from this source in the passage that follows below.

52. Smith v. California, 361 U.S. 147 (1959).

53. Ibid. at 152.

54. Ibid. at 153–154.

55. Ibid. at 154–155.

56. Ibid. at 160–161 (Frankfurter, J., concurring).

57. Ibid. at 161.

58. Ibid. at 160 (Black, J., concurring).

59. Ibid. at 159 (Douglas, J., concurring).

60. Ibid. at 169–170 (Harlan, J., concurring in part and dissenting in part).

61. U.S. Social Security Death Index, 1935–2014.

62. New York Times v. Sullivan, 376 U.S. 254, 279 (1964).

63. See Robert W. Welkos, *Board Rejects Police Pension for TV Actor,* L.A. TIMES (Nov. 7, 1986).

64. Ken Osmond and Christopher J. Lynch, *Eddie: The Life and Times of America's Pre-eminent Bad Boy* (2014).

65. Osmond v. EWAP, 153 Cal.App.3d 842, 847 (Cal. Ct. App. 1984).

66. Ibid.

67. Ibid.

68. Ibid. at 848.

69. Ibid.

70. Ibid.

71. Ibid.

72. Ibid. at 849.

73. Ibid.

74. Ibid. at 852.

75. Ibid. at 854.

76. Ibid.

77. Miller v. California, 413 U.S. 15 (1973).

78. Carrie Weisman, *A Brief but Totally Fascinating History of Porn,* ALTERNET (June 5, 2015).

79. Julia Bindel, *What Andrea Dworkin, the Feminist I Knew, Can Teach Young Women,* THE GUARDIAN (March 30, 2015).

80. American Booksellers Ass'n, Inc. v. Hudnut, 771 F. 2d 323 (7th Cir. 1985).

81. Dworkin v. Hustler Magazine, Inc., 668 F. Supp. 1408, 1410 (C.D. Cal. 1987).

82. Ibid.

83. Dworkin v. Hustler Magazine, Inc., 611 F. Supp. 781 (D. Wyo. 1985).

84. Ibid. at 785.

85. Ibid. at 786.

86. Interview with Charlie Callaway (May 13, 2017).

87. Dworkin, 611 F. Supp. at 786–787.

88. Ibid.

89. Ibid.

90. Dworkin v. Hustler Magazine, Inc., 867 F. 2d 1188 (9th Cir. 1989).

91. Complaint, Spence v. Hustler, Civil Action No. 6568 (District Court of Teton County, Wyoming, May 12, 1986).

92. Spence v. Flynt, 647 F. Supp. 1266, 1269 (D. Wyo. 1986).

93. Complaint, Spence v. Hustler, Civil Action No. 6568 (District Court of Teton County, Wyoming, May 12, 1986) at ¶ 13.

94. Spence v. Flynt, 647 F. Supp. 1266, 1274 (D. Wyo. 1986).

95. Ibid.

96. Ibid. at 1274.

97. Spence v. Flynt, 647 F. Supp. 1266, 1274 (D. Wyo. 1986).

Chapter 2. The Prodigy Exception

1. Martin Lasden, *Of Bytes and Bulletin Boards,* N.Y. TIMES (Aug. 4, 1985).

2. Affidavit of Robert G. Blanchard, Cubby v. CompuServe, 90 Civ. 6571 (S.D.N.Y. July 11, 1991) at ¶ 2.

3. Ibid. at ¶ 3.

4. Ibid. at ¶ 4.

5. Interview with Bob Blanchard (May 23, 2017).

6. Motion for Summary Judgment, Cubby v. CompuServe, 90 Civ. 6571 (S.D.N.Y. April 5, 1991) at 3–4.

7. Ibid.

8. Exhibit A to Affidavit of Robert G. Blanchard, Cubby v. CompuServe, 90 Civ. 6571 (S.D.N.Y. July 11, 1991).

9. Exhibit C to Affidavit of Robert G. Blanchard, Cubby v. CompuServe, 90 Civ. 6571 (S.D.N.Y. July 11, 1991).

10. Interview with Bob Blanchard (May 23, 2017).

11. Complaint, Cubby v. CompuServe, 90 Civ. 6571 (S.D.N.Y. Oct. 5, 1990).

12. Ibid. at ¶ 25.

13. Memorandum of Law in Opposition to Defendant CompuServe's Motion for Summary Judgment, 90 Civ. 6571 (S.D.N.Y. July 11, 1991) at 6.

14. Ibid.

15. Ibid.

16. Affidavit of Eben L. Kent, Cubby v. CompuServe, 90 Civ. 6571 (S.D.N.Y. April 5, 1991) at ¶ 7.

17. Exhibit A to Affidavit of Jim Cameron, Cubby v. CompuServe, 90 Civ. 6571 (S.D.N.Y. April 5, 1991).

18. Affidavit of Jim Cameron, Cubby v. CompuServe, 90 Civ. 6571 (S.D.N.Y. April 5, 1991) at ¶ 7.

19. Exhibit B to Affidavit of Jim Cameron.

20. Memorandum of Law in Support of Defendant CompuServe's Motion for Summary Judgment, Cubby v. CompuServe, 90 Civ. 6571 (S.D.N.Y. April 5, 1991) at 6.

21. Ibid.

22. Ibid. at 5.

23. Memorandum of Law in Opposition to Defendant CompuServe's Motion for Summary Judgment, 90 Civ. 6571 (S.D.N.Y. July 11, 1991) at 3.

24. Ibid. at 4.

25. Ibid. at 8.

26. Cubby v. CompuServe, 776 F.Supp. 135 (S.D.N.Y. 1991).

27. Ibid. at 138.

28. Ibid. at 140.

29. Ibid.

30. Interview with Bob Blanchard (May 23, 2017).

31. Ibid.

32. Interview with Leo Kayser (June 26, 2017).

33. Ibid.

34. Jonathan M. Moses & Michael W. Miller, *CompuServe Is Not Liable for Contents,* WALL ST. J. (Oct. 31, 1991).

35. *Column One,* L.A. TIMES (March 19, 1993).

36. Barnaby J. Feder, *Towards Defining Free Speech in the Computer Age,* N.Y. TIMES (Nov. 3, 1991).

37. Associated Press, *CompuServe Wins Libel Suit, Question of Bulletin Boards Remains,* ASSOCIATED PRESS (Nov. 1, 1991).

38. David J. Conner, *Cubby v. Compuserve, Defamation Law on the Electronic Frontier,* 2 GEO. MASON INDEP. L. REV. 227 (1993).

39. Linette Lopez, *A Former Exec at the 'Wolf of Wall Street' Firm Has a Few Bones to Pick with the Story,* BUSINESS INSIDER (Dec. 10, 2013).

40. Second Amended Verified Complaint, Stratton Oakmont v. Prodigy Services Co., Index No. 94–031063 (N.Y. Sup. Ct., Nassau County, Jan. 9, 1995) at ¶ 18.

41. Ibid. at ¶ 19.

42. Ibid. at ¶ 20.

43. Ibid. at ¶ 21.

44. Ibid. at ¶ 22.

45. Interview with Jake Zamansky (June 14, 2017).

46. Verified Complaint, Stratton Oakmont v. Prodigy Services Co., Index No. 94–031063 (N.Y. Sup. Ct., Nassau County, Nov. 7, 1994).

47. State of New York, Commission on Judicial Conduct, In the Matter of the Proceeding Pursuant to Section 44. subdivision 4, of the Judiciary Law in Relation to Stuart L. Ain (Sept. 21, 1992).

48. Interview with Jake Zamansky (June 20, 2017).

49. Second Amended Verified Complaint, Stratton Oakmont v. Prodigy Services Co., Index No. 94–031063 (N.Y. Sup. Ct., Nassau County, Jan. 9, 1995) at ¶ 6.

50. Ibid. at ¶¶ 60–61.

51. Interview with Jake Zamansky (June 20, 2017).

52. Peter H. Lewis, *Libel Suit against Prodigy Tests on-Line Speech Limits,* N.Y. TIMES (Nov. 16, 1994).

53. Plaintiffs' Memorandum of Law in Support of Motion for Partial Summary Judgment, Stratton Oakmont v. Prodigy Services Co., Index No. 94–031063 (N.Y. Sup. Ct., Nassau County).

54. Ibid. at 4.

55. Ibid.

56. Deposition of Jennifer Ambrozek, 154.

57. *Electronic Bulletin Boards Need Editing. No They Don't,* N.Y. TIMES (Mar. 11, 1990).

58. Plaintiffs' Memorandum of Law in Support of Motion for Partial Summary Judgment, Stratton Oakmont v. Prodigy Services Co., Index No. 94–031063 (N.Y. Sup. Ct., Nassau County) at 4.

59. Ibid. at 6.

60. Ibid.

61. Ibid. at 14.

62. Memorandum of Law of Defendant Prodigy Services Company in Opposition to Plaintiffs' Motion for Summary Judgment, Stratton Oakmont v. Prodigy Services Co., Index No. 94–031063 (N.Y. Sup. Ct., Nassau County Feb. 24, 1995) at 1–2.

63. Ibid. at 11.

64. Ibid. at 11.

65. Ibid. at 12–13.

66. Ibid. at 13.

67. Ibid. at 4.

68. Short Form Order, Stratton Oakmont v. Prodigy Services Co., Index No. 94–031063 (N.Y. Sup. Ct., Nassau County May 24, 1995).

69. Ibid. at 7.

70. Ibid. at 9.

71. Interview with Jake Zamansky (June 20, 2017).

72. *Netwatch . . . Unease after Prodigy Ruling,* TIME (May 26, 1995).

73. *Prodigy on Trial,* ADVERTISING AGE (June 5, 1995).

74. Peter H. Lewis, *After Apology from Prodigy, Firm Drops Suit,* N.Y. TIMES (Oct. 25, 1995).

75. Ibid.

76. Interview with Jake Zamansky (June 20, 2017).

77. Stratton Oakmont v. Prodigy Services Co., Index No. 94–031063 (N.Y. Sup. Ct., Nassau County Dec. 11, 1995).

78. Ibid. at 4.

79. Katharine Stalter, *Prodigy Suit a Tough Read,* VARIETY (Nov. 12, 1995).

80. R. Hayes Johnson Jr., *Defamation in Cyberspace: A Court Takes a Wrong Turn on the Information Superhighway in Stratton Oakmont, Inc. v. Prodigy Services Co.,* 49 ARK. L. REV. 589 (1996).

81. David Ardia, *Free Speech Savior or Shield for Scoundrels: An Empirical Study of Intermediary Immunity under Section 230 of the Communications Decency Act,* 43 LOY. L. A. L. REV. 373 (2010).

Chapter 3. Chris and Ron Do Lunch

1. Interview with Chris Cox (April 14, 2017).

2. Interview with Ron Wyden (June 6, 2017).

3. Interview with Chris Cox (April 14, 2017).

4. Interview with Ron Wyden (June 6, 2017).

5. Interview with Chris Cox (April 14, 2017).

6. Ibid.

7. Interview with Rick White (June 26, 2017).

8. Interview with Bill Burrington (May 18, 2017).

9. Stephen Levy, *No Place for Kids?* NEWSWEEK (July 2, 1995).

10. Interview with Chris McLean (June 26, 2017).

11. S. 314, 104th Congress (1995).

12. 141 Cong. Rec. 8386 (June 14, 1995).

13. Center for Democracy and Technology, *Gingrich Says CDA Is a Clear Violation of Free Speech Rights* (June 20, 1995).

14. Interview with Bill Burrington (May 18, 2017).

15. Interview with Chris Cox (April 14, 2017).

16. Interview with Ron Wyden (June 6, 2017).

17. The bill, as introduced, is largely identical to the version of Section 230 that was signed into law the next year. However, the enacted statute has some minor wording differences. Unless otherwise noted, this book quotes from the bill as it was signed into law.

18. 47 U.S.C. § 230(c)(1).

19. 47 U.S.C. § 230(f)(2).

20. 47 U.S.C. § 230(f)(3).

21. 47 U.S.C. § 230(c)(2).

22. 47 U.S.C. § 230(e)(2).

23. 47 U.S.C. § 230(e)(1).

24. 47 U.S.C. § 230(e)(4).

25. 47 U.S.C. § 230(e)(3).

26. 47 U.S.C. § 230(a).

27. 47 U.S.C. § 230(b).

28. Interview with Jerry Berman (June 23, 2017).

29. Charles Levendosky, *FCC and the Internet? Disastrous Combination,* CASPER STAR-TRIBUNE (July 18, 1995).

30. 141 Cong. Rec. H8470 (Aug. 4, 1995).

31. Ibid.

32. Interview with Rick White (June 26, 2017).

33. 141 Cong. Rec. H8470 (Aug. 4, 1995).

34. 141 Cong. Rec. H8571 (Aug. 4, 1995).

35. Ibid.

36. Ibid.

37. 141 Cong. Rec. H8569 (Aug. 4, 1995).

38. *House Votes to Ban Internet Censorship; Senate Battle Ahead,* WASH. POST (Aug. 5, 1995).

39. Interview with Jerry Berman (June 23, 2017).

40. Sec. 502 of S.652(enr.) (104th Cong.).

41. Ibid.

42. Ibid.

43. Interview with Rick White (June 26, 2017).

44. Interview with Chris McLean (June 26, 2017).

45. Archive.org copy of website of Congressman Rick White, *available at* https://web.archive.org/web/19970616062841/http://www.house.gov:80/white/internet/initiative.html.

46. Interview with Chris McLean (June 26, 2017).

47. Conf. Report 104–458 (104th Cong.) at 194.

48. Howard Bryant and David Plotnikoff, *How the Decency Fight Was Won,* San Jose Mercury News (March 3, 1996).

49. FCC v. Pacifica Foundation, 438 U.S. 726 (1978).

50. Interview with Jerry Berman (June 23, 2017).

Part II. The Rise of Section 230

1. Andy Greenberg, *It's Been 20 Years since This Man Declared Cyberspace Independence,* Wired (Feb. 8, 2016).

2. 141 Cong. Rec. H. 8469 (Aug. 4, 1995).

3. Reno v. American Civil Liberties Union, 521 U.S. 844, 850 (1997).

Chapter 4. Ask for Ken

1. June 26, 1995, Letter of Leo Kayser III to Jane M. Church, attachment to Brief in Opposition to Defendant's Motion for Judgment on the Pleadings, Zeran v. America Online, Civ-96–1564 (E.D. Va. Feb. 13, 1997) ("Kayser Letter") at 1.

2. Ibid.

3. Ibid. at 1–2.

4. Ibid. at 2.

5. Attachment A to Kayser Letter.

6. Kayser Letter at 2.

7. Ibid. at 3.

8. Zeran v. Diamond Broadcasting, Inc., 203 F. 3d 714, 718 (10th Cir. 2000).

9. Ibid.

10. Kayser Letter at 3.

11. Letter from Ken Zeran to Ellen Kirsh (May 1, 1995).

12. Kayser Letter at 4.

13. Ibid.

14. Mark A. Hutchison, *Online T-Shirt Scam Jolts Seattle Man,* Sunday Oklahoman (May 7, 1995).

15. Kayser Letter at 5.

16. May 17, 1994, Letter of Jane M. Church to Ken Zeran, attachment to Brief in Opposition to Defendant's Motion for Judgment on the Pleadings, Zeran v. America Online, Civ-96–1564 (E.D. Va. Feb. 13, 1997) at 1.

17. Interview with Leo Kayser (June 26, 2017).

18. Kayser Letter at 5.

19. Interview with Leo Kayser (June 26, 2017).

20. Associated Press, *Judge in Manafort Trial Is a Navy Vet* (Aug. 3, 2018).

21. *See* Reporter's Transcript, United States v. Franklin, Case No. 05-cr-225 (E.D. Va. June 11, 2009) at 38.

22. Memorandum in Support of Defendant's Motion for Judgment on the Pleadings, Zeran v. America Online, Civil No. 96–1564 (Jan. 28, 1997) at 9–10.

23. Ibid. at 7.

24. Ibid. at 8.

25. Brief in Opposition to Defendant's Motion for Judgment on the Pleadings, Zeran v. America Online, Civil No. 96–1564 (Feb. 13, 1997) at 11.

26. Ibid. at 10.

27. Ibid. at 12.

28. All dialogue from this court hearing is as transcribed in Reporter's Transcript, Hearing on Motions, Zeran v. America Online, Civil No. 96–1564 (E.D. Va. Feb. 28, 1997).

29. Zeran v. America Online, 958 F.Supp 1124, 1133 (E.D. Va. 1997).

30. Ibid. at 1134–1135.

31. Brief of Appellant, Zeran v. America Online, Case No. 97–1523 (4th Cir. June 2, 1997) at 32.

32. Brief of Appellee, Zeran v. America Online, No. 97-1523 (4th Cir. July 7, 1997).

33. Judge J. Harvie Wilkinson, U.S. Court of Appeals for the Fourth Circuit, *available at* http://www.ca4.uscourts.gov/judges/judges-of-the-court/judge-j-harvie-wilkinson-iii.

34. Melody Peterson, *Donald S. Russell Dies at 92, Politician and Federal Judge,* N.Y. TIMES (Feb. 25, 1998).

35. Boyle, Terrence William, Federal Judicial Center, *available at* https://www.fjc.gov/history/judges/boyle-terrence-william.

36. Zeran v. America Online, Inc., 129 F.3d 327, 330 (4th Cir. 1997).

37. Ibid. at 331.

38. Ibid.

39. 47 U.S.C. § 230(b)(1).

40. 47 U.S.C. § 230(b)(2).

41. 47 U.S.C. § 230(b)(3).

42. 47 U.S.C. § 230(a)(3).

43. 141 Cong. Rec. H. 8471 (Aug. 4, 1995).

44. Ibid. at H8472.

45. *Zeran* 129 F.3d at 332.

46. Ibid.

47. Ibid.

48. Ibid. at 333.

49. Ibid.

50. Interview with Ron Wyden (June 6, 2017).

51. Interview with Leo Kayser (June 26, 2017).

52. Zeran v. Diamond Broadcasting, 203 F.3d 714 (10th Cir. 2000).

53. Order, Doe v. America Online, Case No. CL 97–631AE (Fl. Cir. Ct. June 26, 1997).

54. Ibid.

55. Opinion, Doe v. America Online, Case No. 97–25 87 (Fl. Ct. App. Oct. 14, 1998).

56. Doe v. America Online, 783 So.2d 1010, 1017 (Fl. 2001).

57. Ibid. at 1019 (Lewis, J., dissenting).

58. Ibid. at 1022.

59. Ibid. at 1024.

60. Complaint, Blumenthal v. Drudge, Case No. 1:97-cv-01968-PLF (D.D.C. Aug. 27, 1997) ("Blumenthal Complaint") at ¶ 204.

61. Ex. 5 to Blumenthal Complaint.

62. Ibid.

63. Ex. 1 to Blumenthal Complaint.

64. Howard Kurtz, *Blumenthals Get Apology, Plan Lawsuit,* WASH. POST (Aug. 12, 1997).

65. Blumenthal Complaint at ¶ 557.

66. Memorandum of Points and Authorities in Support of Defendant America Online, Inc.'s Motion for Summary Judgment, Blumenthal v. Drudge, Civil Action No. 97-CV-01968 (D.D.C. Oct. 20, 1997).

67. Plaintiffs' Memorandum of Points and Authorities in Opposition to Defendant America Online, Inc.'s Motion for Summary Judgment, Blumenthal v. Drudge, Civil Action No. 97-CV-01968 (D.D.C. Jan. 23, 1998) at 13.

68. Senior Judge Paul Friedman, U.S. District Court for the District of Columbia, *available at* http://www.dcd.uscourts.gov/content/senior-judge-paul-l-friedman.

69. Blumenthal v. Drudge, 992 F. Supp. 44, 51–52 (D.D.C. 1998).

70. Ibid. at 52.

71. Ibid. at 52–53.

72. Ibid. at 49.

Chapter 5. Himmler's Granddaughter and the Bajoran Dabo Girl

1. Ed Whelan, *Reinhardt Day at the Supreme Court,* NAT'L REVIEW (May 25, 2010).

2. Ben Feuer, *California's Notoriously Liberal "9th Circus" Court of Appeals Is Growing More Centrist,* L.A. TIMES (Sept. 11, 2016).

3. Ibid.; Dylan Matthews, *How the 9th Circuit Became Conservatives' Least Favorite Court,* Vox (Jan. 10, 2018).

4. Interview with Chris Cox (April 14, 2017).

5. Interview with Ellen Batzel (July 14, 2017).

6. Ibid.

7. Batzel v. Smith, 372 F. Supp.2d 546, 547 (C.D. Cal. 2005).

8. Batzel v. Smith, 333 F.3d 1018, 1021 (9th Cir. 2003).

9. Jori Finkel, *The Case of the Forwarded E-mail,* SALON (July 13, 2001).

10. Ibid.

11. Batzel v. Smith, 333 F.3d at 1022.

12. Appellant's Opening Brief, Batzel v. Smith, Case No. 01–56380 (9th Cir. April 30, 2002) at 21.

13. Ibid. at 22.

14. Brief of Appellee, Batzel v. Smith, Case No. 01–56380 (9th Cir. May 10, 2002) at 28–29; Interview with Ellen Batzel (July 14, 2017).

15. Ibid.

16. Interview with Ellen Batzel (July 14, 2017).

17. Appellant's Opening Brief, Batzel v. Smith, Case No. 01–56380 (9th Cir. April 30, 2002) at 24.

18. Ibid. at 25.

19. Ibid. at 24–27.

20. Interview with Ellen Batzel (July 14, 2017).

21. Ibid.

22. Ibid.

23. Ibid.

24. Appellant's Opening Brief, Batzel v. Smith, Case No. 01–56380 (9th Cir. April 30, 2002) at 39.

25. Brief of Appellee, Batzel v. Smith, Case No. 01–56380 (9th Cir. May 31, 2002) at 38–39.

26. Ibid. at 39–40.

27. Brief of Public Citizen as Amicus Curiae Urging Reversal and Remand, Batzel v. Smith, Case No. 01–56380 (9th Cir. May 31, 2002) at vii.

28. Ibid. at 23.

29. Batzel v. Smith, 333 F.3d 1018, 1020 (9th Cir. 2003).

30. Ibid. at 1028.

31. Ibid. at 1031.

32. Ibid.

33. Ibid. at 1032.

34. Ibid. at 1033.

35. Ibid. at 1035.

36. Ibid. at 1038 (Gould, J., dissenting).

37. Ibid.

38. Batzel v. Smith, 351 F. 3d 904, 907 (2003) (Gould, J., dissenting from denial of re-hearing en banc).

39. Sebastian Rupley, *Fre-er Speech on the Net; A Court Ruling Sets New Libel Definitions for Bloggers, Discussion, and Forums on the Internet,* PC MAGAZINE (July 3, 2003).

40. Juliana Barbassa, *Court Decision Protects Bloggers from Libel Suits,* ASSOCIATED PRESS (July 2, 2003).

41. Interview with Chris Cox (April 14, 2017).

42. Interview with Ellen Batzel (July 14, 2017).

43. Ibid.

44. Appellant's Opening Brief, Carafano v. Metrosplash, No. 02–55658 (9th Cir. Oct. 16, 2002) at 5–6.

45. Complaint, Carafano v. Metrosplash, Case No. BC239336 (California Superior Court, Los Angeles, Oct. 27, 2000) ("Carafano Complaint") at 2–3.

46. Ibid. at 3.

47. Ibid.

48. Ibid. at 4.

49. Carafano v. Metrosplash, 207 F. Supp. 2d 1055, 1061 (C.D. Cal. 2002).

50. Ibid.

51. Carafano Complaint at 4.

52. Ibid. at 5.

53. Ibid.

54. Carafano v. Metrosplash, 207 F. Supp. 2d 1055, 1066–67 (C.D. Cal. 2002).

55. Ibid. at 1066.

56. Ibid. at 1068–1077.

57. Brief of Appellee Lycos., Inc., Carafano v. Metrosplash, Case No. 02-55658 (9th Cir. Jan. 6, 2003) at 62.

58. Carafano v. Metrosplash, 339 F.3d 119, 1124 (9th Cir. 2003).

59. Ibid. at 1125.

Chapter 6. The Flower Child and a Trillion-Dollar Industry

1. Christian M. Dippon, ECONOMIC VALUE OF INTERNET INTERMEDIARIES AND THE ROLE OF LIABILITY PROTECTIONS (June 5, 2017).

2. Ibid.

3. Anupam Chander, *How Law Made Silicon Valley,* 63 EMORY L.J. 639, 650 (2014).

4. Ripoff Report home page, www.ripoffreport.com.

5. Ibid.

6. Ibid.

7. Interview with Ed Magedson (June 11, 2017).

8. Ibid.

9. Ibid.

10. Ibid.

11. Ibid.

12. Ibid.

13. Email, *Why Ripoff Report Will Not Remove a Report Even When the Author of the Report Asks Ripoff Report to Do So* (provided by Ed Magedson on June 11, 2017).

14. Interview with Ed Magedson (June 11, 2017).

15. Ibid.

16. Order, Global Royalties v. Xcentric Ventures, LLC, No. CV-07–0956-PHX-FJM (D. Ariz. Feb. 28, 2008).

17. Exhibit to Complaint, Global Royalties v. Xcentric Ventures, LLC, No. CV-07–0956-PHX-FJM (D. Ariz. July 11, 2007).

18. Ibid.

19. Amended Complaint, Global Royalties v. Xcentric Ventures, LLC, No. CV-07–0956-PHX-FJM (D. Ariz. Nov. 1, 2007) at ¶ 26.

20. Order, Global Royalties v. Xcentric Ventures, LLC, No. CV-07–0956-PHX-FJM (D. Ariz. Oct. 10, 2007).

21. Amended Complaint, Global Royalties v. Xcentric Ventures, LLC, No. CV-07–0956-PHX-FJM (D. Ariz. Nov. 1, 2007) at ¶ 13.

22. Motion to Dismiss Amended Complaint, Global Royalties v. Xcentric Ventures, LLC, No. CV-07–0956-PHX-FJM (D. Ariz. Nov. 12, 2007) at 5.

23. Plaintiff's Responsive Memorandum in Opposition in Response to Defendants' Motion to Dismiss Amended Complaint, Global Royalties v. Xcentric Ventures, LLC, No. CV-07–0956-PHX-FJM (D. Ariz. Nov. 30, 2007) at 10–12.

24. Order, Global Royalties v. Xcentric Ventures, LLC, No. CV-07–0956-PHX-FJM (D. Ariz. Feb. 28, 2008) at 3.

25. Ibid. at 5–6.

26. Interview with Anette Beebe (June 7, 2017).

27. Ibid.

28. Interview with Ed Magedson (June 11, 2017).

29. Ibid.

30. Angela Balcita, *The Startup Boys: A Conversation with Yelp.com Founders Russel Simmons and Jeremy Stoppelman,* Imagine (Jan./Feb. 2008).

31. Saul Hansell, *Why Yelp Works,* N.Y. Times (May 12, 2008).

32. Jean Harris, *For Some Yelpers, It Pays to be Elite,* L.A. Times (May 1, 2015).

33. Leigh Held, *Behind the Curtain of Yelp's Powerful Reviews,* Entrepreneur (July 9, 2014).

34. Hillary Dixler, *Yelp Turns 10: From Startup to Online Review Dominance,* Eater (Aug. 5, 2014).

35. Ibid.

36. Evelyn M. Rusli, *In Debut on Market, Yelp Stock Surges 64%,* N.Y. Times (Mar. 2, 2012).

37. News Release, *Yelp Reports First Quarter 2018 Financial Results* (May 10, 2018).

38. Michael Anderson & Jeremy Magruder, *Learning from the Cloud: Regression Discontinuity Estimates of the Effects of an Online Review Database* (May 23, 2011).

39. Joyce Cutler, *Counsel at Leading Social Sites Describe Crush of User Content Takedown Requests,* BNA (Mar. 7, 2011).

40. Kimzey v. Yelp! Inc., 836 F. 3d 1263, 1266 (9th Cir. 2016).

41. Ibid. at 1267.

42. Ibid.

43. Complaint, Kimzey v. Yelp, Case No. 13-cv-1734 (W.D. Wash. Sept. 28, 2013) at ¶¶ 19–23.

44. Kimzey v. Yelp Inc., F. Supp. 3d 1120, 1123 (W.D. Wash. 2014).

45. Kimzey v. Yelp! Inc., 836 F. 3d 1263, 1266, 1271 (9th Cir. 2016).

46. Ibid. at 1269.

47. Ibid.

48. Ibid. at 1265.

49. Wikipedia: Size Comparisons, https://en.wikipedia.org/wiki/Wikipedia:Size_comparisons (last visited July 30, 2017).

50. Alexa Top 500 Global Sites, http://www.alexa.com/topsites (last visited July 30, 2017).

51. Interview with Ward Cunningham (Aug. 3, 2017).

52. Ibid.

53. Ibid.

54. Ibid.

55. History of Wikipedia, https://en.wikipedia.org/wiki/History_of_Wikipedia (last visited July 30, 2017).

56. Ibid.

57. Ibid.

58. Interview with Ward Cunningham (Aug. 3, 2017).

59. Peter Meyers, *Fact-Driven? Collegial? This Site Wants You,* N.Y. Times (Sept. 20, 2001).

60. *History of Wikipedia,* https://en.wikipedia.org/wiki/History_of_Wikipedia (last visited July 30, 2017).

61. Wikipedia: Policies and Guidelines, https://en.wikipedia.org/wiki/Wikipedia:Policies_and_guidelines (last visited July 30, 2017).

62. Wikipedia Seigenthaler Biography Incident, https://en.wikipedia.org/wiki/Wikipedia_Seigenthaler_biography_incident (last visited July 31, 2017).

63. John Seigenthaler, Sr., *A False Wikipedia "Biography,"* USA Today (Nov. 29, 2005).

64. Ibid.

65. Ibid.

66. Katharine Q. Seelye, *A Little Sleuthing Unmasks Writer of Wikipedia Prank,* N.Y. Times (Dec. 11, 2005).

67. Second Amended Complaint, Bauer v. Glatzer, Docket No. L-1169–07 (Superior Court of N.J., Monmouth County, Jan. 31, 2008) at 25.

68. Exhibit 1 to Declaration of Mike Godwin in Support of the Motion to Dismiss the Complaint, Bauer v. Glatzer, Docket No. L-1169–07 (Superior Court of N.J., Monmouth County, April 29, 2008).

69. Memorandum of Law in Support of Motion of Defendant Wikimedia Foundation, Inc. to Dismiss the Complaint, Bauer v. Glatzer, Docket No. L-1169–07 (Superior Court of N.J., Monmouth County, May 1, 2008).

70. Brief in Opposition to Motion to Dismiss, Bauer v. Glatzer, Docket No. L-1169–07 (Superior Court of N.J., Monmouth County, May 12, 2008) at 3.

71. Reply Memorandum of Law in Support of Motion of Defendant Wikimedia Foundation, Inc. to Dismiss the Complaint, Bauer v. Glatzer, Docket No. L-1169–07 (Superior Court of N.J., Monmouth County, May 19, 2008).

72. Mike Godwin, *A Bill Intended to Stop Sex Trafficking Could Significantly Curtail Internet Freedom,* Slate (Aug. 4, 2017).

73. DMR Business Statistics, *available at* https://expandedramblings.com/index.php/resource-how-many-people-use-the-top-social-media/.

74. Total aggregated from companies' Securities and Exchange Commission filings.

75. Internet Live Stats, Twitter User Statistics, http://www.internetlivestats.com/twitter-statistics/ (August 22, 2018).

76. Smart Insights, What Happens Online in 60 Seconds: Managing Content Shock in 2017, http://www.smartinsights.com/internet-marketing-statistics/happens-online-60-seconds/ (Aug. 3, 2017).

77. Julia Angwin & Brian Steinberg, *News Corp. Goal: Make MySpace Safer for Teens,* Wall St. J. (Feb. 17, 2006).

78. Letter from Jim Petro to Chris DeWolfe (March 24, 2006).

79. Plaintiff's Original Petition, Doe v. MySpace, DY-GM-06–002209 (Travis County District Court, June 19, 2006).

80. Ibid.

81. Ibid.

82. Memorandum of Law in Support of Plaintiffs' Response to Defendants' Motion to Dismiss, Case No. 1:06-cv-00983-SS (W.D. Tex. Jan, 16, 2007) at 2.

83. Doe v. MySpace, 528 F. 3d 413, 421 (5th Cir. 2008).

84. Ibid.

85. Doe v. MySpace, 474 F. Supp. 2d 843, 848 (W.D. Tex. 2007).

86. Ibid.

87. Ibid. at 849.

88. Dana Milbank, *Justice Clement: We Hardly Knew You: The Rise and Fall of a Contender,* WASH. POST (July 20, 2005).

89. Doe v. MySpace, Inc., 528 F. 3d 413 (5th Cir. 2008).

90. Heidi Blake, *Google Celebrates 12th Birthday: A Timeline,* TELEGRAPH (Sept. 27, 2010).

91. John Patrick Pullen, *Google's Parent Company Achieves Big Market Cap Milestone,* FORTUNE (April 24, 2017).

92. Internet Live Stats, http://www.internetlivestats.com/google-search-statistics/ (Aug. 3, 2017).

93. Fakhrian v. Google, No. B260705 (Cal. Ct. App. 2016).

94. Ibid.

95. Ibid.

Chapter 7. American Exceptionalism

1. Jack M. Balkin, *Old-School/New-School Speech Regulation,* 127 HARV. L. REV. 2296, 2313 (2014).

2. Continental Congress to the Inhabitants of the Province of Quebec, Journals 1:105–13 (Oct. 26, 1774).

3. Noah Feldman, *Free Speech in Europe Isn't What Americans Think,* BLOOMBERG (March 19, 2017).

4. ARTICLE 19, ISLAMIC REPUBLIC OF IRAN: COMPUTER CRIMES LAW (2013) at 41.

5. Ece Toksabay, *Turkey Reinstates YouTube Ban,* REUTERS (Nov. 3, 2010).

6. *Russian Parliament Approves "Right to Be Forgotten" Law,* DW (July 3, 2015).

7. Sherisse Pham, *Here's How China Deals with Big Social Media Companies,* CNN (April 12, 2018).

8. PEN AMERICA, FORBIDDEN FEES: GOVERNMENT CONTROLS ON SOCIAL MEDIA (June 2018).

9. Judgment, Case of Delfi v. Estonia, Application no. 64569/09 (Grand Chamber, European Court of Human Rights June 16, 2015) at ¶¶ 11–12.

10. Ibid. at ¶ 13.

11. Ibid. at ¶ 14.

12. Ibid. at ¶ 18.

13. Ibid. at ¶¶ 19–20.

14. Directive 2000/31/EC, Article 12.

15. Ibid., Article 14.

16. Judgment, Case of Delfi v. Estonia, Application no. 64569/09 (Grand Chamber, European Court of Human Rights, June 16, 2015) at ¶ 23.

17. Ibid. at ¶ 24.

18. Ibid. at ¶ 26.

19. Ibid. at ¶ 31.

20. Ibid. at ¶¶ 61–65.

21. Ibid. at ¶ 63.

22. Written comments of the Media Legal Defence Initiative, Delfi AS v. Estonia (June 6, 2014).

23. Ibid.

24. Judgment, Case of Delfi v. Estonia, Application no. 64569/09 (Grand Chamber, European Court of Human Rights, June 16, 2015) at ¶ 142.

25. Ibid. at 140–146.

26. Ibid. at ¶ 151.

27. Ibid. at ¶ 156.

28. Ibid. at ¶ 157.

29. Ibid. at ¶ 159.

30. Ibid. at ¶ 127.

31. Joint Dissenting Opinion of Judges Sajo and Tsotsoria, Delfi v. Estonia, Application no. 64569/09.

32. Joint Dissenting Opinion of Judges Sajo and Tsotsoria, Delfi v. Estonia, Application no. 64569/09 at ¶ 2.

33. Press Release, Access, *Worrying Setback in European Court Delfi Decision for Online Free Expression and Innovation* (June 15, 2015).

34. TRUSTPILOT, *What Happens If My Review Is Reported? available at* https://support.trustpilot.com/hc/en-us/articles/207312237-What-happens-when-my-review-is-reported-on-Trustpilot- (Aug. 10, 2017).

35. European Charter of Fundamental Rights, Article 8.

36. Google Spain, SL v. Costeja Gonzalez, Case C-131/12 (Grand Chamber May 13, 2014).

37. Ibid. at ¶¶ 14–15.

38. Ibid. at ¶ 16.

39. Ibid. at 81.

40. Ibid. at 95.

41. Ibid. at 97.

42. Stan Schroeder, *Google Has Received Nearly 350,000 URL Removal Requests So Far,* MASHABLE (Nov. 26, 2015).

43. Google Transparency Report (2017).

44. James Vincent, *Critics Outraged as Google Removes Search Results about Top UK Lawyer and US Banker,* THE INDEPENDENT (July 3, 2014).

45. Jeffrey Rosen, *The Right to Be Forgotten,* Stan. L. Rev. (Feb. 2012).

46. Article 17, General Data Protection Regulation.

47. Remarks of Viviane Reding, *The EU Data Protection Reform 2012: Making Europe the Standard Setter for Modern Data Protection Rules in the Digital Age, Innovation Conference Digital Life, Design* (Jan. 22, 2012).

48. Daphne Keller, *The Right Tools: Europe's Intermediary Liability Laws and the 2016 General Data Protection Regulation,* BERKELEY TECH. L.J. (Mar. 22, 2017, working draft).

49. Ibid.

50. Google, Removal Policies, *available at* https://support.google.com/websearch/answer/2744324?hl=en (Aug. 25, 2017).

51. Carter v. B.C. Federation of Foster Parents Ass'n, 2005 BCCA 398 (Ct. App. British Columbia 2005) at ¶ 1.

52. Ibid. at ¶ 5.

53. Ibid. at ¶ 14.

54. Ibid. at ¶ 21.

55. Brisciani v. Piscioneri (No 4) [2016] ACTCA 32 (Sup. Ct. of Australian Capital Territory, Ct. of Appeal 2016) at ¶ 6.

56. Ibid.

57. Ibid. at ¶ 8.

58. Ibid. at ¶ 9.

59. Piscioneri v Brisciani [2015] ACTSC 106 (Sup. Ct. of the Australian Capital Territory 2015) at ¶ 45.

60. Ibid.

61. Piscioneri v Brisciani [2016] ACTCA 32 (Sup. Ct. of the Australian Capital Territory Ct. of Appeal 2016).

62. 28 U.S.C. § 4102.

Chapter 8. A Lawless No-Man's Land?

1. Plaintiffs' First Amended Complaint for Monetary, Declaratory & Injunctive Relief; Demand for Jury Trial, Fair Housing Council of San Fernando Valley v. Roommate.com, Case No. 03–9386 PA (C.D. Cal. April 9, 2004) at ¶¶ 16–47.

2. Ibid. at ¶ 12; Fair Housing Council of San Fernando Valley v. Roommates.com, 521 F.3d 1157, 1161–1162 (9th Cir. 2008) (en banc).

3. Plaintiffs' First Amended Complaint for Monetary, Declaratory & Injunctive Relief; Demand for Jury Trial, Fair Housing Council of San Fernando Valley v. Roommate.com, Case No. 03–9386 PA (C.D. Cal. April 9, 2004) at ¶¶ 51–65.

4. Henry Weinstein, *Bush Names 2 for Judgeships in L.A.*, L.A. TIMES (Jan. 24, 2002).

5. Memorandum of Points and Authorities in Support of Plaintiffs' Motion for Preliminary Injunction, Fair Housing Council of San Fernando Valley v. Roommate.com, Case No. 03–9386 PA (C.D. Cal. Aug. 9, 2004) at 10–11.

6. Ibid. at 13.

7. Defendant's Notice of Motion and Motion for Summary Judgment; Memorandum of Points and Authorities, Fair Housing Council of San Fernando Valley v. Roommate.com, Case No. 03–9386 PA (C.D. Cal. Aug. 16, 2004) at 10.

8. Reporter's Transcript of Proceedings, Fair Housing Council of San Fernando Valley v. Roommate.com, Case No. 03–9386 PA (C.D. Cal. Sept. 13, 2004) at 4.

9. Ibid. at 4–5.

10. Ibid. at 6.

11. Ibid. at 15.

12. Ibid.

13. Order Granting in Part Defendant's Motion for Summary Judgment and Denying Plaintiffs' Motion for Summary Judgment Fair Housing Council of San Fernando Valley v. Roommate.com, Case No. 03–9386 PA (C.D. Cal. Sept. 30, 2004) at 4.

14. Alex Kozinski biography, National Park Service, *available at* https://www.nps.gov/subjects/pacificcoastimmigration/kozinski.htm.

15. Hon. Sandra Segal Ikuta, The Federalist Society, *available at* https://fedsoc.org/contributors/sandra-ikuta.

16. Wood v. Ryan, 759 F. 3d 1076, 1103 (9th Cir. 2014) (Kozinski, C.J., dissenting from denial of rehearing en banc).

17. Dan Berman & Laura Jarrett, *Judge Alex Kozinski, Accused of Sexual Misconduct, Resigns*, CNN (Dec. 18, 2017).

18. Interview with Alex Kozinski (June 30, 2017).

19. Fair Housing Council v. Roommates.com, 489 F.3d 921 (9th Cir. 2007).

20. Ibid. at 928.

21. Ibid.

22. Ibid. at 929.

23. Ibid.

24. Ibid.

25. Ibid. at 931 (Reinhardt, J., concurring in part and dissenting in part).

26. Ibid. at 933 (Ikuta, J., concurring in part).

27. Adam Liptak, *Web Site Is Held Liable for Some User Postings,* N.Y. TIMES (May 16, 2007).

28. Ninth Circuit En Banc Procedure Summary (Feb. 10, 2017), *available at* http://cdn.ca9.uscourts.gov/datastore/general/2017/02/10/En_Banc_Summary2.pdf.

29. Amicus Curiae Brief of the Electronic Frontier Foundation, et al., Fair Housing Council v. Roommates.com, Nos. 04–59916 and 04–57173 (9th Cir. July 13, 2007) at 3.

30. Hon. M. Margaret McKeown, Circuit Judge, Ninth Circuit Court of Appeals, Judicial Profile, The Federal Lawyer (September 2015).

31. Fair Housing Council v. Roommates.com, 521 F.3d 1157, 1168 (9th Cir. 2008) (en banc).

32. Ibid. at 1166–1167.

33. Ibid. at 1162.

34. Ibid. at 1164.

35. Ibid. at 1165.

36. Ibid.

37. Ibid. at 1171.

38. Ibid.

39. Ibid. at 1172.

40. Ibid. at 1173–1174.

41. Ibid. at 1176 (McKeown, J., concurring in part and dissenting in part).

42. Ibid. at 1182.

43. Ibid. at 1166.

44. Fair Housing Council v. Roommate.com, 666 F.3d 1215 (9th Cir. 2012).

45. Varty Defterdian, *Fair Housing Council v. Roommates.com: A New Path for Section 230 Immunity,* 24 BERKELEY TECH. L. J. 563 (2009).

46. Interview with Alex Kozinski (June 30, 2017).

47. Ibid.

48. Orly Lobel, *The Law of the Platform,* 101 Minn. L. Rev. 87, 146 (2016).

49. Interview with Alex Kozinski (June 30, 2017).

50. Ibid.

51. Order on Cross-Motions for Summary Judgment, FTC v. Accusearch, Case No. 06-CV-105-D (D. Wyo. Sept. 28, 2007) at 2.

52. Ibid. at 3.

53. Ibid.

54. Ibid. at 2.

55. Complaint for Injunctive and Other Equitable Relief, FTC v. Accusearch, Case No. 06-CV-105-D (D. Wyo. May 1, 2006) at ¶ 10.

56. Defendants' Memorandum of Points and Authorities in Support of Motion for Summary Judgment, FTC v. Accusearch, Case No. 06-CV-105-D (Dec. 8, 2006) at 18.

57. Ibid. at 19.

58. Hon. William F. Downes (Ret.), JAMS, *available at* https://www.jamsadr.com/downes/.

59. Order on Cross-Motions for Summary Judgment, FTC v. Accusearch, Case No. 06-CV-105-D (D. Wyo. Sept. 28, 2007) at 11.

60. Ibid. at 12.

61. Ibid. at 11.

62. Brief of Appellants, FTC v. Accusearch, No. 08–8003 (10th Cir. April 23, 2008) at 42–43.

63. Brief of Appellees, FTC v. Accusearch, No. 08–8003 (10th Cir. June 6, 2008) at 14.

64. Brief of Jennifer Stoddart, Privacy Commissioner of Canada, as Amicus Curiae in Support of Appellee and Affirmance of the District Court Decision, FTC v. Accusearch, No. 08–8003 (10th Cir. June 26, 2008) at 3.

65. FTC v. Accusearch, 570 F.3d 1187, 1197 (10th Cir. 2009).

66. Ibid. at 1198.

67. Ibid.

68. Ibid.

69. Ibid. at 1199.

70. Ibid. at 1200.

71. Ibid.

72. Ibid. at 1204 (Tymkovich, J., concurring).

73. Ibid.

74. Eric Goldman, *The Ten Most Important Section 230 Rulings*, 20 Tul. J. Tech. & Intell. Prop. 1 (2017).

Chapter 9. Hacking 230

1. Complaint, Barnes v. Yahoo, Civil Action No. 6:05-CV-926-AA (D. Or. June 23, 2005) at ¶ 3.

2. Ibid. at ¶¶ 4–5.

3. Ibid. at ¶ 6.

4. Ibid. at ¶ 7.

5. Ibid. at ¶¶ 8–13.

6. Defendant Yahoo Inc.'s Memorandum in Support of its Motion to Dismiss the Complaint, Barnes v. Yahoo, Civil Action No. 6:05-CV-926-AA (D. Or. July 27, 2005).

7. Opinion and Order, Barnes v. Yahoo, Civil Action No. 6:05-CV-926-AA (D. Or. Nov. 8, 2005) at 9.

8. Maureen O'Hagan, *You've Heard of Scalia. But Who's O'Scannlain?* Portland Monthly (April 22, 2016).

9. Kimberly Sayers-Fay & Eric Ritigstein, *Hon. Susan P. Graber, U.S. Circuit Judge, U.S. Court of Appeals for the Ninth Circuit*, Federal Lawyer (March/April 2006).

10. Carol J. Williams, *Conservatives Gaining Sway on a Liberal Bastion*, L.A. Times (April 19, 2009).

11. Barnes v. Yahoo!, Inc., 570 F. 3d 1096, 1107 (9th Cir. 2009).

12. Ibid.

13. Ibid.

14. Opinion and Order, Barnes v. Yahoo, Civil Action No. 6:05-CV-926-AA (D. Or. Dec. 11, 2009) at 10–11.

15. Daniel Solove, *Barnes v. Yahoo!, CDA Immunity, and Promissory Estoppel*, Concurring Opinions (May 19, 2009).

16. Ibid.

17. Complaint, Doe v. Internet Brands, Case 2:12-cv-03626-JFW-PJW (C.D. Cal. April 26, 2012) at ¶ 11.

18. Ibid.

19. Ibid. at ¶ 12.

20. Ibid. at ¶ 13.

21. Amended Counterclaim, Waitt v. Internet Brands, 2:10-cv-03006-GHK-JCG (C.D. Cal. Sept. 22, 2010) at ¶¶ 15–17.

22. Motion to Dismiss, Doe v. Internet Brands, Case 2:12-cv-03626-JFW-PJW (C.D. Cal. July 3, 2012) at 6.

23. Civil Minutes, Doe v. Internet Brands, Case 2:12-cv-03626-JFW-PJW (C.D. Cal. Aug. 16, 2012) at 4.

24. Brief of Appellant, Doe v. Internet Brands, Case No. 12–56638 (9th Cir. Feb. 13, 2013) at 19.

25. Brief of Appellee, Doe v. Internet Brands, Case No. 12–56638 (9th Cir. March 15, 2013) at 5.

26. Defendant-Appellee Internet Brands, Inc.'s Petition for Rehearing and Rehearing En Banc, Doe v. Internet Brands, Case No. 12-56638 (Oct. 31, 2014) at 2.

27. Doe v. Internet Brands, 767 F. 3d 894, 898 (9th Cir. 2014).

28. Ibid.

29. Ibid.

30. Ibid. at 899.

31. *See* Daniel P. Collins, Munger, Tolles & Olson, *available at* https://www.mto.com/lawyers/Daniel-P-Collins.

32. Petition for Rehearing and Rehearing En Banc, Doe v. Internet Brands, Case No. 12–56638 (9th Cir. Oct. 31, 2014) at 15.

33. Amicus Brief in Support of Petition for Rehearing and Rehearing En Banc, Doe v. Internet Brands, Case No. 12–56638 (9th Cir. Nov. 10, 2014) at 5.

34. The dialogue from the oral argument was obtained from the Ninth Circuit's video recording of the argument, in Doe v. Internet Brands, Case No. 12–56638, *available at* https://www.ca9.uscourts.gov/media/view_video.php?pk_vid=0000007472.

35. Doe v. Internet Brands, 824 F.3d 846 (9th Cir. 2016).

36. Civil Minutes, Doe v. Internet Brands, Case 2:12-cv-03626-JFW-PJW (C.D. Cal. Nov. 14, 2016) at 6.

37. Jeff Kosseff, *The Gradual Erosion of the Law That Shaped the Internet,* 18 COLUM. SCI. & TECH. L. REV. 1 (2017).

38. Alex Kozinski & Josh Goldfoot, *A Declaration of the Dependence of Cyberspace,* 32 COLUM. J.L. & ARTS 365 (2009).

Chapter 10. Sarah versus the Dirty Army

1. Andrea Dworkin, PORNOGRAPHY: MEN POSSESSING WOMEN 9 (1981).

2. Catharine MacKinnon, ONLY WORDS 9–10 (1993).

3. American Booksellers Ass'n, Inc. v. Hudnut, 771 F. 2d 323 (7th Cir. 1985).

4. Catharine MacKinnon, ONLY WORDS 93 (1993).

5. 475 U.S. 1001 (1986).

6. Danielle Keats Citron & Benjamin Wittes, *The Internet Will Not Break: Denying Bad Samaritans Section 230 Immunity,* 86 FORDHAM L. REV 401 (2017).

7. Ann Bartow, *Online Harassment, Profit Seeking, and Section 230,* B.U. L. REV. ONLINE (Nov. 2, 2015).

8. Jones v. Dirty World Entertainment Recordings LLC, 755 F. 3d 398, 402–403 (6th Cir. 2014).

9. Ibid.

10. TheDirty.com, *Legal FAQs,* https://thedirty.com/legal-faqs/.

11. Jones v. Dirty World Entertainment Recordings, 840 F. Supp. 2d 1008, 1009 (E.D. Ky. 2012).

12. Narrative of Sarah Jones, Jones v. Dirty World, 2:09-cv-00219-WOB-CJS (E.D. Ky. Aug. 25, 2010).

13. Ibid.

14. Jones v. Dirty World Entertainment Recordings, 840 F. Supp. 2d at 1009–1010.

15. Jones v. Dirty World Entertainment Recordings LLC, 755 F. 3d 398, 404 (6th Cir. 2014).

16. Ibid.

17. Narrative of Sarah Jones, Jones v. Dirty World, 2:09-cv-00219-WOB-CJS (E.D. Ky. Aug. 25, 2010).

18. Ibid.

19. Teachers Can't Be Cheerleaders, THE DIRTY, *available at* https://gossip.thedirty.com/gossip/cincinnati/teachers-cant-be-cheerleaders/#post-241723.

20. Ibid.

21. Jones v. Dirty World Entertainment Recordings LLC, 755 F. 3d 398, 404 (6th Cir. 2014).

22. Narrative of Sarah Jones, Jones v. Dirty World, 2:09-cv-00219-WOB-CJS (E.D. Ky. Aug. 25, 2010).

23. Ibid.

24. Ibid.

25. Deposition of Sarah Jones, Jones v. Dirty World, 2:09-cv-00219-WOB-CJS at 59–60.

26. Jones v. Dirty World Entertainment Recordings, LLC, 840 F. Supp. 2d 1008, 1012–1013 (E.D. Ky. 2012).

27. Ibid. at 1012.

28. Transcript of Trial Testimony of Nik Richie, Jones v. Dirty World, 2:09-cv-00219-WOB-CJS (E.D. Ky., filed on Jan. 25, 2013) at 11–12.

29. Ibid. at 19.

30. *Bengals Cheerleader Gets Engaged to the Teen She Was Convicted of Having Underage Sex With*, DAILY MAIL (June 13, 2013).

31. Transcript of Trial Testimony of Sarah Jones, Jones v. Dirty World, 2:09-cv-00219-WOB-CJS (E.D. Ky., filed on Jan. 25, 2013) at 94.

32. Jury Questions, Jones v. Dirty World, 2:09-cv-00219-WOB-CJS (E.D. Ky., filed on Jan. 25, 2013).

33. Jones v. Dirty World Entertainment Recordings LLC, 755 F. 3d 398, 414 (6th Cir. 2014).

34. Ibid.

35. Ibid. at 416.

36. Danielle Keats Citron & Benjamin Wittes, *The Internet Will Not Break: Denying Bad Samaritans Section 230 Immunity*, 86 Fordham L. Rev. 401 (2018).

37. Jones v. Dirty World Entertainment Recordings LLC, 755 F. 3d 398, 417 (6th Cir. 2014).

38. Mary Anne Franks, *Moral Hazard on Stilts: "Zeran's" Legacy,* THE RECORDER (Nov. 10, 2017).

39. Transcript of Trial Testimony of Nik Richie, Jones v. Dirty World, 2:09-cv-00219-WOB-CJS (E.D. Ky., filed on Jan. 25, 2013) at 19–20.

40. Samuel D. Warren & Louis D. Brandeis, *The Right to Privacy*, 4 HARV. L. REV. 193 (1890).

41. Amy Gajda, *What If Samuel D. Warren Hadn't Married a Senator's Daughter: Uncovering the Press Coverage That Led to the Right of Privacy,* ILLINOIS PUBLIC LAW AND LEGAL THEORY RESEARCH PAPERS SERIES, Research Paper No. 07–06 (Nov. 1, 2007).

42. New York Times v. Sullivan, 376 US 254 (1964).

43. Gertz v. Robert Welch, 418 US 323, 344 (1974).

44. Ibid.

45. Abby Ohlheiser, *The Woman behind "Me Too" Knew the Power of the Phrase When She Created It—10 Years Ago,* WASH. POST (Oct. 19, 2017).

46. Lisa Respers France, *#MeToo: Social media flooded with personal stories of assault,* CNN (Oct. 17, 2017)

47. Andrea Park, *#MeToo reaches 85 countries with 1.7M tweets,* CBS NEWS (Oct. 24, 2017).

Chapter 11. Kill. Kill. Kill. Kill.

1. New York Times Co. v. United States, 403 U.S. 713, 719 (1971) (Black, J., concurring).

2. First Amended Complaint, Fields v. Twitter, Case No. 3:16-cv-213-WHO (N.D. Cal. Mar. 24, 2016) at ¶ 71.

3. Ibid. at ¶ 74.

4. Ibid. at ¶¶ 78–80.

5. Ibid. at ¶ 84.

6. Ibid.

7. J. M. Berger & Jonathon Morgan, THE BROOKINGS PROJECT ON U.S. RELATIONS WITH THE ISLAMIC WORLD, THE ISIS TWITTER CENSUS (March 2015) at 59.

8. Hamza Shaban, *FBI Director Says Twitter Is a Devil on the Shoulder for Would-Be Terrorists,* BuzzFeed (July 8, 2015).

9. James Comey, *Encryption Tightrope: Balancing Americans' Security and Privacy,* Statement before the House Judiciary Committee (March 1, 2016).

10. Transcript of Interview with Biz Stone, CNN, Erin Burnett Outfront (June 20, 2014), *available at* http://transcripts.cnn.com/TRANSCRIPTS/1406/20/ebo.01.html.

11. 18 U.S.C. § 2333.

12. First Amended Complaint, Fields v. Twitter, Case No. 3:16-cv-213-WHO (N.D. Cal. Mar. 24, 2016) at ¶ 1.

13. Motion to Dismiss, Fields v. Twitter, Case No. 3:16-cv-213-WHO (N.D. Cal. April 6, 2016) at 2.

14. Plaintiff's Opposition to Defendant's Motion to Dismiss the Amended Complaint, Fields v. Twitter, Case No. 3:16-cv-213-WHO (N.D. Cal. May 4, 2016).

15. The above dialogue is as quoted in Transcript of Proceedings of June 15, 2016, Fields v. Twitter, Case No. 3:16-cv-213-WHO (N.D. Cal. Filed on June 23, 2016).

16. Order, Fields v. Twitter, Case No. 3:16-cv-213-WHO (N.D. Cal. Mar. Aug. 10, 2016) at 1.

17. Second Amended Complaint, Fields v. Twitter, Case No. 3:16-cv-213-WHO (N.D. Cal. Aug. 30, 2016) at ¶ 1.

18. Transcript of Proceedings of Nov. 9, 2016, Fields v. Twitter, Case No. 3:16-cv-213-WHO (N.D. Cal. Filed on Dec. 2, 2016).

19. Fields v. Twitter, Inc., 217 F. Supp. 3d 1116, 1118 (N.D 2016).

20. Appellants' Opening Brief, Fields v. Twitter, No. 16–17165 (9th Cir. March 31, 2017) at 16.

21. The above dialogue was obtained from a video of the oral argument on the Ninth Circuit's website, *available at* https://www.ca9.uscourts.gov/media/view_video.php?pk_vid=0000012737.

22. Fields v. Twitter, Inc., 881 F. 3d 739, 749 (9th Cir. 2018).

23. Statement of Sen. John Thune, Terrorism and Social Media: #IsBigTechDoing Enough?, Hearing of Senate Commerce Committee (Jan. 17, 2018).

Chapter 12. Moderation Inc.

1. 47 U.S.C. § 230(b)(4).

2. 47 U.S.C. § 230(c)(2).

3. J. M. Berger & Jonathon Morgan, THE BROOKINGS PROJECT ON U.S. RELATIONS WITH THE ISLAMIC WORLD, THE ISIS TWITTER CENSUS (March 2015) at 2.

4. Alexander Meleagrou-Hitchens & Nick Kaderbhai, ICSR, DEPARTMENT OF WAR STUDIES, KING'S COLLEGE LONDON, *Research Perspectives on Online Radicalisation* (2017), *available at* https://icsr.info/2017/05/03/icsr-vox-pol-paper-research-perspectives-online-radicalisation-literature-review-2006-2016/.

5. J. M. Berger & Jonathon Morgan, THE BROOKINGS PROJECT ON U.S. RELATIONS WITH THE ISLAMIC WORLD, THE ISIS TWITTER CENSUS (March 2015) at 17.

6. *Combatting Violent Extremism*, Twitter blog (Feb. 5, 2016), *available at* https://blog.twitter.com/official/en_us/a/2016/combating-violent-extremism.html.

7. Jeff Kosseff, *Twenty Years of Intermediary Immunity: The U.S. Experience*, 14:1. SCRIPTED 5 (2017).

8. Google User Content and Conduct Policy, *available at* https://www.google.com/+/pol icy/content.html.

9. *See* Alexis C. Madrigal, *Inside Facebook's Fast-Growing Content Moderation Effort*, ATLANTIC (Feb. 7, 2018); Santa Clara University School of Law, Content Moderation & Removal at Scale, *available at* https://law.scu.edu/event/content-moderation-removal-at-scale/.

10. Ibid.

11. Adelin Cai, *Putting Pinners First: How Pinterest Is Building Partnerships for Compassionate Content Moderation*, TECHDIRT (Feb. 5, 2018).

12. Colin Sullivan, *Trust Building as a Platform for Creative Businesses*, TECHDIRT (Feb. 9, 2018).

13. Ibid.

14. Ibid.

15. Ibid.

16. Kate Klonick, *The New Governors: The People, Rules, and Processes Governing Online Speech*, 131 HARV. L. REV. 1598 (2018).

17. Ibid. at 1644–1645.

18. Tarleton Gillespie, CUSTODIANS OF THE INTERNET (2018) at 98.

19. Susan Wojcicki, *Expanding Our Work against Abuse of Our Platform*, YouTube Official Blog (Dec. 4, 2017), *available at* https://youtube.googleblog.com/2017/12/expanding-our-work-against-abuse-of-our.html.

20. Statement of Juniper Downs, Terrorism and Social Media: #IsBigTechDoingEnough?, Hearing of Senate Commerce Committee (Jan. 17, 2018).

21. Ibid.

22. 18 U.S.C. § 2258A.

23. Ibid.

24. *See, e.g.*, PhotoDNA Cloud Service, Microsoft, *available at* https://www.microsoft.com/en-us/photodna.

25. United States v. Keith, 980 F. Supp.2d 33 (D. Mass. 2013).

26. Alex Stamos, *An Update on Information Operations on Facebook*, FACEBOOK NEWSROOM (Sept. 6, 2017), *available at* https://newsroom.fb.com/news/2017/09/informa tion-operations-update/.

27. Julia Angwin, Madeleine Varner, & Ariana Tobin, *Facebook Enabled Advertisers to Reach "Jew Haters,"* PROPUBLICA (Sept. 14, 2017); Will Oremus & Bill Carey, *Facebook's Offensive Ad Targeting Options Go Far Beyond "Jew Haters,"* SLATE (Sept. 14, 2017).

28. Updates to Our Ad Targeting, Facebook Newsroom (Sept. 14, 2017), *available at* https://newsroom.fb.com/news/2017/09/updates-to-our-ad-targeting/.

29. Improving Enforcement and Transparency of Ads on Facebook, Facebook Newsroom (Oct. 2, 2017), *available at* https://newsroom.fb.com/news/2017/10/improving-enforcement-and-transparency/.

30. 141 Cong. Rec. H8460 (Aug. 4, 1995).

31. Kate Klonick, *The New Governors: The People, Rules, and Processes Governing Online Speech*, 131 HARV. L. REV. 1598 (2018).

32. Charles Riley, *YouTube, Apple, and Facebook Remove Content from InfoWars and Alex Jones*, CNN (Aug. 6, 2018).

33. Interview with Jerry Berman (June 6, 2018).

Chapter 13. Exceptional Exceptions

1. United States Senate, Permanent Subcommittee on Investigations, Staff Report, *Backpage.com's Knowing Facilitation of Online Sex Trafficking* (Jan. 2017) ("Senate Backpage Report") at 6.

2. Ibid.

3. National Association of Attorneys General, Aug. 31, 2011, Letter to Samuel Fifer, Counsel for Backpage.com, LLC, *available at* http://www.naag.org/assets/files/pdf/signons/Backpage%20WG%20Letter%20Aug%202011Final.pdf.

4. Ibid.

5. Ibid.

6. Ibid.

7. Senate Backpage Report at 20–21.

8. Ibid. at 21.

9. Ibid. at 21–23.

10. Ibid. at 25.

11. Ibid. at 28.

12. Ibid. at 29.

13. Ibid. at 32.

14. Ibid. at 34–35.

15. Ibid. at 36.

16. Ibid. at 37–38.

17. Ibid. at 40.

18. Andrew O'Reilly, *Prostitution Still Thrives on Backpage despite Site Shutdown of "Adult" Section*, FOX NEWS (May 1, 2017).

19. Tom Jackman & Jonathan O'Connell, *Backpage Has Always Claimed It Doesn't Control Sex-Related Ads. New Documents Show Otherwise*, WASH. POST (July 11, 2017).

20. 18 U.S.C. § 1595.

21. Second Amended Complaint, Doe v. Backpage, Civil Action No. 14–13870 (D. Mass. Dec. 29, 2014) at ¶¶ 71–89.

22. Ibid. at ¶¶ 90–99.

23. Ibid. at ¶¶ 100–107.

24. Ibid. at ¶¶ 108–147.

25. Ibid. at ¶ 10.

26. Ibid. at ¶ 51.

27. Ibid. at ¶ 14.

28. Motion to Dismiss, Doe v. Backpage, Civil Action No. 14–13870 (D. Mass. Jan. 16, 2015) at 30.

29. Ibid.

30. Opposition to Motion to Dismiss, Doe v. Backpage, Civil Action No. 14–13870 (D. Mass. Feb. 13, 2015) at 15, n. 5.

31. Brief of Amici Curiae in Support of Plaintiffs, Doe v. Backpage, Civil Action No. 14–13870 (D. Mass. Feb. 20, 2015) at 15.

32. MA ex rel. PK v. Village Voice Media Holdings, 809 F. Supp. 2d 1041 (E.D. Mo. 2011).

33. Opposition to Motion to Dismiss, Doe v. Backpage, Civil Action No. 14–13870 (D. Mass. Feb. 13, 2015) at 17.

34. The above dialogue is as quoted in the Transcript of the April 15, 2015, hearing on the motion to dismiss in Doe v. Backpage, Civil Action No. 14–13870.

35. Doe v. Backpage, 104 F.Supp.3d 149, 165 (D. Mass. 2015).

36. Doe v. Backpage, 817 F.3d 12, 15 (1st Cir. 2016).

37. Ibid. at 29.

38. Ibid. at 19, n.4.

39. Ibid. at 22.

40. Darrell Smith, *Money Laundering Charges against Backpage.com Execs Can Proceed, Judge Rules,* Sacramento Bee (Aug. 23, 2017).

41. Sarah Jarvis, *et al., As Allegations Increase Against Backpage, Founders Have Become Big Political Donors in Arizona,* ARIZ. REPUBLIC (April 14, 2017).

42. H.R. 1865 (115th Cong.) (as introduced).

43. S.1693 (115th Cong.) (as introduced).

44. Press Release, Office of Sen. Rob Portman, *Senators Introduce Bipartisan Legislation to Hold Backpage Accountable, Ensure Justice for Victims of Sex Trafficking* (Aug. 1, 2017), *available at* https://www.portman.senate.gov/public/index.cfm/2017/8/senators-introduce-bipartisan-legislation-to-hold-backpage-accountable-ensure-justice-for-victims-of-sex-trafficking.

45. Press Release, Internet Association, *Statement on the Introduction of the Stop Enabling Sex Traffickers Act of 2017* (Aug. 1, 2017).

46. Testimony of Chris Cox, before the U.S. House Committee of the Judiciary, Subcommittee on Crime, Terrorism, Homeland Security, and Investigations (Oct. 3, 2017).

47. Public Law No. 115-164.

48. Ibid.

49. Ibid.

50. Ibid.

51. Craigslist, About FOSTA, *available at* https://www.craigslist.org/about/FOSTA.

52. Alina Seluykh, *Backpage Founders Indicted on Charges of Facilitating Prostitution,* NPR (April 9, 2018).

53. Tom Jackman, *Backpage CEO Carl Ferrer Pleads Guilty in Three States, Agrees to Testify Against Other Website Officials,* WASH. POST (April 13, 2018).

54. Order on Motion to Dismiss, Doe v. Backpage, Civil Action No. 17-11069-LTS (D. Mass., Mar. 29, 2018).

55. Eric Goldman, *Congress Probably Will Ruin Section 230 This Week,* TECHNOLOGY AND MARKETING LAW BLOG, *available at* https://blog.ericgoldman.org/archives/2018/02/congress-probably-will-ruin-section-230-this-week-sestafosta-updates.htm (Feb. 26, 2018).

Conclusion

1. *See* Robert Chesney & Danielle Citron, *Deep Fakes: A Looming Challenge for Privacy, Democracy, and National Security,* California Law Review (forthcoming 2019).

2. Orly Lobel, *The Law of the Platform,* 101 Minn. L. Rev. 87, 91 (2016).

3. Paul Sieminski & Holly Hogan, *The Automattic Doctrine: Why (Allegedly) Defamatory Content on WordPress.com Doesn't Come Down without a Court Order,* TechDirt (Feb. 7, 2018).

INDEX

#MeToo, 225–227, 276

Abika.com, 181–189
Abu Zaid, Anwar, 229–230
Accusearch, 181–189
Aereo, 277
Aiken, Anne, 192–195
Ain, Stuart, 48–56
Airbnb, 277–278
al-Awlaki, Anwar, 237
Alger, Timothy, 118–119, 169–172
algorithms, and Section 230 applicability, 188–189
al-Kassabeh, Maaz, 230
Allow States and Victims to Fight Online Sex Trafficking Act (FOSTA), 265–272
Amazon, 4
Ambrose, Yvonne, 266
Ambrozek, Jennifer, 50

American Booksellers Association v. Hudnut, 211
American Civil Liberties Union, 62–63
America Online (AOL), 10, 35–37, 79–102
Ammori, Marvin, 4–5
Anderson, Percy, 169–171
Anello, Douglas A., 14
anonymity, and Section 230, 221
Anti-Terrorism Act, 231–236
Arabian, Armand, 29–30
Arisohn, Joshua David, 232–235
Arnebergh, Roger, 24
Automattic, 279

Backpage.com, 253–272
Balkin, Jack, 9, 145, 152
Bangert, Harold W., 14
Barlow, John Perry, 77–78

Barnes, Cecilia, 191–195
Barnes v. Yahoo, 191–195, 197,
   199–200, 232, 259, 261, 264
Barron, David, 262
Barton, Joe, 69
Bartow, Ann, 212
Batzel v. Smith, 104–115, 127–128,
   168, 209
Batzel, Ellen, 104–115
Bauer v. Glatzer, 138–139
Bea, Carlos, 175
Becerra, Xavier, 265
Beckerman, Michael, 266
Beebe, Anette, 128–129
Bender, Paul, 22
Berman, Jerry, 61, 62–63, 64, 67, 70,
   76, 251
Bertelsman, William, 216–219
Berzon, Marsha, 111–113, 115
Better Business Bureau, 124
Black, Hugo, 15–16, 24–25, 26, 94,
   228–229
Blanchard, Bob, 38–45
Blumenthal, Jacqueline Jordan, 99–102
Blumenthal, Sidney, 99–102
Blumenthal v. Drudge, 99–102
Boyle, Terrence, 91
Brandeis, Louis D., 223
Brennan, William, 23, 25–26, 27
Brimmer, Clarence Addison, 31–35
Brin, Sergey, 143
Brisciani, Anthony Scott, 161
Brookings Institution, 230, 240–241
Burdick, Quentin, 12–13
Burke, Tarana, 225–226
Burns, John, 161
Burrington, Bill, 61, 63, 64
Butler, Bob, 61, 64

Cai, Adelin, 243
Callahan, Consuelo, 193
Callum, Emerson, 196
Canadian Charter of Rights and
   Freedoms, 159
Canadian Privacy Commissioner, 185
Canby, William, 111
Carafano, Christianne, 115–119

Carafano v. Metrosplash, 115–119,
   170–171, 173, 183
Carlisle, James T., 97
Carome, Patrick, 84–96, 100–102,
   192–195, 200–202, 231–232
*Carter v. B.C. Federation of Foster
   Parents Association*, 159–160
Center for Democracy and
   Technology, 61
Chander, Anupam, 121–122
Chastain, Jessica, 264
Citron, Danielle, 212, 220
Clement, Edith Brown, 142
Clifton, Richard, 198–202
Coats, Bill, 55
Cobain, Kurt, 275
Cogan, Brian M., 198, 200
Cohen, Steve, 163
Collins, Daniel, 200–201
Comey, James, 230–231
Communications Act of 1934, 60
Communications Decency Act, legislative
   history, 58–76
CompuServe, 35–45
copyright law, and Section 230, 66, 121,
   139
Costeja Gonzalez, Mario, 154–156
Cox, Chris, 2–3, 57–76, 78, 85, 92,
   104, 114, 140, 239–240, 248, 252,
   268–269, 280
Craigslist, 122, 180, 254, 270–271
Creach, James Damon, 231
Cremers, Ton, 105–115
Cubby v. CompuServe, 38–45, 86–87,
   133, 160, 250
Cunningham, Ward, 134–135

Danner, Pat, 68–69
dark web, 267
Declaration of Independence of
   Cyberspace, 77–78
deep fakes, 277
Delfi v. Estonia, 148–154
Deters, Eric, 217–218
Digital Millennium Copyright Act, 66,
   121, 139

Dippon, Christian M., 121
Doe v. America Online, 97–99, 203–204
Doe v. Backpage. See *Jane Doe No. 1 v. Backpage*
Doe v. Internet Brands, 195–203, 232, 259
Doe v. MySpace, 140–143, 197
Doran, William, 21
Douglas, William, 26–27
Downes, William F., 183–184
Downs, Juniper, 246
Drudge, Matt, 99–102
Dworkin, Andrea, 30–33, 210–211
Dworkin v. Hustler, 30–33

Easterbrook, Frank, 211
eBay, 4
Edwards, John S., 87
Electronic Commerce Directive (Europe), 148–149
Electronic Frontier Foundation, 62–63, 174–175
Ellis, T.S., III, 84–90
Elrod, Jennifer, 142
Epstein, Charles, 50
Estonia Information Society Services Act, 148–149
European Convention on Human Rights, 149–154
Exon, James, 61–63, 64, 71–72, 74–76

Facebook, 4, 139–140, 143, 146, 244–245, 247, 265
Fair Housing Council of San Fernando Valley v. Roommates.com, 168–181, 187
Fakhrian v. Google, 144
Farmers Educ. & Co–op. Union v. WDAY, Inc., 12–17
FCC v. Pacifica Foundation, 75
Federal Trade Commission, 181–189
Feldman, Noah, 146
Ferrer, Carl, 254, 264, 271
Fields, Lloyd, Jr. (Carl), 229–238
Fields, Tamara, 231
Fields v. Twitter, 229–238, 240

First Amendment, and protection for content distributors, 11–35
Flanders, Lavont, Jr., 196
Fleishman, Stanley, 18–28
Fletcher, William, 175
Flower Children, 123–124
Flynt, Larry, 30–35
Frankfurter, Felix, 16, 22
Franks, Mary Anne, 222
Fredman, Howard, 109–110
Friedman, Paul, 101–102
FTC v. Accusearch, 181–189

Gajda, Amy, 224
Garwood, William, 142
General Data Protection Regulation, 157–158
Gertz v. Robert Welch, 224–225
Gibbons, Julia Smith, 219–221
Giberti, Wendy E., 198
Gillespie, Tarleton, 245
Gingrich, Newt, 57–58, 62, 104
Github, 248
Global Royalties, Inc., 126–128
Global Royalties, Ltd. v. Xcentric Ventures, LLC, 126–128
Godwin, Mike, 139
Goldfoot, Josh, 204–205
Goldman, Eric, 188, 265, 272
Goodlatte, Bob, 70, 93
Google Spain v. Costeja Gonzalez, 154–156
Google, 4, 130, 143–144, 146, 154–156, 242
Gore, Al, 1
Gould, Ronald, 111–113
Graber, Susan, 193
Grant, James C., 260
Green, Howard, 29
Greenbaum, Edward S., 14

Hall, John E., 160
Hamilton, Robert, 40–45, 52–53, 93
Harlan, John Marshall, 27
Hartz, Harris, 185–187
Haskell, Eddie (TV character), 28–30

Herman, Jeffrey, 198, 201
Himmler, Heinrich, 106, 115
Holmes, Jerome, 185
Holmes, John, 28
House Judiciary Committee, hearing on Section 230 and sex trafficking, 268–269
Hustler, 31–35

I Am Jane Doe (documentary), 264
Ikuta, Sandra Segal, 171–174, 234–235
Indianapolis City Council, 211
Infowars, 249
Instagram, 139
International approaches to intermediary liability: Australia, 161–162; Canada, 159–160; China, 147; Europe, 148–159; Iran, 147; Russia, 147; Turkey, 147.
Internet Association, 121, 265–266
Internet Brands, 195–203
Islamic State of Iraq and Syria (ISIS), 229–238, 240–241, 249
Itkin, Jason A., 141

Jacobellis v. Ohio, 23
Jane Doe No. 1 v. Backpage, 256–264
Jones, Alex, 249
Jones, Richard A., 132
Jones, Sarah, 213–223
Jones v. Dirty World Entertainment Recordings LLC, 213–223

Kayser, Leo, 39–45, 83, 85–96, 122, 263, 275
Keller, Daphne, 157
Kennedy, John Fitzgerald, 136–137
Kennedy, Robert Francis, 136–137
Kent, Eben L., 40
Kimzey, Douglas, 131–133
Kimzey v. Yelp, 131–133
Kirsch, Robert R., 20
Klonick, Kate, 244–245, 248, 250
Kozinski, Alex, 171–181, 187, 204–205
KRXO, 81, 83, 96

Lacey, Michael, 264, 271
Larkin, James, 264, 271
La Vanguardia, 154–155
Leave It to Beaver, 28
Leisure, Peter, 40–44
Le Sex Shoppe, 28–30
Letters to the Inhabitants of Quebec, 146
Levy, Paul Alan, 110–111
Lewis, R. Fred, 98–99
LinkedIn, 139
Lobel, Orly, 180, 277–278
Lofgren, Zoe, 69, 93
Lusby, David, 46–49
Lycos, 117–119
Lynch, Michael, 32–35

Macgillivray, Alex, 140
MacKinnon, Catharine, 210–211
Magedson, Ed, 123–129
Mann Act, 270
Martone, Frederick, 127–128
Masterson, Chase. *See* Carafano, Christianne
Matchmaker.com, 115–119
Matingly, Alexis, 216, 218–219
McAuliffe, Steven, 234
McDaniel, William Alden, Jr., 99–100
McGilvray, Sean, 248
McKeown, Margaret, 132–133, 175, 178–179
McLean, Chris, 62, 72
Metrosplash, 117–119
Milano, Alyssa, 226
ModelMayhem.com, 195–203
Montgomery, John, 260–262
Morris, James, 13
Mosler, 108
Museum Security Network, 104–115, 168
My So-Called Life, 273
MySpace, 140–143

National Association of Broadcasters, 14–15
National Center for Missing and Exploited Children, 246, 253

NetChoice, 268
New York Times v. Sullivan, 28, 224
New York Times v. United States
  (Pentagon Papers case), 228–229
Niv, Tal, 248
Nupedia, 135

Oklahoman newspaper, 80, 82
O'Neal, Stan, 156
Orrick, William, 231–234
O'Scannlain, Diarmuid, 193–195
Osmond, Kenneth, 28–30
Osmond v. EWAP, 28–30

Packwood, Bob, 73
Padilla, Adam, 254–255
Padilla, Andrew, 254–255
Paez, Richard, 118
Page, Larry, 143
Park Place Market, 31–35
Patel, Jay, 182
Patreon, 243–244
Paul, Rand, 269
Perri, Jamie S., 138–139
Pinterest, 242–243
Piscioneri v. Brisciani, 161–162
Piscioneri, Gabriella, 161
Pollock, John C., 13
Pope, James H., 19–21
Portman, Rob, 265
Porush, Daniel, 45–56
Powell, Lewis, 224
Prodigy, 2, 10, 36–38, 44–56, 274–275
Promissory estoppel, 193–195
Public Citizen, 110–111
Puckett, Nora, 242

Rankin, J. Lee, 14
Reddit, 4
Reding, Viviane, 157
Reed, Edward C., 118
Reinhardt, Stephen, 104, 171–174,
  175, 178
Reno v. ACLU, 74–76
Rhoades, Gary W., 170
Richie, Nik (Hooman Karamian), 212–223

Right to Be Forgotten (Europe), 154–159
Rijkmuseum, 105
Ripoff Report, 122–130, 144, 153
Robinson, Desiree, 266
Roommates.com, 168–181
Rosen, Jeffrey, 156–157
Rosenwein, Sam, 22–28
Rothweiler, Williams, 17–18, 21
Rumorville, 39–45
Russell, Donald S., 91
Russell, Richard Lee, 97–99
Russia, interference in U.S.
  elections, 247
Rymer, Pamela, 175

Sanger, Larry, 135–136
San Jose Mercury News, 74
Sathre, P.O., 13
Sazonoff, Jonathan, 106–107
Schroeder, Mary, 198
Section 230 provisions: definition of
  "interactive computer service," 64;
  definition of "information content
  provider," 65; exception for Electronic
  Communications Privacy Act,
  66; exception for enforcement of
  federal criminal law, 66; exception
  for intellectual property laws, 66;
  general immunity of 230(c)(1), 64;
  policy and factual findings, 66–67,
  239–240; protection for "good faith"
  moderation of 230(c)(2), 65, 239.
Securing the Protection of our Enduring
  and Established Constitutional Heritage
  Act (SPEECH Act), 162–163, 260
Segal, John L., 144
Seigenthaler, John, Sr., 136–137
Selya, Bruce, 262–263
Senate Commerce Committee, hearing on
  Section 230 and sex trafficking, 265–266
Senate Permanent Investigations
  Subcommittee, report on Backpage.
  com, 253–255
sex trafficking and Section 230, 252–272
Shannon, Mark, 81
Silverman, Barry, 175

Simmons, Russel, 130
Skuttlebut, 38–39
Slater, Abigail, 265–266
Smith, Eleazar, 17–28
Smith, Gordon, 73
Smith, Milan D., Jr., 175, 234–236
Smith, Randy N., 175
Smith, Robert, 105–106
Smith v. California, 17–28, 133
Snapchat, 139
Solis, Pete I., 140–143
Solomon-Page Group, 45–48
Solove, Dan, 194–195
Sorokin, Leo T., 271
Souras, Yiota, 265
Souter, David, 262
Sparks, Sam, 141–142
SPEECH Act. *See* Securing the
    Protection of our Enduring
    and Established Constitutional
    Heritage Act
Spence, Gerry, 31–35
Spence v. Flynt, 33–35
Stamos, Alex, 247
Starkman, Melvin, 29
Stearns, Richard G., 260–262
Stevens, John Paul, 75–76
Stewart, Potter, 23
Stoddart, Jennifer, 185
Stone, Biz, 231, 241
Stop Enabling Sex Traffickers Act
    (SESTA), 265–272
Stoppelman, Jeremy, 130
Stratton Oakmont v. Prodigy, 45–56,
    59–60, 73, 195, 250
Sullivan, Colin, 243–244
Sullivan, Spencer, 126–128
Supercock (adult film), 28–30
Sweeter Than Life, 17–28

TaskRabbit, 277
Telecommunications Act of 1996,
    57–78
Tevrizian, Dickran M., 117–118
TheDirty.com, 212–223

Thomas, Sidney, 118–119
Thune, John, 237
Time (1995 feature on
    "cyberpornography"), 63
Townley, Arthur, 12–13
Trafficking Victims Protection
    Reauthorization Act, 256
Trustpilot, 153–154
Tryon, Mark, 19
Twitter, 4, 139–140, 143, 146, 229–238,
    240–241, 249–250, 265
Tymkovich, Timothy, 185–187

Uber, 277
Union Bank of Switzerland, 45
United States Court of Appeals for the
    Ninth Circuit, 103–104
unmasking anonymous Internet posters,
    221–222

Vimeo, 248
Vixen Press, 19

Wagner, Ann, 264–265
Waitt, Donald, 196
Waitt, Tyler, 196
Wales, Jimmy, 135–137
Walter, John F., 197–198, 202–203
Warren, Samuel D., 223–224
Waxman, Seth, 232–236
WBAI, 274
WDAY, 12–17
Weinstein, Harvey, 226
Wells, Charles T., 98
White, Rick, 61, 69, 71–72
Wikipedia, 4, 134–139, 146, 268
Wilkinson, J. Harvie, III, 91–95, 113
Williams, Dar, 273
Wilson, Laurence, 131
Wilson, Steven V., 109
Wing, Joseph E., 17–18,
Wired, 77
Wittes, Benjamin, 212, 220
Wojcicki, Susan, 246
Wolf of Wall Street, 45

WordPress, 279
Wyden, Ron, 2–3, 57–76, 85, 92,
    95, 239–240, 250–251, 269,
    280

Yahoo, 4, 191–195
Yelp, 129–134, 146
York, Cody, 218–219

Young, Milton, 12–13
YouTube, 4, 245–246, 265

Zamansky, Jake, 48–54
Zeran, Kenneth, 79–96
Zeran v. America Online, 79–96, 113,
    122, 125, 141, 165, 191, 197, 276
ZGeek, 161
Zuckerberg, Mark, 3